Brass Tacks

Brass Tacks

Essays in Medical Demography

A TRIBUTE TO THE MEMORY OF
PROFESSOR WILLIAM BRASS

Edited by

BASIA ZABA and JOHN BLACKER

'Birth, and copulation, and death.
That's all the facts when it comes to brass tacks:
Birth, and copulation, and death.'

T.S.Eliot, *Sweeney Agonistes*

THE ATHLONE PRESS
London & New York

First published in 2001 by
THE ATHLONE PRESS
A Continuum imprint
The Tower Building, 11 York Road, London SE1 7NX
370 Lexington Avenue, New York, NY 10017–6503

British Library Cataloguing in Publication Data
*A catalogue record for this book is available
from the British Library*

ISBN 0 485 11563 8 HB

Library of Congress Cataloging-in-Publication Data

Brass tacks : essays in medical demography : a tribute to the memory
 of Professor William Brass / edited by Basia Zaba and John Blacker
  p. ; cm.
 Includes bibliographical references and index.
 ISBN 0–485–11563–8 (HB: alk. Paper)
  1. Medical statistics – Miscellanea. 2. Demography–Miscellanea. 3.
 Fertility–Miscellanea. 4. Social medicine–Miscellanea. I. Title: Essays in medical
 demography. II. Brass, William. III. Zaba, Basia. IV. Blacker, John, 1929–
 [DNLM: 1. Demography–Essays. 2. Fertility–Essays. 3. Mortality–Essays.
 HB 849.4
 B823 2000]

RA407 .B73 2000
614.4′2–dc21
                                                                00–038985

Typeset by Florence Production Ltd,
Stoodleigh Court, Stoodleigh, Devon
Printed and bound in Great Britain by
MPG Books Ltd, Bodmin, Cornwall

Contents

List of Figures

Editors' preface

At least one of the authors of each of the papers in this volume was a student of Bill Brass at the London School of Hygiene and Tropical Medicine. Some were those whom he supervised for their PhDs; others were master's degree students who attended his lectures for the MSc in Medical Demography, and some whose research projects he supervised. The other co-authors were mostly colleagues and staff members of the Centre for Population Studies in the London School. All of us feel that we owe Bill an incalculable debt for the stimulus he has given to our work, for the benefit of his wisdom, for his patience and his generosity, and for his dry Scottish wit.

The diversity of topics covered by the essays in this volume reflects the variety of paths we have subsequently trodden, but by one means or another Bill set us on our ways: they are 'Brass tacks' in a different sense. Although best known as a demographer and as the originator of the 'Brass methods' for analysing limited and defective data from Third World populations, he also made notable contributions to the study of developed-country demography; he was a brilliant mathematician and statistician, and his interests and knowledge of matters medical, historical, anthropological and archaeological were extensive.

In addition to being head of the Centre for Population Studies and Professor of Medical Demography in the London School, Bill held many other positions which were far from sinecures. Among others, he was head of the Department of Epidemiology and Medical Statistics in the School; he was a member of the Economic and Social Research Council and chairman both of its Statistics Committee and of its Research Grants Board; he was a member of the Council of the British Academy; he was president of the International Union for the Scientific Study of Population; he was a Foreign Associate of the US National Academy of Sciences and a member of their Committee on Population and Demography. All these were time-consuming posts, but he still found time for his teaching and research; indeed at one period he was doing more lecturing on the MSc course than all the other CPS staff members put together. Yet if you poked your head round his door, he would always find the time to talk to you, and if he needed to see you he would not pick up the telephone and ask you to come to his room: he would come to yours.

Einstein once said: 'For the creation of a theory, the mere collection of recorded phenomena never suffices – there must always be added a free invention of the human mind that attacks the heart of the matter'. It was Bill's capacity to add this 'free invention' which made him such an outstanding demographer. His inventions were characterized by two note-worthy features: simplicity and serendipity. He sharpened his techniques of demographic analysis with Ockham's Razor[1] and reduced them to such simple forms that anyone could apply them. He also had a remarkable capacity for discerning the truly significant features of a data set from the obscuring 'noise', and for utilizing information which others had set aside as irrelevant or unuseable. We feel privileged to have had the opportunity of working with him.

Basia Zaba
John Blacker

---

1 *Entia non sunt multiplicanda praeter necessitam* – Entities should not be multiplied beyond necessity.

Introduction to Brass Tacks
Griffith Feeney

Most of us who pursue research for a sustained period have the satisfaction of discovering something new and of sharing it with others. But to discover and populate a vast new frontier in the world of knowledge, as William Brass has done, is given to very few. Serendipity plays a role, as Bill would readily admit. But to seize the opportunity requires ability, stamina, vision and courage. Bill could not, because it would require a wholly alien immodesty, outline his achievement and celebrate the virtues that made it possible. This happy task falls to those of us who have followed him.

When Bill joined the East African Statistical Department in 1948, the world was divided, as it is today, between richer and poorer countries. One aspect of this divide lies in the availability of demographic data. Rich countries had population censuses and vital registration systems that provided reasonably complete and accurate demographic statistics. Poor countries had little demographic data, and what little they had was often of poor quality.

Yet the need for demographic information in poor countries was if anything greater than in rich countries, for their attempts to develop were being complicated by rapidly growing populations. As a nascent demographer, Bill recognized this quickly enough – but so did every other demographer who paid attention to the matter. The divide was easy to see. The challenge was to do something about it.

Where others saw merely a deficit and a nuisance, Bill saw an intellectual challenge of the first order. He saw that the eminently practical problem of securing demographic statistics for developing countries could be resolved into a series of scientific problems, that demographic measurement could be conceived in far more general terms, and that in this way useful estimates could be obtained in the absence of established census and vital registration systems. He responded with an extraordinary and sustained outpouring of effort – of ideas and methods, teaching and research, fund-raising and institutional development, international travel, lecturing and consulting – that ceased only when illness prevented further work.

On return from East Africa in 1955 Bill spent a decade at the University of Aberdeen. While his ideas were stimulated by the experience in East Africa, here they matured and were spread in the academic world. A year's leave spent at the Office of Population Research at Princeton University in 1961 played a key role in this process. In 1965 he moved to the London

School of Hygiene and Tropical Medicine, where he remained until retirement in 1988. He began as a Reader, was awarded a personal Chair in
Medical Demography in 1972, and in 1974 founded the Centre for Population
Studies with support from the Overseas Development Administration. In
time the mission of the Centre was broadened to incorporate the demography of developed countries, to which Bill made numerous distinguished
contributions. The Centre remains today one of the pre-eminent institutions
of world, to say nothing of British, demography.

Most demographers know that 'Brass techniques' are a means of getting
demographic estimates when 'standard' sources, most often a mature vital
registration system, are lacking. But to know this is to know very little. A
detailed enumeration of techniques is certainly not wanted here, but we
ought to try for a less superficial understanding of Bill's achievement.

Bill saw more or less from the beginning that in demography as in war,
frontal assault is not always the best strategy, that demographic data collection should take account not only of what we would like to know, but of
the information respondents are best able to provide. This is not merely a
matter of suitable phrasing of questions, an issue familiar to every census
taker and survey statistician, but of recognizing and exploiting deep relationships that must be expressed in mathematical form and which involve
empirical regularities as well as formal demographic tautologies.

This is illustrated by the most famous 'Brass technique', which estimates
mortality from information on children born and surviving. Life-tables are
what we would like to have, but direct calculation requires a mature vital
registration system to supply numbers of deaths. Vital data may in principle
be obtained, with some limitations, by retrospective questions on a census
or survey, but experience shows that respondents are often unable to respond
accurately to these questions.

An alternative is to recognize that census or survey questions on numbers
of children born and surviving contain information about life-table survival
probabilities, and that respondents may be able to answer these questions
more accurately. But to move from information on children ever born and
surviving to life-table survival probabilities is no simple matter. It requires
both non-trivial mathematics and models of the age pattern of fertility and
mortality. Perhaps the best evidence of the complexity of the problem is
the stream of methodological research it has generated. The earliest published
work seems to be the paper Bill presented to the 1961 conference of the
International Union for the Scientific Study of Population. Every subsequent
decade, going on 40 years now, has seen further contributions, most recently
the paper by Collumbien and Sloggett in the present volume.

The various technical assumptions made by this and similar methods
have bothered many people, since they are never perfectly satisfied and are
a source of error in the estimates. In application, however, the important

questions are, firstly, how serious the errors are, and secondly, how the estimates compare with available alternatives. Census or survey questions that attempt to obtain vital registration data retrospectively are simpler to analyse because they make only one assumption – that responses will be reasonably complete.

Unfortunately, this one assumption often fails disastrously, whereas the numerous technical assumptions made by the 'indirect' method – so called because the information collected is only indirectly related to the quantities estimated – come fairly close to the mark.

Nearly as fundamental as the idea of indirection in data collection is the idea that errors in data act as a kind of filter, blocking the transmission of certain information while letting other information pass. One of the most elegant and enduring of Bill's methods exploits a remarkable complementarity of such filtering in questions on children ever born to women at the time of a census or survey and births to these same women during the immediately preceding year (or other period). Numbers of births in the recent past are likely to be under- or overstated, but the extent of this distortion will usually be similar for women at different ages. Thus the error blocks information on numbers of births but lets the percentage distribution by age through relatively unscathed. Numbers of children ever born are generally reported reasonably accurately by younger women but may be seriously underreported for older women. The obscurely named 'P/F ratio method' – i.e. the comparison of cumulated current fertility and average parity – utilizes both sources of data, exploiting their complementary errors to extract from them an estimate of fertility that neither source alone could supply.

A third fundamental idea is deceptively simple, reminding one of Samuel Johnson's adage that we 'need more often to be reminded, than informed'. Bill once expressed it as the principle of 'no rule', observing that

> There is no method which functions at all times and in all situations. All are based on certain suppositions about how errors are made; it is very difficult, if not impossible, to anticipate patterns of error. While there is only a single truth, there is an infinite number of ways to make errors.

What this means in practice is that producing estimates when data are deficient requires always the exercise of intelligence and judgement beyond that which is incorporated in the estimation procedure.

Obvious, you say, but a persistent tendency in statistics at least since Neyman–Pearson theory has been to maximize the intelligence incorporated in statistical methodology and minimize that required in application. This tempts us to think that, having made the often considerable effort necessary to learn a method, we should have only to apply it in one case after the other to get sensible estimates. Would that it were this easy. Unfortunately, this is more or less equivalent to thinking that ordering up a pile of building materials and a shed full of fancy tools should somehow result in the construction of a house, without the necessity of further effort on our part.

Learning the various methods that Bill and others have developed is one thing. Learning to apply them is a different and considerably more difficult thing. Learning the methods may be non-trivial, but with sufficient effort one masters them, and that is that. Learning to apply the methods is a matter of experience, and the more experience one has the more one learns. New situations raise new challenges, and success in past applications does not assure future success. Most who have pursued such work over a career will have had the experience of deploying with satisfaction several highly sophisticated methods only to obtain drastically inconsistent results. And have been humbled by being at least temporarily mystified as to what precise constellation of errors could have resulted in this outcome.

Bill was famously quick on his feet. One of his minor methods was discussed in detail at a meeting, with many lamentations over the various assumptions made and how they might go wrong. As the discussion wore on an impartial observer might have been forgiven for wondering if the thing were really worth pursuing. At length Bill rose to speak, and one sensed a growing but well-tempered impatience. 'This', he said, 'is a *desperation* method', a method to be used when nothing else is possible, when one is desperate. Of course there are problems, but the method gives results where nothing else would, an imperfect but possibly useful answer in place of no answer at all. With a single sentence he restored perspective to the discussion and, not incidentally, a suitable modicum of respect for his methodological child.

On another occasion, following a tendentiously long enumeration of all the things that could go wrong in applying another of his methods, Bill cut characteristically to the quick by observing that 'not everything that can go wrong, will'. Were this not true, social data collection of all kinds would be far more problematic than it is. The observation is so fundamentally true and important that I take the liberty of christening it 'Brass's Law'. Of course it calls to mind Murphy's Law, 'If anything can go wrong, it will'. It is left as an exercise for the reader (as mathematics textbooks are fond of saying) to show that the contradiction between the two is only apparent.

Bill was quick on his feet in part because he spent a great deal of time there and so had a great deal of practice, not only in formal teaching, but in conferences, workshops and lectures around the world. Once after a particularly tedious conference session he confided to me that he would 'rather talk for six hours than listen for one'. I recall with particular fondness a phrase that shows skill in rhetoric rather than demography. In response to complex and long-winded questions Bill would often begin with a measured pause followed by 'Yes, and no'. This is a wonderfully polite way of saying that the issue is more complicated than perhaps the questioner realized. It prepares listeners for an extended reply, to which they must listen carefully to discern which points are on which side. And has the added bonus of giving the speaker a few extra moments in which to compose his or her thoughts.

Bill once told me of receiving a telephone call whose purpose was to ascertain informally whether he would accept a certain honour from the British Government if it were proffered. This was to avoid embarrassment, he explained (to an ignorant American), for from time to time potential recipients had declined the award. Chasing after awards would have been wholly alien to Bill's character, but so would the arrogance required to decline any reasonable honour.

Some honours come free and clear, or even net a small profit, while others come with a requirement of corvée labour that disciplines impose on their best members. Bill had a surfeit of both. In 1978 he received the Mindel C Sheps Award from the Population Association of America. He was elected a Fellow of the British Academy in 1979 and received the CBE in 1981. In 1984 he was elected Foreign Associate of the United States National Academy of Sciences, the highest honour the Academy can bestow on a foreigner, and in 1985 he was elected President of the IUSSP.

Much has changed in the more than half century since Bill first set foot in the East African Statistical Department. Considerable resources have been expended on collecting better demographic statistics in developing countries, and we certainly have more and better information now than we did then. In the face of this progress we might be tempted to flatter ourselves that the principles and methods Bill worked so assiduously and ardently to create and promote are fading in importance.

In fact, nothing could be further from the truth. Mature vital registration systems are still the exception in developing countries, and populations covered by such systems have generally grown much more slowly than countries not covered. As a result, the fraction of the world's population covered by such systems has probably declined over the past 50 years, for there are relatively few countries whose vital registration systems have matured over the same period.

The limited development of vital registration systems has to some extent been offset by the widespread deployment of sample surveys, but these cannot replace vital registration. The obvious contemporary instance is the glaring absence of information on the demographic impact of HIV/AIDS in many of the countries that suffer most severely from it.

But to think in this way is to look backward into the past, and we ought to attempt to peer into the future, the emerging brave new world of global digital computer networks. We have lived for some time in a world in which – this is an actual case – a resident of the Hawaiian Islands in the middle of the Pacific Ocean can buy a book at Blackwell's in Oxford, England, using a small piece of digitally encoded plastic, with payment, including foreign currency exchange, effected transparently, almost instantly, and at negligible cost.

How long can decennial population censuses, which provide data which is, averaged over time, typically six to seven years out of date, survive in such a world? How long, in such a world, can vital statistic systems continue to issue annual reports that are years, sometimes many years, out of date? Demographers routinely project population forward many decades into the future. What will demographic data collection systems look like in 2050? Already some countries have abandoned traditional population censuses, sometimes for reasons that have as much to do with non-cooperation of respondents as with superior alternatives provided by new information technology.

Population censuses and vital statistics systems will not disappear any time soon, but our use of them may be transformed almost beyond recognition over the next few decades by the availability of alternative sources, commercial, private non-profit and governmental, that contain much of the information we now get from censuses for much of the population. How these matters will play out is a pretty puzzle. One suspects that the developed country statistical systems that developing countries are aiming for will be obsolete in developed countries long before they arrive in developing countries.

In the face of these imponderables, and with the usual risk of looking silly in the future if anyone pays attention, I suggest that demographic data collection will become more complicated rather than simpler in coming decades, that the problems we face everywhere will look more like the current and past situation in developing countries than the familiar and comfortable situation of developed countries. If so, the most important lessons Bill has taught us will be as relevant for the world as a whole in the future as they are for the developing world of yesterday and today.

SECTION ONE

Demographic Estimation

CHAPTER ONE

Child mortality estimation by time since first birth

Kenneth Hill

Department of Population Dynamics,
Johns Hopkins University

Maria-Elena Figueroa

Center for Communications Programs,
Johns Hopkins University

INTRODUCTION

The best-known and most widely applied estimation method developed by William Brass is the measurement of child mortality from the proportions dead of children ever borne by women classified by age group (Brass, 1964, 1975). The basic principle of the method is that age of the mother can serve as a proxy for the exposure time of her children, so that the proportion dead for women of a given age group can be converted into a defined probability of dying for their children. This method has been applied to census and survey data from all parts of the developing world, and has been found to work remarkably well in a wide variety of settings. The original method has been extended by a number of authors, notably Sullivan (1972), who extended the method to groups of women classified by duration of marriage; Feeney (1980), who showed that under conditions of steadily changing mortality the estimates of mortality for particular age groups of women could be related to specified time points prior to the survey; and Trussell (1975; United Nations, 1983), who expanded the model base of the estimation methods. As used today, the proportion dead of children ever borne for each group of women provides an estimate of child mortality, usually converted into the probability of dying by age 5, and a time reference for that estimate in years before the survey.

One of the key assumptions underlying the original Brass method and its extensions is that child mortality risks are uniform across the classificatory variable (age or duration of marriage of the mother) being used as a proxy for exposure to risk of the children. Widespread application of the age of mother based method has shown that this assumption is not valid. The child mortality estimates based on reports of younger women, particularly those aged 15–19 but also often those aged 20–4, are almost always higher than the estimates based on reports of older women. This pattern results from a real age effect, whereby children of young mothers have elevated mortality risks, and also from a selection effect, whereby women of lower socio-economic class tend to start childbearing early, and have children exposed to above-average mortality risk. It is unfortunate that it is the two youngest age groups of mothers that are most affected by this bias, since it is these two age groups that reflect the most recent child mortality experience, and provide estimates with reference dates closest to the time of the survey. The youngest age groups of mothers also have the smallest numbers of children ever borne, so random errors are largest for the estimates based on them. The duration of marriage-based method is less affected both by the age at childbearing selection bias and by small numbers of events, since child-bearing typically occurs rapidly in the first five years of marriage across all social classes. The duration of marriage-based method may, however, be affected by another selection bias, by marital status, in countries where substantial proportions of children are born outside formal unions. The experience of these children would not be captured in the duration of marriage-based method until the mother married, and would then be captured at an inappropriate value of the proxy exposure indicator.

This paper develops and illustrates the application of a third approach, which uses time since first birth as the proxy for exposure. This approach will be little affected by socio-economic selection bias, but will be applicable to populations in which substantial proportions of children are born outside formal unions. The method is developed by using fertility and mortality models to simulate children ever borne and children dead for women grouped by five-year time intervals since first birth, and then to relate the proportions dead to standard mortality measures allowing for different fertility patterns. For the method to be applied, additional questions on month and year of first birth must be included in the census or survey. The number of surveys that have included such questions without collecting a full birth history is small, so the number of applications currently available is also small.

FERTILITY BY TIME SINCE FIRST BIRTH

Fertility by time since first birth is modelled in a manner analogous to that shown by Rodriguez and Cleland (1988) to fit patterns of fertility by time since first union closely. The model assumes a pattern of natural fertility at time since first birth t, $n(t)$, which is modified by two parameters, one determining the level of fertility, the other determining the extent of deviation over time of the actual pattern from the natural pattern. The model is

$$f(t) = n(t) \, exp(\alpha + \beta t) \tag{1}$$

where α is the level parameter and β is a measure of the spread of fertility compared to the standard.

The natural fertility pattern was derived from data for the Hutterites. Births and exposure by time since first birth were calculated, categorized in single-year time intervals, and single-year birth rates were computed. Table 1.1 shows the reported rates by single year, and the rates after applying a LOWESS smoothing procedure to the values for periods greater than three years since first birth (no smoothing is applied to the rates for the first three years, since fluctuations may primarily reflect effects of non-susceptibility).

The model described in equation (1) and the Hutterite standard was then applied to data from 31 Demographic and Health Surveys. Fits by and large were satisfactory, with values of α ranging from -1.05 to -1.97, and values of β from -0.008 to 0.082. Figure 1.1 shows plots of $log(f(t)/n(t))$ against t for two countries, one with a low value of β (Thailand) and one with a

Table 1.1   *Observed Hutterite and smoothed fertility rates by year since first birth*

Time since first birth $(a, a+1)$	Hutterite birth rate	Smoothed birth rate
0	0.0450	0.0450*
1	0.8432	0.8432*
2	0.5592	0.5592*
3	0.6007	0.5947
4	0.5783	0.5742
5	0.5285	0.5545
6	0.5488	0.5365
7	0.5269	0.5201
8	0.4813	0.5039
9	0.4767	0.4870
10	0.4720	0.4695
11	0.4577	0.4517
12	0.4825	0.4329
13	0.4201	0.4126
14	0.3692	0.3903
15	0.3807	0.3653
16	0.3476	0.3371
17	0.3592	0.3065
18	0.2553	0.2744
19	0.2580	0.2414
20	0.2054	0.2074
21	0.1726	0.1717
22	0.1025	0.1349
23	0.1239	0.0986
24	0.0623	0.0644

* Values for 0, 1 and 2 years are not smoothed.

high value of β (Zimbabwe). Examination of the 31 applications showed no systematic relation of α to the overall level of fertility, but did suggest that β tended to be small in low fertility countries and high in higher fertility countries. This relationship was taken into account in choosing combinations of fertility level (total fertility rate) and pattern (α and β) in the simulations of proportions dead of children ever borne. It is an important characteristic of this model that the first birth is automatically excluded. In the simulations, the first birth is exposed to mortality risk for the maximum exposure time possible, while subsequent births are distributed by exposure according to the model. For this reason, fertility level, determining the ratio of first to subsequent births, matters in these simulations, whereas it did not matter in previous versions of the Brass method – neither the one based on maternal age nor the one based on time since first marriage.

MORTALITY RISKS

Mortality risks by single years of age were taken from Coale–Demeny model life-tables (Coale and Demeny, 1983) for three mortality levels (10, 15 and 20, corresponding to expectations of life at birth for females of 42.5, 55 and 67.5 years respectively) for each of the four families of tables. Single-year values of the survivors to exact age x, $\ell(x)$, for values of x from 5 to 25 were obtained by linear interpolation, and a both-sex life-table was

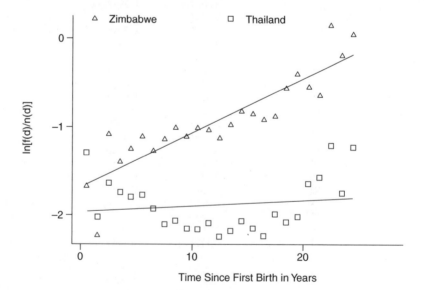

Figure 1.1   Fits of fertility since first birth model to Thailand and Zimbabwe

obtained by combining the male and female tables using a sex ratio at birth of 105 males per 100 females. Survivorship probabilities for single years of age were obtained by assuming linearity of the survivorship curve across one year periods above age 1, and by applying an average age at death of 0.3 years for children dying under 1 for levels 10 and 15, and of 0.2 years for level 20.

POPULATION GROWTH RATE

The fertility model used in the simulations varies with the total fertility rate (TFR), so the population growth rate, used to weight simulations at different times since first birth into five-year groups, also varies with the fertility pattern chosen. The growth rate for a particular simulation was estimated assuming a mean length of generation of 29 years, and an estimate of the Net Reproduction Rate derived from the TFR as $(TFR/2.05)(\ell(29)/l(0))$, where $\ell(29)$ and $\ell(0)$ are life-table survivors to age 29 and 0 respectively.

SIMULATING PROPORTIONS DEAD AMONG CHILDREN EVER BORNE

The number of children ever borne and the number dead among those children is estimated at single-year points since the first birth. The number of children ever borne (CEB) at time since first birth a, CEB (a), is simply 1 (the first birth) plus the sum of the fertility rates by time since first birth up to time a:

$$CEB(a) = 1 + \sum_{t=0}^{a-1} f(t) \tag{2}$$

where f(t) is the fertility rate at t years after first birth. The number of dead children at time since first birth a, CD (a), is the sum of the products of fertility rates and probabilities of dying:

$$CD(a) = q(a) \quad + \sum_{t=0}^{a-1} f(t) \left(1 - {}_1 L_{a-t} / \ell(0)\right) \tag{3}$$

where $q(a)$ is the probability of dying by age a, ${}_1 L_{a-t}$ is the life-table person-years lived at age $(a-t)$, and $\ell(0)$ is the radix of the life-table. The population growth rate, r, is then used to combine average numbers of children ever borne and children dead for five-year time since first-birth intervals, on the assumption that the number of women at each time since first-birth category is given by $exp(-r*a)$ relative to the current number having a first birth. Denoting the five-year groups by time since first birth by the index i, the proportion dead of children ever borne in the group is then obtained as the ratio of *CD(i)/CEB(i)*. The average parity for the group is simply the average *CEB(i)*.

RELATING PROPORTIONS DEAD TO STANDARD MORTALITY INDICES

Proportions dead in a particular interval are affected by mortality risk and by the time distribution of births. A proportion dead is converted into an estimate of a probability of dying by an exact age of childhood by allowing for the time distribution of births. Ratios of observed average parity are used in this conversion, such that

$$_nq_0/PD(i) = a(i) + b(i)\{P(1)/P(2)\} + c(i)\{P(2)/P(3)\} \tag{4}$$

where *P(1)*, *P(2)* and *P(3)* are the average parities in each five-year time since first-birth interval. Linear regression was used to estimate values of *a(i)*, *b(i)* and *c(i)* from the simulated proportions dead and average parities in time since first-birth groups from 0 to 4 through 20 to 24. Separate regressions were run for each family of Coale–Demeny model life table. Values of *a(i)*, *b(i)* and *c(i)* are shown in Table 1.2.

The form of equation (4) is a corollary of the equations used for the age- and duration of marriage-based methods developed by Trussell (1975). Some experimentation with alternative forms was tried before adopting equation (4), because it was not obvious what indicator of fertility timing to use. The method uses time since first birth as the surrogate for child exposure time, but the first birth is exposed throughout the period, and only subsequent births are distributed according to the model. The model pattern might, therefore, be reflected better by ratios of {parity − 1} than by parity. This formulation was tried, but resulted in substantially less good fits for equation (4) than using parity.

The next question to arise was what values of n to use in the $_nq_0$. Again, experimentation showed that the use of values of *n* of 2, 3, 5, 10 and 15 for the time since first-birth groups 0 to 4, 5 to 9, 10 to 14, 15 to 19 and 20 to 24 respectively gave satisfactory results. Average exposure time of children for groups of women defined by time since first birth is somewhat longer than average exposure time for groups defined by duration of marriage, but the same relations work well for both.

REFERENCE DATES OF THE ESTIMATES

Under conditions of changing mortality, each proportion dead identifies an $_nq_0$ from a period life-table for some point in the past, where the point in

Table 1.2   *Coefficients for application of time since first birth mortality estimation*

$$\frac{{}_n q_o}{PD(i)} = a(i) + b(i)\frac{P(1)}{P(2)} + c(i)\frac{P(2)}{P(3)}$$

	Time since first birth (years)				
	0–4 $n = 2$	5–9 $n = 3$	10–14 $n = 5$	15–19 $n = 10$	20–24 $n = 15$
North Model					
a	1.1809	1.1298	1.2037	1.2933	1.3240
b	−0.0787	−0.1609	−0.0107	0.0987	0.1557
c	−0.0182	−0.0746	−0.2856	−0.4629	−0.5678
South Model					
a	1.1697	1.1337	1.2977	1.4860	1.5278
b	−0.1431	−0.2625	−0.0416	0.1566	0.2619
c	0.0034	−0.0859	−0.4335	−0.7602	−0.9135
East Model					
a	1.2023	1.1669	1.2501	1.3243	1.3279
b	−0.1322	−0.1911	−0.0003	0.1220	0.1701
c	−0.0022	−0.0943	−0.3383	−0.5121	−0.5770
West Model					
a	1.1882	1.1410	1.2417	1.3631	1.4240
b	−0.1063	−0.1953	−0.0231	0.1104	0.1934
c	−0.0098	−0.0822	−0.3390	−0.5766	−0.7420

the past lies between the time of the survey and the longest exposure time of the children. Each period life-table in the past is effectively weighted by the number of child deaths that occur in the period, so the reference period of an estimate can be approximated by the average time of occurrence of the deaths of the children reported on. The reference period will be affected to a minor extent by the direction and pace of mortality change. A rapid increase in mortality will bring the reference period closer to the present, whereas a rapid decline will move the reference date further into the past. However, as Coale and Trussell (1977) show, the effect of such change is small relative to the impact of different time distributions of exposure.

The time reference of the estimates based on proportions dead classified by time since first birth is estimated from equation (5):

$$t^*(i) = d(i) + e(i)\{P(1)/P(2)\} + f(i)\{P(2)/P(3)\} \qquad (5)$$

where $t^*(i)$ is the number of years before the survey to which the estimate applies. Values of $d(i)$, $e(i)$ and $f(i)$ estimated by regression are given in Table 1.3 for each family of Coale–Demeny model life tables. These reference points tend to be longer in the past for the time since first birth method

Table 1.3   Coefficients for estimating the time reference of estimates

	Time since first birth (years)				
	0–4	5–9	10–14	15–19	20–24
North Model					
d	1.71	2.16	0.66	−1.96	−3.85
e	1.07	4.36	3.50	−0.90	−6.42
f	−0.35	0.12	6.65	17.66	28.94
South Model					
d	1.68	2.29	1.19	−1.01	−2.68
e	0.96	3.84	3.45	−0.18	−5.06
f	−0.32	−0.01	5.41	15.03	25.21
East Model					
d	1.68	2.19	0.71	−1.96	−4.06
e	0.99	4.28	3.63	−0.71	−6.35
f	−0.33	0.02	6.36	17.42	29.14
West Model					
d	1.70	2.20	0.86	−1.46	−2.97
e	1.03	4.20	3.47	−0.69	−5.80
f	−0.34	0.06	6.21	16.49	26.65

than for the duration of marriage approach because the first birth is exposed to the maximum exposure period.

AN ILLUSTRATIVE APPLICATION

Haiti is a suitable country for using the new approach, since marriage patterns are informal. The 1987 Survey of Mortality, Morbidity and Service Utilization in Haiti (EMMUS) included questions on children ever borne, age of mother and age at first pregnancy. Internal patterns in the data suggest that this latter question was answered as age at first birth, and so has been used to tabulate parous women by time since first birth. The 1994 Survey of Mortality and Morbidity in Haiti (EMMUS-II), part of the Demographic and Health Surveys programme, collected complete birth histories, providing estimates of child mortality for five-year periods back to 15–19 years before the survey. It is therefore possible to apply the technique proposed here to data from the 1987 survey, as well as applying the age-based indirect method, and to compare the resulting estimates to both direct and age-based indirect estimates from the 1994 survey.

Table 1.4 shows the application of the new method to data on proportions dead tabulated by time since first birth. Coefficients from Tables 1.2 and 1.3 for the 'West' family of Coale–Demeny model life-tables have been used, since the direct birth histories from the 1994 survey suggest a close fit of child mortality patterns to that family. The estimates of $_nq_0$ increase

Table 1.4 *Applications of new method to data from Mortality, Morbidity and Service Utilization Survey, Haiti, 1987*

Time since first birth group	Average children ever born	Average children dead	Proportion dead	'West' family k (i)	n	$_nq_o$	'West' family $_5q_o$	Time ago	Reference date
0–4	1.567	0.187	0.1193	1.1294	2	0.1347	0.1755	1.98	85.22
5–9	3.193	0.546	0.1710	0.9895	3	0.1692	0.1955	4.30	83.20
10–14	4.718	0.931	0.1973	1.0009	5	0.1975	0.1975	6.77	80.73
15–19	5.754	1.280	0.2225	1.0271	10	0.2285	0.1974	9.36	78.14
20–24	6.216	1.591	0.2560	1.0167	15	0.2603	0.2104	12.22	75.28

$P(1)/P(2) = 0.491$; $P(2)/P(3) = 0.677$.

monotonically with time since first birth group, and the $_5q_0$ values implied by each $_nq_0$ in the 'West' family of model life-tables also increase, except for a very small decline from the 10–14 to the 15–19 year groups. The reference dates of the estimates also increase with time since first birth, from about two years before the survey for the 0–4 group to about 12 years before the survey for the 20–24 group.

Figure 1.2 shows the estimates of $_5q_0$ plotted against reference date, and includes estimates using other methods and data sources. The 1987 EMMUS data have also been analysed by age group of mother, direct estimates of

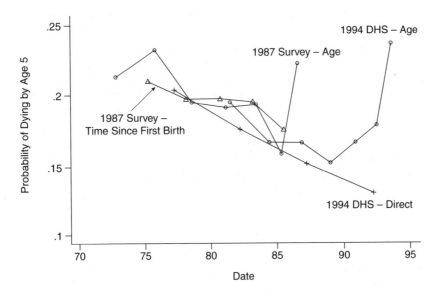

Figure 1.2   Time since first birth estimates of child mortality and other available estimates for Haiti: 1970–94

child mortality by time period are available from the 1994 EMMUS-II, and indirect estimates of child mortality using the age-based methodology have also been made from the 1994 EMMUS-II.

As expected, the age-based indirect estimates, from both the 1987 survey and the 1994 survey, show a sharp upward spike for the estimate nearest the date of the survey (based on women age 15–19). The 1994 direct estimates show a very smooth pattern of decline over time, though at levels generally slightly below the indirect estimates. The new estimates, based on time since first birth, are in general very close to the 1987 indirect estimates based on age group, but the new estimates show a much more consistent time pattern. There is no spike for the most recent estimate, and irregularities observed between the age-group estimates based on reports of women aged 35–39, 40–44 and 45–49 are not evident in the time since first-birth estimates. The new estimates suggest a period of stalled child mortality decline in the early 1980s that is not evident in the trend shown by the direct estimates from the 1994 EMMUS-II. Both the direct and the indirect estimates from EMMUS-II tend to be a bit below the indirect estimates from EMMUS, though the largest difference (excluding mortality estimates based on reports of younger women) between any pair of estimates for a similar time period is less than 25 per thousand.

CONCLUSION

Time since first birth provides an alternative proxy for children's exposure to risk of dying. It shares with time since first marriage the advantages over an age-based proxy of reduced socio-economic selection combined with large numbers of observations in the shortest exposure category, but avoids the disadvantage of the time since first marriage proxy of not being applicable in populations with substantial proportions of births outside formal unions. Birth rates can be reasonably well modelled by time since first birth, and observed proportions dead can be converted into standard mortality indicators both easily and accurately.

A trial application to data from Haiti confirms the expected advantage of the time since first-birth formulation relative to the existing age-based formulation. The new method appears to give good estimates of both levels and trends of child mortality over a 12-year period before the survey.

REFERENCES

Brass, W. (1964) 'Uses of census and survey data for the estimation of vital rates' (E/CN.14/CAS.4/V57), paper prepared for the African Seminar on Vital Statistics, Addis Ababa, 14–19 December 1964.

Brass, W. (1975) *Methods for Estimating Fertility and Mortality from Limited and*

Defective Data. Chapel Hill, NC: Laboratories for Population Statistics, University of North Carolina.

Coale, A.J. and Demeny P. with B. Vaughan (1983) *Regional Model Life Tables and Stable Populations*, 2nd ed. New York: Academic Press.

Coale, A.J. and Trussell, J. (1977) 'Estimating the time to which Brass estimates apply'. Annex 1 to S.H. Preston and A. Palloni, 'Fine-Tuning Brass-Type Mortality Estimates with Data on Ages of Surviving Children'. *Population Bulletin of the United Nations*, No.10.

Feeney, G. (1980) 'Estimating infant mortality trends from child survivorship data'. *Population Studies*, vol 34, No 1.

Rodriguez, G. and J. Cleland (1988). 'Modelling Marital Fertility by Age and Duration: An Empirical Appraisal of the Page Model'. *Population Studies*, vol 42, No 2.

Sullivan, J.M. (1972) 'Models for the estimation of the probability of dying between birth and exact ages of early childhood'. *Population Studies*, vol 26, No 1.

Trussell, T.J. (1975) 'A re-estimation of the multiplying factors for the Brass technique for determining childhood survivorship rates'. *Population Studies*, vol 29, No 1.

United Nations (1983) Manual X: *Indirect Techniques for Demographic Estimation* (Population Studies No. 81). New York: Department of International and Social Affairs, United Nations.

CHAPTER TWO

Adjustment methods for bias in the indirect childhood mortality estimates

Martine Collumbien and Andy Sloggett

Centre for Population Studies, London
School of Hygiene and Tropical Medicine

INTRODUCTION

Retrospective questions on childhood survivorship in censuses and surveys are an important source of information on mortality levels and trends in countries without adequate vital registration systems. The original 'children ever borne – children surviving' method (CEB/CS) as developed by Brass (Brass *et al*, 1968; Brass, 1975) has been improved upon, relaxing some of the assumptions which underlie the method. Reviews of the CEB/CS method for estimating mortality levels and trends with its merits and limitations, as it stands today, can be found in papers by Feeney (1991) and Hill (1991).

The indirect estimation technique converts aggregate proportions dead of children ever born to women, classified in seven reproductive age groups 15–19 to 45–49, into life-table probabilities of dying. Plotting these estimates back in time allows the evaluation of mortality trends. A modelling bias typically affects the most recent estimate which is derived from women 15–19 years old. The strong upward bias is due to the invalidity of the assumption of homogeneity of mortality risk by mother's age at birth. It has been well established that children born to teenage mothers have a higher risk of dying than their peers born to older mothers during the same period, due to higher levels of prematurity and low birth weight (Nortman, 1974). Since a considerable proportion of children of 20–24 year olds were born when the mothers were in their teens, this second most recent estimate also frequently implies higher mortality than the overall trend. The conventional view that higher risks to first births also contribute to this bias has been challenged by multivariate analysis of mortality risk, whereby the apparent adverse effect of first births usually disappears or reverses when controlling for the confounding effect of mother's age at birth (Martin *et al*, 1983; Trussell and Hammerslough, 1983). Our experience of multivariate analysis using the data sets presented here concurred with this finding.

Fernandez Castilla (1989) calculated adjustment factors to correct the retrospective mortality estimates for the bias introduced by assuming constant mortality by birth order and by age of mother at birth. He proposed a functional description of mortality using empirical data and three third-degree polynomials to model the probability of survival as a function of birth order, maternal age and birth concentration. The variation of proportions dead by age of mother and parity relative to the overall mortality level allows the assessment of the impact of the mortality differentials on the levels obtained by the retrospective estimates. Correction factors to adjust the proportions dead by age group are given for different fertility and nuptiality patterns and the user needs an estimate of the mean age at marriage and of the total fertility rate (TFR) to select the appropriate adjustment factors.

Good quality data from retrospective maternity histories collected in the World Fertility Survey (WFS) and the Demographic and Health Survey (DHS) have become available. These large-scale surveys with good questionnaire design, high quality training and supervision have proved to generate sufficiently accurate direct information on mortality levels, trends and age patterns in Third World settings. These birth history data are also valuable for analysing modelling bias in indirect childhood mortality estimates (Hill, 1991).

This paper suggests two adjustment methods to correct the bias caused by the assumption of homogeneity of mortality risk by mother's age. In contrast to the correction factors of Fernandez Castilla the studied adjustments are population-specific. Firstly, a relative risk approach was adopted using birth history data from the DHS to estimate the excess mortality risk associated with mother's age at the time of the birth. The second is a simple method used with census data, with no need for direct estimates from birth histories. It adjusts the proportions dead of children ever borne to women aged 20–24 at the time of survey, based on the proportions dead to children of 15–19 year old women and the parity ratio $P(1)/P(2)$.

RELATIVE RISK ADJUSTMENT

The relative mortality risks associated with births to teenage mothers were calculated using DHS birth history data. Only countries with data available from two DHS rounds were included in this study to allow a more accurate estimation of trends in child mortality. Direct and indirect estimates were used to calculate benchmark levels of period mortality, against which the adjusted mortality estimates could be compared.

Derivation of adjustment factor
The relative mortality risk associated with births to teenage mothers and the proportions of these 'high-risk' births among CEB are calculated from birth history data, limiting the records to births in the last 10 years before the survey. The hazard regression model used to calculate the relative mortality risk of children born to women younger than 20 is presented in equation (1):

$$\log(\text{hazard of dying}) = B_0 + B_1 * \text{YOUNG} \qquad (1)$$

The dependent variable in the model is the hazard of a child death occurring. The risk factor YOUNG is an indicator variable, taking a value of 1 when the age of the mother at birth is below 20 and a value of 0 otherwise. The relative mortality risk associated with a birth to a young mother is equal to $\text{Exp}(B_1)$, compared to a risk of 1 for other births. These relative risks for the 18 surveys are summarized in Table 2.1. The countries are listed according to the level of under-five mortality, Senegal having highest mortality. The three countries with highest mortality showed stable estimates of risk across the two surveys. Kenya and Zimbabwe had a lower risk in the second survey, whereas in the remaining countries teenage births become even riskier. Both trends can be explained: when age at marriage is rising, first births will be delayed to a later, less risky age towards the upper limit of the 15–19 year age group. In the lower fertility countries (Indonesia, Morocco, Peru and Dominican Republic), the women who start childbearing early may come from a increasingly disadvantaged group.

The most recent childhood mortality estimate derived from the 15–19 year olds is based entirely on these 'high-risk' births, whereas among all children born during that period only a small proportion are born to teenage mothers. To adjust the proportions dead derived from the two youngest age groups so they represent period mortality a process of standardization is performed. Consider the example of the Dominican Republic DHS, 1986. For children born during the last 10 years before the survey, the mortality risk for births to teenage mothers was 1.38. With 21.0 per cent of all children being born to women under 20, the average risk of all births is calculated as the weighted average 0.21 * 1.38 + 0.79 * 1 = 1.08. The correction factor for the 15–19 group is then computed as 1.08/1.38 = 0.78 and the proportion

Table 2.1 *Countries included in the study: date of two DHS surveys and the excess mortality risk of births to teenage mothers*

Country	Year of survey DHS I	Excess risk to teenage births	Year of survey DHS II or III	Excess risk to teenage births
Senegal	1986	1.26	1993	1.24
Ghana	1988	1.30	1993	1.28
Egypt	1988	1.55	1992	1.56
Indonesia	1987	1.31	1991	1.53
Morocco	1987	1.45	1992	1.55
Kenya	1989	1.26	1993	1.19
Zimbabwe	1988	1.40	1994	1.17
Peru	1986	1.18	1992	1.33
Dominican Republic	1986	1.38	1991	1.62

dead among CEB are multiplied by this factor to derive the adjusted proportion. For the women aged 20–24 at the time of the survey, 54.5 per cent
of the CEB were born when these women were in their teens. The average
mortality risk for CEB to these women is $0.545 * 1.38 + 0.455 * 1 = 1.21$
and the correction factor is $1.08/1.21 = 0.89$. By multiplying the proportion dead among CEB to mothers 20–24 by this factor the proportions are
adjusted for the surplus of high-risk births to teenage mothers.

Benchmark levels of period mortality
For each survey, three sets of mortality estimates were calculated: the direct
synthetic cohort probabilities of dying and both the age- and duration of
marriage-based indirect estimates. Using information on deaths and exposure
to risk of dying by age during three five-year period intervals before the
survey, synthetic cohort probabilities of death were calculated and aggre-
gated into estimates of under-five mortality. The calculation of these period
estimates of mortality for survey data is clearly explained by Rutstein (1984).
The $_5q_0$ estimates refer to time-points in the middle of each five-year interval.
Truncation bias affecting direct trends was dealt with by restricting births
to children whose mothers were younger than 35 at the time of birth. For
the most recent period, a correct level of under-five mortality was also calculated using births to women of all ages.

Direct estimates of infant mortality $_1q_0$ and child mortality $_4q_1$ were used
to determine the age pattern of child mortality allowing the selection of the
appropriate Coale–Demeny model life-table family for use in the indirect
estimation procedure (United Nations, 1990). All indirect mortality estimates,
based on proportions dead among CEB for each age and each duration group
were converted into indices of $_5q_0$, using the suitable Coale–Demeny model
life-table and Brass's relational logit system. Under-five mortality was taken
as a common index because of its robustness to choice of mortality patterns
in the indirect approach and its lower susceptibility to bias from misreporting
of ages at death in the direct approach.

Finally, a regression line was drawn through all direct estimates of
mortality and the reliable points from the indirect series. In the age-based
approach, the points from the two youngest age groups were always
excluded, and estimates from older cohorts looking questionable were also
rejected. The most recent estimate for the marriage-duration approach was
rejected if biased upwards and the highest duration group (30–34 years of
marriage) has always been excluded, as were other estimates that seemed
badly out of line. This combined regression line was considered to give the
best estimate of period mortality and was used as the benchmark for comparison when evaluating the adjusted mortality estimates.

　　　　Martine Collumbien and Andy Sloggett

Application of relative risk adjustment
The nine graphs in Figure 2.1a-c show the direct and indirect mortality estimates and the adjusted values for the two youngest age groups. Although
all indirect estimates are plotted, only the ones considered reliable were
included in the calculation of the regression line. The selection of reliable
points was guided by the consistency between the surveys overlapping in
time. The adjusted mortality estimates are generally much closer to the
regression line than the unadjusted Brass estimates.

The first panel in Table 2.2 gives the deviations of the unadjusted Brass
mortality estimates and the adjusted values from the assumed 'benchmark'

Table 2.2　*The deviations of the Brass unadjusted and the relative risk (RR) adjusted
under-five mortality estimates from the benchmark mortality level (deaths per 1000)*

	Estimates from 15–19 group			Estimates from 20–24 group		
		Deviation from benchmark*			Deviation from benchmark*	
Country	Bench-mark	Unadjusted Brass	RR adjusted	Bench-mark	Unadjusted Brass	RR adjusted
	$_5q_0$	$_5q_0$	$_5q_0$	$_5q_0$	$_5q_0$	$_5q_0$
DHS I						
Senegal	186	54	18	197	18	0
Ghana	146	−47	−66	149	14	−2
Egypt	113	39	−5	122	27	5
Indonesia	113	61	29	116	−3	−14
Morocco	109	74	26	113	28	8
Kenya	100	71	44	101	10	1
Zimbabwe	90	26	−1	91	−5	−15
Peru	97	67	46	102	4	−3
Dominican Rep.	72	61	33	77	41	29
DHS II or III						
Senegal	131	29	5	141	11	−2
Ghana	132	−26	−45	135	9	−4
Egypt	82	30	−4	91	36	16
Indonesia	103	94	41	106	20	0
Morocco	85	83	30	90	9	−7
Kenya	99	110	85	99	6	−1
Zimbabwe	86	25	12	87	15	9
Peru	70	21	2	76	23	14
Dominican Rep.	52	43	14	57	17	7
	104	53	28	108	16	8

* Deviation from the benchmark in this table refers to the distance of the mortality estimates to the
regression fine through all direct estimates and all reliable age- and duration-based indirect estimates
from the two surveys combined (expressed in deaths per thousand)

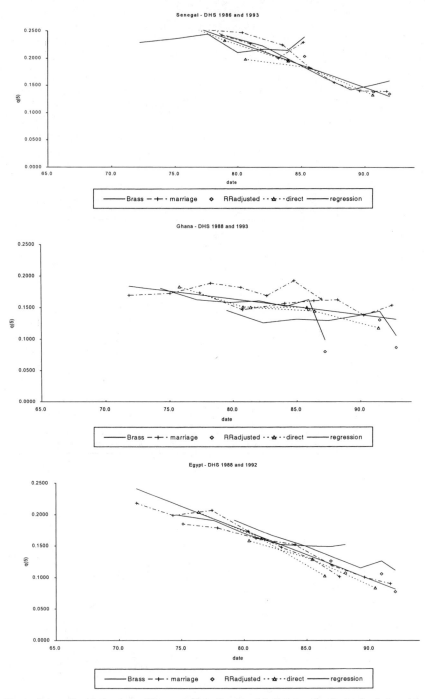

Figure 2.1a   Trends in under-five mortality: direct and indirect estimates and relative risk adjusted values for Senegal, Ghana and Egypt

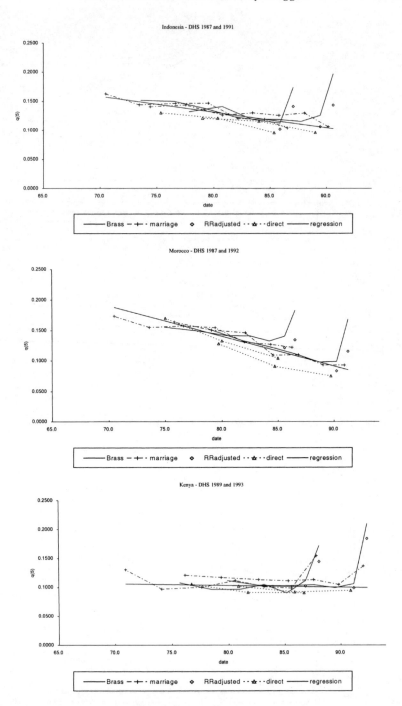

Figure 2.1b   Trends in under-five mortality: direct and indirect estimates and relative risk adjusted values for Indonesia, Morocco and Kenya

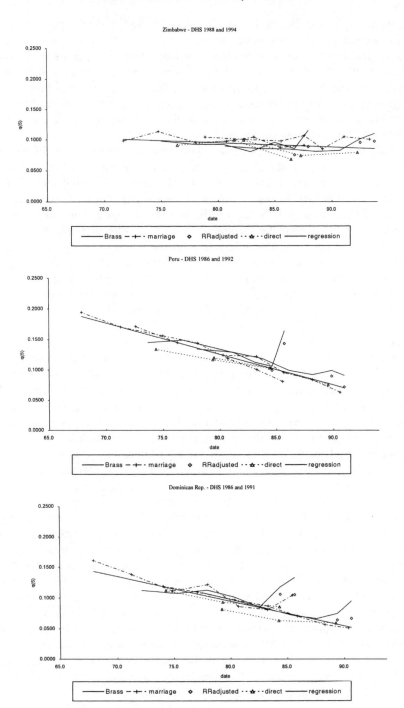

Figure 2.1c   Trends in under-five mortality: direct and indirect estimates and relative risk adjusted values for Zimbabwe, Peru and Dominican Republic

mortality level for the 15–19 age group, expressed in deaths per thousand. The second panel gives these results for the 20–24 year olds. Negative values indicate that the adjusted value lies below the benchmark value. The comparison of distances from the regression line for adjusted and unadjusted estimates allows us to appraise whether the relative risk adjustment significantly improves the consistency among the estimates or whether the remaining errors are large compared to the bias caused by the surplus of high-risk births to teenage mothers.

The results of the relative risk adjustment are summarized for the 18 surveys by averaging the absolute values of the deviations of the adjusted values to the benchmark line. For the 20–24 group the adjusted value differs from the benchmark by an average of 8 deaths per thousand, compared to 16 deaths per thousand for the unadjusted Brass points. The improvement obtained by correcting the estimates for excess risks of births to teenage mothers is 54 per cent. The adjustment for the youngest age group reduced the distance from an average of 53 to 28 deaths per thousand, an improvement of 47 per cent (this improvement would be 56 per cent if the Ghana data set were excluded: the 15–19 estimate is strongly biased downwards and in practice an adjustment would never be applied).

Discussion
Since the 'true' mortality level and trend are not known, the evaluation of the adjustments is necessarily subjective. The validity of the finding that, on average half of the total error affecting the most recent estimates could be eliminated by adjusting for excess mortality risk to teenage births, should be evaluated considering other modelling biases and the sampling variability affecting the survey-based indirect estimates. The benchmark levels of period mortality used for the evaluation of the adjustment may also be flawed by errors affecting both direct and indirect trends. The internal consistency between mortality estimates will therefore be discussed first.

Both the indirect and direct approach to measuring mortality may produce biases in estimated levels and trends of mortality. Non-sampling errors include reporting errors, interviewer misrecording of data, structural errors arising from questionnaire design and errors due to violation of the simplifying assumptions underlying the indirect method. In papers evaluating WFS and DHS data, Preston (1985) and Sullivan (1990) appraise direct information for estimation of recent levels, and especially trends, as superior to the indirect information. Their evaluation is largely based on the same case study in Indonesia, comparing indirect estimates with infant mortality rates calculated on birth cohort basis using WFS data. Hill (1991), discussing the same study, shows that by using synthetic period based rates, nearly all the discrepancy between the direct and indirect levels was eliminated. The direct trends on period basis were shown to be much smoother than those based on birth cohorts.

As shown in Figure 2.1, the agreement between directly and indirectly derived mortality levels and trends for the nine countries is generally high. Overall, the indirect estimates seem to give higher recent mortality levels than the synthetic cohort rates calculated from dated events. Since the number of births and deaths are identical for calculating both the direct and the indirect estimates, any deviations arise from the differences between the direct and indirect allocation of deaths and exposure to risk in specific time periods, explicit for direct estimates and implicit in the case of indirect estimates (Hill, 1991). This is not entirely true here since the direct estimates are adjusted for truncation bias: the implied mortality level is therefore biased downwards a bit, although on average the truncated $_5q_0$ estimate for the most recent period was lower than the one calculated from births to women of all ages by less than 2 per cent (the maximum difference was 3 per cent and for 6 out of the 18 surveys the correct level estimate was actually lower than the one adjusted for truncation).

For most countries the indirect trend is very similar to the trend derived from direct estimates. The indirect approach suggests a steeper mortality decline in Peru and a slower decline in Morocco than the direct trend. The indirect trends referred to here are based on all reliable points from two DHS surveys together. When each indirect series is evaluated separately, some data sets show a less rapid decline in mortality (Ghana, especially the 1993 DHS, the 1986 Senegal DHS). This may be due to selective underreporting of dead children by older mothers or errors in the assumed mortality pattern may also bias the trend. The indirect techniques assume a certain model age pattern of child mortality and also a fixed rate of mortality change over time in order to estimate the underlying trend. Choice of an inappropriate age pattern of mortality will result in misestimation of trends, and Hill (1984) states that the choice of model can affect the estimates of $_xq_0$ from reports of women under 30 by nearly 10 per cent. The use of $_5q_0$ as a common index reduces biases in the estimates obtained, but they cannot be guaranteed to be accurate when the actual mortality pattern is very different from the model life-table used (United Nations, 1990). In this study the choice of model family was guided by using direct information on age pattern from the dated events, and bias introduced should therefore be minimal. Although the Northern pattern of the Coale–Demeny life-table was used for all four countries of Sub-Saharan Africa (Zimbabwe, Kenya, Ghana and Senegal), Senegal and Ghana, with the highest levels of mortality, had a ratio of child to infant mortality still much higher than that represented by the North model.

Recent sharp mortality fluctuations can also give rise to higher recent mortality estimates. Ewbank (1982) analysed the bias introduced by the impact of a mortality peak three years before a survey in Bangladesh where extensive flooding had devastated the country's crops. For older age groups,

any sharp change in mortality is smoothed out as the indirect estimate represents the weighted average of period mortality conditions from the time of
first childbearing by the cohort up to the present (United Nations, 1992).
The effect of recent disasters will therefore be more important for the
youngest group, as their children were all born quite recently.

Another source of bias in the indirect mortality estimates is the violation
of the assumption of constant fertility in the recent past. If fertility is falling
for women under 30, either through a general fall in fertility rates or as a
result of a rising age at marriage, parity ratios $P(1)/P(2)$ and $P(2)/P(3)$ will
not adequately define the current fertility pattern. The Trussell regression
equation (United Nations, 1983) uses these parity ratios to obtain the average
duration of exposure to risk of dying needed in converting proportions of
children dead into probabilities of dying before age x. Since the parity ratios
will be too low, average exposure times will be underestimated and recent
child mortality will tend to be overestimated. However, Feeney (1980) and
Hill (1984) point out that mortality estimates are rather robust against violation of the constant fertility assumption.

The indirect estimates derived by classifying child survival data by duration of marriage give variable results as can be seen in Figure 2.1. As Hill
(1984) points out, the method does not give systematically better estimates
than the age-based one, despite the several theoretical advantages to the
duration classification. In reality it is not clear whether duration of marriage
is more accurately reported than age. The duration-based estimates should
be less model dependent since fertility changes less sharply by marital duration than by age and changes in age at marriage have less effect. The most
recent estimate should be less dominated by higher risk births to young
women and suffer less from selection by social factors. The most recent
duration estimate from the two Moroccan and the two Indonesian surveys
with extremely high mortality from the youngest age groups give a much
lower and very plausible mortality estimate when data are classified by
marriage duration. In the two Kenyan surveys and in the 1986 Dominican
DHS, however, the duration-based estimate is still clearly biased upwards.
In Ghana the duration-based approach gives overall higher mortality than
the age based estimates, as is the case for the first Senegal DHS.

Although not free of error, the direct trends are considered more reliable.
Misreporting of ages at death often bias estimates of infant mortality but have
little effect on the under-five mortality (Rutstein, 1985). The misreporting of
birth dates of children can distort mortality trends and recent levels. DHS
maternity histories have suffered from deliberate displacement of births out
of the period five years before the survey, caused by interviewers avoiding
to ask series of questions on family planning, health and breast-feeding
(Arnold, 1990). Since children are displaced across the same boundary used
to calculate the synthetic cohort rates, mortality rates calculated in this study

may have been affected by the displacement of birth dates. The mortality rates would be overestimated for periods the births are shifted into, and an excessive drop occurs for the most recent period. Sullivan *et al* (1990) simulated that the impact is primarily determined by differential displacement by survivorship status and the effects remain minimal (< 3 per cent).

When looking at cross-survey consistency, the $_5q_0$'s estimated from dated events generally agree well, although the most recent estimate from the 1986 Dominican Republic DHS is 36 per cent higher than that estimated from the 1991 DHS referring to the same period.

Overall, the good agreement between the rates and trends derived directly from dated events and those obtained via models and based on assumptions typical of the two variants of the indirect techniques is quite encouraging. The suggested benchmark mortality level as standard for comparing adjusted and unadjusted mortality estimates against seems therefore quite reliable.

The most serious problem hindering the evaluation of the adjustments is the sampling errors affecting the survey-based indirect estimates, particularly those derived from the youngest age group. Sampling errors (SE) are calculated for the proportions dead D(i) of CEB by age group of mother at the time of the survey (with i = 1 for 15–19 and i = 2 for 20–24). The sampling error is equal to the square root of the product of D(i) and (1 − D(i)) divided by the CEB. The 95 per cent confidence intervals for the estimate are calculated as the D(i) ± 2 * SE and give the range within which the true proportion falls, with 95 per cent certainty. Table 2.3 gives the CEB, the proportions dead and the lower and upper 95 per cent confidence limits for the sample proportions for the two youngest age groups.

The example of Ghana DHS 1988 shows that 6.6 per cent of CEB to the first age group died. With 95 per cent certainty, the real value will be anything within the range of 29 to 102 deaths per thousand children. This translates to corresponding estimates of $_5q_0$ varying from 45 to 151 deaths per thousand. The low mortality estimate as seen in the graph could be entirely due to sampling error. For the first age group, the range (width) of the confidence interval for the proportions dead varies from 51 to 111 deaths per thousand, with an average range of 72 deaths per thousand. The true proportions dead of CEB to women 20–24 lie in intervals with a range of 18 to 42 deaths per thousand (average range is 30 deaths per thousand). Brass *et al* (1968) indeed considered the large sampling variability of the total number of dead children to young women a major reason to mistrust the most recent estimates from sample surveys.

The random errors are thus potentially much bigger than the systematic bias introduced by the assumption of homogeneity of mortality risk. Though this will not be the case in censuses, it does question the suitability of DHS data for evaluating the extent of defects and modelling biases affecting the indirect estimation of mortality levels and trends. Consequently, evaluation

Table 2.3   *The sampling errors of the proportions dead of CEB to the two youngest age groups*

Country	15–19 age group				20–24 age group			
	CEB	D(1)	95% confidence interval		CEB	D(2)	95% confidence Interval	
			Lower limit	Upper limit			Lower limit	Upper limit
DHS I								
Senegal	314	0.153	0.112	0.193	1401	0.171	0.150	0.191
Ghana	183	0.066	0.029	0.102	1086	0.139	0.118	0.160
Egypt	275	0.090	0.055	0.124	2415	0.116	0.103	0.129
Indonesia	362	0.106	0.073	0.138	2945	0.092	0.081	0.103
Morocco	150	0.120	0.067	0.173	1287	0.106	0.089	0.123
Kenya	421	0.117	0.086	0.149	2087	0.088	0.075	0.100
Zimbabwe	192	0.073	0.035	0.110	1091	0.067	0.052	0.082
Peru	153	0.124	0.071	0.178	816	0.085	0.065	0.104
Dominican Rep.	438	0.084	0.058	0.111	1865	0.086	0.073	0.099
DHS II/III								
Senegal	379	0.108	0.076	0.140	1703	0.131	0.115	0.147
Ghana	1086	0.139	0.118	0.160	956	0.115	0.094	0.136
Egypt	2415	0.116	0.103	0.129	2232	0.100	0.087	0.112
Indonesia	2945	0.092	0.081	0.103	4636	0.104	0.095	0.113
Morocco	1287	0.106	0.089	0.123	999	0.078	0.061	0.095
Kenya	2087	0.088	0.075	0.100	2223	0.081	0.070	0.093
Zimbabwe	1091	0.067	0.052	0.082	1397	0.080	0.066	0.095
Peru	816	0.085	0.065	0.104	2431	0.082	0.071	0.093
Dominican Rep.	1865	0.086	0.073	0.099	1444	0.068	0.054	0.081

of the impact of any adjustments on these survey-based indirect estimates cannot be conclusive.

The relative risk adjustment derived from DHS data can be applied to census estimates. However, since both the proportion of teenage births and their associated excess mortality risk will vary over time, the census and survey from which the correction factor has been calculated should not be too far apart in time. The second adjustment method proposed in this paper is therefore entirely based on information available in censuses. The method assumes that the magnitude of the bias in the second estimate logically depends on the mortality of children born to 15–19 year olds and the pattern of fertility at the start of the reproductive ages, more specifically the ratio of the average parties of the first to the second age group (P(1)/P(2)).

SIMPLE ADJUSTMENT METHOD

A method to correct the mortality estimates for the bias introduced by assuming constant mortality by age of mother at birth is developed based on simulations. Firstly, empirical data are used to model the pattern of mortality risk by age of mother. Then the impact of higher mortality of births to teenage mothers on the proportions dead of CEB to the 20–24 age group is simulated for a wide range and combination of different fertility and mortality regimes. The results of these simulations are subsequently used to derive an adjustment factor.

Modelling the effect of age of mother at birth on child survival
Data from the DHS were used to model the mortality risk by age of mother at birth. The effect of maternal age on survival weakens as the child's age increases, with very little impact after the first year of life (Fernandez Castilla, 1989). Therefore only the infant mortality rates (IMR) are considered in the model. The IMR by age of mother was calculated from the 26 DHS-I surveys with complete birth histories (i.e. excluding El Salvador and Ondo State with truncated birth histories). A wide range of mortality experiences is covered by these countries. As Nortman (1974) has shown, the relative mortality risks by age remain much the same regardless of the absolute level of risks. This supports her claim that biological processes predominantly determine the age pattern of reproductive risk whereas social, cultural and ecnomic factors largely determine the degree of risk, whatever the mother's age.

The infant mortality rates were calculated from births (N = 118,532) in a five year period before the survey, pooled for all the DHS data sets. All children born within the year before the survey were omitted, in order to limit the analysis to data on children who had a chance to be observed alive at the end of the age interval. These infant mortality rates by age of mother at birth were also expressed as risks relative to the average infant mortality rate to all children born in that period, as presented in Table 2.4. Children born to teenage mothers have a 27 per cent higher risk of dying in infancy than the average baby born in the same period. Women 20–24 report on children born before they were 20, and on those born when they were 20–24. Using the distribution of births in the second column, the excess risk of dying in infanthood of CEB to a synthetic cohort of women is presented in the last column. Although the IMR for children born when the mother was 20–24 is slightly lower than the average for that time period, the IMR of all CEB to women 20–24 is still 7 per cent higher than the average period rate. From the third age group onwards the IMR of CEB to women is very constant and equal to the period rate, effectively diluting the effect of differential mortality by age of mother at birth.

Although the main concern is the bias introduced by the impact of higher mortality of births to teenage mothers on the proportions dead of CEB to

Table 2.4   *Infant mortality rate by age of mother at birth: pooled data from 26 DHS surveys*

Age group of mother at birth	Births in 5-year interval	Infant mortality rate (IMR)	IMR as risk in excess of average period rate	Age group of mother	IMR of CEB relative to average period rate
15–19	17,681	0.089	1.27	15–19	1.27
20–24	35,559	0.069	0.98	20–24	1.07
25–29	30,220	0.061	0.88	25–29	1.00
30–34	20,044	0.063	0.90	30–34	0.98
35–39	10,669	0.076	1.08	35–39	0.99
40–44	3,952	0.083	1.18	40–44	1.00
45–49	406	0.118	1.69	45–49	1.00
Overall	118,532	0.070			

the 20–24 group, the effect of mother's age at birth is modelled over the whole reproductive age range, since this affects the overall average infant mortality rate. Figure 2.2 plots the IMR against the age of mother in single years. After smoothing these infant mortality rates by taking three-point moving averages, a cubic polynomial was fitted to the rates of 15 to 47 year old mothers. The derived polynomial can be written as

$$IMR_x = Ax^3 - Bx^2 - Cx - D$$

with $A = -2.431 * 10^{-6}$, $B = 0.000439$, $C = -0.019122$, $D = 0.303836$ and $x =$ the age of the mother at birth in completed years.

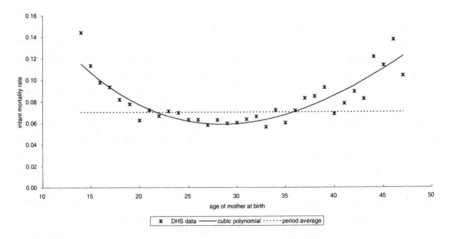

Figure 2.2   Pattern of infant mortality by mother's age at birth: DHS data and modelled approximation

The modelled IMR pattern by age of mother at birth, is also given in Figure 2.2, as is the average period rate. Infant mortality reaches its minimum at maternal age 28 to 29 at birth. Though this may seem high it agrees with the observations by Nortman (1974). She found infant mortality to be lowest at maternal age 26.1 for first births and 34 years as the optimum age for fourth births and explained it by the effect of better socio-economic circumstances typical for women who start childbearing later.

Simulation of proportions dead under conditions of constant and differential mortality by age of mother

The simulation used relational models of fertility and mortality to calculate proportions dead of CEB and average parities for the conventional age groups of women. The fertility pattern was defined using the Gompertz transformation of the Booth standard normalized cumulants by varying the location and spread parameters (Booth, 1984; Brass, 1981). Varying the level parameter is redundant as it has no effect on parity ratios and proportions dead: the estimates depend on the relative distribution of children and are affected only by the age distribution of fertility and not by the level. The mortality schedule was generated by the two-parameter logit system from the general Brass standard by varying the level and slope. To calculate the proportion of children dead for five-year age groups, the ratio of the weighted number of children dead to the weighted number of CEB to women in the corresponding range of ages was obtained. The weights used were based on the proportionate distribution of a female stable population derived from the life-table person-years lived, L_x, describing the mortality in the population, combined with an intrinsic annual growth rate of 3 per cent.

Two distributions of CEB and children surviving were simulated, firstly using constant mortality risk by age of mother at birth, and secondly allowing for differential mortality by age of mother, while ensuring equal total mortality levels. It is important to stress that the simulated effect of mother's age at birth on the proportions dead of CEB only affects survival in the first year of life (mortality at ages over 1 remain unaffected).

Derivation of the adjustment factor

We denote the proportion dead among CEB to women in successive five-year age groups at the time of interview by $D(i)$, with $i = 1$ indicating age group 15–19 up to $i = 7$ for age group 45–49. The subscripts 'con' and 'dif' respectively indicate conditions of constant and differential infant mortality by age of mother. These proportions dead $D(i)_{con}$ and $D(i)_{dif}$ and average parities were calculated for 625 combinations of fertility and mortality schedules by varying the parameters of the relational models.

The object of the simulation is to express $D(2)_{con}$, the hypothetical proportion dead of CEB to 20–24 olds assuming constant mortality by age of mother, as a function of the parity ratio and the proportion dead among children of women in the two youngest age groups $D(1)_{dif}$ and $D(2)_{dif}$, allowing for the higher mortality risk of births to teenage mothers.

The proportion dead of CEB to women 20–24 can be segregated into proportions dead of children borne by them before they reached age 20 and proportions dead of children born when they were 20–24. Let $D(i,j)$ represent the proportion dead among children born to women, aged i at the time of survey, when these women belonged to age group j at the time of birth (with $j < i$), (e.g. $D(2,1)$ represents the proportion dead of children to 20–24 old women, born when they were 15–19). The average parity $P(i)$ is the ratio of children ever borne by women in age group i to the total number of women in that age group irrespective of their marital status.

On average $P(1)$ of the $P(2)$ children were born when the mother was a teenager.[1] The number of dead children for the second maternal age group is the sum of the mean numbers dead amongst children born when the mother was in the first and second age groups, as shown in equation (2)

$$D(2)\ P(2) = P(1)\ D(2,1) + [P(2) - P(1)]\ D(2,2) \tag{2}$$

This equation can be rewritten in terms of the actual proportions dead of CEB to women in the second age group, taking account of differential infant mortality by age of mother at birth (equation 3).

$$D(2)_{dif} = \frac{P(1)}{P(2)} D(2,1)_{dif} + \frac{P(2) - P(1)}{P(2)} D(2,2)_{dif} \tag{3}$$

The proportion dead of children to women 20–24, born when they were teenagers, $D(2,1)_{dif}$ is obviously higher than the hypothetical $D(2,1)_{con}$, but $D(2)_{con}$ must satisfy a similar relationship

$$D(2)_{con} = \frac{P(1)}{P(2)} D(2,1)_{con} + \frac{P(2) - P(1)}{P(2)} D(2,2)_{con} \tag{4}$$

In order to combine both equations and isolate the $D(2)_{con}$ as the 'adjusted' proportion dead of CEB to 20–24 olds assuming constant mortality by age of mother, we have to make some simplifying assumptions. The proportion dead of children born when the mother is aged 20–24, assuming infant mortality is affected by age of mother at birth, $D(2,2)_{dif}$ is not identical to the same proportion under homogeneous mortality risk conditions $D(2,2)_{con}$. However, as can be seen from Table 2.5 infant mortality of births to women 20–24 happens to be very close to the average period rate. This is the case for both the empirical rates and the simulated rates computed from the cubic polynomial: to make the average rates comparable the IMRs were weighted by the number of births in each single-year age group of women as observed

Table 2.5 *Infant mortality by age of mother at birth: empirical and simulated rates*

Age group of mother at birth	DHS data		Simulation with differential mortality		Simulation with constant mortality	
	Infant mortality rate	IMR as risk in excess of average period rate	Infant mortality rate	IMR as risk in excess of average period rate	Infant mortality rate	IMR as risk in excess of average period rate
15–19	0.089	1.27	0.091	1.29	0.070	1.00
20–24	0.069	0.98	0.070	0.99	0.070	1.00
25–29	0.061	0.88	0.060	0.85	0.070	1.00
30–34	0.063	0.90	0.062	0.88	0.070	1.00
35–39	0.076	1.08	0.073	1.04	0.070	1.00
40–44	0.083	1.18	0.093	1.32	0.070	1.00
45–49	0.118	1.69	0.114	1.62	0.070	1.00
overall	0.070		0.070		0.070	

in the pooled DHS data set. The last columns in the table represent the conditions where mortality is independent of age of mother at birth.

Assuming that $D(2,2)_{dif}$ and $D(2,2)_{con}$ are approximately equal, equation (3) can be subtracted from equation (4) to give

$$D(2)_{con} = D(2)_{dif} + \frac{P(1)}{P(2)}(D(2,1)_{con} - D(2,1)_{dif}) \tag{5}$$

Since the effect of the mother's age at birth is assumed to be limited to infant mortality, we can show that the term $(D(2,1)_{con} - D(2,1)_{dif})$ is proportional to $(D(1)_{con} - D(1)_{dif})$ under conditions of fairly constant mortality and fertility over time.

$$D(2)_{con} = D(2)_{dif} + \frac{P(1)}{P(2)}(D(1)_{con} - D(1)_{dif}) \cdot C \tag{6}$$

$D(1)_{dif}$ and $D(2)_{dif}$ are the proportions dead reported by the women in the census. This leaves C and $D(1)_{con}$ as unknown factors on the right-hand side of the equation (6). Using the proportions dead $D(i)_{con}$ and $D(i)_{dif}$ which were simulated for the entire range and combination of mortality and fertility conditions observed in human populations, we can estimate $C.(D(1)_{con} - D(1)_{dif})$ as a function of $D(1)_{dif}$ using linear regression. The difference $(D(2)_{con} - D(2)_{dif})$ was regressed on the whole term $P(1)/P(2) \cdot D(1)_{dif}$ using the results of the 625 simulations, yielding:

$$(D(2)_{con} - D(2)_{dif}) = -0.419677 \frac{P(1)}{P(2)} D(1)_{dif} \tag{7}$$

In practice, we observe the effects of differential mortality by age, but wish to adjust these observations to eliminate the age effects. Symbolically, $D_{obs} \equiv D_{dif}$ and $D_{adj} \equiv D_{con}$, allowing equation (7) to be rewritten:

$$D(2)_{adj} - D(2)_{obs} = -0.419677 \frac{P(1)}{P(2)} D(1)_{obs} \tag{8}$$

An equation to improve the estimate from the first age group can also be derived from the regression of $D(1)_{con}$ on $D(1)_{dif}$, giving a correction to convert the reported proportion dead $D(1)_{obs}$, into an adjusted estimate $D(1)_{adj}$, representative of the mortality experience of all children born in that period.

$$D(1)_{adj} = 0.79184 \, D(1)_{obs} \tag{9}$$

The adjusted proportion dead for the first age group should be treated with more caution than the adjustment for the second age group, since the former is based entirely on the small number of births and deaths observed in the youngest age group.

Application of simple bias adjustment

Adjusted proportions dead have been calculated for censuses of 17 countries using equations (8) and (9) and the results are presented graphically in Figure 2.3, plotting under-five mortality $_5q_0$. The countries can be divided in three groups of 'adjustment performance'. The four countries (Liberia, Burundi, Colombia and Ecuador) in the top left of the graph do not show the typical upward bias in the youngest age group, and in practice the adjustments would not be applied. A second group consists of Brazil, Egypt, Morocco and Sudan, countries with the strongest upward bias in the second most recent estimate, for which the adjustment does not seem to have 'enough' effect. The nine countries for which the adjusted estimates give the most plausible results are displayed in the bottom panels of the graph. These are Guatemala, Indonesia, Mexico, Tunisia, Zimbabwe, Dominican Republic, Thailand, Peru and Botswana (for these last three countries the initial estimates were not strongly biased upward).

With information available from one data source only, it is impossible to establish whether the adjusted estimates adequately represent period mortality since the 'true' period mortality level is never known. As discussed earlier, not all of the upward bias in the mortality estimate derived from the 20–24 olds may be attributable to the impact of higher mortality of births to teenage mothers. Fertility decline, a change in marriage patterns and recent sharp mortality fluctuations could also give rise to higher recent estimates.

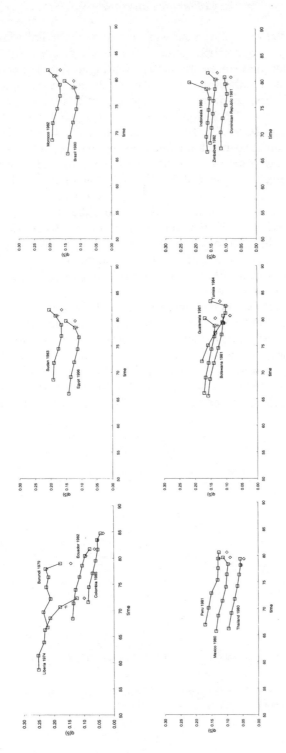

Figure 2.3   Estimates of under-five mortality in censuses: indirect estimates from adjusted value

For Kenya, the bias adjustment was applied to the indirect estimates of four censuses and two DHS surveys. The trends in under-five mortality including the adjusted values are presented in Figure 2.4. The census series gives very steady trends in mortality, showing higher mortality and steeper decline than the survey data, which seem to suffer from event omission. For the 1989 Kenyan DHS, Sullivan *et al* (1990) found evidence of event underreporting in the period 10–14 years before the survey. The upward biases in the estimates derived from the youngest age groups become stronger in the more recent data sets and the survey-based estimates derived from 15–19 are extremely high indeed. In the 1962 census (and to a lesser extent the 1969 census) the estimates seem to be overadjusted; for the 1979 census the adjustment brings the estimate derived from the 20–24 year olds very nicely in line and for 1989 the adjustment seems too weak. However, the performance of the adjustments over time seems consistent with the well-documented fertility changes in Kenyan history, a rise up to the late 1970s and a subsequent decline, which would introduce bias in the direction observed in the graphs.

A change in fertility not only biases the mortality estimates but also influences our adjustment for the bias introduced by the homogeneity of mortality risk by age of mother. The adjustment similarly assumes constant fertility in the recent past, i.e. the average parity of the cohort 15–19 at the time of census is considered to be the same as the parity of the 20–24 cohort five years ago. Both a fertility decline and a trend towards a later start of child-bearing will result in an underestimation of the children born to the 20–24

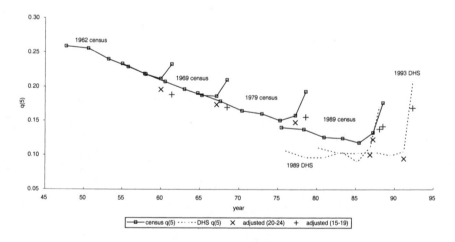

Figure 2.4   Trends in under-five mortality in Kenya: indirect estimates from censuses and DHS surveys with adjusted values for recent estimates

when they were in the high risk teenage years. This will make the adjustment derived using equation (8) too conservative.

For censuses with no data on marriage duration, the proposed adjustment should improve the reliability of levels and trends estimated from that census. When applying the adjustment for higher mortality to births of teenage mothers, information on changes in fertility and recent disasters will help in the interpretation of how well the proposed adjustment produces an estimate of period mortality. For the ultimate evaluation of mortality trends, however, information from more than one data source remains imperative.

REFERENCES

Arnold, F. (1990) 'Assessment of the quality of birth history data in the Demographic and Health Surveys', in *An Assessment of DHS-I Data Quality* (DHS Methodological Reports, No. 1). Columbia, MD: Institute for Resource Development.

Booth, M. (1984) 'Transforming Gompertz's function for fertility analysis; the development of a standard for the relational Gompertz function'. *Population Studies*, 38 (3), pp. 495–506.

Brass, W. (1975) *Methods for Estimating Fertility and Mortality from Limited and Defective Data*. Chapel Hill, NC: Poplab, University of North Carolina.

Brass, W. (1981) 'The use of the Gompertz relational model to estimate fertility', in *International Population Conference*, Manila, vol 3. Liège: International Union for the Scientific Study of Population.

Brass, W., Coale, A.J., Demeny, P., Heisel, D.F., Lorimer, F., Romaniuk, A. and van de Walle, E. (1968) *The Demography of Tropical Africa*. Princeton, NJ: Princeton University Press.

Ewbank, D.C. (1982) 'The sources of error in Brass's method for estimating child survival: the case of Bangladesh'. *Population Studies*, 36 (3), pp. 459–74.

Feeney, G. (1980) 'Estimating infant mortality trends from survivorship data'. *Population Studies* 34 (1), pp. 109–28.

Feency, G. (1991) 'Child survivorship estimation: methods and data analysis'. *Asian and Pacific Population Forum*, 5 (2&3), pp. 51–87.

Femandez Castilla, R. (1989) 'The effects of maternal age, birth order and birth spacing on indirect estimation of child mortality', in *International Population Conference*, New Delhi. Liège: International Union for the Scientific Study of Population.

Hill, K. (1984) 'An evaluation of indirect methods for estimating mortality', in J. Vallin, J. Pollard and L. Heligman (eds), *Methodologies for the Collection and Analysis of Mortality Data*, Liège: Ordina Editions.

Hill, K. (1991) 'Approaches to the measurement of childhood mortality: a comparative review'. *Population Index*, 57 (4), pp. 552–68.

Martin, L.M., Trussell, J., Salvail, F.R. and Shah, N.S. (1983) 'Co-variates of child mortality in the Philippines, Indonesia, and Pakistan: an analysis based on hazard models. *Population Studies*, 37 (3), pp. 417–32.

Nortman, D. (1974) 'Parental age as a factor in pregnancy outcome and child development'. *Reports on Population/Family Planning*, no. 16. New York: The Population Council.

Preston, S. (1985) 'Mortality in childhood: lessons from WFS', in J. Cleland and J. Hobcraft (eds), *Reproductive Change in Developing Countries: Insights from the World Fertility Survey.* New York: Oxford University Press.

Rutstein, S.O. (1984) 'Infant and child mortality: levels, trends and demographic differentials', in *WFS Comparative Studies*, no. 43 Voorburg, Netherlands: International Statistical Institute.

Rutstein, S.O. (1985) 'Assessment of the quality of WFa for direct estimation of childhood mortality', in *WFS Comparative Studies*, no. 44. Voorburg, Netherlands: International Statistical Institute.

Sullivan, J. (1990) 'The collection of mortality data in WFS and DHS surveys', in J. Vallin, S. D'Souza and A. Palloni (eds), *Measurement and Analysis of Mortality.* Oxford: Oxford University Press.

Sullivan, J.M., Bicego, G.T. and Rutstein, S.O. (1990) 'Assessment of the quality of data used for the direct estimation of infant and child mortality in the Demographic and Health Surveys', in *An Assessment of DHS-I Data Quality* (DHS Methodological Reports, No. 1). Columbia, MD: Institute for Resource Development.

Trussell, J. and Hammerslough, C. (1983) 'A hazards-model analysis of the covariates of infant and child mortality in Sri Lanka'. *Demography*, 20 (1), pp. 1–26.

United Nations (1983) 'Manual X. Indirect techniques for child mortality for demographic estimation'. *Population Studies, No. 81*. New York: UN.

United Nations (1990) 'Step-by-step guide to the estimation of child mortality'. *Population Studies No. 107*. New York: UN.

United Nations (1992) 'Child mortality since the 1960s: a database for developing countries'. New York: UN.

CHAPTER THREE

Estimation of adult mortality from data on adult siblings

Ian M. Timæus, Basia Zaba and Mohamed Ali

Centre for Population Studies
London School of Hygiene & Tropical Medicine

Measurement of the mortality of adults in countries that lack effective death registration systems remains a challenge. No fully satisfactory approach exists though demographers have developed a series of ingenious methods that provide in part for this need. William Brass's contribution to this effort has been paramount, both in developing methods to rehabilitate incomplete data on deaths by age (Brass, 1975, 1979a, 1979b) and in pioneering techniques for estimating mortality indirectly from data on the survival of specific categories of relatives (Brass, 1961). Brass and Hill (1973) present the first fully developed method of this type for measuring adult mortality, based on data on the survival of respondents' parents. Brass's associates and others subsequently applied this strategy for the measurement of adult mortality to data on other categories of relatives, including spouses and siblings (e.g. Hill and Trussell, 1977; UN, 1983). The value of the approach was enhanced greatly once Feeney (1980), Brass and Bamgboye (1981) and Brass (1985) had developed methods for estimating the time period to which indirect measures of mortality apply in populations with changing mortality.

The original sibling method for measuring adult mortality has seldom been applied. Trials of it suggested that respondents tend to omit a substantial proportion of siblings from their reports (Blacker and Brass, 1983; Zaba, 1985). Hill and Trussell (1977) point out that in addition to recall errors, respondents might not ever have known about older brothers and sisters who died before the respondent was born or when he or she was very young. Wilson (1985) proposed that one could avoid this problem by asking only about living siblings and those who died in a fixed reference period before the enquiry. This approach has the dual advantages of excluding from the siblings of interest those who are most likely to be omitted from respondents' reports and of generating up-to-date information on mortality. On the other hand, reference period errors may seriously bias mortality estimates made from such data. Moreover, the information collected pertain to both adult siblings and those who are either still children or who died in childhood.

Brass's contribution to the use of reports on siblings for mortality measurement dates from 1989, when he and his collaborators (Graham *et al*, 1989) proposed the sisterhood method for measuring maternal mortality. They suggest that questions should be asked about sisters who survived to age 15 and whether they died subsequently – respondents are then asked whether these adult deaths were associated with pregnancy or childbirth. Restriction of the scope of the questions about survival to adult sisters has two benefits. Firstly, as with Wilson's approach, omission of dead sisters should be far less of a problem than with the original method. Secondly, the resulting data reflect adult mortality alone because those sisters who died as children are excluded from both the numerator and denominator. Because death in the teenage years is uncommon, misclassification of the ages of siblings around age 15 has little impact on the estimated proportion of siblings who died after that age.

Reflecting recent concern about maternal mortality, the sisterhood questions have been asked in numerous surveys (e.g. Graham *et al*, 1989; David *et al*, 1991; Rutenberg and Sullivan, 1991; Hernandez *et al*, 1994; O'Brien *et al*, 1994; Walraven *et al*, 1994; Shahidullah, 1995; Simons *et al*, 1996). By analysing the information on all sisters who have died since age 15, not just the maternal deaths, it should be possible to use these survey data to estimate all-cause adult women's mortality. If data on brothers have been collected, they provide equivalent information on adult men's mortality. Until now, however, no simple method of producing such estimates has existed. This chapter presents such a method.

THEORETICAL BASIS OF THE METHOD

Calculation of the proportion of siblings alive for a given age of respondent requires a model of the distribution of age differences between the respondent and all the other children borne by the respondent's mother. Two approaches have been developed: the first, used by Hill and Trussell (1977), assumes that all mothers experience the age-specific fertility rates of the general population. Thus, a sibling age distribution can be derived as a convolution of the fertility distribution. The second, which is the basis of the Graham *et al* (1989) sisterhood method, assumes that the distribution of age differences of siblings can be represented by a normal distribution. This section discusses the merits of both of these approaches. The term 'fertility distribution' is used here to denote the distribution of age-specific fertility rates in the whole female population, information which is widely available for most populations. The term 'birth distribution' is used to denote the distribution of times since first birth to subsequent births – such distributions are not widely reported in the literature but can be calculated from birth history data.

The first of these two approaches is based on an equation for the proportion of siblings alive by age of respondent in a stable population described by Goodman *et al* (1974). A theoretical attraction of this approach, if the models are developed in the context of stable population structure, is that it yields age distributions of surviving siblings that are consistent with the population age structure when aggregated over all ages of respondent (Zaba, 1987). However conformity at this aggregate level does not ensure that the ages of siblings are realistic for a population in which age patterns of fertility and completed family sizes vary between women, even if the patterns of variation do not change over time.

Keyfitz (1977) has shown that, if family sizes vary, the average size of the family that children are born into, C, must be larger than the average family size borne by women, M, since families of childless women are not represented at all in reports obtained from the children's generation, whilst families of size n are reported n times each. More precisely, $C = M + \sigma^2/M$ where σ^2 is the variance of the distribution of mother's family sizes (Preston, 1976). If the probability of giving birth at any age is independent of whether the woman has given birth at any other age, family sizes will follow a Poisson distribution and the variance of this distribution, σ^2, equals its mean, M. In this special case, a child's average sibship size would be one more than the mothers' average family size. Since larger families would tend to have a wider spread of ages at birth, one might expect that the variance of mothers' birth distributions as reported by the children to be larger than the birth distribution variances measured for all mothers.

The Poisson distribution is not a particularly good approximation for the birth distribution of individual women: the nine-month period of gestation and the period of postpartum amenorrhoea ensure that virtually no children are born in the year before or the year after the birth of a respondent. On the other hand, once a woman enters a stable union and starts bearing children, she is likely to keep up a relatively high tempo of childbearing until she reaches a desired family size or the union breaks up. Unless she enters a new partnership, she then becomes much less likely to bear children. This means, for example, that in a population in which the mean age at first birth is, say, 22 years of age, the few women who bear children at 15 are more likely to also bear children at 18 than other women. For these reasons, Brass has maintained that an adjusted form of the negative binomial distribution is a better representation of birth distributions than the Poisson (Brass, 1958, 1970; Farahani, 1981). If there is a wide scatter of ages at the start of childbearing, but a relatively narrow range of differences between age at first and last birth, as is typical in low fertility populations, we would expect the variance of the birth distribution to be considerably lower than the variance of the fertility schedule. It is the former distribution that determines the sibling age difference distribution.

Graham *et al* (1989) assume that the distribution of sibling age differences can be represented by a normal curve with mean zero and a variance of 80 years-squared. This assumption considerably simplifies the process of estimating the proportion of siblings who remain alive, but is difficult to justify on theoretical grounds. If the distribution of time since first birth to all subsequent births has a variance σ^2, then the age differences between siblings drawn from a cohort of mothers with completed childbearing would have a variance of $2\sigma^2$ and zero mean, but would only be normal if the mother's birth distribution itself was normal. A normal distribution with twice the birth distribution variance constitutes a reasonable approximation for the sibling age difference distribution if the birth distribution is peaked (i.e. $\sigma^2 < 35$), but is less satisfactory for representing sibling age difference distributions in the case of flat birth distributions, such as occur in natural fertility populations. From the discussion of family size, it is clear that the relationship between the variance of the birth distribution and that of the fertility schedule may differ from one population to the next. Therefore, knowledge of the overall shape of the fertility schedule is insufficient to determine the variance of the sibling age difference distribution.

A further problem arises when we consider the distribution of sibling age differences in a growing or shrinking population, rather than a stationary one, which would be equivalent to the cohort considered above. Goldman (1978) proved that, in a growing population, an individual selected at random from those whose mothers have completed childbearing has more younger siblings ever-born than older ones. The opposite is true in a shrinking population. Without repeating her formal mathematical proof here, one can understand this intuitively by considering respondents currently aged 40, all of whose mothers have completed childbearing. In a growing stable population, relatively more of these respondents will have young mothers (say those currently aged under 65 if they have survived) than in a stationary population because, at the time of their birth, there would have been more women aged under 25 than in the corresponding stationary population. But, if the respondents are children of young mothers, they are more likely to have younger than older siblings because their mothers have more child-bearing before them than behind them. This means that the distribution of sibling age differences is not symmetrical: its mean lies below zero in a growing population and the opposite is true in a shrinking population. More precisely, if the variance of the underlying birth distribution is σ^2, then the mean of the sibling age distribution lies at approximately $-r\sigma^2$, where r is the population growth rate. Thus, even if all women experience the same age-specific fertility, the variance of the sibling age distribution in a growing population would still be slightly less than twice the variance of the fertility distribution and the distribution would be positively skewed. The opposite features characterize this distribution in shrinking populations.

Our model synthesizes the approaches of Brass and his colleagues (Graham *et al*, 1989) and Hill and Trussell (1977). We follow the former by deriving an expression for the proportion of siblings alive among those who have survived to age 15 in terms of the distribution of differences in ages between the respondent and their siblings. But, like Hill and Trussell, we relate this to a schedule of age-specific fertility, albeit modified to make it resemble a birth distribution more closely. This enables us to allow for the fact that that the age difference distribution is only symmetrical in a stationary population. The next section uses data collected in fertility surveys to examine the relationship between sibling age difference distributions and the age-specific fertility schedules in real populations and to determine empirically the range of variances found in sibling age difference distributions.

Using the probability approach developed by Goodman *et al* (1974), one can show that in a stable population the number of siblings ever-born z years before a respondent currently aged a is given by $\theta(a,z)$:

$$\theta(a,z) = \int_a^\beta e^{-r(y-a)} f(y) l(y) f(y-z) dy \qquad \text{(for } z \geq 0) \qquad (1)$$

$$\theta(a,z) = \int_a^\beta e^{-r(y-a)} f(y) l(y-z) f(y-z) dy \qquad \text{(for } z < 0) \qquad (2)$$

where equation 1 gives the number of older siblings, equation 2 the number of younger siblings, and:

$l(x)$ = life-table survivorship to age x,
$f(x)$ = the respondents' mothers' probability of giving birth at age x,
r = the growth rate in a stable population,
y = the age of the mother at the birth of the respondent,

and integration is over all ages at childbearing α to β.

The proportion of siblings still alive among those who lived to age 15 for respondents in a five-year age group, x to $x+5$ is given by:

$$_5S^{15+}_x = \frac{\int_x^{x+5} l(a) \int_{15-a}^{\beta-\alpha} \theta(a,z) l(a+z) dz da}{l(15) \int_x^{x+5} l(a) \int_{15-a}^{\beta-\alpha} \theta(a,z) dz da} \qquad \text{for } x \geq 15 \qquad (3)$$

EMPIRICAL EVIDENCE ON AGE DIFFERENCES BETWEEN
SIBLINGS

Ideally, we would like to investigate the relationship between fertility distributions and birth distributions, and then between birth distributions and
sibling age difference distributions, $\theta(a,z)$. This enables us to assess whether
the latter relationship conforms to our theoretical predictions and allows us
to discover empirical relationships between the variances of the fertility and
birth distributions, and between indicators of the timing of fertility and the
variance in completed family size. Unfortunately, birth history data collected
in fertility surveys do not provide enough information to investigate all these
relationships. Such data only furnish a complete picture of cross-sectional
age-specific fertility for the year of the survey: earlier years are affected
progressively by truncation of the fertility data at older ages. On the other
hand, complete birth distributions by time since first birth are only available for the oldest women, with complete fertility. These women are not
representative of the whole cohort as the experience of dead mothers is
omitted. One can construct a complete distribution of the older siblings
ever-born of children born in the survey year. Information on the distribution of younger siblings, however, can only be obtained for children born
in the years preceding the survey. As one moves backward in time, these
children are progressively less representative of all children born in earlier
years, because of truncation of the data on older women and mortality selection. If the population under study was experiencing unchanging age-specific
fertility, various extrapolation procedures could be used to fill in the missing
information. But, in the face of evidence of changing fertility and contam-
ination of retrospective data by dating errors, we do not consider this a
useful approach. Instead, we examine the relationship between current age-
specific fertility distribution and the distribution of older siblings, $\theta(0,z)$,
omitting the intermediate goal of studying the relationship between both of
these distributions and mothers' birth distributions. We can also ascertain
how close the distributions of older siblings are to a truncated normal.

We base this investigation on birth history data from 12 World Fertility
Survey (WFS) studies conducted in the 1970s. The surveys were selected
to provide information on a range of populations with moderate to high
fertility drawn from diverse parts of the developing world. The countries
selected are listed in Table 3.1, together with estimates of their total fertility
at the time when the WFS surveys were conducted.

Figure 3.1 shows the distribution by year of previous births for mothers
who gave birth in the year before the 1975 survey in Thailand, a country
that is fairly typical of those studied. A three-year moving average line
calculated from the data points is also shown. Superimposed on this graph
is part of a normal curve, shown cross-hatched, whose variance ($\sigma^2 = 102$)

Table 3.1   *Fertility and sibling age difference distributions in 12 World Fertility*
Surveys

Country	Total fertility	Variance of the fertility distribution	Variance of the best normal fit to the sibling age difference distribution
Trinidad and Tobago	3.30	40.33	50.00
Sri Lanka	3.75	42.33	43.13
Thailand	4.63	51.10	67.16
Indonesia	4.73	51.68	82.76
Egypt	5.26	50.75	74.39
Ecuador	5.32	55.19	77.35
Dominican Republic	5.71	43.81	48.76
Tunisia	5.85	51.88	62.44
Morocco	5.90	60.60	97.79
Sudan (North)	6.03	58.92	85.23
Mexico	6.20	47.05	89.51
Senegal	7.15	56.97	77.76

is twice the variance of the age-specific fertility schedule and that has its
mean at $-r\sigma^2/2 = -0.053$ (the theoretical mean point of the sibling age
difference distribution in a growing population). The growth rate, $r = 0.103$
per cent, was calculated from the growth in total births during the 15 years
before the survey (United Nations, 1989). The height of this curve depends
on the level of fertility and was fixed by scaling it to obtain the best possible
fit to the observed data in the range 2 to 22 years before the index birth.[1]
Clearly this curve is a poor fit to the observed data, with a variance that is
far too wide. In Thailand, as anticipated, the variance of the sibling age
difference distribution is considerably less than twice the variance of the
population's fertility distribution. The normal curve shown in bold in the
same figure was fitted to the data by a non-linear least-squares minimiza-
tion procedure that allowed both the height of the curve and its variance to
change, subject to the same constraint on the mean, again fitting at ages 2
to 22 years. This best-fitting curve has a variance of 67 years-squared and
a mean at -0.034 years. Fitting a distribution to the data on older siblings
with a mean that is below zero allows largely for the asymmetry of the
sibling age difference distribution. Therefore, we can assume that the variance of this distribution is almost the same as the variance of the complete
birth distribution.

The relationship in Thailand between the variance of the best-fitting normal
and the variance that would be obtained if the birth distribution was normal
with the same variance as age-specific fertility is fairly typical of the twelve
populations that we studied. The data are shown in Table 3.1 and the relationship across the twelve populations is illustrated in Figure 3.2. As expected,

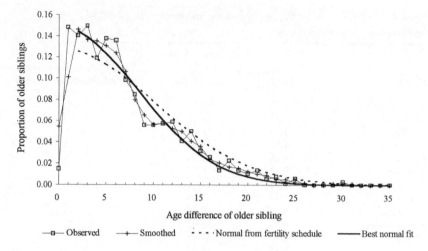

Figure 3.1   Normal fits to the sibling age difference distribution, Thailand

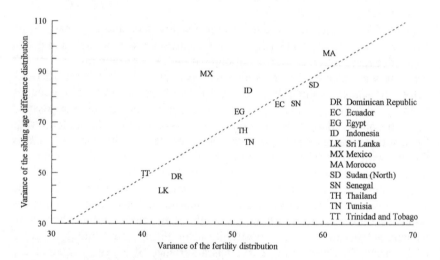

Figure 3.2   Relationship between the variances of the fertility distribution and the sibling age difference distribution in twelve World Fertility Surveys

the variance of the normal fit to the sibling age difference distribution is less than twice that of the fertility distribution in every population. Although the relationship between the variances of these two distributions is a loose one, they are clearly correlated positively. Ignoring the gap in the centre of the distributions, these results suggest that, in populations with moderate to high fertility, sibling age difference distributions have variances that range from about 40 to about 100 years-squared, averaging about 70. Typically, therefore, the variance of sibling age difference distributions is less than the estimate of 80 adopted by Graham *et al* (1989).

To model full sibling age difference distributions for the purpose of calculating the proportion alive of adult siblings, we adapt an existing fertility model to represent birth distributions. The Relational Gompertz model proposed by Brass (1974, 1981) relates two fertility schedules:

$$-\ln(-\ln(F(x))) = \alpha + \beta.-\ln(-\ln(F_s(x)))$$

where $F(x)$ is the proportion of fertility occurring by age x. The α parameter of this model largely affects the location of the fertility distribution while β largely affects its spread. We use the model in conjunction with the standard fertility distribution, $F_s(x)$, proposed by Booth (1984). To allow for the absence of very short birth intervals in human populations, when generating $\theta(a,z)$ using equations 1 and 2 we set $\theta(a,0) = 0$ and $\theta(a,1)$ and $\theta(a,-1)$ to 40 per cent of the model values. The value of 40 per cent reproduces the average of the ratios $\theta(0,1)/\theta(0,2)$ in the twelve WFS populations. Allowing for the gap in the middle of the sibling age difference distribution in this way, raises the range of variances that should characterize the final age difference distributions from 40 to 100 years-squared to about 45 to 110.

As the theoretical discussion suggests, substitution of Booth's standard fertility distribution into equations 1 and 2 in combination with a range of mortality schedules and growth rates generates distributions of age differences between siblings with larger variances than are typical of the twelve populations on which we have WFS data. We therefore used a set of Gompertz models with a mean value of β of more than one to represent the birth distributions (as β increases the variance of the model distributions decreases). The final set of parameters selected is shown in Table 3.2. As a loose relationship exists between the level of fertility and the variance of the fertility distribution (see Table 3.1), we include no broad sibling age difference distributions ($\sigma^2 > 99$ years^2) for the low growth populations and no narrow ones ($\sigma^2 < 55$ years^2) for the high growth populations. The variances of the sibling age difference distributions that result range from 45.4 to 112.6 years-squared with a mean of 77.8. The widest and narrowest distributions of sibling age differences produced in this way are shown in Figure 3.3. They are close in shape to the twelve observed distributions also shown on Figure 3.3 and, allowing for some sampling and reporting errors in the empirical data, more or less span the range of variation of the latter. Small differences remain. Some of the WFS distributions are very highly peaked at two years (e.g. Dominican Republic, Sri Lanka) while others have a rather flat top (e.g. Morocco, Senegal, Sudan). This reflects variation in the mean length of birth intervals between the populations. Thus, by

Table 3.2   *Models used to simulate the proportion of siblings still alive among those who lived to age 15*

Model	Parameter	Values
Mortality – relational logit model	α	−1.0
Brass (1971) General Standard		−0.6
($35.3 < e_0 < 74.1$, mean 55.3)		−0.2
		0.2
	β	0.7
		1.1
Maternity function – relational Gompertz	α	−0.5
model		−0.2
Booth (1984) standard		0.1
($25.0 < \bar{m} < 30.8$, mean 27.5)		0.4
	β	1.0 ($r = 0.03$)
		1.15
		1.4
		1.8 ($r = 0.01$)
Age structure – stable population model	r	0.01
		0.03

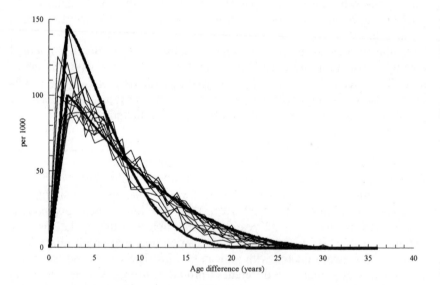

Figure 3.3   Model and observed distributions of the ages of older siblings

combining a range of gaps in the sibling age difference distributions of different width with a slightly different set of Relational Gompertz models, we could probably reproduce the empirical data even more closely. We judge that the gain in the precision of our method for estimating adult mortality would be small and, as students of Brass, restrain ourselves from unwarranted perfectionism.

COEFFICIENTS FOR ESTIMATING LIFE TABLE SURVIVORSHIP

To simplify the estimation of life-table survivorship from data on the survival of adult siblings, we propose a simple regression model of their relationship. We estimate the regression coefficients from data on 192 simulated populations generated from model mortality and birth distribution schedules and the relationships specified in equations 1 to 3. Mortality is represented by relational model life-tables based on Brass's (1971) General Standard. The birth distributions are represented by the Relational Gompertz models of fertility discussed in the previous section. Variation in age structure is represented by the use of two growth rates. These parameters are listed in Table 3.2. Where appropriate, they are the same as those used by Timæus (1991a,b, 1992) to derive coefficients for the estimation of adult mortality from data on orphanhood. Therefore, the adult sibling method should yield estimates of mortality consistent with those from these variants of the orphanhood method.

The adult siblings of respondents aged less than 20 years are, on average, substantially older than the respondents. The relationship between life-table survivorship and the proportion of adult siblings surviving to young respondents is very sensitive to the distribution of age differences between siblings and respondents. The siblings of respondents aged 20 or more years, however, are only slightly older than the respondents on average and the relationship between the respondents' and their siblings' ages varies less. Thus, a close relationship exists between the proportion of siblings still alive among those who survived to age 15 in an age group $n-5$ to $n({}_5S_{n-5}^{15+})$ and life-table survivorship from age 15 to n (l_n/l_{15}). We model this relationship by the regression equation:

$$\frac{l_n}{l_{15}} = \beta_0(n) + \beta_1(n) {}_5S_{n-5}^{15+} + \varepsilon \tag{4}$$

The coefficients of the fitted models are supplied in Table 3.3. It is worth noting that the intercept terms tend to offset the coefficients for the survival of adult siblings. Thus, the adjustments that need to be made to convert the proportion of adult siblings still alive into life-table survivorship from age 15 are small. Despite the wide range of assumptions made about fertility, mortality and age structure to generate these regression equations, the fitted models have high R^2 values and small coefficients of variation. Thus, the relationship between life-table survivorship and the survival of adult siblings

Table 3.3 *Coefficients for the estimation of adult survivorship, l(n)/l(15), from the survival of adult siblings,* $_5S^{15+}_{n-5}$

Age (n)	$\beta_0(n)$	$\beta_1(n)$	R^2	Coefficient of variation[a]
25	−0.0003	1.0011	0.9818	0.0042
30	−0.1546	1.1560	0.9950	0.0034
35	−0.1645	1.1660	0.9981	0.0029
40	−0.1388	1.1406	0.9984	0.0035
45	−0.1140	1.1168	0.9985	0.0042
50	−0.1018	1.1066	0.9986	0.0052

[a] Root mean squared error divided by the mean value of $l(n)/l(15)$

is very robust to variation between populations in their other demographic characteristics. Inspection of the residuals confirms that, apart from moderate heteroscedasticity in older age groups of respondents, the regression models adequately represent the data.

TIME LOCATION OF ADULT SIBLING ESTIMATES

The adult sibling method yields a separate estimate of survivorship from the data on each five-year age group of respondents aged between 20 and 50 years. Each estimate reflects the survivorship of a cohort of siblings from age 15 to just less than the mid-point of the respondents' age group. Estimates based on data supplied by younger respondents equal period mortality at a date relatively close to the time that the data were collected. Estimates based on data supplied by older respondents equal period mortality at a somewhat earlier date.

Brass has demonstrated that the time at which orphanhood- and widowhood-based estimates of adult mortality equal period mortality is unaffected by the rate of change in adult mortality and has developed methods for estimating this time (Brass and Bamgboye 1981; Brass, 1985). The structure of the relationships on which the adult sibling method is based is very similar to that underlying the widowhood method in a population where all men and all women marry at about age 15. Thus, existing time location methods for indirect estimates of adult mortality can be applied to mortality estimates obtained from data on adult siblings.

Brass (1985) shows that the time to which indirect estimates of adult mortality apply is:

$$T = \frac{N}{2}\left(1 - \frac{1n_5S_x}{3} + \frac{\ln\dfrac{80 - M - N}{80 - M}}{3}\right) \tag{5}$$

where:

T = the time in years before the date when the data were collected,

N = the mean time for which the respondent's relatives are exposed to the risk of dying,

M = the mean age of the relatives at the onset of exposure to the risk of dying,

$_5S_x$ = the proportion of the relatives remaining alive in the age group x to $x+5$ years.

This equation states that T is somewhat less than halfway through the mean period of exposure and depends on the level of mortality as indicated by the survival of the relatives compared with mortality in a population in which the survivorship function is linear and everyone dies by age 80.

In the adult sibling method, M, the age at which exposure begins, is exactly 15 years for every sibling. The asymmetry of the sibling age difference distribution means that, in a growing population, they are on average slightly younger than the respondents. This age difference varies between about zero and 1.75 years in those populations in which one is likely to want to apply the method. We suggest using a central value of 0.8 years in all applications. Thus, the duration of exposure, N, becomes $(n-2.5-0.8)-15$, where n is still the upper limit of the age group of respondents. Because M is fixed at 15 years, equation 5 can be simplified for each age group to a linear equation of the form:

$$T = \beta_0(n) - \beta_1(n)\ln {}_5S_{n-5}^{15+}$$

These equations for estimation of the time location of life table indices based on data on adult siblings are presented in Table 3.4.

Table 3.4 *Coefficients for the estimation of the time location (T) of life-table indices based on the survival of adult siblings, $_5S_{n-5}^{15+}$*

Age (n)	$\beta_0(n)$	$\beta_1(n)$
25	3.23	1.12
30	5.46	1.95
35	7.52	2.78
40	9.38	3.62
45	11.00	4.45
50	12.32	5.28

BIASES DUE TO AIDS MORTALITY

The HIV/AIDS epidemic is producing a massive increase in adult mortality in large parts of Eastern and Southern Africa and some other parts of the developing world. This has highlighted the importance of monitoring levels and trends in adult mortality. It has also made this task considerably more difficult. The HIV epidemic poses two problems for indirect methods of estimating mortality based on the survival of relatives. Firstly, both the sexual and vertical routes of transmission produce significant selection biases in data collected in surveys on the survival of relatives. Secondly, the incidence of HIV infection is concentrated among young adults. Thus, populations with significant AIDS mortality have very different age patterns of mortality both from other populations and from the model life-tables used to derive coefficients for converting data on survival of relatives into measures of life-table survivorship.

Focusing first on the selection biases, almost all the mothers of infected children are infected themselves. A disproportionate number of the children of infected women are also infected, as are the spouses of infected adults. Thus, more children, parents and partners of infected individuals die than other people of the same age. When questions are asked about the survival of women's children, about orphanhood or widowhood, the HIV-positive are less likely to have surviving relatives to report on them than the rest of the population.

Methods have been developed that allow one to make an approximate adjustment for the selection bias in data on the survival of women's children and on orphanhood in populations subject to mortality from AIDS (Timæus and Nunn, 1997). These methods require the analyst to have some idea of the severity of the HIV epidemic in a population. However, the widowhood method for estimating mortality seems beyond salvage. A major advantage of the adult sibling method, compared with these existing methods of measuring adult mortality, is that it is free of selection biases arising from direct transmission of the virus. Some residual bias will remain. In particular, the risk of infection tends to vary markedly between localities and siblings often live close to each other. The impact of this, however, will be relatively small.

Bias in the regression coefficients used to estimate life table survivorship remains more of a problem. With respect to equation 3, it is the change in the age pattern of mortality experienced by the siblings as a result of AIDS that is of concern, not the impact of the epidemic on the sibling age difference distribution. For one thing, the latter distribution would only begin to change 15 years after AIDS mortality became significant. Secondly, the main factor shaping this distribution is the age pattern of childbearing, rather than mortality or age structure. Finally, the regression coefficients are affected only moderately by the characteristics of this distribution.

No data on the survival of adult siblings exist for populations that are both subject to AIDS mortality and have reliable mortality statistics. Thus, we can only assess the biases in sibling estimates of adult mortality by combining simulated and actual data. We do this by calculating the proportions of adult siblings still alive by evaluating equation 3, combining our model of the sibling age difference distribution, $\theta(a,z)$, with survivorship data from an AIDS-affected population. Having done this, we use the regression coefficients in Table 3.3 (which were derived for an AIDS-free population) to estimate life-table survivorship from the proportions of siblings alive and compare the results with the actual survivorship values used as input.

The mortality data used for this exercise refer to women. They come from the Medical Research Council study in the Masaka district of Uganda. This prospective study has collected high-quality mortality data on a population of about 10,000 that has been under demographic surveillance since the end of 1989 (Nunn *et al*, 1997; Timæus and Nunn, 1997). Nearly 12 per cent of women of childbearing age are infected with the HIV virus. Death rates among infected women are an order of magnitude higher than those among the seronegative population. The mortality data used here are based on the first five years of surveillance. They are combined with a $\theta(a,z)$ distribution generated using the mean values of the model parameters shown in Table 3.2. Thus, the proportions of adult sisters alive are calculated allowing for high mortality due to AIDS among respondents but assuming that their mothers were unaffected by AIDS mortality.

The results of the analysis are shown in Table 3.5. The level of mortality prevailing in the study population during the first half of the 1990s was very high. At this level, half those surviving to age 15 would die before their 50th birthday. Because the sibling age difference distribution used to generate the proportions of sisters alive is an average one, almost all of the differences between estimated survivorship in the second column of the table and actual survivorship, shown in the third column, reflect the unusual age pattern of mortality in this population. Despite this unusual age pattern of mortality, the adult sibling method produces estimates of survivorship that are close to the actual values for Masaka district. The estimates based on data which represent the reports that would be expected from respondents aged 20–24 years and more than 40 years are extremely accurate. However, those based on data for respondents aged 25–39 years overestimate survivorship. This is because the regression coefficients fail to allow for the concentration of AIDS deaths in this age range. Estimates of sibling survivorship across narrower age ranges (15 to 25 years) and wider ones (15 to 45+ years) are more accurate because the proportions still alive reflect mortality in age cohorts that have experienced both peak and lower AIDS mortality.

Table 3.5 *Errors in adult sibling estimates of survivorship in a female population affected by AIDS*

Age (n)	Proportion of adult sisters alive	Estimated survivorship from 15 to n	Actual survivorship from 15 to n	Relative error (%)	Level of mortality (α)	Estimated survivorship from 15 to 50	Relative error (%)
25	0.8521	0.8527	0.8646	−1.4	0.6757	0.5070	2.1
30	0.7986	0.7686	0.7245	6.1	0.7565	0.4909	−1.2
35	0.7306	0.6874	0.6585	4.4	0.8347	0.4767	−4.0
40	0.6592	0.6131	0.5965	2.8	0.8700	0.4708	−5.2
45	0.5946	0.5500	0.5558	−1.0	0.8306	0.4774	−3.9
50	0.5396	0.4953	0.4968	−0.3	0.7335	0.4953	−0.3

To use sibling estimates of adult survivorship to monitor mortality trends, it is necessary to fit a model life-table to the estimates for specific age ranges and use it to extrapolate to an index referring to a common range of ages. The final three columns of Table 3.5 present the results of extrapolating to survivorship from 15 to 50 years, $_{35}p_{15}$, in this way. The α values indicate the level of mortality in the 1-parameter family of relational model life-tables based on Brass's (1971) General Standard. The proportions of siblings alive were generated using a single period life-table rather than by simulating an AIDS epidemic of growing severity. Thus, except for random fluctuations in the number of deaths by age in the Masaka district study population, one would expect all the estimates to yield the same values of α and of $_{35}p_{15}$. Insofar as each series differs systematically by age, it is because the mortality models used to derive the regression coefficients are inappropriate for populations with significant AIDS mortality.

The results are surprising: the final series of estimates of survivorship from 15 to 50 years, $_{35}p_{15}$, remain fairly accurate. Those obtained from respondents aged 25 to 34 are more accurate than the estimates of l_n/l_{15} on which they are based. Errors due to the failure to allow for the impact of AIDS on the mortality schedule in first calculating the coefficients and then extrapolating to a common measure of survivorship largely cancel out. Further modelling suggests that this finding is robust to variation in background mortality and choice of a mortality standard. It would not necessarily hold, however, in populations where the demography of the AIDS epidemic, in particular the mean age at death from AIDS, is very different from Masaka. Unfortunately, we know too little about trajectories of mortality change in developing country populations affected by AIDS to investigate fully the sensitivity of the finding to such factors. Nevertheless, estimates of $_{35}p_{15}$ obtained from the adult sibling method probably represent relatively robust indices for the monitoring of mortality trends as the AIDS epidemic develops. As with other indirect methods, if successive sets of data are collected for the same population, checks on the consistency of the results for periods when they overlap provide a powerful indication of the robustness of our assumptions.

APPLICATIONS

Figure 3.4 presents estimates of the probability of surviving from age 15 to 50 in three countries that have collected data on the survival of siblings in a recent DHS survey: Peru, Morocco and Zimbabwe. Each plot presents a series of six indirect measures of survivorship for men and women estimated using the adult sibling method. The calculations involved in producing these estimates for Peru are shown as an example in Table 3.6.

The plots also include direct estimates for the periods 0–4 and 5–9 years before the recent DHS surveys calculated using the information on ages and dates of death that these DHS surveys collected in the form of sibling histories (Rutenberg and Sullivan, 1991). The plots for Peru (Timæus, 1995) and Morocco (Timæus, 1991b) also include previously published estimates of survivorship from 15 to 50 for earlier dates. These estimates are based on data on lifetime orphanhood and orphanhood before and since first marriage collected in an earlier DHS survey. In Zimbabwe, the earliest series of estimates are based on the orphanhood data collected in the 1982 Census

Table 3.6 *Calculation of the probability of surviving from age 15 to 50 from data on the survival of adult siblings, Peru Demographic and Health Survey, 1991–2*

Age group of respondents (n−5 to n−1)	Living siblings aged 15+	Dead siblings aged 15+	Proportion of siblings alive ($_5S_{n-5}^{15+}$)	Survivorship from age 15 to n ($_{n-15}P_{15}$)	Mortality level (α)	Time location (T)	Survivorship from age 15 to 50 ($_{35}P_{15}$)
(a) Brothers							
15–19	4539	134	0.9713				
20–24	5713	157	0.9733	0.9740	−0.646	1988.7	0.870
25–29	5642	199	0.9659	0.9620	−0.700	1986.5	0.880
30–34	5074	229	0.9568	0.9511	−0.750	1984.4	0.890
35–39	4481	301	0.9371	0.9300	−0.708	1982.4	0.882
40–44	3472	233	0.9371	0.9326	−0.883	1980.7	0.912
45–49	2533	276	0.9017	0.8961	−0.786	1979.1	0.896
(b) Sisters							
15–19	4543	84	0.9818				
20–24	5488	102	0.9818	0.9825	−0.865	1988.8	0.909
25–29	5430	139	0.9750	0.9725	−0.880	1986.5	0.911
30–34	4809	182	0.9635	0.9590	−0.848	1984.4	0.906
35–39	4290	206	0.9542	0.9495	−0.894	1982.5	0.914
40–44	3533	218	0.9419	0.9379	−0.929	1980.7	0.919
45–49	2339	260	0.9000	0.8941	−0.775	1979.1	0.894

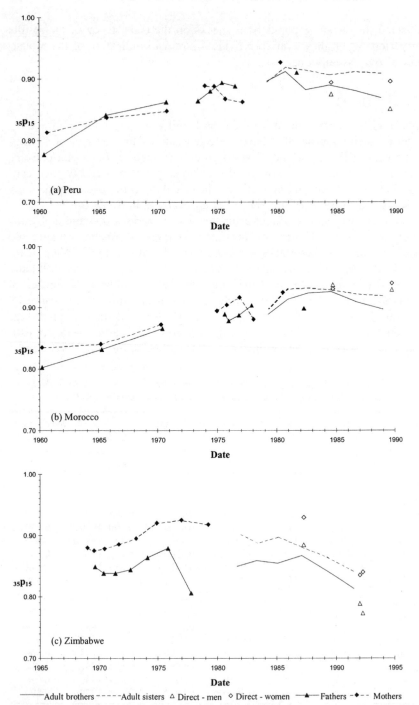

Figure 3.4   Estimates of survivorship from 15 to 50 years: Peru, Morocco and Zimbabwe

(Zimbabwe, 1985). Moreover, direct estimates are also presented for Zimbabwe based on the question about deaths in the last year asked in the 1992 Census (unpublished tables). The latter data have not been adjusted as evaluation using the growth balance and Preston–Coale methods (United Nations, 1983) yielded no clear evidence of underreporting of deaths. Figure 3.4c shows that the Census-based and most recent direct sibling estimates agree very closely.

In Peru, the indirect estimates based on data on adult siblings suggest higher adult survivorship in the late 1980s than the direct estimates based on the same data. The indirect measures may be biased slightly by failure of respondents to report some siblings who died before the reference period for which the direct measures are calculated or by misdating of siblings' deaths. Nevertheless, the two sets of estimates are fairly close. Both suggest that adult women's chances of survival stagnated and adult men's survivorship fell during the late 1980s. Furthermore, the earlier of the indirect estimates of adult mortality obtained from sibling data are very close to the most recent orphanhood-based estimates, which were derived from data on orphanhood since first marriage.

The indirect and direct estimates calculated from data on siblings in Morocco are also in fairly close agreement. Once again, both sets of estimates suggest that the rise in adult survivorship tapered off in the 1980s. Moreover, the earlier estimates made using the adult sibling method are similar to those obtained for the beginning of the 1980s from data on orphanhood since marriage. The indirect estimates for men indicate slightly lower survivorship than the direct estimates. It is possible that it is the latter which are less accurate, perhaps because they have larger sampling errors, as according to them the slight but long-standing excess in adult men's mortality disappeared in the 1980s.

The different series of adult mortality estimates for Zimbabwe also agree quite well. The most recent orphanhood estimates are based on respondents who are still children and may overestimate survivorship somewhat because of the adoption effect. For men, these estimates are erratic. The earlier direct and the indirect adult sibling estimates are consistent with the orphanhood-based estimates. The more recent estimates document a marked decrease in adult survivorship between the first half of the 1980s and the early 1990s. This no doubt reflects the initial rise in AIDS mortality in Zimbabwe. According to the direct estimates, the fall in adult survivorship began later and has been more abrupt than is indicated by the adult sibling method. It was suggested in the last section, that the adult sibling method should perform reasonably well in populations with a high *level* of mortality from HIV/AIDS. Like any indirect method based on the overall proportion of relatives who have died spread out over many years, however, it will tend to smooth out abrupt reversals in the trend in mortality. This seems to have happened in Zimbabwe. Nevertheless, while the most recent adult sibling estimates overestimate adult survivorship in the early 1990s slightly, the method does successfully reveal that a substantial increase in adult mortality has occurred.

DISCUSSION

In this chapter we have investigated the characteristics of the distribution of the age differences between an index individual and his or her siblings as a basis for the development of a simple regression-based method for estimating adult survivorship from data on the survival of a respondent's adult siblings. The data required to implement this method of estimation are straightforward and can be collected in a single-round household survey. Only two questions are required: 'How many living siblings do you have aged 15 years or more?' and 'How many of your siblings died after surviving to age 15 years or more'. Usually, however, one would ask about brothers and sisters separately to improve the quality of the data and to obtain mortality estimates by sex. In addition, one can ask about the residence of siblings to further improve data quality and obtain information that can be used to measure migration (Zaba, 1985). Such data on the survival of adult siblings already exist for many populations as a by-product of efforts to measure maternal mortality by the sisterhood method (Graham *et al*, 1989). They can now be exploited to measure all-cause mortality.

Our initial appraisal of the performance of the adult sibling method suggests that it has several advantages over existing methods for measuring adult mortality in countries with limited and defective data. Firstly, the relationship between the proportion of adult siblings alive and life-table survivorship is a close one that varies little between populations with different patterns of ages at childbirth and of mortality. If the data are accurate, they should yield rather precise estimates. Secondly, the estimates are efficient in terms of the statistical precision of the proportions because data will typically be collected on considerably more siblings than respondents. Of course, siblings tend to have shared risks of dying. Thus, the effective sample size lies somewhere in between the number of respondents and number of siblings reported on. Nevertheless, there is a real gain in sample size. Thirdly, theoretical considerations, simulated data and the application of the method to data for Zimbabwe, all suggest that the adult sibling method should perform better in populations with significant mortality from HIV/AIDS than existing indirect techniques for the estimation of adult mortality. On the one hand, any selection bias resulting from shared risks of infection should be small, while, on the other, the estimation procedure is relatively unaffected by the unusual age pattern of mortality that develops in populations where HIV infection is prevalent.

The initial applications of the adult sibling method presented here confirm that it is a useful new way of measuring adult mortality. Of course, like any indirect method, the results do not yield the detailed information on time trends and age patterns of adult mortality that are provided by accurate direct data. On the other hand, collecting accurate direct data on adult mortality has proved a difficult challenge (Timæus, 1991c). In particular, collecting sibling histories, as has been done in several Demographic and Health Surveys involves a lengthy and, therefore, expensive series of questions. It is unlikely to be successful in enquiries conducted with less well-trained field staff or less experienced professional staff. The simpler questions required to apply the indirect adult sibling method can be used more widely.

Our investigation of the characteristics of sibling age difference distributions and how they relate to the overall fertility distribution presented here is of potential value in other applications. Most obviously, it provides a means for refining the procedure used to estimate maternal mortality from data on sisters who die while pregnant or during the postpartum period (Graham *et al*, 1989). It also bears on the existing literature on the mathematical demography of kinship.

Preston (1996) has recently suggested that indirect methods of estimating mortality have been:

one of the great achievements of demography during the post-war period. They raised the status of demographers in the international health arena, because demographers alone appeared to have the tools needed to measure a central component of a population's health.

Both the original vision underlying these methods and much of the detailed research involved in their development originate with William Brass. Preston goes on to argue that 'improved methods for the assessment of the mortality of adults remain an important piece of unfinished business for demography'. In another paper in the same volume, Brass (1996) concludes that 'There appear to be no insuperable problems to prevent the development of improved techniques for indirect estimation', referring in particular to the issues raised by the increase in the number of deaths from AIDS.

This paper makes a contribution to the enterprise referred to by Brass and Preston. Indirect methods of estimating mortality will always provide less specific measures than detailed, regularly collected direct data. Even the few results presented in this chapter, however, undermine the argument that indirect methods have nothing to contribute to the monitoring of levels and trends in adult mortality. So long as funding remains restricted, administrative capacity limited, and a substantial part of the world's population illiterate, indirect techniques will remain one important approach to the measurement of both child and adult mortality.

In developing the adult sibling method, we have tried to follow the principles that have guided Brass's own research. The method is straightforward to apply and is based on simple questions that avoid making onerous demands on the memories of those who respond in demographic enquiries. As with other indirect methods, however, the technique's apparent simplicity is underlain by careful mathematical description and empirical study of the relationships between the indices of interest. In essence, however, at least for those trained by William Brass, the development of a new indirect technique of estimation is 'normal' science (Kuhn, 1962). Any particular originality in the research described here can be attributed to the man who first established that such things are possible.

REFERENCES

Blacker, J. G. C. and Brass, W. (1983) 'Experience of retrospective enquiries to determine vital rates', in L. Moss and H. Goldstein (eds) *The Recall Method in Social Surveys*, London: University of London Institute of Education, pp. 48–61.

Booth, H. (1984) 'Transforming Gompertz's function for fertility analysis: the development of a standard for the relational Gompertz function'. *Population Studies,* 38, pp. 495–506.

Brass, W. (1958) Models of birth distributions in human populations. *ISI Bulletin,* 36, pp. 165–78.

Brass, W. (1961) 'The construction of life tables from child survivorship ratios', in *Proceedings of the International Population Conference 1961.* Liège: International Union for the Scientific Study of Population, pp. 294–301.

Brass, W. (1970) 'Outlines of a simple birth distribution model for the study of systematic and chance components of variation'. Paper presented at the third conference on the mathematics of population. Chicago, July.

Brass, W. (1971) 'On the scale of mortality', in W. Brass (ed.) *Biological Aspects of Demography.* London: Taylor & Francis, pp. 69–110.

Brass, W. (1974) 'Perspectives in population prediction: illustrated by the statistics of England and Wales'. *Journal of the Royal Statistical Society, Series A*, 137, pp. 532–83.

Brass, W. (1975) 'Estimating mortality from deficient registration data', in W. Brass (ed.), *Methods for Estimating Fertility and Mortality from Limited and Defective Data*, Chapel Hill, NC: International Program of Laboratories for Population Statistics, pp. 117–23.

Brass, W. (1979a) 'Evaluation of birth and death registration using age distributions and child survivorship data'. *Asian and Pacific Census Forum*, 5(3), pp. 9–11 & 20.

Brass, W. (1979b) 'A procedure for comparing mortality estimates calculated from intercensal survival with the corresponding estimates from registered deaths'. *Asian and Pacific Census Forum*, 6(2), pp. 5–7.

Brass, W. (1981) 'The use of the Gompertz relational model to estimate fertility'. *International Population Conference, Manila*, vol 3, Liège: International Union for the Scientific Study of Population, pp. 345–61.

Brass, W. (1985) 'Further simplification of time location estimates for survivorship of adult relatives reported at a survey', in W. Brass (ed.), *Advances in Methods for Estimating Fertility and Mortality from Limited and Defective Data*, London: Centre for Population Studies Occasional Paper, London School of Hygiene & Tropical Medicine, pp. 11–16.

Brass, W. (1996) 'Demographic data analysis in less developed countries, 1946–1996'. *Population Studies*, 50, pp. 451–67.

Brass, W. and Bamgboye, E. A. (1981) *The Time Location of Reports of Survivorship: Estimates for Maternal and Paternal Widowhood and the Ever-Widowed*, London: Centre for Population Studies Research Papers, 81–1, London School of Hygiene & Tropical Medicine.

Brass, W. and Hill, K. (1973) 'Estimating adult mortality from orphanhood', in *International Population Conference, Liège, 1973*, vol 3, Liège: International Union for the Scientific Study of Population, pp. 111–23.

David, P., Kawar, S. and Graham, W. (1991) 'Estimating maternal mortality in Djibouti: an application of the sisterhood method'. *International Journal of Epidemiology*, 20, pp. 551–57.

Feeney, G. (1980) 'Estimating infant mortality trends from child survivorship data'. *Population Studies*, 34, pp. 109–28.

Farahani, M. (1981) 'A model of fertility by birth order and duration of marriage', unpublished PhD thesis, University of London.

Goldman, N. (1978) 'Estimating the intrinsic rate of increase of a population from the average numbers of younger and older sisters'. *Demography*, 15, pp. 499–521.

Goodman, L. A., Keyfitz, N. and Pullum, T. W. (1974) 'Family formation and the frequency of various kinship relationships'. *Theoretical Population Biology*, 5, pp. 1–27.

Graham, W., Brass, W. and Snow, R. (1989) 'Estimating maternal mortality: the sisterhood method'. *Studies in Family Planning*, 20, pp. 125–35.

Hernandez, B., Chirinos, J., Romero, M. and Langer, A. (1994) 'Estimating maternal mortality in rural areas of Mexico: the application of an indirect demographic method'. *International Journal of Obstetrics and Gynecology,* 46, pp. 285–89.

Hill, K. and Trussell, T. J. (1977) 'Further developments in indirect mortality estimation'. *Population Studies*, 31, pp. 313–33.

Keyfitz, N. (1977) *Applied Mathematical Demography*, New York: Wiley.

Kuhn, T. S. (1962) *The Structure of Scientific Revolutions*, Chicago: Chicago University Press.

Nunn A. J., Mulder D. W., Kamali, A. *et al.* (1997) 'Mortality associated with HIV-1 infection over five years in a rural Ugandan population: cohort study'. *British Medical Journal*, 315, pp. 767–71.

O'Brien, J., Wierzba, T., Knott, S. and Pikacha, J. (1994) 'Measuring maternal mortality in developing Pacific Island countries: experience with the sisterhood method in the Solomon Islands'. *New Zealand Medical Journal*, 107, pp. 268–9.

Preston, S. H. (1976) 'Family sizes of children and family sizes of women'. *Demography,* 31, pp. 105–14.

Preston, S. H. (1996) 'Population studies of mortality'. *Population Studies*, 50, pp. 525–36.

Rutenberg, N. and Sullivan, J. (1991) 'Direct and indirect estimates of maternal mortality from the sisterhood method', in *Demographic and Health Surveys World Conference, 5–7 August, 1991, Washington, D.C.*, vol 3. Columbia, MD: IRD/ Macro International, pp. 1669–96.

Shahidullah, M. (1995) 'The sisterhood method of estimating maternal mortality: the Matlab experience'. *Studies in Family Planning*, 26, pp. 101–6.

Simons, H., Wong L., Graham, W. and Schkolnik, S. (1996) 'Experience with the sisterhood method for estimating maternal mortality', in I. M. Timæus, J. Chackiel and L. Ruzicka (eds), *Adult Mortality in Latin America*, Oxford: Clarendon Press, pp. 108–20.

Timæus, I. M. (1991a) 'Estimation of adult mortality from orphanhood before and since marriage'. *Population Studies*, 45, pp. 455–72.

Timæus, I. M. (1991b) 'Estimation of mortality from orphanhood in adulthood'. *Demography*, 27, pp. 213–27.

Timæus, I. M. (1991c) 'Measurement of adult mortality in less developed countries: a comparative review'. *Population Index*, 57, pp. 552–68.

Timæus, I. M. (1992) 'Estimation of adult mortality from paternal orphanhood: a reassessment and a new approach'. *Population Bulletin of the United Nations*, 33, pp. 47–63.

Timæus, I. M. (1995) 'New estimates of the decline in adult mortality since 1950', in I. M. Timæus, J. Chackiel and L. Ruzicka (eds), *Adult Mortality in Latin America*, Oxford: Clarendon Press, pp. 87–107.

Timæus, I. M. and Nunn, A. J. (1997) 'Measurement of adult mortality in populations affected by AIDS: an assessment of the orphanhood method'. *Health Transition Review*, vol 7 (supplement 2), pp. 23–43.

UN (United Nations) (1983) *Indirect Techniques for Demographic Estimation*. ST/ESA/SER.A/81. New York: United Nations.

United Nations (1989) *World Population Prospects, 1988*. ST/ESA/SER.A/106. New York: United Nations.

Walraven, G., Mkanje, R. J., van-Roosmalen, J., *et al.* (1994) 'Assessment of maternal mortality in Tanzania'. *British Journal of Obstetrics and Gynaecology*, 101, pp. 414–17.

Wilson, S. E. (1985) *The Estimation of Recent Levels of Adult Sibling Mortality*, DrPH dissertation, University of North Carolina at Chapel Hill, Ann Arbor: UMI Dissertation Services.

Zaba, B. (1985) *Measurement of Emigration using Indirect Techniques*, Liège: Ordina Editions for IUSSP/CELADE.

Zaba, B. (1987) 'The indirect estimation of migration: a critical review'. *International Migration Review*, 21, pp. 1395–445.

Zimbabwe, Central Statistical Office (1985) *Main Features of the Population of Zimbabwe*. Harare: CSO.

SECTION TWO

Biodemography

CHAPTER FOUR

Use of biomarkers in population-based studies of reproductive function and reproductive health

Ronald H. Gray

*Johns Hopkins University,
School of Hygiene and Public Health*

INTRODUCTION

In the past, it has been difficult to conduct population-based studies of reproduction and reproductive health because clinical examination, or biological measures such as endocrine status or diagnosis of occult disease, generally required invasive procedures and specialized facilities. As a consequence, many biomedical studies were conducted in clinic settings, often on highly selected and atypical populations. This problem of selective observation is particularly acute in developing countries where access to clinical and laboratory facilities is very limited.

At a meeting of the British Society for Population Studies, during the 1970s, I recall a discussion with Professor Brass and Professor R.G. Edwards, regarding the possibility of doing biological or chemical measurements in non-clinic populations. This discussion, and the development of new investigative technologies, has led me to pursue studies of reproductive endocrinology and reproductive health in a number of settings. This paper briefly summarizes our experience with the use of biomarkers for investigation of diverse questions such as the resumption of ovulation and fertility after childbirth, reproductive hazards in the workplace and, more recently, investigations of sexually transmitted diseases (STDs) and other genital tract infections (GTIs) in rural African populations.

STUDIES OF THE POSTPARTUM RETURN OF OVULATION

The effect of breast-feeding on amenorrhoea and delayed conception has long been recognized as an important method of birth spacing. However, information on the relationship between nursing and ovarian inhibition was limited in the 1970s, and health authorities often questioned the utility of breast-feeding as a means of postpartum contraception. Developments in the radioimmunoassay of hormones in small urine samples made population-based studies of physiological processes feasible in postpartum women. We conducted investigations in the United States and the Philippines on non-breast-feeding and breast-feeding mothers. All women collected small, first morning urine samples; in the USA these were stored in a domestic refrigerator, and in the Philippines, the samples were collected from the home daily. We conducted validation studies to show that these urine samples reflected blood levels of the hormones (Gray *et al*, 1987). The samples were assayed for urinary metabolites of oestrogen (oestradiol glucuronide) and progesterone (pregnanediol glucuronide), as well as for pituitary gonadotrophin hormones, luteinizing hormone and follicle-stimulating hormone. In addition, women maintained daily diaries on which they recorded each episode of breast or artificial feeding (bottle, cup, spoon), as well as episodes of vaginal bleeding. We assessed the patterns of lactation associated with ovarian suppression, resumption of ovulatory or non-ovulatory vaginal bleeding episodes, and the adequacy of the hormonal milieu, particularly the luteal phase of the cycle (Gray *et al*, 1990; Campbell and Gray, 1993). This work, particularly the statistical analyses, could not have been accomplished without the contributions of Oona Campbell.

Figure 4.1 shows the pattern of breast-feeding in the two populations. Women in the USA nursed less frequently than women in Manila, but the American mothers suckled for longer periods of time during each episode. Figure 4.2 shows the relative risk of ovulation in relation to the frequency of lactation or the duration of each suckling episode, estimated from a proportional hazards model. These data suggest that only intensive breast-feeding by amenorrhoeic women during the first 6 months post partum, could reliably suppress ovulation. However, beyond 6 months, or after resumption of vaginal bleeding, women could not rely on lactation to prevent conception. These and other data provided the scientific basis for the Lactational Amenorrhea Method of contraception which is now widely promoted among nursing mothers.

STUDIES OF EARLY PREGNANCY LOSS

Although investigations of hormonal patterns during the menstrual cycle were well established during the 1980s, studies of early pregnancy and occult pregnancy loss during the first week after implantation and before the first missed menstrual period were not feasible because sensitive and specific hormonal assays needed to detect an early rise in urine human chorionic gonadotrophin hormone (hCG) were not available until the late 1980s. These assays were developed at Columbia University and in 1989 we initiated studies using urinary hormonal biomarkers to detect menstrual cycle abnormalities, early pregnancy and early pregnancy loss among women employed in semiconductor manufacturing (Campbell and Gray, 1993; Hakim *et al*, 1995;

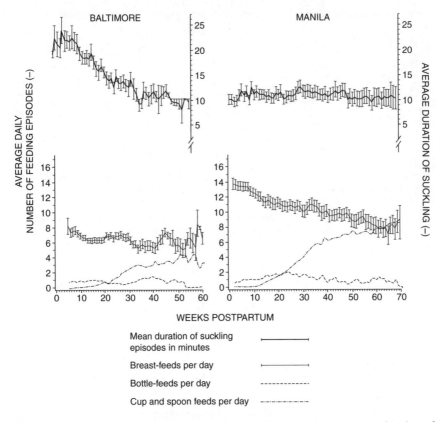

Figure 4.1 The average daily frequency of infant feeding and the average duration of nursing episodes (±SE) for women in Baltimore and Manila

Corea *et al*, 1996; Gray *et al*, 1996). Patterns of rising and falling hCG, indicative of unrecognized early losses are shown in Figure 4.3.

The salient findings from these studies were that, in women with no evidence of infertility, the rate of early, hCG-detected, pregnancy was 21.6 per 100 menstrual cycles, and the rate of early pregnancy loss was 21.0 per cent. However, among women with evidence of subfertility, the conception rate was only 8.8 per 100 cycles, and the rate of early loss was 69.7 per cent (Hakim *et al*, 1995). Some women had occupational exposures to volatile, short-chain glycol ether solvents, which are known reproductive toxins, and among such exposed women, we observed increased rates of subfertility and increased rates of occult and clinical pregnancy loss (Hakim *et al*, 1995; Corea *et al*, 1996; Gray *et al*, 1996). These findings suggested a linkage between the inability to conceive and subclinical pregnancy loss, possibly due to common pathological mechanisms, and emphasized that

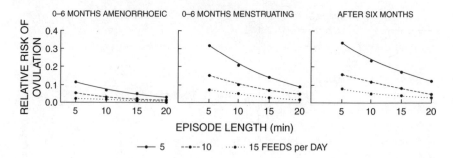

Figure 4.2   Relative risks of ovulation associated with the daily frequency of breast feeds, average duration of nursing episodes, menstrual status and time post partum

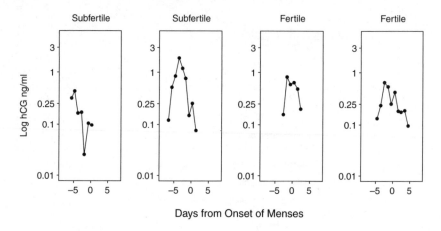

Figure 4.3   Patterns of rising and falling chorionic gonadotrophin hormone (hCG) by days from the onset of menses

studies of reproductive hazards need to investigate both failure to conceive and failure to maintain pregnancy. In addition, as a result of these investigations as well as other animal and human studies, the deleterious glycol ethers have been removed from most manufacturing processes in Western Europe and North America.

COMMUNITY-BASED STUDIES OF SEXUALLY TRANSMITTED DISEASES AND GENITAL TRACT INFECTIONS

Population-based studies of STDs and other GTIs have, in the past, been hampered by diagnostic problems. Many STDs are asymptomatic or manifest symptoms which are not recognized by the individual, so one cannot rely upon a history of illness. Physical examination, particularly genital tract examination, is invasive and difficult to perform outside of a clinical setting; moreover, many infections may be subclinical and inapparent on inspection. Finally, diagnostic tests, particularly those requiring culture of organisms, often have low sensitivity and are difficult to conduct in field settings due to problems of sample collection, transport and lab back-up. These limitations place serious constraints on research in representative, non-clinical populations, particularly in rural areas of developing countries.

There have, however, been major developments in technology which have revolutionized our ability to conduct population-based studies, and we are currently applying these methods to a community-based randomized trial in rural Rakai District of southwestern Uganda. All sample collection and interviews in these studies are conducted in the home. A blood sample is obtained for serological diagnosis of HIV, syphilis, chancroid and herpes infections. Participants are also asked to provide a urine sample which is tested by ligase chain reaction (LCR), a DNA amplification procedure, used to test for gonorrhoea and chlamydia. We are also conducting HIV tests on urine samples, using newly developed immunoassays for HIV antibody excreted in urine. Women provide two self-administered vaginal swabs, one swab is cultured for trichomonas using an InPouch TV culture kit, and the other swab is used to prepare a Gram-stained slide for microscopic diagnosis of bacterial vaginosis in our field laboratory. In addition, we collect swabs on subsamples of women for detection of human papillomavirus, the cause of cervical cancer and genital warts, and samples of ulcers or discharges are collected for polymerase chain reaction (PCR) diagnosis of syphilis, herpes and chancroid. The study also follows up pregnant women and their babies. Samples are collected from the mother for diagnosis of postpartum infections, and mothers are asked to retain the placenta (in a prepared formalin solution) for histopathological examination. Infants are examined by anthropometry and maturity assessment, eye swabs taken for LCR diagnosis of ophthalmia, and blood samples for diagnosis of congenital syphilis or vertically transmitted HIV infection. With the exception of the specialized LCR and PCR tests, all other investigations are conducted in Uganda, either in a field laboratory or at the Uganda Virus Research Institute in Entebbe. All participation is voluntary, and there is no remuneration paid for provision of samples (every person is given soap and access to free medical services, irrespective of their study participation; and fathers or community health workers are compensated for travel costs if they inform the project of new births). Compliance with these investigations has been remarkable, in part because these are relatively non-invasive procedures, and because great effort is made to involve the community in the research. At enrolment, 90 per cent of participants provided blood samples, 95 per cent provided urine and self-administered vaginal swabs, 96 per cent of pregnant women who delivered were followed up post partum, and 78 per cent of mothers collected the placenta. Eye swabs and blood samples were obtained from more than 90 per cent of newborn infants.

This study, which is still ongoing, has provided unique population-based data on the prevalence of STDs and adverse pregnancy outcomes. Infections are extremely common in this underserviced population (Wawer *et al*, 1996). At baseline, the prevalence of serologically positive HIV was 17 per cent, syphilis 12 per cent, and herpes 35 per cent. Among women, 24 per cent had trichomonas infection and 50 per cent of self-administered vaginal swabs showed moderate to severe bacterial vaginosis infections. Chlamydia and gonorrhoea rates varied between 4 and 6 per cent among younger age groups. Among the placentas examined histopathologically, placental membrane inflammation (particularly chorioamnionitis) was observed in 20 per cent of deliveries, and among babies examined within the first week of delivery, low birth weight was observed in approximately 15 per cent. These data provide some insight into the burden of morbidity associated with these infections, and follow up data provide promising evidence of the efficacy of treatment.

In addition to the information on STDs, data are also collected on pregnancy and pregnancy outcomes, including use of hCG testing if women are unsure of their pregnancy status. The prevalence of pregnancy is high in this largely non-contracepting rural population; among women with no evidence of an STD, the prevalence of pregnancy was 21.4 per cent, whereas among woman with HIV infection, the proportion pregnant was 13.4 per cent. After multivariate adjustment for age, marital status, contraception, lactation, sexual behaviour, infertility history and evidence of clinical AIDS, we found that the relative risk of pregnancy among HIV infected women was significantly lower than in HIV-negative subjects (relative risk (RR) 0.45; 95 per cent confidence interval (CI) 0.35 to 57). In addition, HIV infected women experienced significantly higher rates of spontaneous abortion (RR 1.49; 95 per cent CI 1.01 to 2.24) (Gray *et al*, 1998). These findings suggest that HIV infected women may have lower conception rates and increased pregnancy wastage. This has important implications for HIV surveillance, which, in many countries, is conducted among pregnant women attending antenatal or delivery care services. If HIV infected women are less likely to become pregnant or to retain a viable pregnancy, they will be underrepresented among women using these pregnancy-related services. Therefore, surveillance of pregnant women will underestimate the magnitude of the HIV epidemic among women of reproductive age. Figure 4.4 shows HIV prevalence among the pregnant and non-pregnant women in Rakai, and illustrates how biased surveillance based on antenatal or intrapartum care services could be.

In summary, over the past two decades there have been major developments in the availability of investigative procedures that can be applied to population-based studies of reproduction and reproductive health. Selective

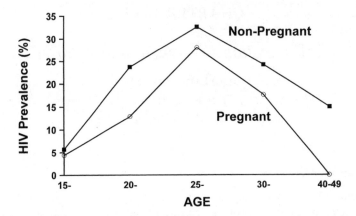

Figure 4.4   HIV prevalence in pregnant and non-pregnant women in Rakai, Uganda

use of such biomarkers could have a major role in future demographic and epidemiological research.

REFERENCES

Campbell, O.M. and Gray, R.H. (1993) 'Characteristics and determinants of post-partum ovarian function in women in the U.S'. *American Journal of Obstetrics and Gynecology*, 169(1), pp. 55–60.

Correa, A., Gray, R.H., Cohen, R., Rothman, N., Shah, F., Secat, H. and Corn, M. (1996) 'Ethylene glycol ethers and risks of spontaneous abortion and subfertility'. *American Journal of Epidemiology*, 143(7), pp. 707–17.

Gray, R.H., Campbell, O.M., Zacur, H.A., Labbok, M.H. and MacRae, S.L. (1987) 'Postpartum return of ovarian activity in nonbreastfeeding women monitored by urinary assays'. *Journal of Clinical Endocrinology and Metabolism*, 64(4), pp. 645–50.

Gray, R.H., Campbell, O.M., Apelo, R., Eslami, S.S., Zacur, H., Ramos, R.M., Gehret, J.C. and Labbok, M.H. (1990) 'The risk of ovulation during lactation and use of breastfeeding for fertility regulation'. *Lancet*, 335, pp. 25–9.

Gray, R.H., Correa, A., Hakim, R., Cohen, R., Shah, F., Rothman, N., Hou, W. and Secat, H. (1996) 'Ethylene glycol ethers and reproductive health in semi-conductor workers'. *Occupational Hygiene* 2, pp. 331–38.

Gray, R.H., Wawer, M.J., Serwadda, D., Sewankambo, N.K., Li, C., Wabwire-Mangen, F., Paxton, L., Kiwanuka, N., Kigozi, G., Konde-Lule, J. Quinn, T.C., Gaydos, C.A. and McNairn, D. (1998) 'Population-based study of fertility in women with HIV-1 infection in Uganda'. *Lancet*, 351, pp. 98–103.

Hakim, R.B., Gray, R.H., Zacur, H. (1995) 'Infertility and early pregnancy loss'. *American Journal of Obstetrics and Gynecology*, 172, pp. 1510–17.

Wawer, M.J., Sewenkambo, N.K., Serwadda, D., Quinn, T.C., Paxton, L., Kiwanuka, N., Wabwire-Mangen, F., Li, C. Lutalo, T., Nalugoda, F., Gaydos, C.A., Moulton, L.H., Meehan, M.O., Ahmed, S. and Gray, R.H. (1999) *Lancet* 353, pp. 525–35.

CHAPTER FIVE

HIV infection in women and children

Marie-Louise Newell

*Department of Epidemiology and Public Health,
Institute of Child Health, London*

INTRODUCTION

The method for deriving estimates of infant and child mortality from census and survey data on proportions of children dead among children ever borne was developed by Brass in the early 1960s. This procedure has provided the basis for most of the estimates of infant and child mortality which have been made in the last 30 years for the majority of Third World countries, particularly in Africa, where death registration is non-existent. Some recent data now show that the long-term decline in mortality in some African countries is coming to an end, and there may even be up-turns in the under-five mortality rates. This is almost certainly mainly due to mother-to-child transmission of HIV infection.

The human immunodeficiency virus (HIV) is a retrovirus, which causes immune suppression through destruction of CD4 lymphocytes. This results in increased susceptibility to common infections which in turn leads to acquired immune deficiency syndrome (AIDS). There are at least two types of HIV of which HIV-1 is the most prevalent and pathogenic. HIV-2 is uncommon in Western countries, and is less transmissable. HIV infection can be acquired through sexual contact, blood or blood products (including contaminated needles and syringes) and vertically from mother to child (Newell and Peckham, 1993; Chin, 1994).

Although molecular evidence suggests that HIV may have been around for several decades or even longer, HIV infection did not occur in epidemic proportions worldwide until the early 1980s. It is estimated that by the year 2000 more than 35 million people will have been infected with HIV. Since HIV began to spread in North America and Sub-Saharan Africa, close to 6 million men, women and children are estimated to have died of AIDS. Over 75 per cent of these deaths occurred in Africa, and around 90 per cent of women who died of AIDS were African (UNAIDS, 1998).

Globally three out of every five adults living with HIV today are men, but the gap between the sexes is narrowing. In Sub-Saharan Africa new infections are already divided equally between men and women. As infection rates rise is women, so does the number of newborns infected with HIV, and it has been estimated that each year 600,000 infants become HIV infected (UNAIDS, 1998).

HIV infection mainly affects adults in the 15–50 year age group, and in East Africa up to three quarters of HIV infections are now occurring among individuals aged under 25 years, while ten years ago this proportion may have been around or below 50 per cent. This exemplifies the changing and maturing epidemic. Although over the years prevalence may remain stable, this can mask high incidence. The virus is spreading, seemingly haphazardly, from urban to rural areas and from Eastern to Western and Southern Africa. HIV spreads at different rates, even within a single country, in different segments of the population. However, despite very high prevalence rates in some countries, HIV prevalence has remained relatively low in the general population of some West African countries, such as Cameroon and Benin.

In Asia the epidemic started a bit later than in Africa, but the rapid increase in the number of infected individuals in recent years was associated with injecting drug use. By the year 2000, it is expected that there will be more cases of HIV in Asia than in Africa (Mertens and Burton, 1996; UNAIDS, 1998).

PREGNANCY IN HIV INFECTED WOMEN

There is a lack of information about the effect of HIV infection on fertility. A study in Kinshasa, Zaire suggested that HIV infected women were as likely to become pregnant during a three-year follow-up period as HIV uninfected women (Ryder *et al* 1994). In a recent study in rural Uganda pregnancy rates among HIV infected women were significantly lower than among HIV uninfected controls (R. H. Gray *et al* 1996).

Results from a number of small studies suggest that HIV infected pregnancies have no increased risk in pregnancy or delivery complications (Selwyn *et al* 1989; Minkoff *et al* 1990; Johnstone, 1993). There is little information about labour and delivery complications in HIV infected women. However, the management of labour is becoming a focus of interest with the findings from several studies about the effect of delivery-associated variables on the risk of vertical transmission (Burns *et al* 1994; European Collaborative Study, 1994a; Duliege *et al* 1995;). In immunocompromised women, it is plausible that the risk of postoperative wound infection or postpartum endometritis may be greater (Semprini *et al*, 1995).

EFFECT OF PREGNANCY ON PROGRESSION OF DISEASE

To counsel women identified as HIV infected before or during pregnancy, the natural history of the infection in pregnant women and its effect on pregnancy outcome must be determined. Both HIV infection and pregnancy exert immunosuppressive effects independently, and it has been suggested that pregnancy and HIV infection might operate synergistically to depress maternal immune function (Mandelbrot and Henrion, 1993). Early in the epidemic it was suggested that pregnancy could accelerate progression of HIV disease. However, most of that information was based on case reports, symptomatic women or studies without appropriate controls, or limited to injecting drug users. Subsequently, findings of prospective studies suggest that pregnancy is unlikely to be associated with HIV disease progression (Alger *et al*, 1993; French and Brocklehurst, 1998; European Collaborative Study and Swiss HIV and Pregnancy Collaborative Study Group, 1997). No gender effect has emerged in several natural history studies (Cozzi Lepri *et al*, 1994). In a Swedish cohort study of people infected through blood transfusion, and thus with known infection date, the progression rate was not related to gender (Blaxhult *et al*, 1990). However, it remains uncertain whether pregnancy further increases the risk of deterioration for women with marked immunosuppression (defined as having CD4 count levels below 200 cells/mm^3), since most studies have looked at asymptomatic women. It is now generally accepted that where there is good access to medical care, women have equivalent if not better survival than men.

HIV INFECTION AND PREGNANCY OUTCOME

The effect of HIV infection on pregnancy outcome requires further research, as studies have had conflicting results. Studies of asymptomatic women in developing countries have not shown an increased risk of obstetric complications and adverse pregnancy outcome in terms of birth weight, gestational age, head circumference, Apgar scores or incidence of chorioamnionitis or endometritis (Johnstone *et al*, 1988; Selwyn *et al*, 1989; Lallemant *et al*, 1990; Minkoff *et al*, 1990; Halsey *et al*, 1991; Lepage *et al*, 1991; Alger *et al*, 1993). However, an increased risk of low birth weight associated with maternal HIV infection has been reported in some African studies (Ryder *et al*, 1989; Temmerman *et al*, 1994; Brocklehurst, 1998); such poor pregnancy outcomes may reflect the health and social status of the mother rather than a direct effect of HIV *per se*. Similarly, no association has been found between HIV infection in the infant and birth weight, head circumference, gestational age, rate of prematurity and incidence of congenital malformations (Blanche *et al*, 1989; European Collaborative Study, 1994; Brocklehurst, 1998).

Studies on T-lymphocyte subsets during pregnancy have reported conflicting results. Some have found a progressive decline in CD4 count throughout pregnancy, while others have reported a U-shaped CD4 cell count profile during pregnancy, or stable levels throughout pregnancy with a postnatal rise (Biggar *et al*, 1989; Miotti *et al*, 1992). In a large European data set there was a gradual linear increase of about 40 CD4 cells over the last six months of pregnancy (European Collaborative Study and Swiss HIV and Pregnancy Collaborative Study Group, 1997). In a study in Nairobi (Temmerman *et al*, 1995), duration of pregnancy was not associated with levels of immunological variables. The CD4 percentage was lower post partum than antenatally, in both infected and uninfected women, but absolute CD4 counts changed little, suggesting that observed changes are due to pregnancy-associated cell count differences rather than to HIV infection. The results from a study in Edinburgh (Brettle *et al*, 1995) comparing immunological markers of infected pregnant and non-pregnant women further confirm these findings and the lack of a short-term synergistic effect of HIV infection and pregnancy on the immune function.

VERTICAL TRANSMISSION

Transmission of HIV infection from mother to child is the dominant mode of acquisition of infection for children. However, in countries where a safe blood supply is not available, and where medically used needles and syringes are in short supply and re-use is routine, acquisition of infection through blood transfusion or contaminated needles and syringes remains a strong possibility.

Estimates of the rates of vertical transmission vary between studies and between population groups. Historically, the rate of vertical transmission in Europe was 15–20 per cent, in the USA 15–30 per cent and in Africa and Asia 25–30 per cent (Working Group on Mother-to-Child Transmission of HIV, 1995). Differences between populations in the rate of mother-to-child transmission are related to differences in the distribution of risk factors associated with increased transmission.

The risk of transmission of HIV-2 infection is reportedly low. In the French Collaborative Study (1994), based on 41 infants born to mothers who were HIV-2 positive, the estimated risk of mother-to-child transmission of HIV-2 was between 0 and 11 per cent. Further evidence that the vertical transmission rate of HIV-2 is likely to be low comes from the Ivory Coast (Adjorlolo *et al*, 1994), where the results of specific immunoglobulin A and polymerase chain reaction (PCR) tests at 6 months of age suggest that 28 per cent (95 per cent confidence interval (CI) 12 to 49) of infants born to HIV-1 infected mothers are infected compared with 3 per cent (95 per cent CI 0 to 15) of infants born to HIV-2 infected mothers.

Vertical transmission of HIV infection can occur before, during or after delivery but the relative importance of each of these stages remains uncertain. There is good evidence to suggest that intrauterine infection does occur, although its contribution to vertical transmission has not been precisely quantified. Studies based on placentas and fetal tissues following pregnancy termination of HIV infected women give conflicting results. Results from studies investigating fetal material suggest a low frequency of early *in utero* HIV infection. There is increasing debate about the importance of intra-partum acquisition of infection. The exchange of blood between mother and child during labour and at the time of delivery, and the detection of the virus in cervical secretions, make acquisition of infection at this stage plau-sible. Postnatal transmission of infection through breast-feeding can occur in infants born to women with established infection, as well as in infants born to mothers who become infected postnatally (Dunn *et al*, 1992).

RISK FACTORS FOR VERTICAL TRANSMISSION

Mother-to-child transmission is associated with maternal factors or factors surrounding the delivery as well as with breast-feeding. Maternal factors linked with increased likelihood of transmission include genetic factors which may be associated with immune response (such as the HLA system). The presence of other sexually transmitted diseases and chorioamnionitis may increase the HIV load in the cervical tract and cause increased exposure to infection for the fetus (Wabwire-Mangen *et al*, 1996). A mother who has recently become infected, with a primary infection, might be more likely to transmit the infection, as her viral load is likely to be higher than in estab-lished infection. Similarly the viral load is increased in advanced disease and the risk of transmission higher than in the clinically latent stage of infection. Recently it has become possible to measure directly the effect of viral load. Several small studies have reported an increase in transmission rate with increasing viral load, and there does not seem to be a threshold below which transmission does not occur (Borkowsky *et al*,1994; Fang *et al*, 1995; Dickover *et al*, 1996; O'Shea *et al*, 1998).

Prematurity has been linked to increased likelihood of transmission (European Collaborative Study, 1992). The time between rupture of mem-branes and delivery, as well as the duration of the second stage of labour, influence the exposure of the infant to HIV infected maternal fluids, and may, therefore, affect the transmission risk (Burns *et al*, 1994; Landesman *et al*, 1996). Results from a large register of twins born to HIV infected mothers suggest that the first-born twin is more likely to be infected than the second-born twin, especially when the delivery was vaginal (Duliege *et al*, 1995). The authors of this study have taken this as evidence of acqui-sition of infection during passage through the birth canal. However, there are methodological concerns regarding this register, which depends on reports from paediatricians in the USA, Europe and Africa.

Information is accumulating on HIV viral load in the genital tract (Kreiss *et al*, 1994; Mostad and Kreiss, 1996) and possible associations with viraemia, and advanced disease. Henin *et al*, (1993) in a cross-sectional study estimated the prevalence of viral excretion in cervico-vaginal secretions of 55 women. Excretion of HIV was significantly higher in pregnant than in non-pregnant women, nearly 40 per cent of whom had evidence of virus replication. More recently, studies have concentrated on the detection of actively replicating virus, HIV-RNA, and with increased sensitivity of the tests, cervical HIV-RNA can be detected in the majority of samples (Goulston *et al*,1996). In the study by Goulston *et al* (1996), cervical shedding of HIV-RNA was associated with increased levels of plasma RNA, but this finding needs to be confirmed in larger studies. In a study in Nairobi the presence of DNA in the genital tract was associated with severe immunosuppression and severe vitamin A deficiency (John *et al*, 1997).

As labour and delivery have been suggested as times of high risk for vertical transmission of HIV from mother to child, much attention has focused on the method of delivery as being an important time for intervention. It has been suggested that an elective caesarean delivery may reduce the rate of transmission because of a reduced exposure to contaminated blood or cervical secretions. Initially evidence from the European Collaborative Study suggested a halving in the risk of vertical transmission in children delivered by elective caesarean section (European Collaborative Study, 1996). A recent meta-analyis of data from 15 prospective perinatal transmission studies, including nearly 8500 mother–child pairs showed a 50 per cent reduction in the risk of vertical transmission after elective caesarean section delivery, defined as before onset of labour and before rupture of membranes (Dunn *et al*, 1994; Read J for the International Perinatal HIV Group, 1998). In France (Mandelbrot *et al*, 1998) and in Switzerland (Kind *et al*, 1998) the effect of elective caesarean section in reducing vertical transmission was especially pronounced in women who also received prophylactic antiretroviral therapy.

BREAST-FEEDING

It is unclear whether infection takes place through cell-free HIV in breast-milk or through HIV infected cells. Cell-free virus could penetrate the mucosal lining of the gastrointestinal tract of infants by infecting cells, or by direct entry into the blood stream via mucosal breaches. If HIV infection only occurs through cell-associated virus then colostral milk may be more infectious because of its high cellular content, although the other components of colostrum may have a protective effect. It is unclear whether damage to the intestinal tract of the infant, caused by the early introduction of other foods, could increase its permeability and thus result in increased rates of acquisition of infection for the infant (Tess *et al*, 1998b). The immature gastrointestinal tract of the newborn may facilitate transmission, however, this is not a requirement as transmission has been reported in infants who begin breast-feeding outside the neonatal period (Datta *et al*, 1994).

Transmission of HIV through breastmilk can occur in situations where the mother acquired the infection shortly after delivery, but also in established maternal infection. Based on a meta-analysis of limited evidence, it has been estimated that the additional risk of acquisition of infection through breast-feeding is between 7 and 22 per cent, and in observational studies from South Africa, Brazil and Europe breast-feeding doubled the overall vertical transmission rate (European Collaborative Study, 1994a; Mayaux *et al*, 1995; G.E. Gray *et al*, 1996; Bobat *et al*, 1997; Newell *et al*, 1997; Tess *et al*, 1998a,b). Transmission may be less related to the amount of exposure and more related to time of exposure, infectivity of milk or specific susceptibility of the infant. It has been suggested that the risk of vertical transmission may be particularly high for infants who receive other foods as well as breastmilk, and there is little evidence to suggest that the risk of transmission is associated with duration of breast-feeding (de Martino *et al*, 1992; Bobat *et al*, 1997; Tess *et al*, 1998a,b).

HYPOTHESIS OF TIMING OF TRANSMISSION

A working definition of the timing of vertical transmission in non-breast-feeding populations has been proposed by Bryson and colleagues in which an infant is defined as infected intrauterine if there is a positive result of a culture or DNA PCR test on a sample drawn in the first 48 hours after birth (Bryson *et al*, 1992). Intrapartum acquisition of infection is assumed if there is a negative culture or PCR test in the first week of life, followed by a positive sample before 3 months of age. However, this definition is not based on experimental data, and the underlying assumption may not hold true if negative early specimens could be due to sequestration of the virus in an inaccessible location (such as lymph nodes or central nervous system). Furthermore, in breast-feeding populations infants are additionally exposed to HIV through breastmilk.

ESTIMATED TIMING OF VERTICAL TRANSMISSION IN NON-BREAST-FEEDING POPULATIONS

There have been several attempts to quantify the relative contribution of each of these routes, using different methodological approaches. One of the first modelling exercises was that of Rouzioux *et al* (1995), who, using a Markov model and results from 95 infected, non-breast-fed infants born to HIV infected women, estimated the timing of transmission, the time from birth to the emergence of detectable virus and the time from birth to sero-conversion. The model indicated that 17 per cent of infected children would be virus culture- or PCR-positive at birth, rapidly rising to 50 per cent by 10 days of age and 95 per cent by 2 months. The model indicated that less than 2 per cent of infected infants acquired the infection more than two months before birth, approximately 35 per cent of vertically infected infants were infected *in utero* less than two months before delivery, and in the remaining 65 per cent of cases (95 per cent CI 22 to 92) the date of infection was estimated as the date of birth. The estimated median period between birth and the emergence of viral markers of infection was 10 days (95 per cent CI 6 to 14), with 95 per cent of infected children having shown markers of infection by 56 days (Busch and Satten, 1997).

Using a different methodological approach, Dunn *et al* (1995) derived age-specific estimates of the sensitivity of PCR using distribution-free methods for interval censored data (Table 5.1). Data on 271 infected children from 12 perinatal studies were combined for analysis. PCR detected HIV-DNA in an estimated 38 per cent (90 per cent CI 29 to 46) of HIV infected children tested on the day of, or the day after, birth. The estimated sensitivity was relatively constant from birth to day 8, increased rapidly in the second week of life, and reached 93 per cent (90 per cent CI 76 to 97) by 14 days of age. Only seven children had negative PCR test results after the neonatal period, the age at the last negative test ranging between 65 and 183 days.

Similar results, also based on the nonparametric method developed by Turnbull (1976), were obtained by others (Table 5.1). Kuhn *et al* (1996) estimated the sensitivity of HIV-DNA PCR in the neonatal period at 22 per cent between birth and day 3, rising to more than 95 per cent by 39 days of age. Chouquet and colleagues (1997) who like Rouzioux used information on children enrolled in the French perinatal cohort, but with a

Table 5.1 *Estimates of mother-to-child transmission rates in the absence of treatment*

	Transmission rate (%)
Europe	14
France	18
Italy	19
Switzerland	20
New York	29
Miami	30
Haiti	25
Zaire	39
Zambia	39
Rwanda	25
Ivory Coast	28

nonparametric method of analysis, showed a PCR positivity at birth of about 25 per cent, rapidly rising to 80 per cent by week 2. Using viral culture rather than PCR, data from 140 infected children in the multicentre Women and Infants Transmission Study suggested an estimated probability of being positive at birth of 27 per cent and 89 per cent by 1 month (Kalish *et al*, 1997) These results are consistent with the estimates derived by others based on DNA PCR.

The statistical method used does not yield a classification of intrauterine or intrapartum transmission for each infant, only an estimate of the population distribution of times at which a viral test would first be positive if monitored continuously. However, these results could be taken to suggest that, in non-breast-feeding populations, about one-quarter to one-third of vertical infection is acquired intrauterine. This is probably a lower estimate as the observed proportion positive at birth will underestimate the true proportion with intrauterine infection as a transmission event shortly before delivery may not have sufficient time for infection to be established and to produce a positive culture at birth, or because of sequestration of the virus (de Rossi *et al*, 1992, 1993; Kalish *et al*, 1997).

TIMING IN BREAST-FEEDING POPULATIONS

The estimates suggesting that three-quarters of vertical transmission occurs during delivery were based on studies in non-breast-feeding populations. However, in populations where breast-feeding is common it is not only impossible to distinguish between late intrauterine and intrapartum transmission, but also between intrapartum transmission and transmission via breast-feeding occurring in the first few weeks of life.

Simonon (Simonon *et al*, 1994) estimated the contribution of intrauterine, intrapartum and postnatal transmission in 47 infected children born to HIV infected mothers in Kigali, Rwanda, using nonparametric methods similar to those used by Dunn *et al*, (1995). In this prospectively followed cohort, 30 per cent of infected childen showed evidence of infection at birth, and 81 per cent at 3 months of age. At 24 months, all infected children had had at least one positive PCR result. In the study by Bertolli (1996) in Kinshasa, Zaire, PCR test results for HIV-DNA on venous blood drawn from children aged 0–2 days and 3–5 months were used to estimate the relative contribution of the three routes. Among 41 infected children, 22 per cent were PCR positive at birth, 83 per cent by 3 months and all by 24 months.

In Kigali, the overall rate of vertical transmission was 25.3 per cent (95 per cent CI 19 to 32) (Simonon *et al*, 1994) (Table 5.2). The estimated rate of intrauterine transmission was 7.7 per cent (taking the 30 per cent of infected children who were PCR positive at birth) and intrapartum plus postnatal transmission rate 17.6 per cent. On the other hand, if the sensitivity of PCR was assumed to be only optimal at 3 months, the intrauterine, intra-partum and early postnatal transmission rate would be 20.4 per cent and the late postnatal transmission rate (after 3 months of age) would be 4.9 per cent. This would give a range of 4.9–17.6 per cent of transmission attributable to breast-feeding and a likely relative contribution of each period of 30, 50 and 20 per cent (before, during and immediately after birth and after 3 months of life respectively). In Kinshasa (Bertolli *et al*, 1996) 23 per cent of infected children were estimated to have had intrauterine, 65 per cent intrapartum/early postpartum and 12 per cent late postpartum trans-mission. The estimated absolute rates for intrauterine, intrapartum/early postpartum and late postpartum transmission (after 3 months of age) were 6, 18 and 4 per cent (Table 5.2). These results again suggest that the risk of transmission is likely to be higher during labour and delivery than during gestation and in addition that breast-feeding beyond 3 months results in a substantial additional risk of transmission.

LATE POSTNATAL TRANSMISSION OF INFECTION THROUGH BREAST-FEEDING

Acquisition of infection after 3–6 months of age through breast-feeding may contribute substantially to the overall rate of infection in breast-feeding populations. The results from Rwanda and Zaire already suggested that about 5 per cent of children born to HIV infected mothers only became infected after 3 months of age, and the relative contribution of this to the overall rate of vertical transmission was 12–20 per cent (Simonon *et al*, 1994; Bertolli *et al*, 1996). Late postnatal acquisition of infection was further confirmed in a study in Ivory Coast by Ekpini *et al* (1997) who defined late postnatal trans-mission to have taken place when a child had a negative PCR at 3 or 6 months

Table 5.2 *Possible risk factors for mother-to-child transmission*

Viral characteristics
Viral load
Background infections, sexually transmitted diseases
Genetic (immune response)
Primary infection during pregnancy
Advanced HIVdisease
Immunological status
   Low CD4 count
   p-24 antigenaemia
   Neutralizing antibodies
Premature delivery
Peripartum procedures and events
Mode of delivery
Breast-feeding

of age, followed by either or both a positive PCR at 9 months or older, or by persistently positive serology beyond 15 months of age. Among the 45 children born to HIV-1 positive mothers whose PCR results were negative at or before 6 months of age, four (9 per cent) became HIV infected. The estimated rate of late postnatal transmission with account taken of loss to follow-up and weaning patterns was 12 per cent (95 per cent CI 3 to 23) or 9.2 per 100 child-years of breast-feeding (Ekpini *et al*, 1997).

To provide a more reliable estimate of late postnatal transmission of HIV through breast-feeding, a meta-analysis of data from four cohorts from industrialized and four cohorts from developing countries was undertaken by the Ghent International Working Group on mother-to-child transmission of HIV-1 (Leroy *et al*, 1998). Results from this analysis indicate an overall risk of acquisition of infection after 3 months of age of about 3 per 100 child-years of breast-feeding, with the similarity between individual studies strengthening the reliability of the overall estimate.

INTERVENTIONS TO REDUCE VERTICAL TRANSMISSION

With increasing evidence to suggest that a substantial amount of infection occurs around the time of delivery, attention is now being given to interventions aimed to reduce vertical transmission, including refraining from breast-feeding; caesarean section delivery; disinfection of the birth canal; antiretroviral drugs; and passive and active immunization (Newell and Peckham, 1994; Consensus Workshop Siena, 1995). Table 5.3 indicates the range of possible areas in which such interventions could be considered.

In most Western countries and Thailand, HIV infected women are advised not to breast-feed. However, in many settings in the developing world the disadvantages of artificial feeding in terms of morbidity and mortality outweigh the reduction in the risk of HIV infection (Nicoll *et al*, 1995). The WHO/UNAIDS continues to recommend breast-feeding in populations where malnutrition and infectious diseases are important causes of infant deaths. To further quantify the additional risk of transmission through breast-feeding a randomized controlled trial of breast- versus bottle-feeding is underway in Nairobi, Kenya. However, concern has been expressed for the need of such trials (Nicoll *et al*, 1995). Much is already known about

Table 5.3   *Prevention of paediatric HIV infection*

Prevention of new infections in women
Avoidance of infection through contaminated blood and syringes
Reduction of mother-to-child transmission
   Avoidance of breast-feeding where safe and affordable
   Modification of obstetric practice
   Therapeutic interventions

---

the risk of transmission through breast-feeding, and it is unlikely that more precise estimates of this risk will change current public health policies. Damage may result from introducing the concept that bottle-feeding may be the better method of feeding. It is known that in settings where infant mortality rates are high, and often due to infectious diseases, bottle feeding carries significant additional risk. Although the trials make special provisions to ensure that bottle-fed infants are not disadvantaged, it remains dubious whether they will be able to ensure this. The generalizability of the results is an accompanying matter. Any estimates of the extent of morbidity and mortality associated with feeding method will only apply to that particular trial population.

In a modelling exercise, assuming different infant feeding practices, infant mortality rates, varying antenatal HIV seroprevalence and HIV incidence postnatally, and HIV transmission rates through breast-feeding. Kuhn and Stein (1997) contributed to the debate about feeding alternatives for infants born to HIV infected women in less developed countries. Complete avoidance of breast-feeding by the whole population always produced the worst outcome. The lowest frequency of adverse outcomes (HIV infection or infant deaths) occurs if no HIV infected women breast-feed and all HIV negative women breast-feed optimally, when infant mortality rates are less than 100 per 1000 and assuming a relative risk of dying in non-breast-fed infants of 2.5 compared to breast-fed infants. If the absolute rate of late postnatal transmission of HIV infection through breast-feeding is 7 per cent or more, early cessation of breast-feeding (3 months after the delivery) by HIV infected mothers would be beneficial, even at high infant mortality rates. However, they show clearly that where HIV infected women are not identified antenatally sustained promotion of breast-feeding is desirable.

MODE OF DELIVERY

Based on recent evidence, there is now sufficient justification to recommend elective caesarean section deliveries for HIV infected women, where this can be done safely (Kind *et al*, 1998; Mandelbrot *et al*, 1998). To avoid acquisition of infection during birth, cleansing of the birth canal with an antiseptic and/or virucidal agent has been proposed (Consensus Workshop Siena, 1995). The agent should inactivate HIV, have little or no local or systemic toxicity and be simple to apply. The agent used should, in addition, be safe for the infant. It is not entirely clear what the most effective and safe agent is, neither is it clear whether there would be a benefit of the agent over and above the action of lavage.

Little information is available regarding HIV viral load in the vagina and cervix, and possible associations with viraemia, and advanced disease. Evidence from a small number of women studied suggests that viral load in vagina/cervix is increased during pregnancy, although less than half of pregnant women are thought to harbour virus in the vagina/cervix. The expected effect of vaginal lavage on reduction of vertical transmission is therefore limited. However, as an intervention it is relatively cheap and easy to apply, and may thus be attractive in many settings. Recently the results of a clinical trial in Malawi were reported on the use of cleansing of the birth canal with chlorhexidine. No adverse reactions to the intervention procedure were seen, but the birth canal cleansing had no significant impact on HIV transmission rates, except when membranes were ruptured more than 4 hours before delivery. These results would indicate either that birth canal exposure is not important in the acquisition of infection for the baby, or that the cleansing was not done to maximum effect. Further trials with different agents, such as chlorhexidine, and benzalkonium chloride, are ongoing or being planned. An important finding from the Malawi trial was the sharp reduction in infant morbidity and mortality due to a decrease in neonatal sepsis, which in itself may be sufficient reason to advocate its introduction generally.

ANTIRETROVIRAL THERAPY

Antiretroviral drugs decrease maternal viral load and/or inhibit viral replication in the infant, thereby decreasing the risk of transmission. Results from an American–French trial suggest that antiretroviral therapy with zidovudine during pregnancy, labour and in the neonatal period can significantly reduce the risk for the infant (Connor *et al*, 1994). These trial results have subsequently been confirmed in observational studies, suggesting the generalizability to the larger population of infected women. However, the optimum timing and method of therapeutic interventions is not yet known, neither is there any information regarding the long-term effect of zidovudine treatment on children, at least 80 per cent of whom are uninfected anyway. Furthermore there is no information about the effect of temporary zidovudine treatment for the subsequent clinical management of the woman. Recently, findings have become available from a trial in Thailand showing that a short course of zidovudine (from 36 weeks of pregnancy and during labour/delivery) resulted in a 50 per cent reduction in the risk, in women who did not breast-feed (Vuthipongse *et al*, 1998). Other antiretroviral drugs are being developed and evaluated as are combination therapies.

The application of antiretroviral therapy to reduce vertical transmission is not likely to be feasible in many resource-poor countries, where HIV prevalence is highest. Furthermore, it is likely that the effect of zidovudine therapy around the time of delivery will not be as effective in breast-feeding populations as in settings where alternative infant feeding is the norm. Infants who 'escaped' infection during the latter stages of pregnancy, or during delivery, are at risk of becoming infected through breast-feeding. This should be borne in mind when discussing the introduction of prophylactic anti-retroviral therapy in settings where breast-feeding remains the norm.

SUPPLEMENTATION WITH VITAMIN A

Based on the findings from studies in Malawi (Semba *et al*, 1995) and the USA (Greenberg *et al*, 1997) that HIV infected women who were severely deficient for vitamin A were at increased risk to transmit the infection to their infant and from a Kenyan study demonstrating an association between severe maternal vitamin A deficiency and a substantial increase in HIV-DNA in breast milk in immunocompromised women (Nduati *et al*, 1995), several randomized trials have started (in Malawi, Zimbabwe, South Africa and Tanzania) to evaluate the effect of micronutrient supplementation with vitamin A in reducing the risk of vertical transmission (Greenberg *et al*, 1997). Vitamin A is essential for maintaining the integrity of the mucosal surfaces, for modulating healthy antibody responses and for the function and growth of T and B cells. Supplementation with vitamin A during pregnancy and lactation may prove to be an inexpensive, simple and effective way of diminishing transmission to infants.

IMMUNOTHERAPY

Maternal immune response, humoral and/or cellular, to HIV infection may play a role in preventing perinatal transmission, although results from various studies are conflicting (Consensus Workshop Siena, 1995). Passive immunization has been investigated in small trials, but currently no effectiveness trials are ongoing. Concern has been expressed regarding the use of blood products from HIV infected donors, and the cost of production. Furthermore, there is unease about the possible adverse effects on the infant, and the effect of passive immunization on viral load and the immune system will need to be carefully assessed.

Active immunization is the most attractive approach because it can potentially induce a long-lasting immunity in the mother, and it may also induce fetal immunity. Several phase I trials are ongoing in the USA (Consensus Workshop Siena, 1995).

ISSUES IN PLANNING TRIALS

It has been implied that trials to evaluate intervention of vertical transmission will be easy, quick and efficient. However, in view of the difficulties in making an early diagnosis, insecurity about the timing of infection, difficulties in ensuring adequate follow-up and high infant mortality in some developing countries, this is unlikely to be the case. Given the relatively low rate of vertical transmission, the number of mother–child pairs needed in these intervention trials is large. For example, to find a reduction in rate from 20 per cent to 15 per cent, with a power of 80 per cent, nearly 1900 mother–child pairs will have to be enrolled, and for a reduction from 15 to 10 per cent nearly 1500 women will be needed.

The WHO/UNAIDS has produced recommendations for future intervention trials, many of which may be carried out in developing countries. These recommendations include the statement that any study conducted should be part of a research strategy which may reasonably be expected to lead to interventions which will be affordable, feasible and sustainable in the same setting. Furthermore, detailed information regarding the timing and mechanisms of transmission should continue to be sought so that optimal interventions can be developed. To ensure that the most relevant scientific questions are addressed, and to achieve complementarity, there is a need for worldwide coordination of research activities.

DIAGNOSIS OF INFECTION

As maternal antibodies cross the placenta, serological diagnosis of infection in infants born to infected mothers is problematic in the first year of life. Passively acquired maternal antibodies may persist until 18 months of age, although the majority of uninfected children will have lost maternal antibodies before their first birthday. An earlier diagnosis of infection can be made by virus culture, PCR, detection of p24 antigen or HIV-specific immunoglobin A antibodies. Culture of HIV is the definitive method of diagnosis but it is slow, expensive and its use is limited to specialized laboratories. The PCR, which detects and amplifies viral genetic material, is increasingly used to make an early diagnosis of infection. This method is less expensive and faster than viral culture (Consensus Workshop, 1992; Dunn *et al*, 1995).

NATURAL HISTORY

HIV infected children most commonly present early in life with non-specific clinical manifestations such as enlargement of liver, lymph nodes or spleen. About one-quarter of infected children will develop AIDS in the first year of life, but the progression of disease in the remainder is much slower. Paediatric HIV infection must now be considered to be a chronic disease. There is great overlap between diseases associated with HIV infection and other common health problems in African children. Measles, but not malaria, has been associated with HIV infection (Lucas *et al*, 1996) reflecting the high mortality under 2 years of age from diseases related to HIV infection. The most common opportunistic infection is *Pneumocystis carinii* pneumonia, which has a high mortality. Syndromes of pulmonary infections, diarrhoea and malnutrition are major causes of death (Lepage *et al*, 1991). However, recognition of HIV disease is often difficult in the absence of a clinical infrastructure and lack of diagnostic facilities. Differences between the disease of AIDS in industrialized and African countries seem less extreme in children than in adults (Lucas *et al*, 1996).

The increasing mortality due to vertical transmission introduces biases into the traditional Brass-type estimates as it violates two of the assumptions on which the procedure is based: there is a clear correlation between the mortality of the mothers and that of the children; and the mortality of the children cannot be assumed to be independent of the age of the mothers, since HIV prevalence varies with age.

CONCLUSION

As the number of infected women and children increases, more attention is being given to issues relating to the care not only of the women, but also of their infected and uninfected children. HIV is a family disease and both infected and uninfected children born to infected mothers will have complex social and medical needs. Orphans in Africa have traditionally been cared for through extended family/kinship systems. However, the extended family system has come under increasing stress due to social trends such as urbanization, and due to the impact of AIDS. The rising morbidity and mortality of HIV infected mothers and fathers threaten to decrease the care and resources spent on children as well as increase the prevalence of orphanhood.

Despite possible obstacles in the provision of care by the extended family, a relative consensus exists on the primacy of the extended family as the principal caretaker of orphans (Preble, 1990). However, some data suggest a reduction in the quality of care as a result of the very low economic resources of the caretakers and an increase in the number of the sick. The impact of the parent's disease on the children starts well before their deaths, involving school absenteeism to care and contribute to the survival of the household (Chevalier and Floury, 1996).

REFERENCES

Adjorlolo, G., de Cock, K., Ekpini, E., Vetter, K.M., Sibailly, T., Brattegaard, K., Yavo, D., Doorly, R., Whitaker, J.P., Kestens, L., Ou, C.Y., George, R. and Gayle, H.D. (1994) 'Prospective comparison of mother-to-child transmission of HIV-1 and HIV-2 in Abidjan, Ivory Coast'. *Journal of the American Medical Association*, 272, pp. 462–6.

Alger, L.S., Farley, J.J., Robinson, B.A., Hines, S.E., Berchin, J.M. and Johnson, J.P. (1993) 'Interactions of human immunodeficiency virus infection and pregnancy'. *Obstetrics and Gynecology*, 82, pp. 787–96.

Bertolli, J., St. Louis, M.E., Simonds, R.J., Nieburg, P.I., Kamenga, M., Brown, C., Tarande, M., Quinn, T. and Ou, C.Y. (1996) 'Estimating the timing of mother-to-child transmission of human immunodeficiency virus in a breastfeeding population in Kinshasa, Zaire'. *Journal of Infectious Diseases*, 174, pp. 722–6.

Biggar, R.J., Pahwa, S., Minkoff, H., Mendes, H., Willoughby, A., Landesman, S. and Goedert, J.J. (1989) 'Immunosuppression in pregnant women infected with human immunodeficiency virus'. *American Journal of Obstetrics and Gynecology*, 161, pp. 1239–44.

Blanche, S., Rouzioux, C., Guihard, M.M.-L., Veber, F., Mayaux, M.J. and Jacomet, C. (1989) 'A prospective study of infants born to women seropositive for human immunodeficiency virus type 1'. *New England Journal of Medicine*, 320, pp. 1643–8.

Blaxhult, A., Granath, F., Lidman, K. and Giesecke, J. (1990) 'The influence of age on the latency period to AIDS in people infected by HIV through blood transfusion'. *AIDS*, 4, pp. 125–9.

Bobat, R., Moodley, D., Coutsoudis, A. and Coovadia, H. (1997) 'Breastfeeding by HIV-1 infected women and outcome in their infants: a cohort study from Durban, South Africa'. *AIDS*, 11, pp. 1627–33.

Borkowsky, W., Krasinski, K., Cao, Y., Ho, D., Pollack, H., Moore, T., Chen, S.H., Allen, M. and Tao, P.-T. (1994) 'Correlation of perinatal transmission of human immunodeficiency virus type 1 with maternal viremia and lymphocyte phenotypes'. *Journal of Pediatrics*, 125, pp. 345–51.

Brettle, R.P., Raab, G.M., Ross, A., Fielding, K.L., Gore, S.M. and Bird, A.G. (1995) 'HIV infection in women: immunological markers and the influence of pregnancy'. *AIDS*, 9, pp. 1177–84.

Brocklehurst, P.F.R. (1998) 'The association between maternal HIV infection and perinatal outcome: a systematic review of the literature and meta analysis'. *British Journal of Obstetrics and Gynaecology*, 105, pp. 836–48.

Bryson, Y.J., Luzuriaga, K., Sullivan, J.L. and Wara, D.W. (1992) 'Proposed definitions for in utero versus intrapartum transmission of HIV-1'. *New England Journal of Medicine*, 327, pp. 1246–7.

Burns, D., Landesman, S., Muenz, L.R., Nugent, R.P., Goedert, J.J., Minkoff, H., Walsh, J.H., Mendez, H., Rubinstein, A. and Willoughby, A. (1994) 'Cigarette smoking, premature rupture of membranes, and vertical transmission of HIV-1 among women with low CD4 − levels'. *Journal of the Acquired Immune Deficiency Syndrome*, 7, pp. 718–26.

Busch, M.P. and Satten, G.A. (1997) 'Time course of viremia and antibody seroconversion following human immunodeficiency virus exposure'. *American Journal of Medicine*, 102, pp. 117–24.

Chevalier, E. and Floury, D. (1996) 'The socio-economic impact of AIDS in sub-Saharan Africa'. *AIDS Yearbook*, 10, SA205–12.

Chin, J. (1994) 'The growing impact of the HIV/AIDS pandemic on children born to HIV-infected women'. *Clinical Perinatology*, 21, pp. 1–14.

Chouquet, C., Burgard, M., Richardson, S., Rouzioux, C. and Costagliola, D. (1997)

'Timing of mother-to-child HIV-1 transmission and diagnosis of infection based on polymerase chain reaction in the neonatal period by a non-parametric method'. *AIDS*, 11, pp. 1183–99.

Connor, E.M., Sperling, R.S., Gelber, R., Kiselev, P., Scott, G., O'Sullivan, M.J., Van Dyke, R., Bey, M., Shearer, W., Jacobson, R.L., Jimenez, E., O'Neill, E., Bazin, B., Delfraissy, J.F., Culnane, M., Coombs, R., Elkins, M., Moye, J., Stratton, P. and Balsley, J. (1994) 'Reduction of maternal-infant transmission of human immunodeficiency virus type 1 with zidovudine treatment'. *New England Journal of Medicine*, 331, pp. 1173–80.

Consensus Workshop (1992) 'Early diagnosis of HIV infection in infants: report of a consensus workshop held in Siena, Italy, January 1992'. *Journal of the Acquired Immune Deficiency Syndrome*, 5, pp. 1169–78.

Consensus Workshop Siena (1995) 'Strategies for prevention of perinatal transmission of HIV infection'. *Journal of the Acquired Immune Deficiency Syndromes and Human Retrovirology*, 8, pp. 161–78.

Cozzi Lepri, A., Pezzotti, P., Dorrucci, M., Phillips, A. and Italian Seroconversion Study (1994) 'HIV disease progression in 854 women and men infected through injecting drug use and heterosexual sex and followed for up to nine years from seroconversion'. *British Medical Journal*, 309, pp. 1537–42.

Datta, P., Embree, J.E., Kreiss, J.K., Ndinya-Achola, J.O., Braddick, M., Temmerman, M., Nagelkerke, N.J.D., Maitha, G., Holmes, K.K., Piot, P., Pamba, H.O. and Plummer, F.A. (1994) 'Mother-to-child transmission of human immunodeficiency virus type 1: report from the Nairobi study'. *Journal of Infectious Diseases*, 170, pp. 1134–40.

de Martino, M., Tovo, P.-A., Tozzi, A.E., Pezzotti, P., Galli, L., Livadiotti, S., Caselli, D., Massironi, E., Ruga, E., Fioredda, F., Plebani, A., Gabiano, C. and Zuccotti, G.V. (1992) 'HIV-1 transmission through breastmilk: appraisal of risk according to duration of feeding'. *AIDS*, 6, pp. 991–7.

de Rossi, A., Ometto, L., Mammano, F., Zanotto, C., del Mistro, A., Giaquinto, C. and Chieco-Bianchi, L. (1993) 'Time course of antigenaemia and seroconversion in infants with vertically acquired HIV-1 infection'. *AIDS*, 7, pp. 1528–9.

de Rossi, A., Ometto, L., Mammano, F., Zanotto, C., Giaquinto, C. and Chieco-Bianchi, L. (1992) 'Vertical transmission of HIV-1: lack of detectable virus in peripheral blood cells of infected children at birth'. *AIDS*, 6, 1117–20.

Dickover, R.E., Garratty, E.M., Herman, S.A., Sim, M.-S., Plaeger, S., Boyer, P.J., Keller, M., Deveikis, A., Stiehm, R. and Bryson, Y.J. (1996) 'Identification of levels of maternal HIV-1 RNA associated with risk of perinatal transmission'. *Journal of the American Medical Asociation*, 275, pp. 599–605.

Duliege, A.M., Amos, C.I., Felton, S., Biggar, R.J., Goedert, J.J. and The International Registry Of HIV-exposed Twins. (1995) 'Birth order, delivery route, and concordance in the transmission of human immunodeficiency virus type 1 from mothers to twins'. *Journal of Pediatrics*, 126, pp. 625–32.

Dunn, D., Brandt, C.D., Krivine, A., Cassol, S.A., Roques, P., Borkowsky, W., de Rossi, A., Denamur, E., Ehrnst, A., Loveday, C., Harris, J.A., McIntosh, K., Comeau, A.M., Rakusan, T., Newell, M.L. and Peckham, C.S. (1995) 'The sensitivity of HIV-1 DNA polymerase chain reaction in the neonatal period and the relative contributions of intra-uterine and intra-partum transmission'. *AIDS*, 9, pp. F7–F11.

Dunn, D., Newell, M.L., Ades, A. and Peckham, C.S. (1992) 'Risk of human immunodefiency virus type 1 transmission through breastfeeding'. *Lancet*, 340, pp. 585–8.

Dunn, D., Newell, M.L., Mayaux, M.J., Kind, C., Hutto, C., Goedert, J., Andiman, W. and Perinatal AIDS Collaborative Transmission Studies (1994) 'Mode of delivery and vertical transmission of HIV-1: a review of prospective studies'. *Journal of the Acquired Immune Deficiency Syndrome*, 7, pp. 1064–6.

Ekpini, E., Wiktor, S.Z., Satten, G.A., Adjorlolo, G., Sibailly, T., Ou, C.Y., Karon, J.M., Brattegaard, K., Whitaker, J.P., Gnaore, E., de Cock, K.M. and Greenberg, A.E. (1997) 'Late postnatal mother-to-child transmission of HIV-1 in Abidjan, Cote d'Ivoire'. *Lancet*, 349, pp. 1054–9.

European Collaborative Study (1992) 'Risk factors for mother-to-child transmission of HIV-1'. *Lancet*, 339, pp. 1007–12.

European Collaborative Study (1994a) 'Caesarean section and risk of vertical transmission of HIV-1 infection'. *Lancet*, 343, pp. 1464–7.

European Collaborative Study (1994b) 'Perinatal findings in children born to HIV-infected mothers'. *British Journal of Obstetrics and Gynaecology*, 101, pp. 136–41.

European Collaborative Study (1996) 'Vertical transmission of HIV-1: maternal immune status and obstetric factors'. *AIDS*, 10, pp. 1675–81.

European Collaborative Study and Swiss HIV and Pregnancy Collaborative Study Group. (1997) 'Immunological markers in HIV infected pregnant women'. *AIDS* 11, pp. 1859–65.

Fang, G., Burger, H., Grimson, R., Tropper, P., Nachman, S., Mayers, D., Weislow, O., Moore, R., Reyelt, C., Hutcheon, N., Baker, D. and Weiser, B. (1995) 'Maternal plasma human immunodefiency virus type 1 RNA level: a determinant and projected threshold for mother-to-child transmission'. *Proceedings of the National Academy of Sciences of the USA*, 92, pp. 12100–4.

French, R. and Brocklehurst, P. (1998) 'The effect of pregnancy on survival in women infected with HIV: a systematic review of the literature and meta-analysis'. *British Journal of Obstetrics and Gynaecology*, 105, pp. 827–35.

French Collaborative Study of HIV infection in Newborns (1994) 'Comparison of vertical human immunodeficiency virus type 2 and human immunodeficiency virus type 1 in the French prospective cohort'. *Pediatric Infectious Disease Journal*, 13, pp. 502–6.

Goulston, C., Stevens, E., Gallo, D., Mullins, J.I., Hanson, C.V. and Katzenstein, D. (1996) 'Human immunodeficiency virus in plasma and genital secretions during the menstrual cycle. *Journal of Infectious Diseases*, 174, pp. 858–61.

Gray, G.E., McIntyre, J.A. and Lyons, S.F. (1996) 'The effect of breastfeeding on vertical transmission of HIV-1 in Soweto, South Africa'. *XI International Conference on AIDS, Vancouver*, Th.C.415, 237(abstract).

Gray, R.H., Wawer, M.J. and Wabwire-Mangen, F. (1996) ,Reduced fertility among HIV-infected women: results of cross-sectional and prospective studies in rural Uganda,. *XI International Conference on AIDS, Vancouver*, vol 1, p. 28(abstract).

Greenberg, B.L., Semba, R.D., Vink, P.E., Farley, J.J., Sivapalsingam, M., Steketee, R.W., Thea, D.M. and Schoenbaum, E.E. (1997) 'Vitamin A deficiency and maternal-infant transmission of HIV in two metropolitan areas in the United States'. *AIDS*, 11, pp. 325–32.

Halsey, N.A., Boulos, R., Holt, E., Ruff, A., Brutus, J.R., Ki, T.C., Coberly, J.,

Adrien, M., Boulos, C., CDC/JHU AIDS Project Team. (1991) Transmission of HIV-1 infections from mothers to infants in Haiti. *Journal of the American Medical Association*, 264, pp. 2088–92.

Henin, Y., Mandelbrot, L., Henrion, R., Pradineaud, R. and Montagnier, L. (1993) 'HIV in the cervicovaginal secretions of pregnant and non- pregnant women'. *Journal of the Acquired Immune Deficiency Syndrome*, 6, pp. 72–5.

John, G.C., Nduati, R.W., Mbori-Ngacha, D., Overbaugh, J., Welch, M., Richardson, B.A., Ndinya-Achola, J., Bwayo, J.J., Krieger, J., Onyango, F. and Kreiss, J.K. (1997) 'Genital shedding of human immunodeficiency virus type 1 DNA during pregnancy: association with immunosuppression, abnormal cervical or vaginal discharge, and severe vitamin A deficiency'. *Journal of Infectious Diseases*, 175, pp. 57–62.

Johnstone, F.D. (1993) 'Pregnancy outcome and pregnancy management in HIV-infected women', in M.A. Johnson and F.D. Johnston (eds), *HIV in Women*, pp. 187–98. Edinburgh: Churchill Livingstone.

Johnstone, F.D., Maccallum, L., Brettle, R., Inglis, J.M. and Peutherer, J.F. (1988) 'Does infection with HIV affect the outcome of pregnancy?' *British Medical Journal*, 296, p. 467.

Kalish, L.A., Pitt, J., Lew, J., Landesman, S., Diaz, C., Hershow, R., Blaine Hollinger, F., Pagano, M., Smeriglio, V., Moye, J. and Women and Infants Transmission Study (1997) 'Defining the time of fetal or perinatal acquisition of human immunodeficiencey virus type I infection on the basis of age at first positive culture'. *Journal of Infectious Diseases*, 175, pp. 712–15.

Kind, C., Rudin, C., Siegrist, C.A., Wyler, C.A., Biedermann, K., Lauper, U., Irion, O., Nadal, D., Schupbach, J. and the Swiss Neonatal HIV Study Group (1998) 'Prevention of vertical HIV transmission: additive protective effect of elective caesarean section and zidovudine prophylaxis. *AIDS*, 12, pp. 205–10.

Kreiss, J., Willerford, D.M., Hensel, M., Emonyi, W., Plummer, F., Ndinya-Achola, J., Roberts, P.L., Hoskyn, J., Hillier, S. and Kiviat, N. (1994) 'Association between cervical inflammation and cervical shedding of human immunodeficiency virus DNA'. *Journal of Infectious Diseases*, 170, pp. 1597–601.

Kuhn, L. and Stein, Z. (1997) 'Infant survival, HIV infection and feeding alternatives in less-developed countries'. *American Journal of Public Health*, 87, pp. 926–31.

Kuhn, L., Abrams, E.J., Chincillla, M., Tsai, W.Y., Thea, D.M. and New York City Perinatal HIV Transmission Collaborative Study Group (1996) 'Sensitivity of HIV-1 DNA polymerase chain reaction in the neonatal period'. *AIDS*, 10, 1181–2.

Lallemant, M., Le Coeur, S., Cheynier, D., Nzingoula, S., Larouze, B., *et al* (1990) 'Morbidity, mortality and HIV1 infection rates in infants born to seropositive mothers, Brazzaville, Congo: 30 months follow-up'. *Fifth International Conference on AIDS in Africa, Kinshasa, Zaire, October 1990* W.R.T.A.3(Abstract).

Landesman, S.H., Kalish, L.A., Burns, D., Minkoff, H., Fox, H.E., Zorrilla, C., Garcia, P., Fowler, M.G., Mofenson, L., Tuomala, R. and The Women and Infants Transmission Study (1996) 'Obstetrical factors and the transmission of human immunodeficiency virus type 1 from mother-to-child. *New England Journal of Medicine*, 334, pp. 1617–23.

Lepage, P., Dabis, F., Hitimana, D.-G., Msellati, P., Van Goethem, C., Stevens, A.M., Nsengumuremyi, F., Bazubagira, A., Serufilira, A., de Clercq, A. and Van de Perre, P. (1991) 'Perinatal transmission of HIV-1: lack of impact of maternal HIV infection on characteristics of livebirths and on neonatal mortality in Kigali, Rwanda'. *AIDS*, 5, pp. 295–300.

Leroy, V., Newell, M.L., Dabis, F., Peckham, C., Van de Perre, P., Bulterys, M., Kind, C., Simonds, R.J., Wiktor, S., Msellati, P. and Ghent International Working Group on Mother-to-Child Transmission of HIV (1998) 'International multicentre pooled analysis of late postnatal mother-to-child transmission of HIV-1 infection'. *Lancet*, 352, pp. 597–600.

Lucas, S.B., Peacock, C.S., Hounnou, A., Brattegaard, K., Koffi, K., Honde, M., Andoh, J., Bell, J. and de Cock, K.M. (1996) 'Disease in children infected with HIV in Abidjan, Cote d'Ivoire'. *British Medical Journal*, 312, pp. 335–8.

Mandelbrot, L. and Henrion, R. (1993) 'Does pregnancy accelerate disease progression in HIV-infected women?' in M.A. Johnson and F.D. Johnston (eds), *HIV in Women*, pp. 157–72. Edinburgh: Churchill Livingstone.

Mandelbrot, L., Le Chenadec, J., Berrebi, A., Bongain, A., Benifla, J.L., Delfraissy, J.F., Blanche, S., Mayaux, M.J. and French Perinatal Cohort (1998) 'Perinatal HIV-1 transmission – interaction between zidovudine prophylaxis and mode of delivery in the French Perinatal Cohort'. *Journal of the American Medical Association*, 280, pp.55–60.

Mayaux, M.J., Blanche, S., Rouzioux, C., Le Chenadec, J., Chambrin, V., Firtion, G., Allemon, M.C., Vilmer, E., Vigneron, N.C., Tricoire, J., Guillot, F., Courpotin, C. and The French Pediatric HIV Infection Study Group (1995) 'Maternal factors associated with perinatal HIV-1 transmission: the French Cohort Study: 7 years of follow-up observation'. *Journal of the acquired Immune Deficiency Syndromes and Human Regovirology*, 8, pp. 188–94.

Mertens, T.E. and Burton, A. (1996) 'Global estimates and epidemiology of HIV-1 infections and AIDS'. *AIDS Yearbook*, 10, S221–8

Minkoff, H.L., Henderson, C., Mendez, H., Gail, M.H., Holman, S., Willoughby, A., Goedett, J.J., Rubinstein, A., Stratton, P., Walsh, J.H. and Landesman, S.H. (1990) 'Pregnancy outcomes among mothers infected with human immunodeficiency virus and uninfected control subjects'. *American journal of Obstretics and Gynaecology*, 163, pp. 1598–604.

Miotti, P.G., Liomba, G., Dallabetta, G.A., Hoover, D.R., Chiphangwi, J.D. and Saah, A.J. (1992) 'T lymphocyte subsets during and after pregnancy: analysis in human immunodeficiency type 1-infected and -uninfected Malawian mothers'. *Journal of Infectious Diseases*, 165, pp. 1116–19.

Mostad, S.B. and Kreiss, J.K. (1996) 'Shedding of HIV-1 in the genital tract'. *AIDS*, 10, pp. 1305–15.

Nduati, R.W., John, G.C., Richardson, B.A., Overbaugh, J., Welch, M., Ndinya-Achola, J., Moses, S., Holmes, K., Onyango, F. and Kreiss, J.K. (1995) 'Human immunodeficiency virus type 1-infected cells in breast milk: association with immunosuppression and vitamin A deficiency'. *Journal of Infectious Diseases*, 172, pp. 1461–8.

Newell, M.L., Gray, G. and Bryson, Y.J. (1997) 'Prevention of mother-to-child transmission of HIV-1 infection'. *AIDS*, 11, pp. S165–72.

Newell, M.L. and Peckham, C. (1993) 'Risk factors for vertical transmission of HIV-1 and early markers of HIV-1 infection in children'. *AIDS*, 7 (Suppl. 1), pp. S591–7.

Newell, M.L. and Peckham, C.S. (1994) 'Working towards a European strategy for intervention to reduce vertical transmission of HIV'. *British Journal of Obstetrics and Gynaecology*, 101, pp. 192–6.

Nicoll, A., Newell, M.L., Van Praag, E., Van de Perre, P. and Peckham, C. (1995) 'Infant feeding policy and practice in the presence of HIV-1 infection'. *AIDS*, 9, pp. 107–119.

O'Shea, S., Newell, M.L., Dunn, D., Garcia-Rodriguez, M.C., Bates, I., Mullen, J., Rostron, T., Corbett, K., Aiyer, S., Butler, K., Smith, R. and Banatvala, J.E. (1998) 'Maternal viral load, CD4 cell count and vertical transmission of HIV-1'. *Journal of Medical Virology*, 54, pp. 113–17.

Preble, E.A. (1990) 'Impact of HIV/AIDS on African children'. *Social Science and Medicine*, 31, pp. 671–80.

Read, J. for the International Perinatal HIV Group (1998) 'Mode of delivery and vertical transmission of HIV-1: a meta-analysis from fifteen prospective cohort studies'. *XII International Conference on AIDS, Geneva* (abstract).

Rouzioux, C., Costagliola, D., Burgard, M., Blanche, S., Mayaux, M.J., Griscelli, C., Valleron, A.J. and HIV Infection in Newborns French Collaborative Study Group (1995) 'Estimated timing of mother-to-child human immunodeficiency virus type 1 (HIV-1) transmission by use of a Markov model'. *American Journal of Epidemiology*, 142, pp. 1330–7.

Ryder, R.W., Kamenga, M., Nkusu, M., Batter, V. and Heyward, W.L. (1994) 'AIDS orphans in Kinshasa, Zaire: incidence and socioeconomic consequences'. *AIDS*, 8, pp. 673–9.

Ryder, R.W., Nsa, W., Hassig, S.E., Behets, F., Rayfield, M., Ekungola, B. Nelson, A.M., Mulenda, U., Francis, H., Mwandagalirwa, K., Davachi, F., Rogers, M., Nz\ilambi, N., Greenberg, A., Mann, J., Quinn, T.C., Piot, P. and Curan, J.W. (1989) 'Perinatal transmission of the human immunodeficiency virus type 1 to infants of seropositive women in Zaire'. *New England Journal of Medicine*, 320, pp. 1637–42.

Selwyn, P.A., Schoenbaum, E.E., Davenny, K., Robertson, V.J., Feingold, A.R., Shulman, J.F., Mayers, M.M., Klein, R.S., Friedland, G.H. and Rogers, M.F. (1989) 'Prospective study of human immunodeficiency virus infection and pregnancy outcomes in intravenous drug users'. *Journal of the American Medical Association*, 261, pp. 1289–94.

Semba, R.D., Miotti, P.G., Chiphangwi, J.D., Liomba, G., Yang, L.P., Saah, A.J., Dallabetta, G.A. and Hoover, D.R. (1995) 'Infant mortality and maternal vitamin A deficiency during human immunodeficiency virus infection'. *Clinical Infectious Diseases*, 21, pp. 966–72.

Semprini, A.E., Castagna, C., Ravizza, M., Fiore, S., Savasi, V., Muggiasca, M.L., Grossi, E., Guerra, B., Tibaldi, C., Scaravelli, G., Prati, E. and Pardi, G. (1995) 'The incidence of complications after caesarean section in 156 HIV positive women'. *AIDS*, 9 , pp. 913–17.

Simonon, A., Lepage, P., Karita, E., Hitimana, D.G., Dabis, F., Msellati, P., Van Goethem, C., Nsengumuremyi, F., Bazubagira, A. and Van de Perre, P. (1994)

'An assessment of the timing of mother-to-child transmission of human immun-odeficiency virus type 1 by means of polymerase chain reaction'. *Journal of the Acquired Immune Deficiency Syndrome*, 7, pp. 952–7.

Temmerman, M., Chomba, E.N., Ndinya-Achola, J., Plummer, F.A., Coppens, M. and Piot, P. (1994) 'Maternal human immunodeficiency virus-1 infection and pregnancy outcome'. *Obstetrics and Gynecology*, 83, pp. 495–501.

Temmerman, M., Nagelkerke, N., Bwayo, J.J., Chomba, E.N., Ndinya-Achola, J. and Piot, P. (1995) 'HIV-1 and immunological changes during pregnancy: a comparison between HIV-1 seropositive and HIV-1 seronegative women in Nairobi, Kenya'. *AIDS*, 9, pp. 1057–60.

Tess, B.H., Rodrigues, L.C., Newell, M.L., Dunn, D.T., Lago, T.D.G. and Sao Paolo Collaborative Study of Vertical Transmission of HIV-1 (1998a) 'Breastfeeding, genetic, obstetric and other risk factors associated with mother-to-child trans-mission of HIV-1 in Sao Paulo State, Brazil'. *AIDS*, 12, pp. 513–20.

Tess, B.H., Rodrigues, L.C., Newell, M.L., Dunn, D.T., Lago, T.D.G. and Sao Paolo Collaborative Study of Vertical Transmission of HIV-1 (1998b) 'Infant feeding and risk of mother-to-child transmission of HIV-1 in Sao Paulo State, Brazil'. *Journal of the Acquired Immune Deficiency Syndrome and Human Retrovirology*, 19, pp. 189–94.

Turnbull, B.W. (1976) 'The empirical distribution function with arbitrarily grouped, censored and truncated data'. *Journal of the Royal Statistical Society B*, 38, pp. 290–5.

UNAIDS (1998) Report on the global HIV/AIDS epidemic. Geneva.

Vuthipongse, P., Bhadrakom, C., Chaisilwattana, P., Roongpisuthipong, A., Chalermchokcharoenkit, A., Chearskul, S., Wanprapa, N., Chokephaibulkit, K., Tuchinda, M., Wasi, C., Chuachoowong, R., Siriwasin, W., Chinayon, P., Asavapiriyanont, S., Chotpitayasunondh, T., Waranawat, N., Sangtaweesin, V. and Horpaopan, S. (1998) 'Administration of zidovudine during late pregnancy and delivery to prevent perinantal HIV transmission – Thailand, 1996–1998'. *MMWR. Morbidity and Mortality Weekly Report*, 47, pp. 151–4.

Wabwire-Mangen, F., Gray, R.H. and Wabinga, H. (1996) 'Placental risk factors for the vertical transmission of HIV-1 in Uganda'. *Abstract book of XI International Conference on AIDS, Vancouver*, vol 1, p. 246(abstract).

Working Group on Mother-to-Child Transmission of HIV (1995) 'Rates of mother-to-child transmission of HIV-1 in Africa, America, and Europe: results from 13 perinatal studies'. *Journal of the Acquired Immune Deficiency Syndrome and Human Retorvirology*, 8, pp. 506–10.

SECTION 3

Developing Country Demography

CHAPTER SIX

Evidence of changes in family formation patterns in Pakistan?

Fatima Juarez

Centre for Population Studies, London School of Hygiene and Tropical Medicine, University of London

Zeba A. Sathar

Pakistan Institute of Development Economics/ The Population Council

INTRODUCTION

While other South Asian countries such as Sri Lanka, India and Bangladesh have already experienced major changes in fertility, there was little evidence to support the onset of transition in Pakistan until 1991. Fertility has remained high, relatively homogeneous and unchanging for the last two or three decades (Alam, 1984; Booth and Shah, 1984; Casterline, 1984; Sathar, 1993). With a population of 130.6 million, Pakistan has continued to contend with a high growth rate of 2.4 per cent according to the 1998 Census (Population Census Organization, 1998). While the growth rate remains high in comparison to other neighbouring countries, the intercensal growth rate of 2.6 for the years 1981–98 does represent a waning trend. In fact the Pakistan Demographic and Health Survey (PDHS) of 1991 was not the first source to reveal a decline in fertility. The Pakistan Demographic Survey (PDS; an ongoing multi-round operation which collects information on births and deaths of a large sample at three-monthly intervals) had shown a drop in the total fertility rate from about 7 births per women in 1984–7 to 6.5 in 1988 and 6.0 in 1991. However, the PDS results were themselves controversial and the data do not permit the analysis of changes in family building which can best be made with birth histories.

Such birth histories were collected in the PDHS, and they too showed a decline in total fertility from over 7 in the late 1970s to 5.4 for 1986–91. But these results were also controversial, for good reason, as we will describe below. The most recent Pakistan Fertility and Family Planning Survey (PFFPS) of 1997–8 also shows a fertility decline, this time from 7.3 in 1987–91 to 5.4 in 1992–6. Thus while all these surveys would appear to agree in showing that fertility has declined in Pakistan, they are clearly contradictory as regards the rates they show for different time periods.

Unlike many other developing countries, Pakistan has a long history of fertility surveys. Some of them provide more detailed information than others, but all of them provide enough data to generate estimates of fertility levels and trends at the national level. Despite the abundance of data, reporting of ages and dates has made it difficult to present a coherent and consistent picture of reproductive behaviour. The various data sets have each been problematic particularly in terms of producing unreliable signals of the beginning of any significant fertility change. Based on this past experience, the most facile explanation is that the PDHS is also plagued with data problems, and that the most recent fertility decline is in fact an artefactual finding. However, the PDHS comprising full birth histories and contraceptive use data also supported a rise in prevalence levels from 5.5 per cent of non-pregnant currently married women in the Pakistan Fertility Survey of 1975 to 14.0 per cent in 1991; subsequent surveys have shown this rise to be continued to 20.5 per cent in the 1994–5 Contraceptive Prevalence Survey and 28.2 per cent in the 1996–7 PFFPS.

This paper is motivated by two main concerns. The first is to document the exact fertility levels for the early 1990s – a particularly pertinent question for basing future projections. The second is to identify some of the problems inherent in the PDHS data, and to assess any genuine changes in family formation patterns. The PDHS data are analysed using techniques especially developed by Professor Brass and colleagues to see if information can be adjusted and methods adapted to utilize data from a country which has had a long history of data problems.

DOUBTS ABOUT THE VERACITY OF PREVIOUS SOURCES OF DATA

Data problems are known to plague *all* past Pakistani surveys which have attempted to collect fertility information. These biases have led to considerable confusion about fertility levels and even prematurely heralded a fertility reduction at the turn of the decade of the 1970s based on the Pakistan Fertility Survey 1975 (PFS-1975) (Alam, 1984). This fertility decline was refuted by data from the later survey, the Population Labour Force and Migration Survey (PLM-1979), which showed a similar decline in fertility over the last five years but not for the same period as seen in the PFS-1975 (Alam *et al*, 1983). Later on, an application of the own children method confirmed that the fertility decline seen in the PFS-1975 was an artefact of the data (Retherford *et al*, 1987).

The range of estimates available for fertility levels based on the measure of the total fertility rate show a wide divergence. Table 6.1 and Figure 6.1 present total fertility rate estimates from various surveys carried out to measure fertility starting from the Population Growth Estimation (PGE) in

Table 6.1   *Total fertility rates (TFR) from various surveys and periods*

Survey	Period	Estimated TFR
Population Growth LR	1963–5	6.1
Estimation (PGE) 1962–65-CD	1963–5	8.0
National Impact Survey (NIS) 1969	1968–9	5.0
Population Growth Survey (PGS)	1968–71	6.0
1968–71 and 1976–9	1976–9	6.9
Pakistan Fertility Survey (PFS)	1960–5	7.1
1975	1965–70	7.1
	1970–5	6.3
Population, Labour Force and	1970–5	7.1
Migration Survey (PLM) 1979	1975–9	6.5
Pakistan Contraceptive Preval-	1984–5	6.0
ence Survey (PCPS) 1984–85		
Pakistan Demographic Survey	1984	6.9
(PDS) 1984–92	1985	7.0
	1986	6.9
	1987	6.9
	1988	6.5
	1989	6.4
	1990	6.2
	1991	6.0
	1992	5.8
Pakistan Demographic and	1976–81	7.1
Health Survey (PDHS) 1991	1981–6	7.6
	1986–91	4.9
Pakistan Integrated Household	1986–91	7.4
Survey (PIHS) 1991		
Pakistan Integrated Household	1987–9	7.6
Survey (PIHS) 1995–6	1990–2	6.6
	1993–5	5.3
Pakistan Integrated Household	1987–9	7.3
Survey (PIHS) 1996–7	1990–2	6.9
	1993–5	5.5
Pakistan Fertility and Family	1982–7	7.7
Planning Survey (PFFPS) 1996–7	1987–92	7.1
	1992–7	5.3

1962. The divergence in these estimates is partially attributable to differences in methodology and coverage across these surveys. The PGE Experiment 1962–5, the Population Growth Surveys of 1976–9 and the PDS of 1984–92, are all cross-sectional surveys which collected information on vital events quarterly or annually, while the National Impact Survey 1969, the Pakistan Fertility Survey of 1975, the Population Labour Force and Migration Survey

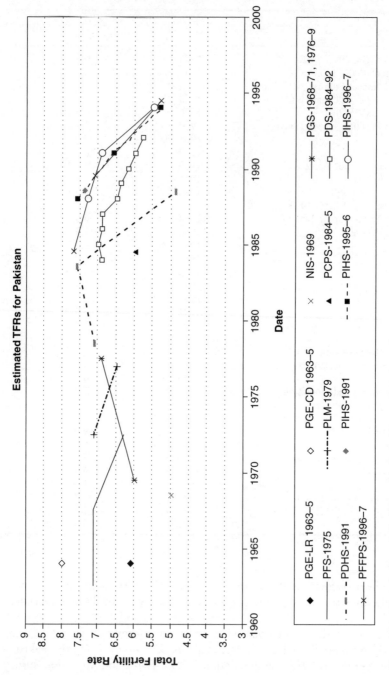

Figure 6.1 Estimated total fertility rates for Pakistan, 1960–97

of 1979 and the Pakistan Integrated Household Survey 1991 all collected full birth histories of all ever married women of reproductive ages. The Pakistan Contraceptive Prevalence Survey PCPS) of 1984–5 was also a fertility survey but only collected a partial birth history (i.e. births in the last three years) for currently married women. No clear trend emerges from this range of estimates, with fertility falling over a very wide range between 5 and 7 births per woman. The PCPS of 1994–5 has information on contraceptive prevalence and indirect measures of current fertility though the date of the last birth places the total fertility rate (TFR) at 5.6. As noted above, the latest PFFPS of 1997–8 follows much the same trend as earlier surveys of an incredibly sharp decline in fertility from a total fertility rate of 7.3 in 1987–91 to a TFR of 5.4 in the period 1992–6 (Hakim *et al*, 1999).

THE DISARRAY OF THE RECENT SOURCES OF DATA

The results of the PDHS show a sharp decline in fertility in the five year period before the date of the survey (NIPS, 1992).[1] The question is whether there was a genuine fertility reduction in the five years prior to the date of the survey, particularly since previous experience of Pakistani surveys has demonstrated that similar declines were an outcome of data distortions. Since estimates of fertility as reported by the findings of the PDHS 1990–1 and past analyses have relied mainly on conventional measures such as total fertility rates and children ever borne, which may have severe shortcomings, a more definitive answer has to be sought elsewhere. We intend to do this through a meticulous evaluation of the birth histories and by utilizing other measures of changes in fertility.

What are the elements that surround this dilemma about the fertility levels in Pakistan? Do these elements support or disprove a possible fertility decline at present? The keen expectation of a fertility decline in Pakistan was based on a family planning programme initiated in 1965. In fact, Pakistan was one of the pioneers in starting a family planning programme in Asia. The round of fertility surveys described above have largely been motivated by the anti-natalist policy pursued by Pakistan since the Third Five Year Plan (1965–70). Nevertheless, the evidence from these surveys shows that, based on fertility levels and the prevalence of contraceptive use, the family planning programme has had a minimal impact. Contraceptive use levels have remained low and have been increasing at a slow pace: 5 per cent in 1975, 9 per cent in 1985 and 12 per cent in 1991. Only recently in the late 1990s was there a much more rapid uptake in the levels of contraceptive use (Sathar and Casterline, 1998). Rises in age at marriage of females from 18 years in 1961 to almost 22 years in 1991 are probably responsible for any change in fertility in that period. Further, the major impact of the programme has mainly been restricted to urban areas. Figures from the PDHS 1990–1 indicated that contraceptive use in major urban cities had risen to almost 30 per cent, a proportion which is rather impressive in comparison with the rest of Pakistan. The PCPS 1994–5 shows even higher rates for urban Pakistan. Unmet need, i.e. women who state that they want no more children and are not using any method of contraception, is estimated to be 28 per cent (NIPS, 1992). This level is even higher at 37 per cent in the PCPS 1994–5 (Sathar and Casterline, 1998). It has been argued with substantial conviction that the family planning programme in Pakistan has failed due to problems of its chequered history and changes in management and strategy (Robinson *et al*, 1981; Rukanuddin and Hardee-Cleveland, 1992). In contrast, a counter-argument has been made that even though women may desire fewer children, they are still not prepared to adopt family planning as the next logical step (Sathar, 1993). The ideal family size has not changed much over time and remains at about four children (NIPS, 1992); however, the proportion of currently married women wanting no more children had risen in 1994–5 (Population Council, 1995).

DATA AND METHODS

The analysis is based mainly on the reproductive histories of 6611 women of the PDHS 1990–1. The main comparison will be made with the PFS-1975 in order to observe the overlap of fertility trends based on the oldest cohorts in the PDHS 1990–1 and the youngest cohorts in the PFS-1975. For the purposes of supporting our estimates, we will also utilize the Pakistan Integrated Household Survey of 1991 (PIHS-1991), which also collected full reproductive histories for practically the same year as the PDHS 1990–1, and the PDS 1984–8 and some preliminary analysis of the PFFPS 1997–8. The proposed study seeks to reconcile fertility estimates from the different data sources and, since our primary objective is to present evidence of the beginnings of marital fertility changes, our emphasis is on the interpretation of the PDHS 1990–1.

In this paper we are shifting the focus away from conventional fertility measurements to other gauges of fertility. Estimates of the family building process based on unbiased measurements equivalent to parity progression ratios are obtained. The advantage of this approach (developed by Juarez, 1983 and Brass and Juarez, 1983) is that it addresses the problem inherent in conventional fertility rates which may be disguising any real trend in current fertility due to data deficiencies. In order to confirm a decline in fertility at the national level based on traditional measurements such as the TFR, we would need to find evidence of modifications in the way that couples build up their families. While fertility levels may have remained constant, this may not necessarily be accompanied by lack of changes in the family formation processes.

The strategy followed is one that combines a period and a cohort approach. Different methods of fertility estimation are used: P/F ratios for evaluating maternity histories (ratio of cumulated current fertility to average parity), the Gompertz function adapted to make full use of the retrospective birth histories (Brass, 1981; Brass and Rashad, 1992) for modelling the fertility schedule, and the Parity Progression Ratio Truncation Approach (Brass and Juarez, 1983; Juarez, 1983) for capturing changes in family formation. The application of these techniques enables us to evaluate the type of errors affecting the data and provides information on real current fertility levels, thereby confirming or rejecting a fall in fertility.

To adjust for the time allocation distortions, fertility measures by age groups of women and time periods have been graduated by fitting Relational Gompertz Models. The method used was that devised by Zaba (1981). P_i values, i.e. the mean parities of the cohort at ages 15–19, 20–24, were calculated up to the last available group at the time of the survey. From these the Z_i (double the logarithms of the ratios of successive pairs of P_i values) are calculated. Zaba has shown that Z_i values are linearly related to functions derived from the standard fertility pattern. The parameters β and α representing the slope and intercept of the linear relationship can be estimated from the set of Z_i measures found from the observations. The strength of the Zaba procedure is that the shape parameters of the model, α and β, are estimated independently of the fertility level. The estimates of total fertility rates after fitting the Relational Gompertz Model are presented in the paper.

After evaluating the data and establishing trends in fertility, we proceed to apply the 'Parity Progression Ratio Truncation Approach' developed by Juarez and Brass (Brass and Juarez, 1983; Juarez, 1983). This allows us to obtain estimates of the quantum of fertility by adapting the life-table analysis of birth intervals using the measure of B_{60}, the proportion of women progressing from one parity to the next in 5 years. This approach uses an 'adjustment factor' that takes into account the possible bias of the estimates, thus generating indices of the real pace of fertility. These refined measures are ideally suited to capture the onset of fertility decline as reflected in the altering shape of family formation patterns, documenting the reduction of the progression of women from one parity to another. Such changes, though very critical in what they reflect in terms of family limitation, may not cause prominent changes in the total fertility rate. However, these measures help to identify groups of women who are experiencing changes in family formation and also the parities at which these changes are occurring. We are thereby able to identify women who are pioneers in the process of adoption of small family size norms.

EVIDENCE OF A DECLINE IN FERTILITY

Table 6.2 shows the average parities by age group of women derived from the PFS, the PDHS, the PFFPS and from three rounds of the PIHS. The trends shown by these figures are very erratic. The PDHS figures are lower at all ages than those from the PFS, but the 1991 PIHS, done in the same year as the PDHS, are, except for the 15–19 age group, consistently higher than the latter, and show no systematic change on the PFS. The 1996–7 PFFPS also gives higher figures than the PDHS, but lower than the 1991 PIHS and the 1975 PFS (except the 45–49 age group); the PFFPS is also in reasonably good agreement with the PIHS done in the same year.

It would therefore appear that it is the 1991 PDHS which is the odd one out. The increase in average parities between the PDHS and the PFFPS can be accounted for in only three ways: either there had been a rise in fertility; or births had been underreported in the PDHS; or they had been overreported in the PFFPS. Of these, the first can be ruled out: a 'synthetic cohort' calculated from the inter-survey parity changes gives a total fertility of over 9 births per woman! The third is also implausible: the general agreement between the PFFPS and the contemporaneous PIHS is reassuring, and other tests which have been imposed on the PFFPS data suggest that the birth histories are more likely to have suffered from omissions than faulty inclusions. We are left therefore with the inescapable conclusion that the birth histories compiled in the 1991 Demographic and Health Survey (DHS) suffered not only from massive misdating of the births (described below) but also from serious omissions. A similar conclusion was reached by Curtis and Arnold (1994) in their evaluation of the Pakistan DHS based on a reinterview survey.

When considering the cumulated fertility by ages of women for different time periods before the survey, the pattern presented in Table 6.3 makes it clear that the time location of births reported is greatly distorted. The apparent large fall in fertility for the five years before the survey, with a TFR of 4.8 for this period and 7.6 for the 5–9 years before the survey (indicating a

Table 6.2　*Average parities from surveys*

Age group of women	1975 PFS	1990–1 PDHS	1991 PIHS	1995–6 PIHS	1996–7 PIHS	1996–7 PFFPS
15–19	0.23	0.16	0.1	0.1	0.1	0.11
20–24	1.47	0.95	1.2	0.9	0.9	1.02
25–29	3.08	2.61	3.0	2.6	2.6	2.75
30–34	4.80	4.29	4.7	4.2	4.3	4.62
35–39	5.88	5.49	6.2	5.6	5.7	5.60
40–44	6.87	6.26	6.8	6.6	6.5	6.46
45–49	6.82	6.42	7.0	7.0	7.2	7.18

Table 6.3   *Cumulated fertilities by age of women in time periods. PDHS 1990–1*

Age of women	Time period before survey (years)						
	0–4	*5–9*	*10–14*	*15–19*	*20–4*	*25–9*	*30–4*
15–19	0.158	0.236	0.219	0.259	0.191	0.269	0.192
20–24	0.874	1.441	1.343	1.201	1.093	1.007	
25–29	2.063	3.207	2.990	2.751	2.622		
30–34	3.205	4.995	4.643	4.218			
35–39	4.126	6.441	6.019				
40–44	4.568	7.287					
45–49	4.838						

fertility fall of 2.8 children in the last five years), is totally implausible. Such a sharp decrease in fertility at all ages can only happen in very specially disturbed conditions such as in the late 1950s in China. There is no evidence of any such special circumstances for the late 1980s in Pakistan. Even stranger is the reported level of fertility 5–9 years before the survey. For the full age range the TFR approaches 7.6, a value entirely discrepant with other evidence. For earlier time periods, cumulated fertility at all ages appears to have been rising consistently over time between the period 20–24 years before the survey and 5–9 years before, which again contradicts other information. However, there are time location distortions with births in the five years before the survey pushed backwards, and those which occurred more than 15 years previously, brought forward. Inspection of the corresponding PFS (1975) measures reveals a similar pattern of misrepresentation but to a much lesser degree.

The huge distortions in the time location of births of the PDHS 1990–1 birth histories needed to be 'adjusted' using a suitable approach with the shape parameters of the model estimated independently of the fertility level. To adjust for the time location distortions, the fertility measures by age group of women and time period were graduated by fitting the Relational Gompertz Models. The calculations described below were in fact made by Professor Brass himself in 1993. We present them here in homage to the fact that they were one of the last substantive pieces of demographic analysis which he undertook before he was incapacitated by illness. But he himself would have urged that great caution is needed before interpreting the results.[2] We have not attempted to replicate the calculations which Brass made for the PDHS with the PFFPS or the later rounds of the PIHS.[3] When this is done the extent of the agreement of the fertility rates obtained for the overlapping time periods will constitute a powerful validation of the procedure.

With measures as erratic as those found in the Pakistan PDHS, determination of the best fitted β and α is problematic. The discrepancies at the

extremes of the range were not allowed to influence the fitting calculations
because of the huge distortion in the reporting of births in the last five years
and the sensitivity of the fitting to model and reporting deviation at the
lower tail of the fertility distribution. The combination of erratic observations
and the small number of points made specific fitting of the model for the
younger cohorts impracticable. Instead, the β and α estimates for the cohort
aged 30–34 years were assumed to apply at younger ages also. From the
fitted parameters, the P_i/F are calculated from the basic Gompertz equation
$Y_i = \alpha + \beta Y_s(i)$, where $Y_i = -l_n[-l_n\{P_i/F\}]$ and $Y_s(i)$ is the corresponding function from the standard distribution which is tabulated. The total
fertility, F, is then estimated from the value of P_i/F for the age group of
the cohort at the time of the survey and the series of P_i hence obtained for
the younger age groups. The values for cohorts are then translated into time
period fertility cumulated as in Table 6.4.

The trend pattern of these fitted values is plausible. They indicate that
the level of fertility started to decline from about 10–14 years before the
PDHS (supported by the PDSs) with a marginal fall at 5 to 9 years previously and a larger reduction in the five years up to 1990–1. The drop of
about 0.7 to 0.8 births per woman in the TFR from some 15 years before
is appreciable but much less than suggested by the unadjusted PDHS data.
As before, a substantial part of the fall occurs for early ages of women,
suggesting an important effect of age at marriage. Based on this evidence,
the fall in fertility at the later ages of women (over 30 years in 1990–1 say)
cannot be attributed to effects stemming from increased ages at marriage.
In fact, the pattern of change at later ages suggests that family limitation
within marriage is the major contributor to change. Although the severe
distortion in the time allocation of births makes the model fitting less secure,
the results are sensible.

The birth histories from the PFS data were also graduated using the
Relational Gompertz Model, and the results are shown in Table 6.5. Since

Table 6.4 *Cumulated fertility by age of women in time periods from fitted Relational
Gompertz Model. PDHS 1990–1*

Age of women	Time period before survey (years)						
	0–4	*5–9*	*10–14*	*15–19*	*20–4*	*25–9*	*30–4*
15–19	0.158	0.112	0.136	0.150	0.090	0.094	0.148
20–24	0.998	1.132	1.264	1.091	1.042	0.959	
25–29	2.455	2.742	2.901	2.734	2.409		
30–34	3.858	4.345	4.521	4.194			
35–39	5.076	5.587	5.830	.			
40–44	5.787	6.525					
45–49	6.118						

Table 6.5 *Cumulated fertilities by age of women in time periods from fitted Relational Gompertz Model. PFS-1975*

Age of women	Time period before survey (years)						
	0–4	5–9	10–14	15–19	20–4	25–9	30–4
15–19	0.230	0.332	0.362	0.357	0.368	0.402	0.377
20–24	1.373	1.578	1.684	1.670	1.750	1.715	
25–29	2.850	3.205	3.269	3.308	3.316		
30–34	4.349	4.652	4.750	4.730			
35–39	5.516	5.840	5.892				
40–44	6.300	6.595					
45–49	6.550						

the time allocation distortion is much less in the PFS, the fitting is more robust. The evidence seemed good enough to fix β at 0.95. An important feature of the two sets of estimates is the satisfactory agreement between the fertility measures for the five years before the PFS and the 15–19 years before the PDHS 1990–1, closely corresponding calendar periods. The agreement at 20 years and more before the PDHS is not so impressive but less reliance can be placed on these estimates at the tails of the distributions.

The mean parities from the PDHS and the PIHS birth histories for urban and rural residents are shown in Table 6.6. In both surveys the differences in

Table 6.6 *Mean parities by urban–rural residence*

Age group of women	PDHS Urban	1990–1 Rural	PIHS Urban	1991 Rural
15–19	0.1	0.19	0.1	0.1
20–24	0.77	1.04	0.9	1.3
25–29	2.47	2.7	2.8	3.1
30–34	4.18	4.33	4.6	4.7
35–39	5.42	5.53	5.7	6.4
40–44	6.33	6.22	6.7	6.8
45–49	6.32	6.46	7.1	7.0
Age group of women	PFFPS Urban	1996–7 Rural	PIHS Urban	1996–7 Rural
15–19	0.06	0.14	0.0	0.1
20–24	0.71	1.18	0.7	1.0
25–29	2.30	2.94	2.4	2.7
30–34	4.23	4.80	4.0	4.5
35–39	5.20	5.80	5.4	5.9
40–44	6.30	6.54	6.2	6.7
45–49	6.38	7.59	6.9	7.3

the mean parity levels between the urban and rural residents are small. Examination of the reported distribution of births over time for the PDHS data shows that the distortions for the rural areas are much the same as for the national pattern. Births in the urban areas also show a substantial under-count in the five years before the survey but fewer signs of error in the reports for more distant periods. Period fertility rates for urban and rural areas adjusted by the Relational Gompertz Model are presented in Table 6.7.

For both urban and rural residents there is a downward trend in fertility but the size of the reduction and the duration of the fall are appreciably larger for the former. In the urban areas, there appear to have been slight falls in fertility some 20 years before the PDHS with a sharp acceleration about 10 years before. The urban TFR in the five years before 1990–1 was around 1.3 births less than at 10–14 years before. The corresponding reduc-tion for rural residents was roughly 0.5 births. The effect of these trends was the differential in fertility between urban and rural residents of some 1.2 births for the period just prior to 1990–1. The lower urban fertility despite the near equality of the cohort measures of Table 6.6 appears odd until it is noted that the Gompertz fits imply that urban rates were in fact higher than the rates 15 years earlier, up to the mid 1970s. The slightly higher urban fertility was, in fact, pointed out in the reports analysing the PFS (Sathar, 1979; Yusuf and Retherford, 1981). Despite the problems of the distortion in the true location of past births, a consistent picture emerges

Table 6.7   *Cumulated fertilities by age of women in time periods from fitted Relational Gompertz Model. PDHS 1990–1*

Age of women	Time period before survey (years)						
	0–4	*5–9*	*10–14*	*15–19*	*20–4*	*25–9*	*30–4*
Urban residents							
15–19	0.096	0.097	0.138	0.156	0.139	0.098	0.120
20–24	0.774	1.060	1.229	1.275	1.229	1.069	
25–29	2.145	2.612	2.886	3.072	2.794		
30–34	3.525	4.079	4.514	4.608			
35–39	4.563	5.214	5.720				
40–44	5.142	5.935					
45–49	5.340						
Rural residents							
15–19	0.189	0.117	0.134	0.146	0.072	0.091	0.150
20–24	1.114	1.172	1.279	0.998	0.969	0.909	
25–29	2.622	2.810	2.892	2.579	2.265		
30–34	4.028	4.483	4.500	4.018			
35–39	5.358	5.764	5.844				
40–44	6.124	6.787					
45–49	6.516						

of fertility falls operating over a longer period and more sharply in urban than in rural areas, reversing the direction of the historical differentials.

Further comparisons can be made with the fertility estimates from the first five years of the PDS 1984–8. The mean parities were obtained for the sample of women by questions on children ever borne in 1984 and 1988, and the results are presented in Table 6.8. The last column in this table was calculated by subtracting the births in the preceding five years, as adjusted by the Relational Gompertz Model, from the reports of the PDHS of 1990–1. The agreement of the PDHS-based estimates with the PDS results is notably good.

The primary purpose of the PDS series is the collection of current birth and death statistics. From the recorded births, age-specific fertility rates for the calendar years 1984 to 1992 have been derived. Differences among the years 1984–7 are small and the measures have been averaged for Table 6.9. The reported 1988 levels are somewhat lower. As pointed out by Blacker (1990) in his analysis of the data, the TFR for 1984–7 is appreciably higher

Table 6.8   Mean parities by age of women from surveys

Age of women	1984 PDS	1988 PDS	1985–86 PDHS (backdated)
15–19	0.165	0.145	0.112
20–24	1.200	1.189	1.156
25–29	2.902	2.894	2.888
30–34	4.369	4.407	4.271
35–39	5.486	5.487	5.551
40–44	6.111	6.046	6.087
45–49	6.196	6.300	

Table 6.9   *Age-specific fertility rates from the Pakistan Demographic Survey 1984–1992*

Age group of women	1984–7	1988	1989	1990	1991	1992
15–19	0.060	0.066	0.076	0.075	0.069	0.073
20–24	0.270	0.264	0.266	0.275	0.258	0.261
25–29	0.362	0.333	0.323	0.313	0.315	0.313
30–34	0.313	0.278	0.274	0.276	0.259	0.254
35–39	0.227	0.203	0.197	0.176	0.186	0.163
40–44	0.045	0.111	0.102	0.097	0.082	0.074
45–49	0.045	0.042	0.042	0.030	0.027	0.028
TFR	6.964	6.486	6.400	6.215	5.989	5.835

than the cohort mean parities of 1984 and 1988 of Table 6.8 for the women near the end of the reproductive period. He suggests that the explanation of the discrepancy is an increase in fertility during the 1980s followed by a decline at the end of the decade, as suggested by the 1988 fertility rates. In fact, this is also the trend indicated by the PDHS birth histories, as adjusted by the Relational Gompertz Model.

In Table 6.10, the age specific fertility rates of 1984–7 are translated into cumulated fertilities by age group and compared with the retrospective PDHS estimates from Table 6.4. The agreement is quite good at ages over 30 years. The discrepancies at the younger ages of women are not unexpected in view of the sensitivity of both birth reporting and model fitting to small variations in the pattern of childbearing near the start of the reproductive period. Although there must still be reservations about the fertility trends revealed by the adjusted birth histories of the PDHS because of the severely distorted time allocation, the consistency of the estimates with the measures from the PFS and the 1984–8 PDS is impressive.

CHANGES IN THE FAMILY FORMATION PROCESS (PPRS)

From the Gompertz fitting and reconciliation of the various fertility estimates, there are indications that the recent slight fall in fertility was only partially due to the influence of an increase in age at marriage. There are clear indications that fertility falls within marriage at later ages have contributed to the trend as well as changes in risk exposure. To capture the inclination among Pakistani couples for family limitation and spacing strategies, we turn to the detailed analysis of family formation as measured by the 'Parity Progression Ratio Truncation Approach'. The Juarez–Brass procedures for the estimation of parity progression changes for cohorts of incomplete fertility have been applied (Brass and Juarez, 1983; Juarez, 1983). These require the calculation of B_{60} measures (the proportion of women having an (n + 1)th birth within five years of the nth) by life-table methods.

Table 6.10   *Cumulated fertility rates (mean parities) from surveys*

Age of women	PDS 1984–7	PDHS 1980–1 to 1985–6
15–19	0.062	0.112
20–24	0.912	1.132
25–29	2.550	2.742
30–34	4.275	4.345
35–39	5.645	5.587
40–44	6.500	6.525
45–49	6.902	

The measures are corrected for pace selection biases by making a series of comparisons of successive age groups with the births in the past five years removed from the older. This is to provide equal truncation (that is incompleteness) for the cohorts compared. The possible effects of the errors in the time location of births on the truncation adjustments were examined, and the method was found to be very robust to the distributions. Table 6.11 and Figure 6.2, present adjusted estimates for the PFS, PDHS and PFFPS surveys. Access to the latter survey data has recently been made possible thanks to the National Institute of Population Studies, Islamabad, and the Centre for Population Studies at the London School of Hygiene and Tropical Medicine.

Changes in family formation patterns were absent in 1975, while 15 years later there is evidence of a fall in fertility through the alteration in the build-up of families and a greater inclination towards smaller families. The indices of parity progression for the PFS birth history indicated only a negligible change in family formation: there is a faint indication of a fall only at higher birth orders, seventh and eighth interval, but only because of two individual values, and little weight can be placed on this suggestion (Brass and Juarez, 1983). However, the PDHS and PFFPS birth histories provide results which

Table 6.11 B_{60}'s adjusted using indices of relative change. Truncation approach. PFS-1975, PDHS 1990–1 and PFFPS 1996–7

Cohort	U–1	1–2	2–3	3–4	4–5	5–6	6–7	7–8
PFS-1975								
20–24	0.8454	0.9215	0.9026	0.8771				
25–29	0.8439	0.8939	0.8888	0.8754	0.8642	0.8055		
30–34	0.8456	0.9009	0.9096	0.9031	0.8685	0.8270	0.7390	0.6980
35–39	0.7781	0.8848	0.8981	0.8919	0.8770	0.8270	0.8181	0.6735
40–44	0.8072	0.9121	0.9187	0.9032	0.8685	0.8349	0.8330	0.6914
45–49	0.8094	0.8962	0.8740	0.8781	0.8855	0.8179	0.7977	0.7442
PDHS 1990–1								
20–24	0.8184	0.8969	0.7944	0.7507				
25–29	0.8673	0.9235	0.8333	0.7782	0.6788	0.5855		
30–34	0.8411	0.9280	0.8893	0.8370	0.7299	0.6951	0.5618	0.4561
35–39	0.8567	0.9190	0.9111	0.8787	0.8093	0.7253	0.6114	0.6102
40–44	0.8316	0.9278	0.9227	0.8539	0.8350	0.7864	0.7070	0.6651
45–49	0.8024	0.9212	0.9128	0.8706	0.8650	0.7853	0.7429	0.7776
PFFPS 1996–7								
20–24	0.9014	0.8506	0.8167	0.7205				
25–29	0.9203	0.9025	0.8741	0.7874	0.7396	0.6229		
30–34	0.9163	0.9266	0.9051	0.8142	0.7865	0.7155	0.6756	0.6358
35–39	0.8985	0.9086	0.8950	0.8677	0.8115	0.7985	0.7457	0.6069
40–44	0.9053	0.9271	0.9153	0.8640	0.8442	0.7998	0.7347	0.7102
45–49	0.8827	0.9043	0.9026	0.8808	0.9294	0.8500	0.7851	0.7568

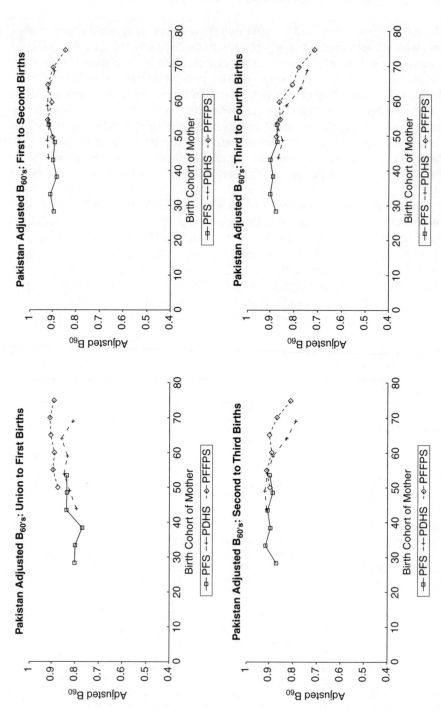

Figure 6.2 Pakistan adjusted B_{60}'s from the Pakistan Fertility Survey (1975), the Pakistan Demographic and Health Survey (1991) and the Pakistan Fertility and Family Planning Survey (1996–7)

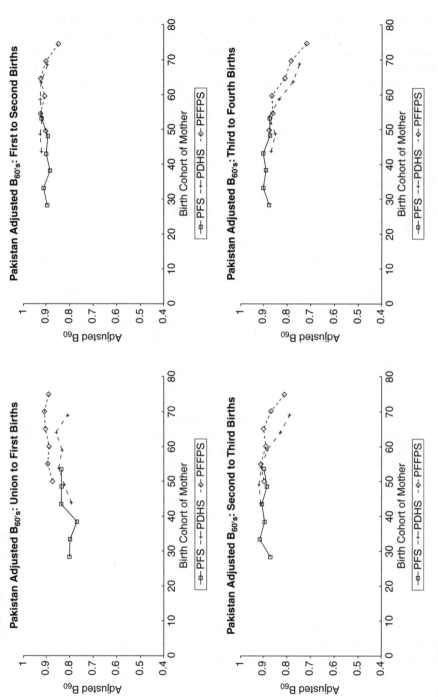

Figure 6.2b

are fully consistent with the pattern in the initial stages of fertility falls through family limitation. While parity progression from marriage to first and first to second births remain constant over the cohorts, there are consistent declines in the progression from second to third parities and upwards. Thus the PDHS and PFFPS findings are in contrast with the corresponding analysis of the PFS birth histories where no significant decreases at any birth order were detected (Brass and Juarez, 1983).

The main intervals contributing to the fertility fall according to PDHS 1990–1 are the fourth and fifth – that is to say, proportionately fewer women with a fourth birth who go on to have a fifth. Similarly the probability of women achieving a sixth birth having had a fifth child has been falling. The pattern is stronger for younger cohorts. This is interesting in the light of the consistently reported desire for about four children in Pakistan for the last 20 years.

From the adjusted values we can observe that women of the birth cohort 1951–6, aged 35–39 at the date of interview, are most probably the pioneers in exhibiting this new reproductive behaviour. Women who started forming their families in the first half of the 1970s are the ones who initiated the trend of declining fertility, and are now being followed by younger cohorts. It was in the decade of the 1980s when these 'innovators' consolidated this decisive change which came about with the reduction of higher parity progression ratios (in the 1980s they would have been reaching their fifth, sixth or higher order births). Data do show that these women are more likely to have ever used contraception (31 per cent) than any other cohort. Younger women seem to be following suit. In a period of 15 years, 25–29 year old women have managed to reduce their probability of achieving a fifth birth from around 85 to 70 per cent. Furthermore, younger women aged 20–24 in 1990–1 are increasingly opting for families of two children, as seen from the trend in transition from second to third birth. The comparison of the adjusted B_{60}'s derived from both the PDHS and the PFFPS for the same cohorts of women show generally good agreement at the lower parities. But above parity 4 there are appreciable discrepancies, which increase as the parities get higher. Both data sets show fertility to be declining across the cohorts, but the parity progression ratios shown by the PFFPS are consistently higher than those of the PDHS for the same cohorts. One is left with the suspicion that the PDHS ratios were biased downwards by the omission of births to high parity women noted earlier in this paper. Nevertheless, the initial decisive declines of the adjusted PPRs occur at the fourth parity continuing consistently into the later parities. As before, the threshold of change, between earlier uncontrolled large families to a distinctly smaller family size, is the decision to stop at the fourth child as opposed to continue to the fifth birth.

CONCLUSIONS

The main findings of the assessment of data quality of the reproductive histories of the PDHS 1990–1 survey, the modelling of the fertility schedule and the exploration of the timing and quantum of fertility, show that fertility in Pakistan has commenced to decline in the last 10 years. However, this decline is not as drastic as portrayed by unadjusted measurements such as the TFR. The TFR is about 6.1 for 1986–91 and this is supported by the TFR of 5.6 for 1994–5 from the PCPS. This is an important confirmation that the Government of Pakistan was not wrong in accepting 5.95 as the base figure for the Eighth Plan 1993–8, rejecting a drastic fall in fertility as depicted by unadjusted PDHS data.

The decline as depicted in the TFR, though slight, started about 10 years ago. Further, there is firm evidence that fertility has declined more sharply in urban areas and the adjusted TFR for urban areas is over 1.5 children less than the rural TFR. This depicts the emergence of the urban–rural fertility differential which was practically negligible or even in the reverse direction in the 1970s.

The changes underway are found to be parity dependent as well as an outcome of recent rises in age at marriage of females. The pioneers leading the transition towards lower fertility are the cohort born approximately between 1951 and 1956 which began to modify their reproductive behaviour in the early 1980s. However, it is important to note that the change identified is not restricted to urban areas and is well represented in the data on rural women who of course dominate national patterns. This change is supported by the quite notable rise in the use of contraceptives documented for the 1994–5 PCPS and the PFFPS 1997–8 (Sathar and Casterline, 1998).

Finally, we can confidently predict that the family limitation process which appears to have started is likely to continue for younger generations with a reduction in their completed family size. Family formation patterns seem to be converging towards an achieved family size of about four children, unexpectedly in agreement with the stated desired family size which has remained consistent across all fertility surveys in Pakistan. Furthermore, the larger changes in postponing higher parity births or even limiting family size at lower parities can be anticipated among younger cohorts. Therefore, we can expect quite a sharp decline in fertility in the near future.

REFERENCES

Alam, I. (1984) 'Fertility levels and trends', in I. Alam and B. Dinesen (eds), *Fertility in Pakistan. A Review of Findings from the Pakistan Fertility Survey.* Voorburg, Netherlands: World Fertility Survey, International Statistical Institute.

Alam, I., Irfan, M. and Farooqui, N.I. (1983) 'Fertility levels, trends and differential in Pakistan: evidence from the Population Labour Force and Migration Survey 1979–80'. Islamabad, Pakistan: Pakistan Institute of Development Economics.

Blacker, J. (1990) 'Population growth in Pakistan. New data and new methods', document presented at the Training Workshop at the Population Studies Centre, University of Karachi 12–17 May.

Blacker, J. and Hakim, A. 'Fertility and mortality in Pakistan: new evidence from the 1996–97 Pakistan Fertility and Family Planning Survey', NIPS Working Paper, forthcoming.

Booth, H. and Shah, I. (1984) 'The data and their quality', in I. Alam and B. Dinesen (eds), *Fertility in Pakistan. A Review of Findings from the Pakistan Fertility Survey*, Voorburg, Netherlands: World Fertility Survey, International Statistical Institute.

Brass, W. (1981) 'The use of the Gompertz Relational Model to estimate fertility', in *Proceedings XIX International Population Conference, Manila 1981*. Liège, Belgium: IUSSP.

Brass, W. and Juarez, F. (1983) 'Censored cohort parity progression ratios from birth histories'. *Asian and Pacific Census Forum*, vol 10, no 1, August.

Brass, W. and Rashad, H. (1992) 'Evaluation of the reliability of data in maternity histories', in A. Hill and W. Brass (eds), *The Analysis of Maternity Histories*, Liège, Belgium: IUSSP, Ordina Editions.

Casterline, J. (1984) 'Fertility differentials', in I. Alam and B. Dinesen (eds), *Fertility in Pakistan. A Review of Findings from the Pakistan Fertility Survey*. Voorburg, Netherlands: World Fertility Survey, International Statistical Institute.

Curtis, S. and Arnold, F. (1994) 'An evaluation of the Pakistan DHS Survey based on the reinterview survey', Occasional Papers 1. Columbia, MD: Macro International.

Hakim, A., Cleland, J. and Bhatti, M. (1999) *The Pakistan Fertility and Family Planning Survey 1997–98 : Main Report*, Islamabad: NIPS/CPS.

Juarez, F. (1983) 'Family formation in Mexico: a study based on maternity histories from a retrospective fertility survey', Ph.D. thesis, University of London, London.

NIPS (National Institute of Population Studies) (1992) *Pakistan Demographic and Health Survey 1990–1991*. Columbia, MD: Demographic and Health Survey, IRD/Macro International Inc, July.

Population Census Organization. (1998) *Population and Housing Census 1998*, Bulletin No.1, Islamabad: Statistics Division.

Population Council (1995) *Pakistan Contraceptive Prevalence Survey 1994–95: Basic Findings*. Islamabad: Ministry of Population Welfare and Population Council.

Retherford, R., Mujtaba Mirza, G., Irfan, M., and Alam, I. (1987) 'Fertility trends in Pakistan: The decline that wasn't', *Asian and Pacific Population Forum*, vol 1, no 2.

Robinson, W.C., Shah, M. and Shah, N. (1981) 'The family planning programme in Pakistan: What went wrong?' *International Family Planning Perspectives*, vol 7, no 3.

Rukanuddin, R. and Hardee-Cleveland, K. (1992) 'Can family planning succeed in Pakistan?' *International Family Planning Perspectives*, vol 18, no 3.

Sathar, Z. (1979) 'Rural-urban fertility differentials in Pakistan'. *Pakistan Development Review*, vol 18, no 3.

Sathar, Z. (1993) 'The much awaited fertility decline in Pakistan: wishful thinking or reality? *International Family Planning Perspectives*, December.

Sathar, Z and Casterline, J. (1998) 'The onset of fertility transition in Pakistan' *Population and Development Review*, vol 24, no 4.

Yusuf, F. and Retherford, R. (1981) 'Urban-rural fertility differentials in Pakistan. *Journal of Biosocial Sciences*, vol 13, no 4.

Zaba, B. (1981) 'Use of the relational gompertz model in analysing fertility data collected in retrospective surveys', CPS Working Paper No. 81–2, London: Centre for Population Studies, London School of Hygiene and Tropical Medicine, University of London, March.

CHAPTER SEVEN

A comparative analysis of fertility in Arab countries: Explaining the anomalies

Hoda Rashad

Social Research Center (SRC),
American University in Cairo (AUC)

The comparative study of the fertility of the Arab countries has generally been constrained by the lack of accurate data that allows an investigation of the nature of change and its precipitating factors. Recently, the information base in Arab countries has improved considerably with the launching of three regional comparative efforts [Demographic and Health Surveys (DHS), Pan Arab Project for Maternal and Child Health (PAPCHILD) and Gulf Child and Family Health Surveys (GHS and GFHS)]. These surveys are major international or regional efforts fielded in a number of Arab countries during the late 1980s and early 1990s. They provide a unique opportunity for an accurate reconstruction of the fertility history of Arab countries, as well as a better understanding of the anomalies observed in fertility differentials across Arab countries. Such an understanding provides a platform for revisiting existing transition theories and their relevance to explaining the experience of Arab countries.

The paper is divided into four sections. The first specifies the Arab countries and the data sources used in the analysis. The second provides an overview of the fertility transition and investigates the distinctiveness of the experience. The third addresses the direct determinants of change within and differentials across Arab countries. In particular, this section compares the Sudan, Syria and Yemen. The three countries represent interesting case studies for comparative analysis. Sudan and Yemen are at close levels of socio-economic development and contraceptive prevalence, but with large differences in total fertility rates (TFR); Syria and Sudan are different in contraceptive levels and socio-economic development, but their TFR are very close. The search for explanations of the anomalies invites a revisit to transition theories and their relevance to explaining the experience of Arab countries. This is attempted in the last section of the paper.

SPECIFICATION OF COUNTRIES AND DATA SOURCES

The League of Arab States includes 22 Arab countries. Among these, four countries (Djibouti, Comoros, Somalia and Mauritania) are excluded from the analysis. These countries, while part of the Arab region, are suspected of being influenced by a different set of cultural and social forces (history, language and religious composition) shaping their fertility transition.

The remaining 18 Arab countries, which appear to be much more socially and culturally homogeneous, differ a great deal in the amount and type of information that could be used. The focus here is on cross-sectional national demographic or health surveys that are part of international or regional efforts utilizing comparable sampling designs, strict quality control and detailed birth histories and are accessible in published and/or tape format.

Eight Arab countries have collected at least two national retrospective demographic surveys (including a detailed birth history). Seven of these participated in the World Fertility Survey (WFS) programme in the late 1970s (Egypt (1980), Morocco (1979–80), Sudan (1979), Tunisia (1978), Jordan (1976), Syria (1978), Yemen (1979)) and have also collected at least another health survey, a DHS or a Maternal and Child Health Survey (MCHS), in the late 1980s or early 1990s.[1] Also, Algeria had a national fertility survey (1986–87) and a recent (1992) maternal and child health survey.

The three Gulf countries of Bahrain, Oman and Qatar participated in the Gulf Survey programme conducted in the late eighties as well as the mid-nineties. For these three countries retrospective fertility measures from the Child Health Surveys (CHS) conducted in the late eighties have been published and, as of yet, only one estimate from the Fertility and Family Planning surveys conducted in the mid-nineties has been published for Bahrain and Oman.

Of the remaining seven countries, Libya has retrospective estimates of TFR available for the last three five year periods preceding a recent survey (Libya MCHS (1995)). United Arab Emirates has two point estimates from the two Child Health and Fertility and Family Health Surveys. Four countries (Iraq, Kuwait, Lebanon, Saudi Arabia) have only one recent survey estimate of the TFR for the most recent period.[2] The TFR estimate of a recent cross sectional survey for Palestinian people cannot be used (the baseline report on a survey of living conditions (Heiberg and Ovensen, 1993) uses indirect techniques for estimation and there is no earlier time series accessible).

In addition to the aforementioned data sources, The United Nations (UN) revised 1995 edition provides a historical base for a general overview of fertility trends from the early 1950s. Many of the UN revised measures for recent periods did incorporate the findings of the three major survey pro-grammes conducted in the Arab region (DHS, PAPCHILD, GHS).[3] Further-more the decision to adopt a certain estimate in the UN report appeared to benefit from other additional information derived from censuses, registra-tion and national surveys other than the ones mentioned above. Despite the overall appropriateness of using the UN revised measures (particularly in view of the length of the data series available), it appeared necessary to investigate first whether any further revisions are needed and also to high-light unresolved discrepancies between the revised UN estimates and those provided by the many recent cross sectional retrospective surveys. This was called for by the observation that the findings of some of the most recent surveys have not been considered or adopted in the UN series,[4] and also by the fact that the analysis will combine the findings from surveys with those provided in the UN report. Such movement across and within many sets of data requires some caution.

Inspection of Table 7A.1 in the appendix, which provides different measures of TFR by source of information, reveals that the different survey data for as many as 11 countries (Algeria, Egypt, Libya, Morocco, Sudan, Tunisia, Bahrain, Jordan, Qatar, Saudi Arabia and Syria) are reasonably consistent with UN series up till 1985–9. It also indicates that survey estimates post-1990 for the majority of these countries are more or less within the expected levels assuming a continuation of earlier trends. The clear exceptions to this rule are Libya, Sudan and Syria, which show a major decline between 1985–9 and 1990–4. For these countries (except for the Gulf countries of Bahrain and Qatar), the TFR measures presented in UN (1995) for 1950–89 were retained and extrapolated to 1990–4 using the inferred recent trends from surveys (when available) or from the UN (1995). For the two Gulf countries, the survey measures referring to nationals only were retained for 1975 to 1989 and extrapolated. The data for nationals are of course more appropriate for an explanatory analysis of fertility trends.

The survey estimates for the remaining countries of: Iraq, Kuwait, Oman, United Arab Emirates, and Yemen are not in good agreement with UN findings. For both Oman and Yemen, the survey and UN estimates confirm that the current levels of TFR remain very high (in the neighbourhood of 7 and 8). The implications of the two sets of data are similar when viewing long-term declines from the early 1950s to the present. However, the recent picture is quite different. The estimates in the UN report portray recent constant fertility while the survey estimates present a picture of steady decline from the extremely – and rarely observed – high levels of TFR around 11 births per woman. The survey estimate for Oman and Yemen for the period 1975–94 replaces the UN measures. Iraq and UAE limited survey data on fertility do not provide any basis for ironing out the differences between them and UN estimates. For these countries, the analysis will use the estimates provided in the UN report.

As for Kuwait, given the marked difference between the survey and UN measures, further investigation was needed. Fargues (1989) provides the following civil registration measures for Kuwaiti nationals:

Year	1970	1975	1980	1985
TFR	7.21	7.08	6.60	6.47

Given that these measures are in full agreement with the recent child health surveys and the earlier (1970) UN measures, we can infer that: (1) Fertility measures for Kuwait are currently at a much lower level and has experienced appreciable change. (2) Fertility measures for Kuwaiti nationals remain high and have been through some decline.

For the purpose of the current analysis, the UN reported TFR for the periods 1970 to 1989 are replaced by the corresponding vital statistics for Kuwaiti nationals.

To sum up, while it is true that some of the estimates in the UN report for a limited number of countries are not in total agreement with survey estimates and may benefit from further probing, it is clear that the level of consistency between the measures from different sources is high enough to allow the overview to be generally based on UN statistics integrated with more recent findings. The integration is guided by the consistency of the many recent survey findings but is also careful to avoid too many movements across different sources of data (to reduce the effect of sampling and response variations on the inference of trend). Table 7A.2 in the appendix provides the data used for trend analysis. It should be noted that there are two estimates provided for 1990–4. The first extrapolates the UN series using the best possible estimate for recent trends. The second adjusts the most recent survey estimate to refer to 1990–4. For the analysis of current levels (post-1990) and the very long term trend from 1950 to 1990, the adjusted survey estimated is used. For shorter term analysis the extrapolated measures are recommended.

OVERVIEW

Levels, timing and magnitude of decline
Table 7.1 provides measures of TFR, during the early 1950s, for Arab countries and for major regions in the world. Comparing TFR levels in the early fifties for most Arab countries with the averages for other regions in the world indicates that TFR for most Arab countries are closer (slightly higher) to those in other regions in Africa (except middle Africa) and to Central America. These levels of TFR are markedly higher than those in regions that have already been through their fertility decline (Europe and North America). They are also higher by nearly one birth per woman than almost all the averages for the remaining regions that do not appear to have started their fertility transition (Asia, the Caribbean and South America).

The obvious exception to this statement is Lebanon, with a level of TFR (5.7) comparable to most regions of Asia, the Caribbean and South America.

A closer look at TFR levels in individual countries (not regional averages) reveals that the TFR levels prevailing in Arab countries during the early fifties are similar to those in many countries in other regions (excluding

Table 7.1   *Measures of TFR, during the early 1950s, for Arab countries and major regions in the world*

Region	TFR
Arab Countries	6.99*
North Africa	6.82
Algeria	7.28
Egypt	6.56
Libya	6.87
Morocco	7.17
Sudan	6.67
Tunisia	6.87
West Asia	7.04*
Bahrain	6.97
Iraq	7.17
Jordan	7.38
Kuwait	7.21
Lebanon	5.74
Oman	7.20
Qatar	6.97
Saudi Arabia	7.17
Syria	7.09
Emirates	6.97
Yemen	7.61
Other regions	
Eastern Africa	6.90
Middle Africa	5.91
Southern Africa	6.46
Western Africa	6.58
Eastern Asia	5.61
South-Central Asia	6.08
South-Eastern Asia	6.03
Eastern Europe	2.69
Northern Europe	2.32
Southern Europe	2.65
Western Europe	2.39
Caribbean	5.22
Central America	6.79
South America	5.69

Source: United Nations (1995)
* Calculated as a simple average using United Nations (1995) country estimates.

the countries in Europe, North America and Oceania – Australia and New Zealand – whose fertility transition started much earlier). Table 7.2 shows that close to half (54 out of 122) of the countries considered fall within the levels experienced by Arab countries.

It is interesting that this similarity is not confined to countries within Africa, but to many countries in Asia, Latin America and Oceania.

Another observation relates to the small range of variations observed among Arab countries during the 1950s. With the exception of Lebanon, TFR for all Arab countries range between 6.5 and 7.6. Indeed, during the second half of the fifties 15 of the 17 Arab countries considered had a TFR between 7.0 and 7.6.

The small variability among Arab countries during the early fifties can be compared to the degree of variability within different regions in the same time period. Table 7.3 provides the interquartile range for TFR for the Arab countries within Asia and Africa and non-Arab countries within different regions in the world. Clearly, the Arab West Asian countries reflect minimum variability and are clustered around the TFR value of 7. The Arab African countries' range of variability is similar to that of other regions in Africa but much less variable than any other region in the world.

It is probably true that the picture of high Arab fertility in the early 1950s is more a result of the clustering of TFR than its extreme excess over the levels in other developing countries.

It should be emphasized that the wider range of variations among non-Arab, and non-African countries cannot be explained by the fact that many of these countries have already started their transition and hence the regional variations are simply echoing the different transitional stages. Indeed, the fertility transition in most countries of Asia, the Caribbean and most regions

Table 7.2   *Number of countries within different regions whose TFR during early 1950s fall within indicated range*

	< 6.5	6.5–6.9	7.0–7.6	Subtotal 6.5–7.6	Total
Arab countries	1	7	9	16	17
Africa	20	17	9	26	46
Asia	27	6	4	10	37
Latin America & Caribbean	17	10	4	14	31
Oceania	4	2	2	4	8
Total non-Arab	68	35	19	54	122*

Source: United Nations (1995)
* Excluding countries in Europe, North America, New Zealand and Australia whose fertility transition started much earlier than 1950s.

Table 7.3 *The interquartile range for TFR during 1950–4 for Arab and non-Arab countries within different regions in the world*

Region	TFR	N	25 %	50 %	75 %	Range (75–25 %)
Arab countries						
North Africa	6.82	6	6.64	6.87	7.20	0.56
West Asia	7.04*	11	6.97	7.17	7.21	0.24
Other regions						
Eastern Africa	6.90	17	6.46	6.78	7.09	0.63
Middle Africa	5.91	8	5.51	5.68	5.94	0.44
Southern Africa	6.46	5	5.92	6.50	6.51	0.59
Western Africa	6.58	16	6.30	5.69	6.90	0.60
Eastern Asia	5.61	6	4.02	5.18	6.03	2.01
South-Central Asia	6.08	14	5.91	6.01	6.67	0.76
South-Eastern Asia	6.03	11	6.05	6.40	6.83	0.78
Eastern Europe	2.69	10	2.51	2.71	3.51	1.00
Northern Europe	2.32	10	2.15	2.57	3.07	0.92
Southern Europe	2.65	11	2.57	3.05	4.82	2.25
Western Europe	2.39	7	2.10	2.28	2.73	0.63
Caribbean	5.22	11	4.22	5.30	5.71	1.49
Central America	6.79	8	6.51	6.74	7.35	0.84
South America	5.69	12	5.25	6.62	6.76	1.51

Source: Calculations based on United Nations (1995).
* Calculated as a simple average using United Nations (1995) country estimates.

in the Americas (consult Table 7A.3 in the appendix providing the dates at the start of fertility transition) had not yet picked up by the early fifties.

The little variations in TFR for Arab countries contrast sharply with experiences observed in some other regions of the world prior to their fertility transition. For example, Casterline (1991) noted that traditional reproductive regimes (particularly nuptiality and postpartum practices) in major areas of Asia did inhibit fertility and that the total fertility rate at the onset of transition in Asia ranged between 5.5 and 7.0. For the Arab region only one country (Lebanon) approached that lower level. Similarly, Coale (1986) highlighted the moderate levels – TFR from about 4.1 to 6.2 – in preindustrial European populations. The modes of behaviour that limited the fertility of these populations were, as in the Asian model, non-parity specific.

The small variations and the relative stability of TFR remained till the early 1960s. By the second half of the sixties, changes in fertility started to set in. By that time, many Arab countries had already been through or were experiencing some rises in fertility that seem to precede their fertility decline.

Table 7.4 *Distribution of Arab and non-Arab countries by the date marking the onset of fertility decline*

Region	1950–9	1960–74	1975–9	1980+	Total
Arab countries	0	10	3	4	17
Non-Arab countries					
Africa	2	4	5	1	12
Asia	8	16	0	1	25
West Asia (non-Arab)	3	2	1	0	6
Caribbean	6	4	1	0	11
America	3	14	0	3	20
Oceania	4	3	0	1	8
Total non-Arab countries	26	43	7	6	82*

Source: Calculated from Table 7A.3 in the appendix.
* Excluding the countries whose fertility transition started much earlier than the 1950s and those (40 countries) who have not started their transition yet.

Table 7.4 presents the distribution of Arab and non-Arab countries whose fertility fall did not precede the early fifties by the date marking the onset of fertility decline.

All the Arab countries have now joined the fertility transition while as much as a third of non-Arab countries where fertility had not begun to fall before 1955 have not yet begun their transition. Among the Arab countries, none are early starters. Around three-quarters began their transition during the sixties and early seventies and one quarter are clearly late starters.

The timing of the fertility transition in the Arab region is of course quite late when viewing the European and North American experience. Also, while the timing of change in the Arab region is similar to that in many developing countries (half of the non-Arab countries considered declined during the same time span, 1960 to 1974, as nearly two thirds of the Arab countries) and even preceded a number of countries (particularly in Africa), the overall timing is relatively later. Around a third of non-Arab countries, among those experiencing a transition, had started their transition before the sixties, while no Arab country showed signs of decline at that time. The span of the onset of the fertility decline is closely clustered in the Arab region (between 1960 and 1974) while it is much more dispersed (over 1950 to 1980) for other countries.

When the trend and its magnitude are followed over a longer period of 15 years (Table 7A.3), the following observations are called for. With the exceptions of Iraq whose decline was around one birth per woman, and perhaps Yemen (which calls for more in depth investigation), all the Arab countries reduced their TFR by between 1.5 to 3 births per woman. The magnitude is quite reasonable compared to other non-Arab countries. Very few countries in the world managed to exceed the 2.5 decrease in TFR over the period of 15 years. Also many non-Arab countries have not managed to reach the 1.5 decline.

It is indeed noticeable that the three countries of Libya, Sudan and Syria, with declines of 2.4, 1.9 and 2.5 respectively between 1985–9 and 1990–4,[5] managed in a period of five years to catch up with and even surpass other countries who had quite a head start.

It should be noted that the survey data for the two countries of Oman and Yemen also support the occurrence of fast declines in fertility. Furthermore, the Gulf health survey data indicate faster declines in fertility in some Gulf countries (Farid, 1996). It is indeed possible that these more recent surveys are capturing real changes that are not yet reflected in the UN report.

Figures 7.1, 7.2 and Table 7.5 reflect the movement from a highly clustered TFR of the early fifties to a more dispersed TFR in the seventies (suggesting a difference in transitional route) and a reclustering for African Arab Countries around a lower level in the nineties ranging between 3 and 4.5. Asian Arab countries – particularly in view of the remaining high fertility levels for Yemen, Oman and Palestine – have not yet completed their transition but appear to be in the midst of a declining path.

The level of recent fertility in the Arab region has departed considerably from its earlier close ties with other regions in Africa, it remains higher than many regions in Asia, Latin America and Caribbean but the indications post-1990s suggest that the gap will narrow.

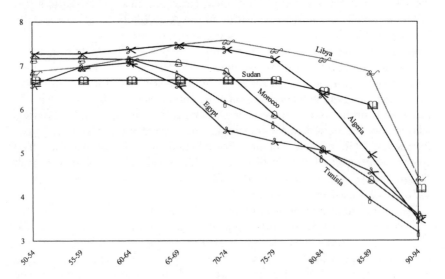

Figure 7.1   Total fertility rates in Africa Arab countries, 1950–95

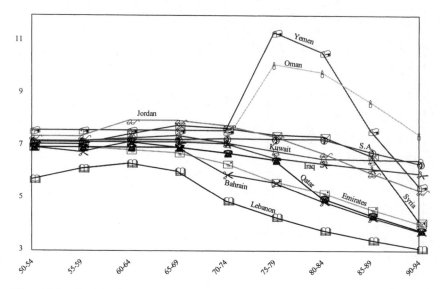

Figure 7.2   Total fertility rates in Asian Arab countries, 1950–95

Thus, it is true that earlier fertility in the Arab region was on average somewhat higher and later in beginning to fall, but the differences in level and timing are not truly exceptional to place it as a world apart. The Arab pretransitional levels and its transitional path are found in many other countries in Asia and Central and South America and the magnitude of change allowed some catching up of the region average with other regions. What is very distinct in the Arab experience is its tendency to cluster in terms of level and timing of change.

Direct determinants of prevailing levels
The relatively (compared to pretransitional fertility levels in developing societies) high and close TFR's at the early 1950s, slightly late but also clustered timing of decline as well as a tendency for TFR's to converge again at the early nineties invite a picture of an Arab region governed by the same dynamics and proximate determinants. Is this a true representation of reality?

Data on underlying determinants for early fifties fertility levels are rather sparse. Utilization of parity-specific measures to control fertility (particularly contraceptives) is expected to be low. Also, the fertility inhibiting effect of universal and long duration of breast-feeding – that remains above 88 per cent in prevalence and nine months in duration up till the nineties (Farid, 1996, Table 7.9) – is known to operate.

In terms of nuptiality, Table 7.6 provides the singulate mean age at marriage (SMAM) prior to fertility transition. With the exception of Morocco, SMAMs prior to transition are closely clustered and their quartiles lie between

Table 7.5 *Grouping of Arab countries by fertility levels at different time periods*

Date	2.5–2.9	3–3.9	4–4.9	5–5.9	6–6.9	7 and over
1950–4				Lebanon	Egypt Libya Sudan Tunisia Bahrain Qatar Emirates	Syria Morocco Iraq Saudi A. Oman Kuwait Algeria Jordan Yemen
1970–4			Lebanon	Egypt Bahrain	Tunisia Emirates Sudan Qatar Morocco	Libya Syria Yemen Jordan Iraq Kuwait Oman Saudi A. Algeria
1975–9			Lebanon	Egypt Bahrain Tunisia Emirates Morocco	Qatar Iraq Sudan Kuwait	Algeria Saudi A. Yemen Oman Libya Jordan Syria
1990–4 extrapolation from UN		Lebanon Tunisia Algeria Morocco Egypt Bahrain Qatar	Emirates Syria Sudan Libya	Iraq Jordan Yemen	Saudi A. Oman Kuwait	
1990–4 Adjusted latest Survey estimate	Lebanon	Tunisia Bahrain Algeria Morocco Syria Qatar Egypt	Emirates Sudan Jordan Libya	Iraq	Saudi A. Yemen Kuwait	Oman

Table 7.6 *Singulate mean age at marriage (SMAM) in Arab countries in different years*

Date of fertility decline	Country	1950	1955	1960	1965	1970	1975	1980	1985	Post 1995
1960–	Bahrain									25.4
	Egypt		19.8				21.4	21.4		21.3
	Lebanon									
	Tunisia		19.3		20.9		22.6		24.3	25
1965–	Emirates						18			22.9
	Kuwait				18.9	19.6	20.5	21.7	22.4	21.7
	Morocco	17.3		17.5		19.4		22.3		22.2
	Qatar									22.9
1970–	Algeria		19.4		18.3	19.3	21			26
	Jordan		20.4					21.5	22.8	
	Iraq		20.6		20.6		20.8			
	Libya					18.7				
	Saudi Arabia									21.8
	Sudan					18.7		21.5		25.3
	Syria			19.6		20.7		21.5	22.1	24.5

Source: United Nations (1990)
* Different years corresponding to the recent DHS, MCHS and GCHS surveys.

18.9 and 20.6, a value that is higher than expected and is comparable to that in many developing countries at pretransition levels. That none of the Arab countries portray the very young patterns of marriage (SMAM of 15 and 16) that were observed in some countries prior to their transition – e.g. the UN (1995) measures for Chad (1963), Guinea (1955), Mali (1960), Niger (1959), Bangladesh (1974), India (1951), Nepal (1961) – is probably worth further investigation.

This scanty information suggests that both breast-feeding and nuptiality curbed fertility levels in Arab countries during the early fifties. It should be noted, however, that the inhibiting role of these forces is such as to result in TFR's of 4 and 5 witnessed in other regions. It is interesting to note that the extreme levels of TFR of 10 and 11 found in health surveys of Yemen and Oman are most likely a result of low SMAM combined with a decrease in breast-feeding. It is also possible that the figures have been biased by mis-dating of the births in the birth histories.

The movement in SMAM across time from the early fifties to the onset of the transition, while difficult to document properly due to paucity of data, does not appear to be very strong. The maximum change is in the neighbourhood of one year.

It may be appropriate at this stage to point out that similar values of SMAM do not necessarily establish similar contributions of marriage in shaping fertility levels. The contribution of marriage is shaped by the inter-action of proportion married at different ages and the age-specific marital rates. However, since the marital fertility schedule prior to the transition is expected to be close given the low uptake of contraceptive use and universal and long duration of breast-feeding, values of SMAM during the fifties are likely to be closely associated with the role of marriage in shaping fertility levels. But this statement does not hold true once parity-specific measures to control fertility are introduced.

Thus, the existing scanty data do not refute the notion of similar direct determinants sustaining the close values of TFR during the early fifties.

The study of direct determinants sustaining the recent fertility levels can benefit from the rich surveys of the nineties. A cursory look at Table 7.6 shows much variance in values of SMAM post-1985. They move from a low of 21.3 to 26.0 and the quartiles are between 21.8 and 25.3.

Table 7.7 shows that in most Arab countries marriage is a major force in inhibiting potential fertility. With the exception of Egypt, it is more or roughly as important as contraception.

The range of the Bongaarts marriage indices (Cm from 0.49 to 0.70) across Arab countries suggests that its similar contribution in the early fifties has given way to different contributions during the nineties. Also, while the contribution of breast-feeding does not vary much across Arab countries (after excluding Sudan, the range of Bongaarts breast-feeding index (Ci) falls within 0.71 to 0.82), the variability in contraceptive uptake (Cc from 0.53 to 0.91) is quite noticeable. Clearly different direct determinants are shaping the close recent TFR levels.

Table 7.7 *Components of Bongaarts Model in some Arab countries whose total fertility rates falls within 3 to 5*

Country	Source	TFR	Cm	Ci	Cc	TF
North Africa						
Algeria	MCHS, 92	4.40	0.53	0.77	0.53	20.36
Egypt	DHS, 92	3.93	0.69	0.74	0.54	14.36
Sudan	MCHS, 92/93	4.60	0.64	0.64	0.91	12.34
Tunisia	DHS, 88	4.50	0.52	0.71	0.65	18.75
West Asia						
Bahrain	GCHS, 89	4.19	0.56	0.80	0.54	17.45
Qatar	GCHS, 87	4.49	0.49	0.82	0.74	15.08
Syria	MCHS, 93	4.20	0.57	0.75	0.63	15.59

Source: Calculated using Decomposition Method presented in Bongaarts and Potter, 1983.
Cm: marriage index; Ci: breast-feeding index; Cc: contraceptive uptake.

DETERMINANTS OF CHANGE AND DIFFERENTIALS

The study of direct determinants of fertility change and differentials is crucial in any attempt to understand why and how the change took place. The examination of the applicability of transition theories to the change observed in Arab countries is attempted in the following section, such an examination is closely dependent on the findings of this section.

Determinants of change within Arab countries

Many specific country studies have attempted to decompose the fertility change between WFS surveys and the more recent surveys that followed during the late 1980s and early 1990s. It should be recalled, however, that WFS surveys were conducted during the late seventies and early eighties. At that time many Arab countries had already started their fertility decline and WFS surveys captured different stages in their fertility transition. Egypt, Morocco and Tunisia were many years into their transition (estimates of TFR from WFS were: 5.3, 5.9 and 5.9 respectively), Jordan had just started its downward move (TFR estimate from WFS was 7.3, which probably reflects the increase in fertility that usually precedes a decline). For these countries an accurate documentation of the main forces responsible for the change (particularly the early change) is difficult to achieve through a simple decomposition exercise. However WFS data are available for three countries whose decline is of a more recent origin. These are Sudan, Syria and Yemen (whose TFR estimates from WFS were 6.2,[6] 7.3 and 8.5 respectively).

Table 7.8 provides a decomposition of factors responsible for the change in TFR between WFS and recent surveys.

Table 7.8 *Decomposition of factors responsible for the change in TFR in WFS and recent years*

	Egypt	Sudan	Tunisia	Syria
TFR at base year	5.27	6.20	5.90	7.30
Source	WFS, 80	WFS, 79	WFS, 78	WFS, 78
TFR at end year	3.90	4.60	4.50	4.20
Source	DHS, 92	MCHS, 92/93	DHS, 88	MCHS, 93
*% Distribution of change attributed to different factors**				
Cm (marriage)	−26.15	−71.72	−114.71	−52.20
Ci (breast-feeding)	34.12	−32.68	−12.23	−11.50
Cc (contraception)	−133.50	−23.60	−48.90	−56.82
TF	46.15	20.79	91.82	4.16
Interaction	−20.62	7.21	−15.98	16.36
Total	100	100	100	100

* Calculated using Decomposition Method presented in Bongaarts and Potter, 1983.

With the exception of Egypt, where contraception is leading the decline across time, marriage is playing a key role in bringing down fertility in the Arab countries considered. A detailed study on the role of nuptiality in fertility decline using standardization techniques to decompose the change in TFR to changes in marital status and marital fertility confirms that: 'in countries of sub-Saharan Africa and North Africa marriage is the dominant factor responsible for most or all of the fertility decline' while 'marriage as a factor in recent fertility declines in the countries of Asia and Latin America is of lesser importance' (Adlakha *et al*, 1991, p. 953).

The fact that changes in marital status have been more influential than other experiences is further confirmed by the studies of fertility declines in the West. Freedman (1982) notes that 'the demographic transition in the West resulted mainly from a decline in marital fertility while nuptiality levels were relatively stable' and that in terms of the Coale nuptiality index (usually denoted Im) that has often been used in the study of demographic transition in the West: 'Im (nuptiality) remained stable at relatively low levels. Im had fallen to relatively low levels much earlier – perhaps at the end of the Middle Ages, according to Hajnal's classic work (1965)' (p. 1).

Determinants of differentials among Arab countries.
An investigation of fertility differentials across Arab countries would invite many questions. For example, why the change in some Arab countries began earlier than others, why the decline was so late in some Arab countries and why some of the late starters had such a precipitous decline, why a country like Lebanon has been so different from the early fifties and is currently supporting a level of near replacement in the early nineties, why are some oil rich countries with reasonable low mortality indicators (like Saudi Arabia) sharing the same level of TFR with the poorest country and highest mortality in the Arab region (Yemen for example), what is keeping the level of TFR in a few Arab countries to a pretransitional level, have these countries succeeded in resisting the wave of change sweeping the Arab region (as reflected in UN reports) or is the recent survey information capturing a strong movement that is about to set in, what explains the non-systematic relation between the adoption of family planning policies and the magnitude of decline in TFR as well as the general weak link between socio-economic levels and fertility among Arab countries?

This section is one step towards the search being proposed. It uses the comparative approach to understand the differentials in fertility across the countries of Sudan, Syria and Yemen.

The specific questions being posed are:

(i) Knowing that the contraceptive prevalence rate (CPR) is equal in both Sudan and Yemen, what sustains the exceptionally large difference in TFR between the two countries: 4.6 in Sudan (for the 5 years preceding the

1992/93 MCHS and 7.7 in Yemen (for the 3 years preceding the 1991/92 MCHS)? Also, as the two countries are at close levels of socio-economic development, why do they not conform to the prevailing transition theories?

The search for the answers is not only prompted by the observed differences in TFR but also by the fact that Sudan and Yemen were identified as interesting case studies. The first is a country of observed delayed but strong change in fertility and the second of remaining pretransitional high fertility levels.

(ii) Syria and Sudan present the opposite picture. They are quite different in contraceptive levels and socio-economic development, but their TFR are very close. What are the direct and underlying determinants for such similarity?

(i) Comparative analysis of Sudan and Yemen Table 7.9 provides a summary of direct determinants generally believed to be mainly responsible for differentials in fertility levels. Bongaarts proximate indices are also provided. Table 7.9 suggests that marriage is the major explanatory variable justifying the difference in TFR between Sudan and Yemen. Contraceptive prevalence is equal. Also breast-feeding practice and its duration are quite close. Bongaarts indices provide a simple summary of such an observation.

A closer look at the data would lead us to question that the marriage distribution (proportions married by age) is the main explanatory variable for the difference between TFR in Sudan and Yemen. Table 7.10 reveals that the age-specific marital fertility rates for Sudan and Yemen appear to

Table 7.9 *Direct determinants of TFR and components of Bongaarts Model for Sudan and Yemen*

	Country	
	Sudan	*Yemen*
TFR	4.57	7.7
CPR (modern)	10 (7)	9.7 (6.1)
% Breast-feeding*	97	94
Mean duration of breast-feeding	19	17
SMAM	25.3	20.8
% Currently married 15–49	51%	72%
Source	MCHS, 92/93	MCHS, 91/92
Bongaarts Proximate Determinants		
Cm (marriage)	0.64	0.83
Ci (breast-feeding)	0.64	0.68
Cc (contraception)	0.91	0.91
TF	12.34	14.6

* Based on last birth.

Note: the TFR of 7.7 for Yemen differs from that shown in Table 7A.2 (5.49 for 1990–94). The latter figure was based on an extrapolation of the apparent rapid decline from 1980–84.

Table 7.10 Relevant statistics for Sudan and Yemen

Age group	% Single		A.S.M. Rates 0–4 before survey		% Currently married from those ever married		% Of currently married women in polygynous marriages	
	Sudan	Yemen	Sudan	Yemen	Sudan	Yemen	Sudan	Yemen
15–	89.4	75.3	0.306	0.295	96.2	95.1	8.5	3.0
20–	60.1	28.2	0.327	0.354	91.2	96.6	10.1	2.1
25–	32.8	9.1	0.291	0.327	93.3	94.8	15.6	5.0
30–	16.5	2.5	0.237	0.291	90.6	93.7	20.3	5.8
35–	7.0	1.0	0.173	0.254	91.1	93.4	25.3	8.1
40–	3.3	0.2	0.078	0.171	85.4	94.2	21.8	8.1
45–49	1.6	0.0	0.033	0.120	86.6	90.0	24.0	9.8
Total (15–49)	53.6	23.9			89.9	94.0	16.8	5.9

Age group	% Of ever married Women experiencing a pregnancy loss		Proportion of births breast-fed and given other types of milk by age of child		
	Sudan	Yemen	Age	Sudan	Yemen
15–	0.060	0.170	0–3	21.3	37.7
20–	0.097	0.205	4–11	31.4	51.0
25–	0.191	0.256			
30–	0.251	0.383			
35–	0.285	0.412			
40–	0.333	0.422			
45–49	0.339	0.439			
Total	0.235	0.344			

Source: Demographic and Maternal and Child Health Survey for Yemen (1991–2); Maternal and Child Health Survey for Sudan (1992–93)

be relatively close at young age groups; however, the difference between these rates for ages 35 onwards is extremely large. Yemen marital fertility rates are 1.5- to 3.5-fold the rate for Sudan. This in itself would tell us that differences within marriage are responsible for some of the differences between TFR for Sudan and Yemen.

The calculation of TFR standardized by the age marriage pattern for Yemen provides a TFR for Sudan (assuming that Sudan had the same proportions currently married by age as Yemen) of 5.1. In other words the marriage distribution only explains 0.5 of the difference between TFR for Sudan and Yemen and that as much as a 2.6 difference needs to be explained by within-marriage variations.[7]

Other statistics in Table 7.10 would guide us to the source of variations between Sudan and Yemen. Marriage dissolution in Sudan appears more frequent than Yemen and may explain some of the differences in marital rates.[8] However, other factors presented in Table 7.10 may be better candidates for the observed differences: these are polygyny (influencing exposure to the risk of pregnancy) and intensity of breast-feeding (affected by supplementation and influencing the resumption of ovulation). It is interesting to note that intrauterine mortality (reducing the number of live births) does not explain the low marital fertility rates for Sudan. Two other factors in Sudan may contribute to its reduced marital fertility: the high prevalence of circumcision and the high rural-to-urban movement of men in search of jobs and internal displacement connected to the war.

The prevalence of circumcision in Sudan is around 89 per cent, the pharaonic circumcision reaches 82 per cent (DHS 89–90). The Rushwan (1980) study shows that the incidence of pelvic inflammatory diseases (PID) is more than three times as great in patients with pharaonic circumcision. The Aziz (1980) study reveals that PID is linked to infertility and difficult child-birth. Caesarean sections in Sudan constitute around 20 per cent of hospital deliveries (MCHS 1993) while it is only 10 per cent in Yemen (MCHS 91–92).

Also, while both Sudan and Yemen experience temporary migration of husbands to work in Saudi Arabia and the Gulf states, 'Sudan experiences of drought, civil war and armed conflict produced unprecedented displacement problems, it is believed that at least six million persons are involved (*in mass movement*) and that Khartoum alone is host to at least two million, mainly from the south and west' (Eltigani, 1995, p. 52).

The analysis, so far, reveals that many direct determinants of fertility that are generally believed less important and ignored in proximate determinants analysis are playing a key role in inhibiting marital fertility in Sudan. It is these factors that underlie the differences in TFR between Sudan and Yemen. Once the direct causes of fertility differentials are identified, the reasons justifying why socio-economic development indices across countries do not follow the demographic wisdom (as illustrated in Table 7.11) become obvious.

Table 7.11   *Indicators of development for Sudan, Syria and Yemen*

	Year	Sudan	Syria	Yemen
Human Development Index	1993	0.359 (low)	0.69 (medium)	0.366 (low)
Urban population as % of total population	1992	52	67	53
IMR	1992	99	36	106
Adult illiteracy (%)	1990			
Females		88	49	74
Males		73	36	62
Female share of labour force (as % of total population)	1992	22	18	14

Source: World Development Report, 1994 (World Bank, 1994).

Transition theories do not posit a one way relation between economic development and polygyny, breast-feeding supplementation, spousal separation, circumcision. etc. What first appears as a contradiction serves as a reminder that: 'fertility is a social feature. Individuals must not be described by certain personal characteristics (*or even a macro summation of these*), but their situation must be seen in a social context' (Fargues, 1989, p. 148).

(ii) Comparative analysis of Sudan and Syria   Sudan and Syria summary statistics presented in Table 7.12 provide the complementary picture for Yemen and Sudan. They appear to have similar marriage patterns; slightly

Table 7.12   *Direct determinants of TFR and components of Bongaarts Model for Sudan and Syria*

	Country	
	Sudan	Syria
TFR	4.57	4.2
CPR (modern)	10 (7)	40 (28)
% Breast-feeding*	97	92
Mean duration of breast-feeding	19	13
SMAM	25.3	24.5
% Currently married 15–49	51 %	54 %
Source	MCHS, 92/93	MCHS, 93
Bongaarts Proximate Determinants		
Cm (marriage)	0.64	0.57
Ci (breast-feeding)	0.64	0.75
Cc (contraception)	0.91	0.63
TF	12.34	15.59

* Based on last birth.

different breast-feeding patterns but markedly different contraceptive prevalence rate. On the face of it one would expect that the TFR for Sudan would be much higher than for Syria. The earlier analysis for Sudan would suggest that factors other than those presented in the table have reduced the expected difference between Sudan and Syria.

Table 7.13 confirms this notion. Polygyny is much more widely practised in Sudan than Syria, marriage is less stable, circumcision and displacement are not playing a role in Syria. It is interesting to note that the pattern of breast-feeding in Sudan in which supplementation is more prevalent than in Syria, may be offsetting some of the fertility reducing effect of longer and more widely practised breast-feeding in Sudan. Consulting Table 7.11, which places Syria at a higher development scale than Sudan, the large difference between contraceptive prevalence in the two countries (40 per cent against 10 per cent) follows the expected relation.

Given the effect of factors other than contraceptive practice and breast-feeding duration in reducing marital fertility in Sudan, the relevant question is not why TFR's are similar but why both countries are experiencing similar marriage patterns in terms of SMAM and proportions single.

Courbage (1994) provides concise and very revealing insights into fertility transition in Syria. The following summarizes the main points of his analysis with minor additional supporting statistics. He points to the reluctance of the Syrian government to intervene directly to reduce the population growth and its reliance on economic development and the education and employment of women to reduce family size. He asserts that despite positive changes in the economic and social environment, fertility in Syria between 1960 and 1985 was slow to respond. 'This lack of change in reproductive behaviour, in contrast with the definite progress made in most political, economic and social areas, shed some doubt on the assumption that there is an automatic link between modernization and population growth' (Courbage, 1994, p. 143).

The Courbage analysis contrasts two phases in Syria's transition from 1960 to 1985, where fertility was not showing a strong declining movement, and from 1985 to 1990, when the sharp decline was felt.

Phase (1) was characterized by an increased standard of living (9.4 per cent average annual growth in national wealth between 1970 and 1981), a drop in child mortality (in 1981, the average woman had 6.6 surviving children at the end of her childbearing years, compared with 4.9 in 1960), and above all an improvement in female education. The percentage distribution of women 15–49 by level of education showed clearly a decline in the uneducated and a major improvement at all other educational categories. All these changes failed to be translated into a decline in TFR.

The second phase in Syria's transition occurred after the mid-1980s; Courbage argues that the main difference between the two phases was in a serious economic recession (decline in average annual growth rate of gross

Table 7.13 Relevant statistics for Sudan and Syria

Age group	% Single		A.S.M.Rates 0–4 preceding survey		% Currently married from those ever married		% Of currently married women in polygynous marriages		Proportion of births breast-fed and given other types of milk by age of child		
	Sudan	Syria	Sudan	Syria	Sudan	Syria	Sudan	Syria	Age of child	Sudan	Syria
15–	89.4	86.1	0.306	0.376	96.2	94.2	8.5	1.3	0–3	21.3	12.9
20–	60.1	57.7	0.327	0.350	91.2	98.5	10.1	3.0	4–11	31.4	18.8
25–	32.8	30.5	0.291	0.304	93.3	97.4	15.6	5.1			
30–	16.5	17.0	0.237	0.222	90.6	98.1	20.3	7.3			
35–	7.0	8.8	0.173	0.142	91.1	96.4	25.3	7.0			
40–	3.3	6.3	0.078	0.068	85.4	93.4	21.8	7.9			
45–49	1.6	5.2	0.033	0.012	86.6	89.9	24.0	8.9			
Total	53.6	42.6			89.9	96.5	16.8	5.8			

Source: Maternal and Child Health Survey for Sudan (1992–93); Maternal and Child Health Survey for Syria (1993).

domestic product (GDP) from 9.9 to 1.8 per cent during 1970–80 to 1980–92) and an increased income tax (an income tax that made up only 6.8 per cent of revenue during the prosperous 1970s reached in some recent years a quarter to a third of government revenues). Economic hardships forced females into the employment market. (The proportion of women employed in non-agricultural work that had dropped from 10 per cent in 1960 to 8 per cent in 1981, rose to 12 per cent in 1989; the World Development Report (1994) (World Bank, 1994) shows that the female share of labour force in 1992 was around 18 per cent.)

Finally Courbage states: 'It took a serious economic recession for fertility to decrease in Syria. Educating women without integrating them into the job market has little effect on fertility' (Courbage, 1994, p. 146).

Turning to the Sudan case, Sudan statistics do show a drop in infant mortality (from 149 per 1000 in 1970 to 99 per 1000 in 1992), improvement in female education (from 7 per cent net enrolment in secondary education in 1970 to 22 per cent in 1991) and a small change in employment across time (from 20 per cent in 1970 to 22 per cent in 1992). It is interesting to observe that the level of female employment in Sudan as early as 1970 was much higher than the comparable levels for Syria (12 per cent) and is even higher than the 1992 female employment in Syria (18 per cent).

Sudan data also show deteriorating economic conditions. According to World Bank estimates, the average annual growth rate of GNP per capita declined from 0.8 per cent during the period 1965–80 to −2.4 per cent during 1980–91 (UNICEF, 1994). As Table 7.6 indicates, the change in SMAM was moderate between 1970 and 1980 (from 18.7 to 21.5) and accelerated to reach the level of 25.3 during the nineties.

For both Syria and Sudan, economic hardships leading to postponement of marriage accelerated the fertility decline. For Syria, hardships were coupled by positive improvements in education. Employed educated women faced with economic constraints changed their reproductive strategies and opted for utilization of family planning methods. Both marriage delays and use of contraceptives were the direct determinants of transition.

For Sudan, the high percentage of employed women in a context of low educational levels did not change their reproductive strategies but led to some delays in marriage. The increased hardships of the 1990s further delayed marriage and decreased fertility. Sudan experienced only small increases in contraceptive practice and possibly an increased practice in polygyny. According to Sudanese scholars, the practice of polygyny is associated with poverty. The search for extra working hands and the low costs of marriage within subsistence economies support the high prevalence of polygyny (Eltigani, 2000). For Sudan the increase in age at marriage was not mainly prompted by education or even by high employment. It is clearly blamed on economic hardships.

THEORIES OF TRANSITION

Fertility changes and their underlying determinants have captured the attention of demographers for centuries. The demographic literature is abundant with empirical evidence linking decline in mortality, economic development, education, employment of women, family planning programmes and fertility decline. The hypothesis being advanced range from: the movement from fatalistic attitudes to some control of one's life facilitated by community-level reductions in child loss[9] to another formulation (more closely attached to socio-economic stimulants) where conscious and complex calculations lead to a calculated choice of a smaller number of children. The calculations are heavily governed by the costs and benefits of children. Urbanization, child employment and expected future remittances are key indicators used to ascertain the relation between socio-economic development and fertility change. The theory, while heavily influenced by economic considerations, leaves ample room to allow for other more socially oriented factors. For example, changes in the definition of women's role and improvements in her status can be introduced in the calculus formula by accounting for self-fulfilment (outside the home boundaries) and lost employment opportunities. Indeed, recent developments have assigned women's education and employment a central role in explaining fertility change. While the specific factors advocated and their level of operation (aggregate level of education, gross national product or individual traits) tend to vary, the main theme is that, the driving force is in the existence of micro level considerations and judicious calculation of costs and benefits.

A third stance that is receiving more and more recognition is in ideational innovations, where societies become more at ease in grasping and adopting new ideas and behaviour. Here the movement to smaller size is more in conformity with acceptable modes of practice. A latent desire for a smaller (than actual) number of children that may not have been explicitly formulated gains more strength to be translated into actual adoption of family planning. The shift here to smaller number is less a result of micro-economics but more of a diffusion of new standards and acceptable technology. Many believers in the power of family planning programmes in speeding fertility decline have argued that such programmes do not only provide the means for those wanting a smaller number of children through better accessibility and more convenient contraceptives but that they also influence the desire through legitimizing and obtaining societal approval for the value of smaller families and birth control methods.

The focus of traditional transition theory (development, demand, costs–benefits) was generally on motivation, while the applications of the diffusion approach emphasized the means to fertility control.

Greenhalgh (1996) comments that while the search for the diffusion theorization was prompted by a realization that social and economic variables,

stressed in classic transition theory, were not sufficient to guide the interpretation of fertility change and that cultural variables hold more promise,
it turned out that the 'notion, diffusion, was embedded in the theory of
modernization developed at mid century. Thus, instead of moving beyond
modernization theory when they moved beyond social and economic
hypotheses, demographers succeeded in building important parts of it back
into theory of culture' (Greenhalgh, 1996, p. 57). She also states: 'Diffusion
theory's long life span rests in part on its ability to provide an ostensibly
scientific concept that reflects many demographers' abiding belief that
fertility decline and its means, as well as the cultural notions about the
family that give rise to it, are Western innovations that "diffused" to backward third-world peoples' (p. 58).

Whatever theory, indicators or level of analysis adopted there exist a
number of studies that purport to support the underlying hypothesis. There
also seems to be enough empirical evidence to refute the same hypothesis.
Those different theories and conflicting evidence are not necessarily proof
of the futility of the prevailing wisdom but they are simply an indication
that in areas of human behaviour there are a complex interplay of factors
and many contradictory decisions that may have to go hand in hand. The
resulting change in reproductive behaviour is more of a balance of forces
and the question is where such a balance lies. The answer to determinants
of change needs to go beyond cross-national evidence to detailed country-
level investigations that give due recognition to the cultural and normative
context in which reproduction occurs.

The current analysis is sensitive to this need, it does not attempt to advance
a particular theory of change or even refute it. Indeed, the analysis clearly
indicates that one transition theory cannot explain or guide the interpretation of change across a region that embodies immense diversity of economic
and political organizations. The number of case studies, discussed so far,
challenge the main theme that prevails in all the different transition theories
– that is, modernization and motivation. The idea that a decline in fertility
is synonymous with a population becoming more Western and advanced
and is prompted by motivation and desire for smaller numbers does not
apply to the Arab countries considered here. Economic hardships are driving
the change and the change is occurring despite remaining ideals favouring
large families.

Tables 7.14 and 7.15 provide some relevant statistics on fertility desires
and their change across time. Among the three countries that managed to
reduce their TFR to moderate levels, only Egypt shows a desire compat-
ible with actual fertility. Both Sudan and Syria retain larger family ideals
which are comparable to the ideals for Yemen, whose TFR is still at
maximum levels observed in human societies. The change in TFR in Egypt
appears to be responding to the change in desire and in Syria to respond

Table 7.14 *Percentage not wanting additional child*

Age	Egypt	Sudan	Syria	Yemen
15–	9.4	2.9	5.6	6.2
20–	34.3	5.1	18.5	17.7
25–	59.6	10.9	32.3	29.8
30–	77.8	15.5	50.8	39.9
35–	81.3	26.8	59.7	46.6
40–	81.4	35.0	65.2	52.4
45–	58.9	35.9	53.5	47.5
Total	63.0	19.0	42.0	35.0

Source: MCHS reports for different countries.

Table 7.15 *Desired number of children and TFR in different countries and time periods*

	Egypt		Sudan		Syria		Yemen	
Time periods	Desired	TFR	Desired	TFR	Desired	TFR	Desired	TFR
Late 1970s*	4.1	5.27	6.4	6.20	6.1	7.30	5.4	8.51
Early 1990s**	3.1	4.60	6.0	4.60	5.0	4.20	5.4	7.70

* WFS Reports.
** MCHS Reports.

partially to changes in desires and partially to change in marriage pattern. For both Sudan and Yemen, the change is occurring despite the lack of change in desire.

CONCLUSION

The analysis did confirm that fertility levels for the Arab region during the early 1950s were quite close and relatively high. The level itself was shared by many non-Arab countries but its dispersion was much smaller in the Arab region. Also, the timing of the decline, while again similar to many non-Arab countries, is much more centred (during the sixties and early seventies). This tendency to cluster in terms of level and timing of change is the main distinctive feature of the Arab fertility transition. The clustering was very much supported by patterns of marriage and breast-feeding that did not play a significant role in inhibiting fertility.

The picture of an Arab region with excessive fertility, late and slow changes is much more attributable to the fact that the regional non-Arab pretransitional experiences have included quite variant fertility levels and dispersed timing of change. Contrary to the Arab experience, traditional reproductive regimes (particularly nuptiality and postpartum practices) did inhibit pretransitional fertility in many parts of Asia and Europe.

The period of the mid-sixties to mid-eighties reflected much wider variations in fertility levels among Arab countries as well as different paths of change. The mid nineties TFR are showing a movement towards reclustering again between 3 and 4. However, this new move is being supported by widely different proximate determinants, particularly marriage and contraception.

The decline across time has been strongly affected by changes in marital status. Also, the current lower levels, in many Arab countries, are not necessarily (or at least solely) a result of a high contraceptive uptake.

These two features are seen as a justification of some of the anomalies observed when transition theories are advanced to explain the decline in fertility. These theories are geared more to describe changes in reproduction that are led by changes in marital fertility shaped by contraceptive uptake. The latter expresses a controlled act to reduce family size that responds to articulated desires rather than an indirect exposure effect of delayed marriage, spousal separation or a biological health effect.

The detailed comparative analysis of Sudan, Syria and Yemen has identified worsening economic conditions (rather than development) as a key determinant of fertility decline and has shown how different contextual forces (educational levels for example) interact with the same determinant producing different dynamics that nevertheless have produced similar levels of fertility.

It was illustrated by these studies how the comparative detailed country level investigations with due recognition of contextual forces would explain the similarity of (or the large difference in) TFR in Arab countries that are widely different (or similar) in their socio-economic development and in their desires for a smaller family size.

The analysis also challenges the main themes of transition theories that link fertility reductions to modernization and motivation. It was illustrated that the decline in fertility in some Arab countries is not synonymous with a population becoming more advanced, and that the reduction is not motivated by a search for a lower number of children but despite the desire for a higher number.

ACKNOWLEDGEMENTS

This paper is produced under the framework of a project on the 'New Demography of the Arab Region'. The project is a collaborative effort between Arab scholars, and national and international institutions. It is coordinated by SRC and supported by Mellon, Hewlett and Ford Foundations.

The assistance of Mr. Amr El-Sayed in compiling the statistics and tables for this paper is appreciated.

Table 7A.1 Measures of TFR for different Arab countries by year of reference and source of data

	Source	75	76	77	78	79	80	81	82	83	84	85	86	87	88	89	90	91	92	93	94	95
North Africa																						
Algeria	MCHS 92						7.10					6.30					4.40					
	UN 95			7.17					6.35					4.97								
Egypt	WFS 80				5.27	5.28																
	DHS 88		5.70					5.10			4.85		4.66	4.38								
	MCHS 91					5.84					5.17					4.55	4.31	4.13				
	DHS 92						5.70					5.20					4.23	3.93				
Libya	UN 95			7.38					7.17					6.87								
	DHS 95			5.27					5.06	5.60				4.58	4.84				3.78			
	UN 95									7.91					6.35						4.10	
Morocco	MCHS 95				5.90					5.80					4.84			4.13				
	WFS 79/80			5.90																		
	DHS 87						6.30		5.10			4.84	4.90	4.40								
	DHS 92																4.13	4.04				
Sudan	UN 95			6.67					6.42					6.10					4.57			
	DHS 95							7.30					6.66					4.25				
	WFS 79			6.02	7.15																	
	DHS 89/90									6.33					4.96	4.60						
Tunisia	MCHS 93																			3.43		
	UN 95								4.88					3.94								
	WFS 78		5.80					5.40														
	DHS88		5.80					5.40					4.40									
	U.N 95											4.40										
	MCHS 95																					3.20

Source	75	76	77	78	79	80	81	82	83	84	85	86	87	88	89	90	91	92	93	94	95
North Asia																					
Bahrain																					
CHS 89			5.62					4.90					4.29								
UN 95			5.23					4.63					4.08								
GULF 95																					3.13
Iraq																					
CHS 89			6.56					6.35						5.25							
UN 95													6.15								
Jordan																					
WFS 76	7.4																				
FFHS83							6.60														
DHS 90				8.53					7.48					5.86							
UN 95			7.38					6.76													
Kuwait																					
CHS 87			5.89					4.87					3.94								
UN 95												6.00	6.5								
Lebanon																					
MCHS 96																			2.53		
UN 95			4.30					3.79					3.42								
Oman																					
CHS 88/89				10.13				9.82					8.70	7.84							
UN 95			7.20				7.20						7.20								
GULF 95																					6.65
Qatar																					
CHS 87			6.49					5.02				4.49									
UN 95			6.11					5.45					4.70								
Saudi Arabia																					
CHS 87			7.28					7.28					6.5								
UN 95													6.80								
Syria																					
WFS 78						7.50															
MCHS 93																		4.22			
UN 95							7.73					6.76				4.20					
U.A. Emirates																					
CHS 87			7.44					7.38					6.66								
UN 95			5.66					5.23				5.9	4.6								
Yemen																					
WFS 79			8.51																		
MCHS 91/92							11.36				10.60				7.62		7.70				
UN 95			7.61				7.60						7.60								

Source: UN: United Nation report 1995 for Total Fertility Rates during 1950–89.
CHS: Child Health Surveys in Gulf Countries MCHS: Maternal and child health surveys conducted under the framework of Pan Arab Project for Child Development
WFS: World Fertility Surveys DHS: Demographic and Health Survey FFHS: Fertility and Family Health Survey

Table 7A.2 *Total fertility rates for Arab countries*

Arab Countries (Size of pop. in thousands during 1990–5)	Years 50–54	55–59	60–64	65–69	70–74	75–79	80–84	85–89	90–94	Latest survey adjusted 90–94**
North Africa										
Simple average	6.90	7.01	7.10	7.02	6.70	6.34	5.83	5.14	3.74	3.90
Weighted average	6.82	7.00	7.08	6.85	6.33	5.99	5.55	4.89	3.67*	3.89*
Algeria (24,935)	7.28	7.28	7.38	7.48	7.38	7.17	6.35	4.97	3.47[a]	3.64
Egypt (56,312)	6.56	6.97	7.07	6.56	5.53	5.27	5.06	4.58	3.58[a]	3.99
Libya (4,545)	6.87	6.97	7.17	7.48	7.58	7.38	7.17	6.87	4.44[a]	4.55
Morocco (24,334)	7.17	7.17	7.15	7.09	6.89	5.90	5.10	4.40	3.55[a]	3.69
Sudan (25,585)	6.67	6.67	6.67	6.67	6.67	6.67	6.42	6.10	4.19[a]	4.15
Tunisia (8,080)	6.87	6.97	7.17	6.83	6.15	5.66	4.88	3.94	3.18[b]	3.37
West Asia										
Simple average	7.04	7.06	7.21	7.20	6.89	7.19	6.70	5.92	5.08	4.87
Weighted average	7.18*	7.20*	7.33*	7.37*	7.27*	7.67*	7.39*	6.52*	5.49*	5.29*
Bahrain (490)	6.97	6.79	7.17	6.97	5.94	5.62[c]	4.90[c]	4.29[c]	3.76[c]	3.57
Iraq (18,078)	7.17	7.17	7.17	7.17	7.11	6.56	6.35	6.15	5.97[b]	5.25(85–9)
Jordan (4,259)	7.38	7.38	7.99	7.99	7.79	7.38	6.76	6.00	5.33[b]	4.56
Kuwait (2,143)	7.21	7.21	7.31	7.41	7.14[d]	6.83[d]	6.53[d]	6.50[d]	6.47[d]	6.47
Lebanon (2,555)	5.74	6.15	6.35	6.05	4.92	4.30	3.79	3.42	3.09[b]	2.53(91–5)
Oman (1,751)	7.20	7.20	7.20	7.20	7.20	10.13[c]	9.82[c]	8.70[c]	7.46[c]	7.42
Qatar (485)	6.97	6.97	6.97	6.97	6.76	6.49[c]	5.02[c]	4.37[c]	3.80[c]	3.70
Saudi Arabia (16,048)	7.17	7.17	7.26	7.26	7.30	7.28	7.28	6.80	6.35[b]	6.35
Syria (12,348)	7.09	7.09	7.46	7.79	7.69	7.44	7.38	6.66	4.13[a]	3.69
Emirates (1,671)	6.97	6.97	6.87	6.76	6.35	5.66	5.23	4.60	4.05[b]	4.05
Yemen (11,311)	7.61	7.61	7.61	7.61	7.60	11.36[c]	10.60[c]	7.62[c]	5.49[c]	5.49
Total										
Simple average	6.99	7.04	7.17	7.13	6.82	6.89	6.39	5.65	4.6	4.48
Weighted average	6.95*	7.07*	7.16*	7.04*	6.68*	6.58*	6.19*	5.45*	4.27*	4.31*

Source: United Nations (1995) for pop. size and TFR during 1950–89, unless indicated. For TFR 1990–4.
a: The relative decline in the last two periods preceding the most recent health survey is used to extrapolate 85–9 UN measures.
b: TFR was estimated using UN measures and assuming the relative decline prevailing during 80–84 to 85–9 applies between 85–9 and 90–4.
c: The last survey estimates replacing UN measures for 1975 to 1989 and extrapolated for 1990–4.
d: Using vital registration data until 1985–9 and extrapolated for 1990–4.
* Weighted using pop. size (World Population Prospects, UN, 1994).
** Adjusted to correspond to 1990–4 using the last two fertility measures from the latest survey (when two measures are available, or the latest survey estimate if lower than extrapolated (Iraq, Lebanon). Otherwise, the extrapolated measures for 1990–4 is retained (Kuwait, Saudi Arabia, United Arab Emirates).

Table 7A.3 Date of the onset of fertility decline* and magnitude of decline over 15 years** for Arab countries and other countries

Country	1950	1955	1960	1965	1970	1975	1980 +
Arab countries							
North Africa			Egypt (1.8) Tunisia(1.51)	Morocco(1.99)	Algeria(2.41)		Libya Sudan
West Asia			Bahrain(1.55) Lebanon(2.05)	Emirates(1.53)	Iraq(0.96) Jordan (1.79) Qatar (2.39)	Syria(3.31) Oman (2.71) Yemen (5.81)	Saudi Arabia Kuwait +
Other countries							
Africa							
Eastern Africa		Mauritius (2.72) Reunion (1.92)		Zimbabwe (1.31)		Kenya Rwanda Zambia	Djibouti +
Middle Africa							
Southern Africa			South Africa (1.42)		Botswana (1.36) Cape Verde (2.3)	Swaziland Mauritania	
Western Africa							
Asia							
Eastern Asia	Japan (0.75)	Rep.of Korea (1.96)	China (2.35) Hong Kong (2.99)	Dem. Peo. Korea (4.23)		Mongolia +	
South Central Asia		Kazakhstan (1.09) Sri Lanka (1.44)	Iran (0.76)	India (1.22) Kyrgystan (0.91) Tajikistan (1.18) Turkmenistan (1.55) Uzbekistan (1.44)	Bangladesh (2.22)		
South Eastern Asia	Singapore(2.94)	Brunei Darussalam (1.6) Malaysia (1.79) Philippines (1.59)	Thailand (2.15) Cambodia (2.19)	East Timor (0.77) Indonesia (1.51) Myanmar (1.1)	Viet Nam (1.63)		

continued

Table 7A.3 *(continued)*

Country	1950	1955	1960	1965	1970	1975	1980+
West Asia (non-Arab)	Turkey (1.23)	Armenia (1.45) Cyprus (1)	Azerbaijan (2.02)	Georgia (0.34) +		Israel +	
Caribbean	Netherlands (2.35)	Barbados (1.93) Dominican (1.77) Martinique (1.63) Puerto Rico (1.82) Trinidad Tobago (1.85)	Bahamas (1.12) Cuba (2.54) Guadeloupe (2.55)		Jamaica (2.4)	Haiti +	
Central America		Costa Rica (2.78)	El Salvador (1.15) Panama (1.86)	Honduras (1.42) Mexico (2.4) Nicaragua (1.17)	Belize (1.55)		Guatemala +
South America		Brazil (1.45) Chile (1.7)	Colombia (2.62) Ecuador (1.3) Guyana (2.21) Paraguay (1.92) Peru (1.47) Suriname (2.36) Venezuela (2.19)	Bolivia (1.26)			Argentina + Uruguay +
Oceania	New Caledonia (1.74) Guam (1.71) Samoa (1.4)	Fiji (2.59)	French Polynesia (2.27)	Vanuatu (1.4)	Solomon Islands (1.41)		Papua New G. +

Source: Based on United Nations (1995).

* The date of the decline is the date followed by a decrease in TFR of at least (0.7) over a period of 10 years or if such a precipitous decline has not occurred it is the date marking a fall of 10% in fertility from its pretransitional maximum.

The dates calculated by the latter criteria are identified by +.

** Figures in parentheses are the magnitude of decline over 15 years for those countries whose decline started at or prior to 1970.

REFERENCES

Abdel-Azeem, F., Farid, S. and Khalifia A. (eds) (1993) *Egypt Maternal and Child Health Survey 1991*. Cairo: Central Agency for Public Mobilization and Statistics and PAPCHILD/League of Arab States.

Adlakha, A., Ayad, M. and Kumar, S.(1991) 'The role of nuptiality in fertility decline: a comparative analysis'. *Proceedings of the Demographic and Health Surveys World Conference*, Washington. DC. vol 2, pp. 947–64. Columbia, MD: Macro International Inc.

Algeria Maternal and Child Health Survey (1994) Cairo: National Office of Statistics (Algiers) and PAPCHILD/League of Arab States.

Al-Mazrou, Y. and Farid, S. (eds) (1991) *Saudi Arabia Child Health Survey*. Riyadh: Ministry of Health.

Al-Muhaideb, A., Abdul-Ghafour, A. and Farid. S. (eds) (1991) *United Arab Emirates Child Health Survey*. Abu Dhabi: Ministry of Health.

Aloui, T., Ayad, M. and Fourati, H. (1989) *Enquete Demogrphique et de Sante en Tunisie 1988*. Columbia, MD: Office National de la Famille et de la Population (Tunis) and IRD/Macro Systems Inc.

Al-Rashoud. R. and Farid, S. (1991) *Kuwait Child Health Survey*. Kuwait: Ministry of Health.

Azelmat, M., Ayad, M. and Housni, E. (1993) *Maroc: Enquete Nationale sur la Population et la Sante 1992*. Columbia, MD: Ministere de la Sante Publique (Rabat) and Macro International Inc.

Azelmat, M., Ayad. M. and Housni, E. (1996) *Maroc: Enquete de Panel sur la Population et la Sante 1995*. Calverton, MD: Ministere de la Sante Publique (Rabat) and Macro International Inc.

Aziz, F.A. (1980) 'Gynecologic and obstetric complications of female circumcision'. *International Journal of Gynaecology and Obstetrics*, 17 (6), pp. 560–3.

Bongaarts, J. and Potter, P.G. (1983) *Fertility, Biology, and Behavior: An Analysis of the Proximate Determinants*. New York/London: Academic Press.

Caldwell, J. (1986) 'Routes to low mortality in poor countries'. *Population and Development Review*, 12 (2), pp. 171–220.

Caldwell, J.C. and Caldwell, P. (1988) 'Is the Asian family planning model suited to Africa'. *Studies in Family Planning*, 19 (1), pp. 19–28.

Casterline, J.B. (1991) 'Fertility transition in Asia', paper presented at seminar on 'The course of Fertility Transition in Sub-Saharan Africa', IUSSP Committee on Comparative Analysis of Fertility and University of Zimbabwe, Harare, Zimbabwe.

Cleland, J. (1987) 'Demand theories of the fertility transition: an iconoclastic view'. *Population Studies*, no 41, pp. 5–30.

Coale, A. (1986) 'The decline of fertility in Europe since the eighteenth century as a chapter in demographic history', Chapter 1 in A.J. Coale and S. Watkins (eds), *The Decline of Fertility in Europe,* The revised proceedings of a conference on the Princeton European Fertility Project, Princeton: Princeton University Press.

Courbage, Y. (1994) 'Fertility transition in Syria: from implicit population policy to explicit economic crisis'. *International Family Planning Perspectives,* 20 (4), pp. 142–6.

Egypt Demographic and Health Survey 1995: Preliminary Report (1996) Calverton, MD: National Population Council (Cairo) and Macro International Inc.

El-Khorazaty, N. (1996) 'Characterization and determinants of reproductive patterns in the Arab world: 1976–1995'. *Proceeding of the Arab Regional Population Conference*, vol 1, pp. 375–434. Cairo: CDC Press.

Eltigani El, E. (1995) 'Health implications of displacement in Sudan', in E.E. Eltigani (ed.), *War and Drought in Sudan*. University Press of Florida.

Eltigani, E.E. (2000) 'Understanding the fertility decline in Northern Sudan: An analysis of determinants. *Genus*, 57 (no. 1–2).

El-Zanaty, F., Sayed, H., Zaky, H. and Way, A. (1993) *Egypt Demographic and Health Survey 1992*. Calverton, MD: National Population Council (Cairo) and Macro International Inc.

Enquête Nationale sur la Fécondité et la Planification Familiale au Maroc 1978 (1979–80) Ministere de la Sante Publique Direction des Affaires Techniques Service D'Exploitation Mecanographique.

Enquête Nationale sur la Planification Familiale, la Fécondité et la Santé de la Population au Maroc 1987 (1989) Azelmat, M., Ayad, M., Ayad, M. and Belhachmi, H. Rabat: Ministere de la Sante Publique, Rabat et Institute for Resource Development/Westinghouse.

Fargues, P. (1989) 'The decline of Arab fertility'. *Population* 44, (English selection) (1), pp. 47–175.

Farid, S. (1996) 'Transitions in demographic and health patterns in the Arab region'. *Proceeding of the Arab Regional Population Conference*, vol 1, pp. 435–62. Cairo: CDC Press.

Freedman, R. (1982) 'Introduction in L.T. Ruzicka (ed.), *Nuptiality and Fertility*. Proceedings of a IUSSP Seminar held in Bruges (Belguim), 1979.

Freedman, R. (1995) 'Asia's recent fertility decline and prospects for future demographic change'. *Asia Pacific Population Research Reports*, no 1.

Greenhalgh, S. (1996) 'The social construction of population science: an intellectual, institutional, and political history of twentieth-century demography'. *Society for Comparative Study and History*, 38 (1), pp. 26–62.

Hajnal, J. (1965) 'European marriage patterns in perspective', in D.V. Glass and D.E.C. Eversley (eds), *Population in History*. Chicago: Aldine.

Hallouda, A.M., Amin, S.Z. and Farid, S. (eds) (1983) *The Egyptian Fertility Survey*, vol II. Cairo: Central Agency for Public Mobilization and Statistics.

Heiberg, M. and Ovensen, G. (1993) *Palestinian Society in Gaza, West Bank and Arab Jerusalem; A Survey of Living Conditions*, FAFO reports 151. Oslo: Falch Hurtigtrykk.

Iraq Child Health Survey 1989: Preliminary Report (1990) Baghdad: Ministry of Health.

Jordan Fertility Survey 1975 (1976) Amman, Hashemite Kingdom of Jordan: Department of Statistics.

Lebanon Maternal and Child Health Survey 1995: Preliminary Report (1996) Cairo: Ministry of Health (Beirut) and PAPCHILD/League of Arab States.

Libya Maternal and Child Health Survey 1995: Preliminary Report (1996) Cairo: General Committee for Health and Social Security (Tripoli) and PAPCHILD/League of Arab States.

Lutz, W. (1987) 'Culture, religion, and fertility: A global view'. *Genus*, 43, 3–4, pp. 15–35.

Nagi, M. (1984) 'Trends and differentials in Moslem fertility'. *Journal of Biosocial Science*, 16, pp. 189–204.

Obermeyer, C.M. (1995) 'Reproductive rights in the West and in the Middle East: a cross-cultural perspective, in C. Makhlouf Obermeyer (ed) *Family, Gender, and Population in the Middle East Policies in Context.* Cairo: The American University in Cairo Press.

Obermeyer, C.M. (1992) 'Islam, women and politics'. *Population and Development Review*, 18 (1), 33–57.

Raftery, A.E., Lewis, S.M. and Aghajanian, A. (1995) 'Demand and ideation? Evidence from the Iranian Martial Fertility Decline'. *Demography*, 32 (2).

Rushwan, H. (1980) 'Pelvic inflammatory disease in Sudanese women', *unpublished paper prepared for the International Symposium on Pelvic Inflammatory Disease, Atlanta, GA.*

Salman, A., Al-Jaber, K. and Farid, S. (eds) (1991) *Qatar Child Health Survey.* Doha: Ministry of Health.

Sayed, H., Osman, M., El-Zanaty, F. and Way, A. (1989) *Egypt Demographic and Health Survey 1988.* Columbia, MD: National Population Council (Cairo) and Institute for Resource Development/Macro Systems, Inc.

Sudan Demographic and Health Survey 1989/90 (1991) Columbia, MD: Department of Statistics (Khartoum) and Macro International Inc.

Sudan Fertility Survey 1977 (1979) Khartoum: Ministry of National Planning, Department of Statistics.

Sudan Maternal and Child Health Survey 1993 (1995) Cairo: Federal Ministry of Health (Khartoum) and PAPCHILD/League of Arab States.

Suleiman, M., Al-Ghassany, A. and Farid, S. (eds) (1992) *Oman Child Health Survey (1992).* Muscat: Ministry of Health.

Syria Fertility Survey 1977 (1982) Damascus: Central Bureau of Statistics in collaboration with The World Fertility Survey.

Syria Maternal and Child Health Survey 1993 (1995) Cairo: Central Bureau of Statistics (Damascus) and PAPCHILD/League of Arab States.

Tunisia Maternal and Child Health Survey 1994/95 (1996) Cairo: Ministry of Health (Tunis) and PAPCHILD/League of Arab States.

United Nations (1990) *Patterns of First Marriage: Timing and Prevalence.* New York : United Nations.

UNICEF (United Nations Children's Fund) (1994) *The State of the World Children.* Oxford: Oxford University Press.

United Nations (1995) *World Population Prospects*, 1994 rev. New York: United Nations.

World Bank (1994) 'World Development Report, 1994: Infrastructure for development'. New York: Oxford University Press.

Yacoub, I. and Farid, S. (eds) (1992) *Bahrain Child Health Survey.* Manama: Ministry of Health.

Yemen Arab Republic Fertility Survey 1979 (1979) Central Planning Organization, Department of Statistics.

Yemen Demographic and Maternal and Child Health Survey 1991/92 (1994) Columbia, MD: Central Statistical Organization (Sana'a), PAPCHILD/League of Arab States (Cairo), and Macro International Inc.

CHAPTER EIGHT

Fertility trends and population policy in Kenya

S.M. Macrae, E.K. Bauni and J.G.C. Blacker

INTRODUCTION

When the Committee on Population of the United States National Academy of Sciences decided, in 1989, to set up a panel on the population dynamics of sub-Saharan Africa, William Brass was invited both to be a member of the panel, and to be chairman of a working group on Kenya. It was a most appropriate appointment, for not only was Brass the doyen of demographers concerned with techniques for the analysis of limited and defective data, but he also had a long-standing and particular interest in the demography of Kenya, having lived in Nairobi from 1948 to 1954, when he worked in the East African Statistical Department. During that time he analysed the demographic data which had been collected in the East African Medical Survey, conducted in selected districts of Kenya and Tanganyika (as it then was) in the early 1950s; it can be seen as the beginning of his distinguished career as a demographer.

The results of the work of the panel and its working groups were published in a series of monographs which were presented to the public at a conference held in Washington, DC in August 1993. The monograph on Kenya, entitled *Population Dynamics of Kenya*, was edited by Brass and Jolly, and was largely devoted to the evidence which had emerged from the 1989 Kenya Demographic and Health Survey (KDHS), to the effect that fertility in Kenya had started to decline.

At the Washington conference, the third author of this paper was invited to be the discussant of the monograph, and he had the temerity to question the validity of the conclusion: the 1989 KDHS was the only source of evidence (other than some small localized studies) that fertility was falling; it was based on a sampling frame, in rural areas, which was five years out of date, and its data were incompatible with those derived from the 1984 Contraceptive Prevalence Survey. His remarks, which were subsequently published in *Population and Development Review*, concluded:

Of course one cannot conclude from this that the evidence of fertility decline in Kenya which emerges from the Demographic and Health Survey is necessarily spurious. But in my view the case for its innocence has not been entirely proven, so that doubts and reservations still linger. Nor will such doubts be fully dispelled if the second DHS held in 1993 produces similar evidence: similar surveys are liable to suffer from similar biases. But if the fertility data from the 1989 census were also to show a consistent fall in fertility, the case would be much more convincing. Students of Kenya's demography are still hoping, perhaps forlornly, that these data will one day be released. (Blacker, 1994),

Hardly had these words been printed when news reached London that the first volume of tables from the 1989 census had been published. After years of delay, an injection of funds by the United Nations Fund for Population Activities (provided through the initiative of the first author of this paper) enabled the Central Bureau of Statistics in Nairobi to embark on an ambitious programme of analysis and publication, so that the 'forlorn hope' was realized. The second author was appointed the manager of the census project and the third acted as a visiting consultant. The results have now been published in ten volumes, together with a popular report and an atlas (Kenya, 1994a, 1996f).

In this paper we shall seek to update the topics covered in three chapters of the *Population Dynamics of Kenya*:

Chapter 3 on fertility trends; we examine the new data from the 1989 census and from the second DHS of 1993; we also include the results of some calculations we have made from the third DHS of 1998, the preliminary report of which became available in time to include here.

Chapter 5 on the proximate determinants of fertility; we examine the new data on marriage, contraception, postpartum infecundability and sterility from the 1993 DHS, and assess their impact on fertility trends.

Chapter 6 on government programmes and their effect on fertility; we review developments in the Government of Kenya's policies and programmes in the field of population from 1993 to 1996.

FERTILITY TRENDS

The 1989 census

As in the previous censuses of Kenya, the 1989 census included questions on the numbers of children ever borne by all females aged 12 and over, and on the date of their most recent live birth. The data so obtained were therefore more limited than those compiled in the Kenya Fertility Survey (KFS) of 1977–8 and the DHS's of 1989 and 1993, which asked for the date of every birth, not just the most recent. Table 8.1 shows the mean numbers of children ever borne, or average parities, by age group, from the last four censuses, and from the KFS and two DHS's. The average parities from the 1989 census show a consistent drop, for all age groups except

Table 8.1   *Average numbers of children ever borne by Kenya women, 1962–93*

Age group	Census 1962	Census 1969	Census 1979	Census 1989	KFS 1977–8	DHS 1989	DHS 1993	DHS 1998
15–19	0.357	0.355	0.321	0.265	0.345	0.280	0.200	0.210
20–24	1.652	1.882	1.853	1.560	1.843	1.580	1.360	1.280
25–29	3.009	3.653	3.652	3.252	3.741	3.470	3.130	2.700
30–34	4.204	5.112	5.388	4.891	5.576	5.010	4.530	4.030
35–39	5.072	6.002	6.470	6.052	6.828	6.480	6.130	5.320
40–44	5.608	6.441	7.021	6.871	7.551	7.360	6.950	6.370
45–49	5.902	6.687	7.173	7.207	7.898	7.630	7.870	6.940

45–49, on those from the 1979 census; they are also marginally lower than those from the 1989 DHS.

However, census data on children ever borne tend to suffer from a variety of errors and biases, of which perhaps the most important is that relating to the numbers of childless women. When a woman has never borne any children, some enumerators tend to leave the questions blank rather than complete them with zeros. There are therefore appreciable numbers of 'not stated' women, most of whom are in fact childless, but some of whom may have borne children whom the enumerators, for various other reasons, have failed to record. The standard technique for correcting for this error is that devised by El Badry (1961). We have applied this correction to the data from the 1969, 1979 and 1989 censuses with seemingly plausible results; when used with the 1962 census, however, they were clearly misleading and unacceptable. Table 8.2 shows the adjusted average parities from the last three censuses. Comparison of the adjusted 1989 figures in Table 8.2 with those of the 1989 DHS in Table 8.1 shows the two data sets to be in reasonably good agreement, and what discrepancies remain probably lie within the sampling errors of the DHS.

Table 8.2   *Average parities 1969–89 adjusted with the El Badry correction*

Age group	1969	1979	1989
15–19	0.366	0.321	0.273
20–24	1.939	1.899	1.610
25–29	3.764	3.743	3.357
30–34	5.267	5.523	5.049
35–39	6.186	6.632	6.247
40–44	6.637	7.197	7.093
45–49	6.891	7.353	7.440

In order to obtain an estimate of the level of fertility during the 1969–79 and 1979–89 intercensal periods, we have used the technique of constructing a 'synthetic cohort' from the increments in average parities for the same cohorts of women in consecutive censuses (e.g. 15–19 in 1979 and 25–29 in 1989; 20–24 in 1979 and 30–34 in 1989, etc.). We used the adjusted average parities shown in Table 8.2 above, and the results were graduated by fitting Gompertz fertility models to the average parities of the synthetic cohorts. The results are shown in Table 8.3.

The estimated TFR of 6.58 for the 1979–89 intercensal period is slightly lower than the 6.7 shown by the 1989 DHS (and which Brass accepted) for the five years prior to the survey. It also represents a compromise between estimates derived from other parts of the census data. The numbers of children under 10 years of age, when allowance is made for mortality, would give an average total fertility of about 6.0. Such children were certainly under-enumerated, but the degree of under-enumeration is problematical. Acceptance of the 6.58 implies that such children had been under-enumerated by nearly 9 per cent. On the other hand the births reported as occurring in last 12 months, adjusted by the P/F ratio and similar techniques, gave TFRs of over 7.2, which would have implied an undercount of children under 10 of over 18 per cent, which is so large as to strain our credulity.

We may conclude, therefore, that the 1989 census did indeed confirm the fall in fertility shown by the DHS, and that it had been sudden and substantial. But our estimates of the extent of the fall, and the actual levels of fertility at different times in the 1980s, remain subject to large margins of uncertainty.

Table 8.3 *Average parities of hypothetical cohorts, 1969–79 and 1979–89 with fitted Relational Gompertz Fertility models*

Age group	Hypothetical cohort: average parities		Age group	Fitted models: age-specific fertility rates	
	1969–79	*1979–89*		*1969–79*	*1979–89*
			10–14	0.0033	0.0019
15–19	0.321	0.273	15–19	0.1883	0.1583
20–24	1.899	1.610	20–24	0.3745	0.3344
25–29	3.698	3.309	25–29	0.3688	0.3231
30–34	5.483	4.760	30–34	0.3006	0.2522
35–39	6.566	5.813	35–39	0.2132	0.1685
40–44	7.413	6.331	40–44	0.0963	0.0697
45–49	7.733	6.622	45–49	0.0122	0.0077
			Total(×5)	7.7858	6.5789

The 1993 Demographic and Health Survey

When the report of the 1993 DHS was published in 1994, considerable interest was focused on the fertility data. The results were in fact so dramatic that they were greeted with widespread scepticism. They showed a total fertility rate for the three years prior to the survey of 5.4, implying a drop of 1.3 births on the 1989 DHS estimate of 6.7 (Kenya and IRD/Macro, 1993, p. 29, Table 3.3). Such a large fall in so short a period was considered by many to be implausible. Suspicions arose that the fertility rates for the various time periods had been distorted by mis-dating of the births, those in the most recent period being displaced backwards in time. Although Brass had found little evidence of such biases in the 1989 DHS, any such tendency might have been aggravated in the 1993 survey by the inclusion of questions on the heights and weights of children under 5.

Thus a critical analysis, similar to that made by Brass of the 1989 KDHS and the 1977–8 KFS, was clearly called for. We have endeavoured to carry out such an analysis, though at national level only.

In the first place the numbers of births by single years prior to the survey strongly suggest that such displacement occurred:

0–1 1187; *1–2* 1221; *2–3* 1238; *3–4* 1341; *4–5* 1141
5–6 1300; *6–7* 1431; *7–8* 1239; *8–9* 1219; *9–10* 1139

The deficit at 4–5, followed by the upsurge at 5–6 and 6–7 years before the survey can be seen as *prima facie* evidence that some children who were in fact under 5 had their dates of birth pushed back so as to avoid the necessity of asking the additional questions and making the physical measurements required of children under 5.

Table 8.4a shows the distribution of births per 1000 women in each age group by five-year periods prior to the survey; Table 8.4b shows the cumulated rates by cohort, giving the average parities at 5, 10, 15, etc. years prior to the survey; Table 8.4c shows the rates cumulated by time period, together with the extrapolated total fertility rates obtained by completing the missing cells (created by the truncation of the survey at age 49) with the appropriate age-specific rates from the neighbouring time periods. These tables therefore correspond with the tables created by Brass from the two previous surveys (Brass and Jolly 1993, pp. 59–63).

It will be seen that while the total fertility rate (TFR) reported for the last five years before the survey was 5.53 births per woman, that for the preceding quinquennium was 7.35. The latter is substantially higher than the estimates for the same period derived both from the 1989 DHS and from the 1989 census, described above. It therefore lends weight to the suspicion that the fertility rates for the period 5–9 years before the survey had been inflated at the expense of those in last five years.

Table 8.4a   *Births per 1000 women by age group and time period, 1993 KDHS*

Age at	Time preceding survey (years)							
KDHS(2)	*0–4*	*5–9*	*10–14*	*15–19*	*20–24*	*25–29*	*30–34*	*35+*
15–19	198	7						
20–24	1016	323	17					
25–29	1359	1339	411	24				
30–34	1153	1628	1363	368	17			
35–39	909	1526	1822	1389	456	22		
40–44	571	1240	1616	1636	1335	492	58	
45–49	325	963	1505	1675	1680	1272	408	39
Total	5530	7026	6733	5092	3488	1786	466	39

Table 8.4b   *Cumulated births per 1000 women by age group, 1993 KDHS*

Age at	Time preceding survey (years)							
KDHS(2)	*0*	*10*	*20*	*30*	*40*	*50*	*60*	*70*
15–19	205	7						
20–24	1357	340	17					
25–29	3133	1774	435	24				
30–34	4528	3376	1748	385	17			
35–39	6124	5215	3689	1867	478	22		
40–44	6948	6378	5138	3522	1886	550	58	
45–49	7866	7541	6578	5074	3399	1719	447	39

Table 8.4c   *Cumulated births per 1000 women by time period,*
1993 KDHS

Age at	Time preceding survey (years)			
KDHS(2)	*0–4*	*5–9*	*10–14*	*15–19*
30–34	3726			
35–39	4634	4823		
40–44	5205	6062	5229	
45–49	5530	7026	6733	5092
Extrapolated	5530	7350	8022	7885
Adjusted	5793	6452	6893	7237

Table 8.4d   *Births per 1000 women by age group and time period: observed and model*

Age at		Time Preceding Survey (years)				Total
KDHS(2)	Source	0–4	5–9	10–14	15–19	Births
30–34	Observed	1153	1628	1363	368	4528
	Model	1226	1464	1350	422	
35–39	Observed	909	1526	1822	1389	6124
	Model	1027	1366	1626	1508	
40–44	Observed	571	1240	1616	1636	6948
	Model	661	1060	1399	1660	
45–49	Observed	325	963	1505	1675	7866
	Model	231	732	1160	1520	

Table 8.5 shows the average parities from the 1993 DHS back-dated first by four years and compared with those reported in the 1989 DHS, and second by 15 years and compared with the 1977–8 KFS.

In general the agreements are quite good, but the back-dated parities for 1989 are higher for all age groups except 25–29 and 35–39 than those from the 1989 DHS. This could also be seen as further evidence that the numbers of births in the last four years, which were subtracted from the 1993 parities in the process of back-dating, had been too small.

We have therefore attempted to redistribute in time the births for each cohort of women, using the Relational Gompertz Fertility model. The fitting procedure we have used follows (with minor differences) that described by Brass in his 1981 Manila paper (Brass, 1981). The results are shown in the 'adjusted' TFRs in Table 8.4c and in Table 8.4d. Thus the TFR for 1988–93 has been increased slightly from 5.5 to 5.8, while that for 1983–8 has been reduced from 7.4 to 6.5. However, it should be emphasized that the adjustments are sensitive to the choice of Gompertz parameters, and there are no objective criteria for determining the 'best' choice.

Table 8.5   *Comparison of average parities from the 1989 DHS and 1977–8 KFS with back-dated 1993 DHS*

Age group	1989 DHS	1993 DHS back-dated to 1989	1977–8 KFS	1993 DHS back-dated to 1978
15–19	0.281	0.289	0.345	0.385
20–24	1.580	1.674	1.843	1.867
25–29	3.472	3.326	3.741	3.522
30–34	5.015	5.166	5.576	5.074
35–39	6.474	6.357		
40–44	7.362	7.436		

Finally we have repeated the calculation of the 'synthetic cohort' used with the 1979 and 1989 censuses, but this time with the average parities from the 1989 and 1993 DHS's. To facilitate the calculations we have assumed a five-year rather than a four-year interval between the surveys. The results, shown in Table 8.6, give a TFR of 5.6 or 5.7, but the assumption of the five-year interval will have led to a small downward bias, suggesting that the figure of 5.8 given by the earlier calculations was of the right order of magnitude.

The 1998 Demographic and Health Survey

As only the preliminary results of the 1998 DHS are available at the time we write, we have not been able to make the detailed analyses such as we have made for the 1993 survey.

The published results include age-specific and total fertility rates for the three-year period prior to the survey, and the distribution of women by age group and parity. The estimated TFR for the period 1995–8 was 4.703. If this figure is taken at its face value, it implies a fall of 0.7 on that of the 1993 DHS, and more if our adjusted figure is accepted.

To validate these dramatic changes, we have constructed a 'hypothetical cohort' from the average parities from the 1993 and 1998 surveys, in the same way as we did for 1969–79 and 1979–89 intercensal periods and for the 1989–93 period between the two DHS's. The results are shown in Table 8.7. They give a TFR of about 4.6 births per woman – a fraction lower than the direct estimate, suggesting that the latter had not exaggerated the fertility decline.

Table 8.6 *Hypothetical cohort from the 1989 and 1993 Demographic and Health Surveys*

Age group	Average parities			Fitted model	
	1989 DHS	*1993 DHS*	*Hypothetical cohort*	*Average parity*	*Age-specific fertility rates*
15–19	0.281	0.205	0.205	0.192	0.1288
20–24	1.580	1.357	1.280	1.307	0.2909
25–29	3.472	3.133	2.833	2.795	0.2867
30–34	5.015	4.528	3.889	4.097	0.2239
35–39	6.474	6.124	4.998	5.037	0.1479
40–44	7.362	6.948	5.472	5.577	0.0599
45–49	7.625	7.866	5.977	5.714	0.0064
				TFR	5.7229

Table 8.7   *Hypothetical cohort from the 1993 and 1998 Demographic and Health Surveys*

Age group	DHS 1993	DHS 1998	Hypothetical cohort	Average parity	Age-specific fertility rates
				Fitted model	
15–19	0.20	0.21	0.21	0.22	0.125
20–24	1.36	1.28	1.29	1.35	0.277
25–29	3.13	2.70	2.63	2.64	0.237
30–34	4.53	4.03	3.53	3.61	0.158
35–39	6.13	5.32	4.32	4.22	0.087
40–44	6.95	6.37	4.56	4.51	0.028
45–49	7.87	6.94	4.55	4.57	0.002
				TFR	4.577

Parity progression ratios and conclusions on fertility trends in Kenya
How, then, can we splice together the information gleaned from the various censuses and surveys so as to produce a coherent picture of fertility trends in Kenya? For this purpose we have used what are perhaps the most powerful and sensitive indices of measuring fertility trends from data on children ever born: parity progression ratios (PPRs), or the proportion of women with n children who go on to have $n + 1$. We have also followed the simple and elegant procedure advocated by Feeney (1988), which not only enables one to reconstruct fertility trends across cohorts, but also provides a powerful test of internal consistency.

The women who were aged 50–54 in 1969 are the same women (mortality and migration apart) as those aged 60–64 in 1979 and 70–74 in 1989; since these women had completed their childbearing, their proportionate distributions by parity as recorded in the three censuses, and hence their PPRs, should broadly correspond. By plotting the PPRs for successive cohorts as shown in different censuses on a graph, one can quickly assess both the compatibility of the censuses, and whether the PPR's had been changing from cohort to cohort. As originally formulated by Feeney, the method could only be applied to women who had completed their childbearing. However, Brass (1985) devised a method of projecting the PPRs of younger women up to the end of childbearing, using data on births in the last 12 months (derived from the question on the date of the woman's last birth) tabulated by age group and parity. We have applied this technique to the 1969, 1979 and 1989 censuses and thereby extended Feeney's method to the younger women; it could not be used with the 1962 census as the current births were never tabulated by parity. The results are shown in Table 8.8 and are illustrated in Figure 8.1.

Table 8.8 *Cohort parity progression ratios*

1962 Census

Age group	Birth cohort	1 to 2	2 to 3	3 to 4	4 to 5	5 to 6	6 to 7	7 to 8	8 to 9
45–49	1912–17	0.957	0.935	0.918	0.894	0.867	0.832	0.799	0.729
50–54	1907–12	0.945	0.932	0.918	0.894	0.858	0.833	0.806	0.742
55–59	1902–07	0.953	0.940	0.918	0.911	0.878	0.838	0.824	0.773
60–64	1897–1902	0.938	0.926	0.907	0.892	0.85	0.829	0.807	0.729
65–69	1892–7	0.945	0.939	0.913	0.891	0.867	0.836	0.797	0.742
70–74	1887–92	0.945	0.928	0.909	0.873	0.858	0.791	0.797	0.705
75+	Before 1887	0.948	0.926	0.909	0.875	0.848	0.787	0.772	0.714

1969 Census

Age group	Birth cohort	1 to 2	2 to 3	3 to 4	4 to 5	5 to 6	6 to 7	7 to 8
20–24	1944–9	0.953	0.962					
25–29	1939–44	0.977	0.982	0.955	0.957			
30–34	1934–9	0.972	0.976	0.966	0.966	0.916		
35–39	1929–34	0.969	0.962	0.955	0.944	0.914	0.881	
40–44	1924–9	0.959	0.953	0.944	0.919	0.904	0.868	
45–49	1919–24	0.956	0.954	0.940	0.910	0.887	0.857	0.815
50–54	1914–19	0.946	0.943	0.927	0.908	0.884	0.836	0.804
55–59	1909–14	0.945	0.942	0.926	0.907	0.882	0.850	0.804
60–64	1904–09	0.931	0.938	0.921	0.900	0.873	0.836	0.804
65+	Before 1904	0.920	0.938	0.920	0.884	0.852	0.808	0.762

1979 Census

Age group	Birth cohort	1 to 2	2 to 3	3 to 4	4 to 5	5 to 6	6 to 7	7 to 8	8 to 9
20–24	1954–9	0.933							
25–29	1949–54	0.961	0.953	0.935					
30–34	1944–9	0.972	0.967	0.963	0.948	0.932			
35–39	1939–44	0.972	0.965	0.959	0.944	0.925	0.894	0.840	0.791
40–44	1934–9	0.968	0.963	0.955	0.939	0.918	0.888	0.843	0.791
45–49	1929–34	0.965	0.959	0.948	0.932	0.908	0.876	0.834	0.782
50–54	1924–9	0.959	0.952	0.942	0.923	0.899	0.866	0.828	0.779
55–59	1919–24	0.958	0.951	0.939	0.921	0.897	0.863	0.827	0.779
60–64	1914–19	0.951	0.946	0.934	0.912	0.886	0.851	0.813	0.768
65–69	1909–14	0.951	0.948	0.932	0.910	0.883	0.845	0.812	0.763
70–74	1904–09	0.946	0.945	0.929	0.904	0.880	0.841	0.805	0.756
75+	Before 1904	0.944	0.940	0.919	0.893	0.858	0.813	0.774	0.729

Table 8.8   *(continued)*

1989 Census

Age group	Birth cohort	1 to 2	2 to 3	3 to 4	4 to 5	5 to 6	6 to 7	7 to 8	8 to 9
20–24	1964–69	0.921							
25–29	1959–64	0.944	0.923	0.889					
30–34	1954–59	0.966	0.953	0.924	0.902	0.872			
35–39	1949–54	0.971	0.960	0.938	0.918	0.887	0.849	0.811	
40–44	1944–49	0.972	0.962	0.947	0.931	0.907	0.872	0.829	0.773
45–49	1939–44	0.972	0.963	0.950	0.935	0.910	0.876	0.836	0.778
50–54	1934–39	0.968	0.960	0.948	0.934	0.912	0.878	0.838	0.787
55–59	1929–34	0.967	0.959	0.948	0.933	0.910	0.879	0.840	0.792
60–64	1924–29	0.960	0.953	0.940	0.922	0.898	0.866	0.825	0.776
65–69	1919–24	0.960	0.953	0.939	0.920	0.896	0.862	0.825	0.775
70–74	1914–19	0.955	0.948	0.933	0.910	0.883	0.850	0.809	0.766
75+	Before 1914	0.954	0.946	0.928	0.902	0.871	0.831	0.795	0.749

1993 and 1998 Demographic and Health Surveys

Age group	Birth cohort	1 to 2	2 to 3	3 to 4	4 to 5	5 to 6	6 to 7	7 to 8	8 to 9
15–19/ 20–24	1973–78	0.8151	0.7069	0.6339					
20–24/ 25–29	1968–73	0.8810	0.7307	0.7161	0.7005	0.8597	0.6183	0.4259	0.7518
25–29/ 30–34	1963–68	0.9599	0.8381	0.7843	0.7070	0.8261	0.6018	0.5395	0.4511
30–34/ 35–39	1958–73	0.9736	0.9205	0.8516	0.7834	0.8500	0.6732	0.6341	0.6259
35–39/ 40–44	1953–58	0.9880	0.9588	0.9022	0.8792	0.8700	0.7379	0.7337	0.6662
40–44/ 45–49	1948–53	0.9774	0.9569	0.9484	0.9177	0.8914	0.8116	0.8185	0.6951

Secondly, from the parity distributions from the 1993 and 1998 surveys, we constructed PPRs for the cohorts of women born between 1950 and 1975, using a modified version of a rather similar procedure devised by Brass and Juarez (1983).[1] These have been plotted on the graphs in Figure 8.1 so that they can be seen in relation to the PPRs derived from the censuses. Three principal features emerge from these graphs.

(i) The consistency of the PPRs from the four censuses is remarkable, and boosts our confidence in the validity of the data. The trends shown by the youngest cohorts of mothers tend to be rather more erratic, since they were based largely on projected data rather than achieved fertility. The consistency is also remarkably good between the PPRs for the older women

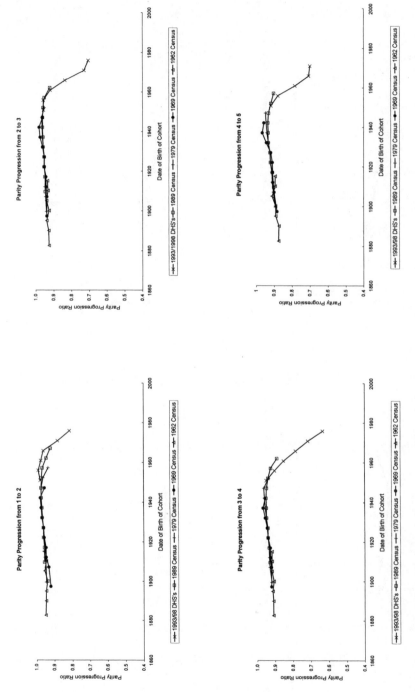

Figure 8.1 Cohort parity progression ratios for Kenya, 1880–1980

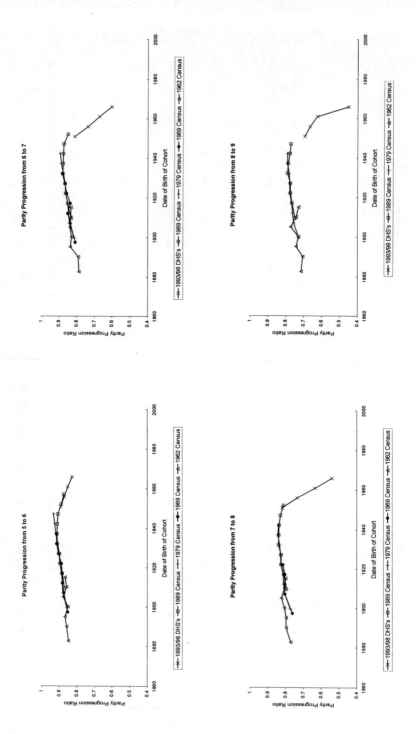

Figure 8.1b

in the 1993 and 1998 DHSs where they overlap with those from the 1989 census.

(ii) There was a general rise in the PPRs, starting with the earliest cohorts of women covered by the data – those born in the late nineteenth century – and increasing steadily up to those born in the 1940s. These increases were minimal at the lower parities, and the lines of points for the proportions of women going from a first to a second birth, and from a second to a third are almost flat; but they then get steeper with increasing parity.

(iii) There was a marked downturn in the PPRs for the women in the youngest cohorts shown by the 1989 census, and it is continued with precipitous steepness for the younger women in the two DHSs. This decline is apparent at all parities, even those going from a first to a second birth. This feature confirms Brass's similar finding from the DHS data, not only for Kenya, but also for Botswana, Nigeria and Zimbabwe, and provides a contrast to the patterns of change in most Asian and Latin American countries when they embarked on their fertility transitions (Brass and Jolly 1993, pp. 75–8).

In order to quantify the rise in fertility noted in (ii) above, regression lines were fitted to the various estimates of PPRs for the cohorts of women born between 1880 and 1945 shown in Table 8.4 and Figure 8.1; the smoothed PPRs so obtained were then chained together to give estimates of completed family size for the different cohorts of women. The results suggested that family size had risen from about 6 births for women born before 1900 to nearly 8 births for women born in the 1940s.

We may conclude therefore that from the end of the First World War until the late 1970s, fertility in Kenya was rising slowly but steadily. The causes of this rise were complex, and probably included declines in pathological sterility, particularly in the coastal districts, shortening birth intervals due to reductions in breast-feeding, and declines in adult mortality reducing the prevalence of widowhood. Total fertility, which was probably of the order of 6 births per woman in the early 1920s, rose to about 8 in the 1970s, when it was one of the highest in the world.

Then somewhere in the late 1970s or early 1980s (the date cannot be pinpointed precisely), there was an abrupt and dramatic change, and fertility began to fall with a rapidity which few people could have predicted. By the late 1980s total fertility, as shown by both the 1989 DHS and the 1989 census, had fallen to well under 7 births per woman; by the early 1990s it was under 6, and by the late 1990s to less than 5, as shown by the 1993 and 1998 DHS's, which our calculations have broadly validated. The causes of this remarkable decline will now be discussed in the next sections of this paper.

PROXIMATE DETERMINANTS OF FERTILITY

The preceding analysis of fertility has shown that Kenya entered the fertility transition era somewhere between the late 1970s and early 1980s. The decline in fertility seems to affect all women irrespective of parity, age, education, residence or region, albeit in different degrees. This analysis throws more light on the factors (proximate determinants) that affect fertility directly. Their effect on fertility is quantified using Bongaarts model (1982), and their trend examined since the 1970s.

The eleven intermediate variables described by Davis and Blake (1956) were reduced to seven by Bongaarts (1982, p. 179) as follows:

1. proportions married among females
2. contraceptive use and effectiveness
3. prevalence of induced abortion
4. duration of postpartum infecundability
5. fecundability (or frequency of intercourse)
6. spontaneous intrauterine mortality
7. prevalence of permanent sterility

These variables influence fertility directly. There are other factors such as cultural, psychological, economic, social, health and environmental which affect fertility indirectly through the above proximate determinants. Bongaarts showed that four of the above proximate determinants of fertility explain 96 per cent of the variation in fertility (Bongaarts, 1982, p. 184). The four variables are:

1. percentage of women in sexual union
2. contraception
3. postpartum infecundability
4. induced abortion

An index ranging from 0 to 1 is estimated for each variable, and the effect on fertility of each determinant depends on the value of the index. The value 0 has the greatest inhibiting effect and the value 1 has the least inhibiting effect.

Percentage of women in sexual union
In the 1950s and 1960s, sexual intercourse outside marriage was socially stigmatized, and marriage marked the start of a socially accepted active sexual life (Molnos, 1973, vol. 3, p. 13; Kenyatta, 1938, p. 164). Marriage was almost universal, since the proportion never married by age 45–49 was very small. In 1969, 1979, 1989 and 1993, it was 3, 2, 2 and 3 per cent respec-

tively (Kenya and IRD/Macro, 1993, p. 62). Although marriage was universal, a large proportion of women were delaying entry into marriage. The proportion of never-married women increased from 26.0 per cent in 1989 to 30.2 per cent in 1993, while the proportion married or 'living together' fell from 66.7 per cent to 61.4 per cent. The trend in the singulate mean age at first marriage (SMAM) was estimated using the 1962, 1969, 1979 and 1989 census data (Hajnal, 1953) and the results are illustrated in Figure 8.2, where a clear rise is evident. Similarly, the trend in the mean age at first birth was estimated from the proportions of childless women in each age group using the 1969, 1979 and 1989 census data,[2] and are also shown in Figure 8.2: the change is small, but rising. The most interesting feature in Figure 8.2 is the crossing of the two trend lines depicting a period in the 1960s when the first birth generally came after marriage contrasting with the period starting in the 1970s when the first birth tended to come before marriage. In fact, the gap between age at first birth and age at marriage seems to be widening with time. Thus the effect of the rise in age at marriage on fertility has been undermined by the increase in births to unmarried women.

The index measuring the effect of marriage patterns on fertility (Cm) takes the value of 1 when all women of reproductive age are in union and 0 when none are in union. It measured 0.91, 0.86, and 0.81 in 1977–8, 1988–9 and 1993 respectively. The trend suggests that the fertility-inhibiting effect of the index has increased over the years, largely due to the rising age at first marriage.

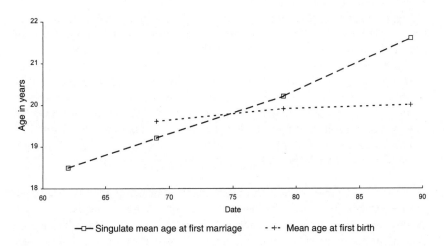

Figure 8.2   Mean ages at marriage and first birth in Kenya – estimates from census data

Contraception

The use of contraception is a deliberate attempt to minimize the risk of becoming pregnant, but at the same time, to have sexual intercourse. Contraceptives are used by most Kenyan women either to delay the first birth, or to space births, or to stop childbearing altogether. Several methods both modern and traditional are available in Kenya. The pill, injection and female sterilization are the most popular modern methods whereas post-partum abstinence is the most popular traditional method.

There has been a marked increase in the use of contraception rising from about 7 to 27 and to 33 per cent in 1977–8, 1989 and 1993 respectively. Except for the barrier methods (condom, diaphragm, foam, jelly), the use of modern methods of family planning increased between 1989 and 1993. The use of traditional methods, mainly periodic abstinence, also apparently increased between 1977–8 and 1989, but then declined between 1989 and 1993.

The increased use of contraceptives has a negative impact on fertility, and the index of contraception (Cc) declined from 0.95 to 0.76 to 0.70 from 1977–8 to 1989 and to 1993 respectively.

Postpartum infecundability

Postpartum infecundability is the period following a birth when a woman is not at risk of getting pregnant because she is either not ovulating (post-partum amenorrhoea) or she is abstaining from sexual intercourse. Abstinence is fairly short in Kenya, about 3 to 4 months, while postpartum amenorrhoea is about 11 to 12 months (Ferry and Page, 1984, p. 25). Prolonged breast-feeding on demand delays the return of ovulation. On average, postpartum amenorrhoea increases by 60 to 70 per cent of the length of breast-feeding (Lesthaeghe *et al*, 1981, p. 7).

The trends in postpartum infecundability shown by the data from the 1977–8, 1989 and 1993 surveys are in some respects puzzling. Thus the 1989 DHS showed a small increase in the average length of breast-feeding on the KFS, but a small decrease in that of amenorrhoea (Brass and Jolly, 1993, pp. 98–101). The 1993 DHS, however, showed increases in the length of both breast-feeding and amenorrhoea, as well as in that of abstention, on 1989. Thus the mean length of the insusceptible period (defined as either amenorrhoeic or abstaining, whichever is longer) apparently fell from 12.7 months in 1977–8 to 11.7 months in 1989, and then increased to 13.7 months in 1993[3] (Brass and Jolly, 1993, pp. 99–100; Kenya and IRD/Macro, 1989, p. 15, 1993, p. 69).

The index of postpartum infecundability (Ci) measures the effect of post-partum amenorrhoea and abstinence on fertility. When there is no breast-feeding or postpartum abstinence Ci equals 1 and 0 if the duration of infecundability is infinite. Thus the index of postpartum infecundability rose from 0.64 in 1977–8 to 0.66 in 1989 and then declined to 0.62 in 1993.

Primary sterility

This is the biological inability of a woman to bear a child. It is generally measured by the proportion of women aged 40–49 who have never borne a child. Bongaarts *et al* (1984) estimated a standard rate of childlessness in developing countries to be about 3 per cent. The index of primary sterility (Ip) is calculated based on the 3 per cent standard. When the rate of childlessness is less than 3 per cent, (Ip) is greater than 1, implying that primary sterility is not inhibiting fertility. On the other hand, if primary sterility exceeds 3 per cent, (Ip) is less than 1, suggesting that primary sterility has an inhibiting effect on fertility.

In 1989 and 1993, the proportion of childless women aged 40–49 was 2.4 and 1.7 respectively (KDHS, 1989 and 1993). Doubts have been cast on such low levels, and these figures will have been subject to large sampling errors. However, it is clear that the level of sterility in Kenya is small. Therefore the impact of primary sterility on fertility is assumed to be negligible and the Ip value has been taken to be 1.0 in all three surveys.[4]

Abortion

Abortion may be defined as the termination of a pregnancy before the fetus is capable of extrauterine life. Spontaneous abortion occurs mainly in the first 4 weeks of gestation while induced abortion may occur at any time of gestation when the woman herself or any other person deliberately terminates it.

Except when a woman's life is threatened, abortion is illegal in Kenya, and data to estimate its prevalence are scarce. Some studies (Rogo, 1990; Robinson, 1992) suggest that abortion is a fairly common practice in Kenya. An abortion rate of 25 procedures per 1000 women per year (assuming that for every woman admitted to a hospital for abortion complication, four other women attempted an abortion) was estimated by Robinson and Harbison (1993) using data from government hospitals. Brass and Jolly (1993, p. 108) used the same information to derive an estimate of an index of abortion of 0.92, which, due to lack of any new and reliable information, has not been changed in this paper.

Estimated total fecundity and consistency check

The Bongaarts indices provide measures of the amount by which fertility is reduced from a hypothetical 'total natural fecundity rate' (TF) by the various proximate determinants. As Brass and Jolly state, 'no one knows what TF really is, but Bongaarts and Potter (1983) estimated that it ranges from 13 to 17, with an average of approximately 15', Brass and Jolly (1993, p. 108) used the same information to derive an index of abortion (Ca) of 0.92. TF can, however, be estimated by dividing the observed TFR by the product of the Bongaarts indices: i.e. $TF = TFR/(Cm.Cc.Ci.Ip.Ca)$. The results for Kenya are shown in Table 8.9 and Figure 8.3. The estimated TF

Table 8.9   *Proximate determinants of fertility, 1977–8, 1989 and 1993*

	TFR	Cm	Cc	Ci	Ip	Ca	Product	Implied TF
1977–8	8.15	0.91	0.95	0.64	1.00	0.92	0.51	16.0
1989	6.62	0.86	0.76	0.66	1.00	0.92	0.40	16.7
1993	5.40	0.81	0.70	0.62	1.00	0.92	0.32	16.7
Ratio 1	81.2	94.5	80.0	103.1	100.0	78.7		
Ratio 2	81.6	94.1	92.1	93.9	100.0	80.7		

Ratio 1 = $100 \times$ 1989 values/1977–8 values.   Product = $Cm \times Cc \times Ci \times Ip \times Ca$.
Ratio 2 = $100 \times$ 1993 values/1989 values.   Implied TF = TFR/product

of 16.7 from the 1989 DHS was slightly higher than the 16.0 from the 1977–8 KFS, but the difference can be regarded as trivial, and the 1993 DHS gave an indentical figure to that of 1989.

Although this agreement may have been achieved as a result of compensating errors, it is nevertheless gratifying. It implies that the changes in observed fertility both from 1977–8 to 1989 and from 1989 to 1993 were largely consistent with the information on proximate determinants. Table 8.9 shows that the observed total fertility rate declined by 19 per cent between 1977 and 1989, and by about 18 per cent between 1989 and 1993, while the changes in the product of the proximate determinants were of 21 per cent and 19 per cent respectively.

Conclusion on trends in the proximate determinants of fertility
Figure 8.3 shows that postpartum infecundability, contraceptive use and proportions married have continued to reduce fertility since the late 1970s.

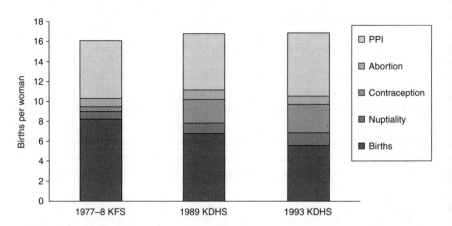

Figure 8.3   Proximate determinants of fertility in Kenya

Postpartum infecundability is the most important proximate determinant of fertility, and has been so since the 1970s. However, the proportions married and the use of contraception have changed ranks, with the latter taking the second position in the 1980s and 1990s.

Increased length of breast-feeding, use of modern contraception and reduced proportions of married women have consistently reduced fertility. These will be the key factors to determine the future pace of fertility decline in Kenya. Their impact on fertility will also depend on the quality and strength of the existing population policy and programmes to enhance breast-feeding, use of modern contraception, including single women, who would like to delay their marriage without the risk of pregnancy.

DEVELOPMENTS IN THE GOVERNMENT OF KENYA (GOK) POPULATION POLICIES AND PROGRAMMES SINCE 1993

Chapter 6 of the US National Academy of Sciences' monograph *Population Dynamics of Kenya* was devoted to 'Socio-economic and program factors related to fertility change' and was drafted by Warren Robinson. It was not confined to the GOK's policies on population and family planning; it reviewed also the impact of developments in the fields of transport and communications, education, health and land policy. Thus although this section of our paper is concerned primarily with innovations in the population and related policies, we also discuss briefly the trends in education and health in the context of the general economic condition of the country.

Following periods of economic change, the national economy (for reasons too numerous to detail here) was in a parlous state in 1992 and, by the beginning of 1993, the GDP growth rate had declined to a mere 0.1 per cent (Kenya, 1992,1993). This decline, coupled with high rates of inflation (53 per cent) and of interest rates (70 per cent) arising from inappropriate macro-economic policies, with the still high, albeit declining, population growth rate, and with increasing unemployment levels (20 per cent), led to a proportionate decrease in the availability of adequate basic services. However, since the introduction of economic reforms in 1993, there have been indications that the economy has managed to emerge from the period of low economic growth which had prevailed in the years immediately up to then. Indicators of the positive developments in 1995 include the increase in GDP growth rate to 4.9 per cent, the fall in inflation to less than 1.6 per cent and the fall in interest rates to less than 30 per cent (Kenya, 1995).

Despite these recent improvements in the national economy, there are continuing declines in the welfare of the people, with glaring discrepancies between social groups and between geographical locations. Widespread poverty therefore remains the major challenge to development efforts. In 1992, it was estimated that in the rural areas the population below the absolute poverty line (those with per capita incomes lower than US$32 per month) was 46 per cent, while in the urban areas the incidence of poverty was approximately 30 per cent (World Bank, 1994). The introduction (albeit a decade or so ago) of indirect taxation through commodity taxes on even basic items has contributed to this, as the poor are as affected by such taxes as are the rich. In addition, Structural Adjustment Programmes (SAPs), introduced in the late 1980s and designed to reduce the levels of government subsidies, have had several adverse side-effects. Aware of these, the GOK, in 1994, introduced the Social Dimensions of Development programme to help mitigate them, but this programme has had limited impact to date, and poverty persists.

Although the government in 1994–5 spent 16.1 per cent of its total recurrent and development budgets on education (Kenya, 1995), the SAP reforms involving cost-sharing have had a negative impact, and the quality of educational services has declined. With inadequate 'safety nets' to limit these negative consequences, many children from poor families are not enrolling in or are dropping out of school. This leads to wastage in formal education estimated in the range of 30 to 47 per cent at both primary (ages 6–13) and secondary (ages 14–17) levels. Parents currently contribute over 50 per cent of the total cost of education and, since the introduction of cost-sharing in schools, some communities in Kenya have reverted to giving girls second priority in families with boys. The national completion rates for girls at primary school level is only 35 per cent against 55 per cent for boys (Kenya, 1994b). Causes of female student drop-outs are, however, not just economic or gender-linked; a survey conducted in some districts revealed that about 10 per cent of these drop-outs (i.e. approximately 10,000 girls per annum) is accounted for by unplanned pregnancy (Kenya, 1988). Out of this number, 66 per cent became pregnant while in primary school. Of even greater concern, 40 per cent of all documented school-girl pregnancies terminated in abortion (Rogo, 1993). While the Ministry of Education agreed in 1994 to re-accept postpartum/postabortum girls back into school, the government is less willing (due to the opposition from religious leaders) to promote Family Life Education in schools and to educate the youth about how to prevent such pregnancies. A UNESCO survey in a few districts in 1993 showed that, in addition to being exposed to the widespread risk of sexual abuse by teachers, there was more ill-health and lower nutritional levels among school-going children than among out-of-school youth, indicating declining standards of health care and of school feeding, and emphasizing also that with widespread poverty, parents may have paid for education at the expense of food and health care. These issues, concerns and gender disparities need to be addressed, as education of children nevertheless remains of primary importance to Kenyans. It is considered by many that one of the issues influencing decision-making over family size is that Kenyans only wish to have the number of children they can educate; given the current economic situation, this number is necessarily fewer than previously. Research currently under-way may give this thinking a more solid basis.

Adolescents (aged 10–19 years) make up about 25 per cent of Kenya's population and, within this group, inaccurate information and inadequate access to services are not only closely associated with the observed high rates of unplanned and unwanted pregnancies – within and out of school – but also of HIV/AIDS (higher in teenage girls than boys). About 75 per cent of AIDS cases reported in the period 1986–96 occurred among adults aged 20–45, with the peak at 25–29 for females and 30–34 for males.

The emergence of the HIV/AIDS pandemic, which received only a cursory mention in the National Academy of Sciences monograph, has been the major feature of the health scene in Kenya in the last five years: it is prob-ably the greatest social, political and development disaster to have hit the country. HIV prevalence (i.e. the proportion of the adult population who are HIV positive) is thought to have increased from 3.1 per cent in 1990 to 7.5 per cent in 1995, and is optimistically predicted to level out at 10 per cent at the end of the century (Kenya, 1996b). These prevalence figures, however, which are based on the whole population over 15 years of age, do not convey the full magnitude of the disaster; realistic models of age-specific prevalence suggest that the 7.5 per cent prevalence for 1995 would be equivalent to a lifetime risk of dying from AIDS of about 30 per cent: in other words about 1 child in 3 born in Kenya could expect, sooner or later, to die of AIDS (Blacker and Zaba, 1997).

Projections published by the Central Bureau of Statistics show not only a dramatic rise in adult mortality rates, but also that infant and child mortality, which had been falling steadily up to the late 1980s, could at best be expected to level out, and more probably rise, due to the vertical transmission of HIV from mothers to children, despite the fact that the projections assume, contro-versially, that mortality from causes other than AIDS will continue to decline (Kenya, 1996f, vols. III and VII). What effect, it may be asked, will the AIDS epidemic have on the trends in fertility in Kenya? The possible ways in which AIDS could interact with fertility are diverse and complex; some could be seen to increase it and others to depress it (Zaba and Collumbien, 1997). On balance, however, it seems more likely that it will accelerate the decline which we have described above, and this conclusion is supported by the evidence of longitudinal studies in Uganda and Zimbabwe (Carpenter *et al*, 1997; Gray *et al*, 1997; Gregson *et al*, 1997).

Apart from effects of AIDS, health services have also been adversely affected by the reforms related to cost-sharing, by the limited government spending on health – only 5.3 per cent of the total recurrent and develop-ment budget in 1994–5 (Kenya, 1995) – and by problems of cost containment and sustainability. In addition, quality of health care in the government services is now seriously compromised by: inadequate physical infrastruc-ture; shortage of equipment, essential drugs and supplies; unattractive schemes of service and hence low self-esteem of health workers; and weak supportive supervision. With particular respect to maternal and child health/family planning (MCH/FP) services, problems relate to: personnel not being prepared for the newly emerging concept and scope of repro-ductive health care; occasional negative personnel attitude; and minimal follow-up of family planning clients. However, on the positive side, the Ministry of Health has made remarkable progress in the last five years with respect to the supply and distribution of FP commodities and especially of contraceptives. There is in place an excellent system of distribution to the district level, thus ensuring that there is an adequate supply of a variety of contraceptives in Service Delivery Points – government, non-governmental and private.

The improved supply and distribution of contraceptives is a significant achievement of the national population programme, since the decline in fertility has been attributed largely to the increase in the use of contraception, as discussed above. Hence, a particular programme intervention has been shown to have a direct impact on fertility levels, and the programme focus on contraception rather than on health and economic development as previ-ously has been proved justified. While the study of proximate determinants is based on the 1993 KDHS, there is every indication that the trend indicated in Figure 8.3 above will be continued and contraception possibly become the most important factor in the limitation of fertility.

Despite the increased contraceptive prevalence, the 1989 and 1993 KDHS's both indicated that there is still a high unmet need for family plan-ning services, with over one-third of women interviewed in 1993 saying that they wanted either to stop or to space their childbearing, but were not prac-tising contraception (Kenya and IRD/Macro, 1989, 1993). Reasons given included concerns about side-effects and about quality and adequacy of service delivery. In addition, varied accessibility of services contributes to contraceptive uptake: of all the women interviewed in the 1993 KDHS, 50 per cent reported being within 5 km of both family planning services and of a facility that offered antenatal care, while only 32 per cent of married women interviewed lived within 5 km of a facility that provided delivery care services. The government is now the most important provider of family plan-ning services accounting for 68 per cent of the services nationally. Currently, of the existing 3,500 health facilities (government and non-governmental), 1,879 offer MCH/FP services with varied accessibility. In addition to these static services, outreach workers are forming an increasingly important network of service delivery. The Ministry of Health is fully aware of the need to address identified constraints to quality of care, and has prepared, in col-laboration with national and international partners, a Health Policy Framework (Kenya, 1994c), which has as its overall goal to promote and improve the health status of all Kenyans through the restructuring of the health sector to make all health services more effective, accessible and affordable.

A further reason for not practising contraception was given in the 1993 KDHS as being related to disapproval by men. Many communities still entrust women's reproductive capacity to men. Thus the sexual and reproductive health and rights of women are still being compromised because of traditional norms and cultures. These also limit the decision-making capacity of the large number of women left as *de facto* heads of households in areas with high male labour out-migration, as well as of the many single-parent families formed by teenage pregnancies. Although efforts to involve men in family planning – and now broader issues of reproductive health – have been continuing for many years, their participation is still negligible. These social constraints call for well-designed and targeted programmes with improved advocacy and information, education and communication (IEC) to influence more male participation, in particular.

One of the major changes since the National Academy of Sciences monograph was written has been the recognition by the government, in early 1993, of the priority need to strengthen the coordinating role of the National Council for Population and Development (NCPD), to enable it better to address both changing circumstances and some unchanging opinions. A workshop was therefore convened, under funding from UNFPA, to assess the role and functions of the NCPD. As a result, in January 1994 the NCPD was relocated into a more appropriate Ministry (the Office of the Vice President and Ministry of Planning and National Development) and a Government Task Force established to assess its structure, staffing, etc. The number of District Population Officers (DPOs) – a Civil Service position created in 1986 following the government's increased commitment both to the population sector and to decentralization – was, as a result, increased from a previous complement of 12 to one of 18 in 1995. Each DPO works in one or more districts to promote issues related to population and development and to incorporate these into district planning. However, while the concept is good, much still needs to be done to improve the impact and effectiveness of DPOs. Further strengthening of the NCPD in toto with physical, financial and human resources (with a scheme of service which attracts and retains qualified staff) still needs to be addressed by the government.

The International Conference on Population and Development (ICPD) held in Cairo in September 1994 stimulated a radical revision of Kenya's population policy, involving a widening of the objectives outlined in the 1984 Population Policy Guidelines (Kenya 1988). Initially efforts were made to develop a National Programme of Action based directly on that of the ICPD, adapting it to national and local conditions. However, it was soon realized that such a programme-related implementation plan could only be prepared under the umbrella of an already-formulated population policy. Hence, throughout 1995, there were several national workshops to prepare a draft population policy and this document was discussed at four regional seminars, under UNFPA funding. These seminars gave the chance for people at provincial and district level to comment on the draft document and on the issues it addressed. Many diverse views were heard and incorporated where possible and appropriate. The final draft was discussed in detail in a further workshop. The process of policy formulation was thus indeed a national one and a sense of ownership thereby fostered. After clearance with relevant ministerial authorities, the document, entitled 'A National Population Policy for Sustainable Development', was cleared by the Cabinet and at the time of writing (1996) awaiting approval by Parliament for publishing as a Sessional Paper (Kenya, 1996c)

The Policy represents a substantial advance in national thinking on the issues of concern discussed above: reproductive health (including family planning, sexual health and reproductive rights) replacing the more restricted MCH/FP and separate IEC approaches; HIV/AIDS; the needs of adolescents and youth; gender issues; poverty; environmental degradation; population issues in development planning, etc. It also notes the eventual goal of sustainability. It outlines Kenya's goals, objectives and targets to guide the implementation of the population programmes up to the year 2010. These include an infant mortality rate of 59, a total fertility rate of 2.5, and a contraceptive prevalence rate of 62 per cent (compared with 33 per cent shown by the 1993 KDHS).

The actual implementation of the National Population Policy for Sustainable Development will take cognizance of the Health Policy Framework (Kenya 1996a) and be closely guided by major other Government documents prepared in the course of 1996. Of paramount importance amongst these are two strategies – a Reproductive Health Strategy (Kenya, 1996d) and a Population Advocacy and IEC Strategy (Kenya, 1996e) – and an HIV/AIDS Sessional Paper.

The Reproductive Health Strategy goes far beyond the previous narrow focus on family planning and outlines strategies to address relevant elements of both the Health Policy Framework and also the Population Policy, with particular emphasis on quality of care, integrated service delivery and accessibility of services to identified target groups (especially adolescents and men) and underserved communities. It also builds on the lessons learned from the programme to date and incorporates the many diverse forms of service delivery (in addition to the hierarchy of static services), which have been implemented in recent years and which have, in several instances, had considerable success in reaching clients. Such channels include: the use of outreach workers – community-based distribution workers, community health workers, and traditional birth attendants – from static services, and of others such as agricultural extension workers and cooperatives leaders; the use of condom dispensing units associated with the work of Public Health Technicians to reach the men in rural areas; and of social marketing in urban areas. The Population Advocacy and IEC Strategy identifies the issues to be addressed under both reproductive health and also population and development strategies and clearly delineates the various approaches which could be adopted to achieve the different objectives.

An updated policy, though necessary to guide programme implementation and to ensure cohesion and agreement on the priority objectives and issues, is nevertheless not sufficient by itself to ensure appropriate development and behavioural change. The formulation of a policy, and of related strategies, is meaningless without the commitment, resources and institutional structure to ensure the full and active implementation of appropriate, multidimensional programmes. Within such programmes, the national implementors – government agencies, non-governmental organizations, private sector and individuals – as well as the international and donor partners need to focus on areas in which they have comparative strengths and advantages. At this stage of the demographic transition in Kenya, it is particularly important that limited resources are indeed deployed to maximum effect.

During 1997, a National Implementation Plan will be developed which more closely identifies the actual activities, target groups and/or geographical areas, actors and required resources (human/technical, financial and material) associated with each aspect. This Plan will – within the framework of the Population Policy and Strategy documents – link national activities and donor support thereto. Key donors to the national population programme are the World Bank, UNFPA, European Union, ODA, United States Agency for International Development, Gesellschaft für Technische Zusammenarbeit (GTZ) and many other bilateral agencies. UNFPA's Fifth Country Programme, 1997–2001, has been formulated within the 'umbrellas' of the national policy and strategy documents described above – most of which have been prepared under UNFPA funding (UNFPA, 1996). It will focus on three main areas of assistance: reproductive health; population and development strategies; and advocacy. The component subprogrammes will be prepared in parallel with, or immediately following, the preparation of the National Implementation Plan, and in a manner which complements the inputs of other donors. Coordination of the many donor inputs, as well as of programme elements, is a pivotal role of the NCPD. There is thus a unique opportunity for the Kenyan Population Programme to be implemented henceforth in a fully cohesive and cost-effective manner, with close collaboration and coordination between all partners.

In conclusion, it can be noted that Kenya is in many ways a paradox, particularly of the political system. On the one hand, the government is notably and negatively influenced by a minority of vocal religious and other leaders who continue publicly to oppose the teaching of Family Life Education in schools and the access to services (including information and counselling) to adolescents and youth. These opinions have considerably constrained progress with respect to meeting the reproductive health needs of the younger generation, and have surely contributed to their high rates of pregnancy and HIV/AIDS. On the other hand, the government is prepared to formulate, and then at the highest levels formally to ratify, innovative and pioneering documents such as the above population policies and strategies, which in large part clearly focus on addressing those same constraints.

Whatever the publically-expressed opinions of political and religious leaders, individual couples have taken their own decisions to reduce family size and to practise family planning, as evidenced by the continuing demographic transition. The new population policy has certainly been prepared in response to and in recognition both of these changes in individual fertility behaviour – which in turn were influenced in part by the prevailing population policy and programmes – as well as of the global, national and subnational changes in the overall environment. The process of formulation of the National Population Policy for Sustainable Development, and of the related Reproductive Health and Advocacy/IEC Strategies, may be seen as an example for Sub-Saharan Africa and, if the ensuing National Implementation Plan can be fully effected, then Kenya can be proud of its blended policies–programmes approach to overall population management. It is certainly leading the countries of Sub-Saharan Africa in conceptualizing such documents.

CONCLUSIONS

Bill Brass used to tell a story of how, when he was in the East African Statistical Department, he would select sample plots for measuring agricultural yields by attaching a stone to a handkerchief which would form an improvised parachute; he would throw this in the air, and the spot where it came to earth (after being carried some distance by the wind) would mark the selected plot. Kenya's statistics have come a long way since those days of *ad hoc* sample selection. Where demographic statistics are concerned Kenya has a more comprehensive and coherent data base than any other country in sub-Saharan Africa. This situation is largely due, directly and indirectly, to Brass's influence.

The questions on fertility and mortality which have been included in the censuses and surveys, and the tabulations derived from them, have largely been dictated by the analytical techniques which he has devised. They have enabled demographers to piece together the components and trends of fertility and mortality, and the knowledge thus generated has undoubtedly had an impact on policy and human welfare. It is no coincidence that Kenya was also the first country in sub-Saharan Africa to adopt a population policy, and among the first to enter the fertility transition.

ACKNOWLEDGEMENTS

We are indebted to Fatima Juarez and Mohammed Ali of the Centre for Population Studies, London School of Hygiene and Tropical Medicine, for preparing special tables from the 1993 Kenya DHS which enables us to make the calculations contained in Tables 8.6 and 8.7. We are also indebted to the Director of the Central Bureau of Statistics, Nairobi, for permission to reproduce tables and diagrams previously published in the Analytical Report on the 1989 Kenya Census.

REFERENCES

Blacker, J. (1994) 'Some thoughts on the evidence of fertility decline in Eastern and Southern Africa'. *Population and Development Review*, 20 (1), pp. 200–5.

Blacker, J. and Zaba, B. (1997) 'HIV prevalence and life-time risk of contracting AIDS'. *Health Transition Review*, Supplement to vol 7, pp. 45–62.

Bongaarts, J. (1982) 'The fertility effects of the intermediate fertility variables'. *Studies in Family Planning*, 13, (6/7), pp. 179–89.

Bongaarts, J., Frank, O. and Lesthaeghe, R. (1984) 'The proximate determinants of fertility in sub-Saharan Africa'. *Population and Development Review*, 10 (3), pp. 511–37.

Brass, W. (1981) 'The use of the Gompertz Relational Model to estimate fertility'. *International Population Conference Manila 1981*, vol 3, pp. 345–62.

Brass, W. (1985) 'P-F synthesis and parity progression ratios', in W. Brass (ed.), *Advances in Methods for Estimating Fertility and Mortality from Limited and Defective Data*. London: London School of Hygiene and Tropical Medicine.

Brass, W. and Jolly, C.L. (eds) (1993) *Population Dynamics of Kenya*. Washington, DC: National Academy Press.

Brass, W. and Juarez, F. (1983) 'Censored cohort parity progression ratios from birth histories'. *Asian and Pacific Census Forum*, vol 10, no 1.

Carpenter, L.M., Nakiyingi, J.S., Ruberantwari, A., Malamba, S., Kamali, A. and Whitworth, J. (1997) 'Estimates of the impact of HIV infection on fertility in a rural Ugandan population cohort'. *Health Transition Review*, Supplement to vol 7, pp. 113–26.

Davis, K. and Blake, J. (1956) 'Social structures and fertility'. *Economic Development and Cultural Change*, 4, pp. 211–35.

El Badry, M.A. (1961) 'Failure of enumerators to make entries of zero: errors of recording childless cases in populations censuses', *Journal of the American Statistical Association*, 56 (296), pp. 909–24.

Feeney, G. (1988) 'The Use of Parity Progression Models in Evaluating Family Planning Programmes', *African Population Conference, Dakar 1988*, Vol.3 pp.7.1.17–30.

Ferry, B. and Page, H.J. (1984) *The Proximate Determinants of Fertility and their Effect on Fertility Patterns: An Illustrated Analysis applied to Kenya*. Voorburg/London: WFS Scientific Reports No. 71.

Gray, R.H., Wawer, M.J., Serwadda, D., Sewankambo, N., Li, C., Wabwire-Mangen, F., Paxton, L., Kiwanuka, N. Kigozi, G., Konde-Lule, J., Quinn, T.C., Gaydos, C.A. and McNairn, D. (1997) 'Population-based study of fertility in women with HIV infection in Uganda', *Lancet*, 351, pp. 98–103.

Gregson, S., Zhuwau, T., Anderson, R. and Chandiwana, S. (1997) 'HIV and fertility change in rural Zimbabwe'. *Health Transition Review*, Supplement to vol 7, pp.89–112.

Hajnal, J. (1953) 'Age at marriage and proportions marrying'. *Population Studies*, 7 (2), pp. 111–36.

Kenya, Republic of (1984) *Population Policy Guidelines*. Sessional Paper No. 4 of 1984. Nairobi: National Council for Population and Development, Office of the Vice President and Ministry of Home Affairs.

Kenya, Republic of (1988) *School Girl Pregnancy in Kenya: Report of a Study of Discontinuation Rates and Associated Factors*. Nairobi: Division of Family Health, Ministry of Health and GTZ Support Unit.

Kenya, Republic of (1992) *Economic Survey, 1992*. Nairobi: Central Bureau of Statistics, Office of the Vice President and Ministry of Planning and National Development.

Kenya, Republic of (1993) *Economic Survey, 1993*. Nairobi: Central Bureau of Statistics, Office of the Vice President and Ministry of Planning and National Development.

Kenya, Republic of (1994a) *Kenya Population Census 1989*: vol I and II. Nairobi: Central Bureau of Statistics, Office of the Vice President and Ministry of Planning and National Development.

Kenya, Republic of (1994b) 'Kenya: national report on population and development', presented at the International Conference on Population and Development. Nairobi: National Council for Population and Development, Office of the Vice President and Ministry of Planning and National Development.

Kenya, Republic of (1994c) *Kenya's Health Policy Framework*. Nairobi: Ministry of Health.

Kenya, Republic of (1995) *Economic Survey, 1995*. Nairobi: Central Bureau of Statistics, Office of the Vice President and Ministry of Planning and National Development

Kenya, Republic of (1996a) *Kenya's Health Policy Framework: Implementation and Action Plans – The First Steps*. Nairobi: Ministry of Health.

Kenya, Republic of (1996b) *AIDS in Kenya: Background, Projections, Impact, Interventions*, 3rd ed. Nairobi: National AIDS and STDs Control Programme, Ministry of Health, and National Council for Population and Development, Office of the Vice President and Ministry of Planning and National Development.

Kenya, Republic of (1996c) *National Population Policy for Sustainable Development*. Sessional Paper of 1996. Nairobi: National Council for Population and Development, Office of the Vice President and Ministry of Planning and National Development.

Kenya, Republic of (1996d) *National Reproductive Health Strategy*. Nairobi: Ministry of Health.

Kenya, Republic of (1996e) *National Population Advocacy and IEC Strategy for Sustainable Development, 1996–2010*. Nairobi: National Council for Population and Development, Office of the Vice President and Ministry of Planning and National Development.

Kenya, Republic of (1996f) *Kenya Population Census 1989: Analytical Reports, Volumes III -X; Popular Report; Atlas.* Nairobi: Central Bureau of Statistics, Office of the Vice President and Ministry of Planning and National Development.

Kenya, Republic of, and IRD (Institute for Resource Development)/Macro International Inc. (1989) *Kenya Demographic and Health Survey 1989.* Nairobi: National Council for Population and Development, Office of the Vice President and Ministry of Planning and National Development.

Kenya, Republic of, and IRD (Institute for Resource Development)/Macro International Inc. (1993) *Kenya Demographic and Health Survey 1993.* Nairobi: National Council for Population and Development, Office of the Vice President and Ministry of Planning and National Development.

Kenyatta, J. (1938) *Facing Mount Kenya,* London: Secker and Warburgh.

Lesthaeghe, R., Ohadike, P.O., Locher, J. and Page, H.J. (1981) 'Child spacing and fertility in sub-Saharan Africa: An overview of issues', in H.J. Page and R. Lesthaeghe (eds), *Child Spacing in Tropical Africa*, pp. 3–23. London: Academic Press.

Molnos, A. (1973) *Cultural Source Materials for Population Planning in East Africa,* vol 1–3. Nairobi: East African Publishing House.

Robinson, W.C. (1992) 'Kenya enters the fertility transition'. *Population Studies,* 46 (3), pp. 445–57.

Robinson, W.C. and Harbison, S.F. (1993) 'Components of fertility decline in Kenya: Prospects for the future', in *Population Research Center Working Paper.* University Park, PA: Pennsylvania State University.

Rogo, K.O. (1993) *Analysis and Documentation of Research on Adolescent Sexuality and Unsafe Abortion in Kenya.* Nairobi: Centre for the Study of Adolescence.

UNFPA (United Nations Fund for Population Activities) (1996) Support to the Population Programme of Kenya, 1997–2001. New York: Programme Review Committee.

World Bank (1994) *Kenya: Poverty Assessment.* Washington, DC: World Bank, Population and Human Resources Division, Eastern Africa Department, Africa Region.

Zaba, B., and Collumbien, M. (1997) 'HIV and fertility: modelling the effects of changes in union dynamics', International Population Conference, Beijing 1997, vol 2, pp. 283–610.

CHAPTER NINE

Populations of the Northern Sahel: demographic problems and solutions

Sara Randall

Department of Anthropology, University College London

If the Sahel is the band of countries which run from West to East across Africa, south of the Sahara, some including sizeable areas of Sahara (Mali, Mauritania, Niger, Chad), the Northern Sahel can be defined as the band of land closest to the Sahara, where rainfall is lowest (under 350mm per annum) and most unpredictable both in time and space. Much of this area is ideally suited to extensive pastoralism; cattle in southern and riverine zones, camels in the more arid areas and small ruminants everywhere. The countries concerned are very poor[1] and in most of them the Northern Sahelian area includes the least developed zones in terms of conventional measures of well-being: health services, education, housing standards and water facilities. This situation has led to a plethora of development projects who have an all too common refrain, blaming high population growth, poor agricultural practices and extensive pastoralism for a range of sins which culminate in poverty.

Although rapid population growth, either of the population as a whole, or of particular subsets is frequently referred to in daily development discourse, and has probably entered into public understanding (at least the development public understanding) as a known fact, little is known about population dynamics in the zone and little thought has gone into defining which populations are being talked about, whether they really do have high population growth, and if so, whether it is a problem.

The aim of this paper is to consider the different populations in this area, the problems faced both in defining them and subsequently in measuring their demographic dynamics, and to show that where the unknowns are substantial, yet the issues are crucial, the range of indirect methods pioneered by Brass are the only ways possible for addressing this demographic lacuna in the foreseeable future.

Census data are probably the main source of preoccupations with population growth issues. All these Sahelian countries have had high national population growth rates in the past and continue to have high fertility and growth (Table 9.1) but this fact alone does not confirm that development problems in the northern Sahelian zones are necessarily a function of population

Table 9.1 *Annual population growth in Sahelian countries*

Country	Annual % population growth 1960–93	Annual % population growth 1993–2000	TFR 1992
Niger	3.2	3.4	7.4
Mali	2.6	3.1	7.1
Burkina Faso	2.4	2.6	6.5
Chad	2.1	2.8	5.9
Senegal	2.8	2.7	6.1
Gambia	3.3	3.1	5.6
Mauritania	2.4	2.6	5.4

Source: Table 21: *Human Development Report 1996* (UNDP, 1996)

growth. A major problem with the census data is the spatial demarcation of population by administrative area including national boundaries; these bear little relationship to human distribution and groupings, however they are defined. Linguistic, ethnic and occupational groups all straddle many boundaries. Examination of net change in both numbers and distribution of bodies between censuses is very misleading. To understand this we must consider in more detail the nature of the ethnic groups, the production systems and mobility in these zones. These issues will be addressed using research on the Northern Sahelian zones of Mali and Burkina Faso.

POPULATION MOVEMENT

Mobility is an essential aspect of survival in the northern Sahel. Traditional extensive pastoralism depends on movement of herds, and therefore people, to maximize production and use of natural resources, and to minimize risk of herd loss. This movement also increases substantially the number of animals (and people) that an area can support (see for example Thébaud, 1995) – a fact lost if agencies restrict themselves to calculating carrying capacities. These movements can be broken down into different types.

Nomadism
Nomadic pastoralists have mobile homes (tents made of leather, cloth or mat) and tend to move as family groups (See Table 9.2a: Fulbe Djelgobe, Table 9.2b: pastoralist). They move because their primary economic activity is animal husbandry and they need pasture and water for the herds, both of which are rather sparse and change in their distribution both between and within seasons. In the long hot dry season, nomadic groups are normally less mobile, remaining within walking distance of a well system or other water supply for both animal and human provision. They may still move short distances every few weeks when camp sites get dirty. In the wet season

Table 9.2 *Northern Burkinabe Fulani transhumance*[a]

(a) By ethnic sub-group[b]

Ethnic subgroup: % Going on transhumance in preceding year

	Males	N	Females	N
Fulbe Djelgobe	62.1	739	59.8	701
Fulbe Gaobe	24.4	1314	19.8	1237
Fulbe Oudalan	4	361	1.2	332
Fulbe Liptaako	3.1	983	1.2	829
Rimaibe Gaobe	0.6	173	0	151
Rimaibe Liptaako	0	762	0	696

(b) By household production system

Household production: % Going on transhumance in preceding year

	Males	N	Females	N
Pastoralist	63.3	724	62.7	644
Agropastoralist	13.1	2220	10.5	1981
Small agropastoralist[c]	8.3	748	8.1	676
Cultivator	1.0	684	0.5	649
Contract herder	90.9	11	100	8
Contract herder + agric.	13.3	60	15.2	46

[a] Transhumance here refers to any residential movement with, and because of livestock. Both nomadic and transhumant populations are included.
[b] The data in Tables 9.2a and 9.2b were collected in 1995 by Kate Hampshire as part of an EEC funded research programme on 'Household viability and migration in the Sahel' EU DG XII PROGRAMME STD3, reference 921028.
[c] Small agropastoralists were households where both agriculture and pastoralism were practised, but pastoralism was only a minor part of the household economy.

such groups move with their animals to wherever the pastures are best – this varies from year to year according to the spatial distribution of rainfall. Usually the movements of any one domestic unit are within a fairly well-demarcated range of options, but if climatic conditions are extreme they may move much further to different areas altogether and across international boundaries; the domestic unit may split to try and minimize herd losses and reduce risks. The movements are not, however, random and continuous wanderings. Within a nomadic pastoralist population there may be subgroups who move more and further; for example, young men who take groups of animals off to salt licks, or long distance contract herders who take animals down to the coast. In Mali, with the dry season attraction of the inner Niger Delta, the seasonal spatial distribution of pastoralists is extremely variable (Gallais, 1967), and demographic data collection and interpretation must take account of this.

Transhumance

Some pastoralists also practise cultivation, either from economic necessity or out of choice. This reduces their mobility somewhat because they have to be near the fields at key times such as sowing and harvesting, although agricultural labouring inputs are often relatively low. Forms of mobility vary more once agriculture enters into the production equation (see Table 9.2b: agropastoralist). Often, at the first rains, the animals are taken off by part of the human population, others plant the fields and then join up with the first group, only returning to harvest. In other groups, sections of either families or communities stay behind to tend the fields while others move with the herds. They may regroup later in the year, either by the fields or somewhere else. Most movement combinations and permutations are possible.

For households or groups where agriculture is more important, mobility patterns differ again (see Table 9.2b: small agropastoralist). Availability of water also determines where people live. In the wet season some groups move near the fields, and those with the herds can be wherever there is good pasture, because standing water is used for both human and animal consumption. Once the standing water dries up then households and villages may move to be near a water hole or a reliable well. In Northern Burkina Faso, Fulani Liptaako (Table 9.2a) villages of mudbaked brick suggest a fairly fixed population. However, even within those villages there are subgroups – usually young men – who move long distances with the herds at different times of year.

So there is primary production system-related mobility. Although it might be possible to predict probabilities of movement, and patterns of dispersion and regrouping, spatial movements differ from year to year, being largely dependent on the spatial and temporal pattern of the rains, and within households or larger social groups – camps or villages – the membership may also change from season to season and year to year, although there is usually a core of individuals who stay together.

Labour migration

In Burkina Faso, Sahel region (Oudalan, Seno and Soum provinces) is the area with least labour migration (Blion, 1990) in a country where international labour migration has long been a major feature of life (Cordell *et al*, 1996). Whereas elsewhere in Burkina Faso, much of the circular labour out-migration is long term (several years), in this area seasonal labour migration is the norm, at least among the Fulani groups studied. Mobility of subsections of the population is still substantial with 22.8 per cent of the adult Fulani men (aged 18–64) having been on labour migration in the 12 months preceding May 1995, staying for a median stay of 5 months (Hampshire and Randall, 1996). Most of these men go to Ivory Coast. In areas of the northern Sahel in Mali some seasonal migrants move shorter distances going to the large towns of Mopti, Segou and Bamako, others also go to the coastal areas. Whichever movement is being considered it can cause a serious distortion of the recorded population in both the giving and the receiving area, and because of the periods involved, often around six months, classic census definitions of resident or non-resident risk misinterpretation.

Other movements
Droughts are a major cause of population movement in the Sahel. At first such movements are indistinguishable from transhumance, but if a drought persists then those with animals may go much further afield – even down towards the coast – and those who have lost animals tend to congregate around towns or areas of food supply. In terms of population distribution these movements are substantial and are often across administrative boundaries. The 1984–5 drought in the northern Sahel caused severe livestock loss in the pastoral population, and the population distribution recorded by the censuses in Mali in 1987 and in Burkina in 1985 is distorted by this event (Pedersen, 1995, Randall, 1998).

To make matters worse there are all sorts of other short-term movements which make comparisons between different censuses very difficult particularly if the censuses have been taken at different times of year or if the rainy seasons preceding the census were of significantly different quality. Many of the movements are far more likely to occur in the dry season (the slack season for those without animals) but the proportions who move vary from year to year depending in part on the previous rains, harvest and therefore hardship. Such movements include temporary movement of individuals and whole households to gold mines, and to small, medium and large urban areas to look for temporary manual labour.

Population movement and the census
Thus however defined (ethnically, linguistically, economically) people in the Northern Sahel move, with serious repercussions for any attempts to understand net population change using census data. An examination of intercensal changes in Mali between 1976 and 1987 demonstrates this. The 1976 census was done in early December (the cold season) whereas the 1987 one was done in April, mid-hot season. Tables 9.3 and 9.4 demonstrate the consquences[2] of these seasonal differences at cercle (Tenenkou and Gourma Rharous) and arrondissement level.

Much of Tenenkou cercle is in the Niger inner delta to which access is strictly controlled, expanding as the dry season progresses, starting with a massive entry of pastoralists and their cattle in December at Diafarabe. Over the next three months new pasture areas are opened up and the human and cattle populations are allowed to enter. Arrondissements which are totally within the Delta such as Togguere Koumbe and Sossobe have fairly small

Table 9.3   *Intercensal change in de jure population Tenenkou December 1976–April 1987*[a]

Arrondissement	Pop. 1987	% Annual change 1976–87	Comments
Tenenkou urban	12,708	2.16	
Tenenkou rural	29,073	1.46	
Diafarabe urban	5,726	−2.09	Dec: big pop because pastoralists have just entered. April: small pop.
Diafarabe rural	5,858	0.01	as pastoralists have moved on
Diondori	17,936	2.82	
Togguere Koumbe	21,631	5.63	Inner delta: small pop. in Dec. – pastures not available. Large pop in
Sossobe	11,622	4.95	April because of dry season delta pastures
Dioura	13,624	−1.01	Dry land: pastoralists waiting zone in Dec. No pasture in April
Tenekou Cercle	118,178	2.02	

[a] Source for Tables 9.3, 9.4 and 9.5 are the census reports for the two Malian censuses: 1976, vol 1, table p-1; 1987, vols 5, 6, 7, table p-1.

Table 9.4   *Intercensal change December 1976–April 1987, Gourma Rharous Cercle*

Arrondissement	Pop. 1987	% Annual change	Comments
Gourma Rharous town	4,989	0.96	
Gourma Rharous rural	1,3683	−4.31	Dec: pastures April: no water
Bambara Maounde	1,0285	−3.79	Formerly rich area with lakes.
Haribomo	8,613	−2.01	Depopulation since lakes dried up
Madiakoye	10,437	−3.62	
Inadiatafane	9,624	4.53	Permanent water: focus for
Gossi	23,038	4.01	pastoralists in hot season
Ouinarden	6,695	−0.82	Dec: pastures and wild grains April: little water
Gourma Rharous Cercle	87,364	−0.91 m: −1.4 f: −0.45	Mainly pastoral cercle: Drought and cattle loss induced out-migration Also traditional hot season out-migration towards Niger Delta

populations in the wet season and early cold season, because most of the pastoralists and herds are elsewhere. By April (census in 1987) all the pastoralists have been admitted and are making full use of flood plain pastures. Dryland arrondissements outside the delta (Dioura) are more populated in the rainy and cold seasons and less in the hot. Table 9.3 shows the effect of these movements on the census figures. It would be unwise to interpret any of these figures as genuine indications of natural population growth, and had the second census been done at the same time of year the pattern of changes would have been totally different.

Table 9.4 shows similar data for a more typical north Sahelian zone, dominated by pastoralism. Here, in December many pastoralists are still exploiting small standing pools alongside gathering wild grains such as cramcram (*Cenchrus biflorus*). By April these pools have dried up and the majority camp within 10km walking distance of major permanent or semi-permanent pools the largest of which is Gossi mare, with two large water systems in Inadiata-fane. Such redistribution is quite clear from the intercensal growth rates.

Thus census figures only reiterate former knowledge, but require that knowledge for sensible interpretation. Changing data collection quality between the two censuses may have contributed to an underestimation of pastoralists in 1987, but the distributional changes suggest that seasonal patterns are equally important. Certainly in northern Mali there is no evidence from the censuses of the annual growth rates of 2.6 per cent cited in Table 9.1. In fact for the three Northern regions (which contain substantial numbers of nomadic pastoralists and agropastoralists) the Regional intercensal growth rates were substantially smaller (Table 9.5).

THE 'POPULATION PROBLEM' IN THE NORTHERN SAHEL

One problem in defining the population for a Northern Sahelian zone is a consideration of who should be included. Various possibilities can be envisaged:

(a) The census de facto population
(b) The census de jure population (used in Tables 9.3, 9.4, 9.5 above)
(c) Those who could reasonably be expected to claim to a right to live in the area which could include many long-term but temporary labour out-migrants and people who were forced to become a floating population on the town edges.

Table 9.5   *Intercensal growth rates 1976–87, North Mali*

| Region | % Annual intercensal growth | | |
	Urban[a]	Rural	Total
Mopti	3.03	1.01	1.25
Tombouctou	4.25	−1.36	−0.63
Gao	5.59	−0.73	0.25

[a] Calculated from census tables outlined in FN 6 above. Where villages were transformed into urban areas through intercensal population growth they were retained as rural.

Census or census-like data can only generate the first two of these. Yet, many out-migrants, either labour migrants or drought refugees, retain family and economic links in their area of origin and usually intend to return there. Thus to an extent they are part of the 'population' of the area and certainly need to be taken into account when considering whether there is a 'population problem'. Assuming we can get around the theoretical issue of who has a right to be labelled a 'member' of an area, the next issue in relationship to understanding whether 'population growth' is the major cause of environmental problems and underdevelopment is establishing how different 'populations' should be defined. Perceptions of the 'population' problem may clarify this a little. The various baseline stories are:

(a) Rapid population growth (undifferentiated) is causing overuse of natural resources, decreasing fallow, overgrazing, unsustainable use of firewood and leads to desertification.
(b) Population growth in extensive agricultural populations further south has led to a gradual movement of these populations northwards, and extension of agriculture into zones previously used by pastoralists, thus reducing their flexibility and the security provided by their production system.
(c) Human and associated animal population growth in pastoral populations is one factor exacerbating overgrazing leading to poor productivity and economic precariousness. One consequence of this is a gradual transformation of pastoralists into agropastoralists, and herd owners into contract herders.
(d) Extensive pastoralism is economically and environmentally irrational (Hardin's tragedy of the commons) and most pastoralists should be encouraged to destock and invest more in agriculture whilst more intensive modes of livestock production are developed and adopted by a few. Population growth exacerbates this irrationality.
(e) Changes in rainfall are the major causes of hardship in this area and of the problems faced by pastoralists. However, if population growth continues, per capita animal holdings are unlikely to be maintained because of poor environmental conditions, and therefore human welfare will suffer (and pastoralists will probably have to transform into agriculturalists or urban labourers).

Testing any of these hypotheses would require an examination of population growth and demographic dynamics in at least three economic subgroups of the population: agriculturalists, agropastoralists and pastoralists.

Here, however, we encounter a whole series of definitional problems because not only is there a continuum between the different economic activities, there are also lifetime changes, life-cycle effects and economic diversity within families and households. For example, in a large Fulani household with several brothers, one brother may continuously look after the extended family herd, going off with his wife and children on transhumance in the wet season, whereas two others cultivate the extended family fields along with a few privately owned fields and stock the granaries of everyone. The fourth brother spends much of his life on labour migration in the Ivory Coast. In this fairly typical case, who is a pastoralist? who is an agriculturalist? All own animals, all draw grain out of a household granary filled through family production (rather than purchased). In years of poor rainfall and harvest more brothers may go to Abidjan; over a lifetime each brother will probably have a few years in each speciality.

There are temporal changes too. Some former pastoralists, who have lost all or most of their animals, move into agriculture. For many this is seen as a temporary strategy whilst they gradually build up their herd with the ultimate aim of eventually abandoning agriculture (Bonfiglioli, 1990; Cisse, 1981). The proportion of the former pastoral population in this position will clearly vary according to the recent climatic past. A recent severe drought will have left more destitute herders than a series of good years. Even within a good period some pastoralists fail through bad management or bad luck.

A final problem in defining pastoralists is whether the critical group is the population of animal owners, animal herders (in which case herd owners and/or contract herders) or people who depend on livestock herding for their survival even though they do not participate in the actual herding. In the Northern Sahel most people invest in livestock and many of the animals observed grazing are not owned by the herders. Civil servants, merchants and farmers all invest in cattle. In fact the latter, who in the past may have invested in cattle herded by traditional herders, may be turning more and more to herding their own animals and moving towards the pastoral end of the economic spectrum (Cisse, 1980; Toulmin, 1992). But let us consider for the moment the farmer who has invested surplus in cattle, and the civil servants, who rarely see their animals, and have little day to day contact, yet can mobilize substantial resources through cattle sales. Are these pastoralists? Certainly any increase in the numbers of animals in the Northern Sahel is closely related to these peoples' investments.

Thus the human dynamics are problematic. If we consider the animal demography and population dynamics, is this likely to be any more informative? It would inform on the changing livestock population density, although this is also subject to substantial fluctutation, and nomadism (where do the animals 'belong'), but it would say little about the strategies and well-being of pastoralists since recently there has been substantial transfer of ownership, and it would be wrong to automatically condemn the irrational pastoralist for any increase in animal numbers.

It appears impossible to examine issues of population growth within production system for the reasons outlined above, yet unfounded conclusions about differential growth or rapid growth are often the premises for 'development'/'aid' programmes.

In what other meaningful ways can one define populations in the Northern Sahel? Are these populations coherent and consistent groups and can they be used to throw any light on changing population dynamics?

Ethnicity-specific demography

Ethnicity has long been recognized as an important determinant of demographic behaviour (Lestaeghe 1989) and in most African countries where the issue is not politically and demographically sensitive, data on ethnicity have been collected. It was once considered that ethnic group was a fairly stable and unambiguous concept which brought with it a package of behaviours which could be quantified and opposed – hence the use that has been made of the Murdock Ethnographic Atlas. Anthropology has moved from an interpretation of African societies as essentially culturally stable – to be written about in the 'ethnographic present' – to a recognition of constant change, lack of homogeneity, internal contradictions and transformation. Transformations occur from one ethnicity to another either relatively voluntarily, agropastoral Jie to pastoral Turkana in East Africa two centuries ago (Gulliver, 1970), camel herding Rendille into cattle herding Samburu (Spencer, 1973), or through force and slave raiding such as *iklan* in West African Kel Tamasheq society (Winter, 1984). Many of these *iklan* are now adopting Fulani or Songhay surnames which may well be part of further transformations. Within ethnic groups, normative behaviour changes for a variety of reasons which include economic exigencies and contacts with new ideas. Nevertheless most people in the Northern Sahel can ascribe themselves fairly unequivocally to an ethnic group and the ethnically determined norms of behaviour still seem to have quite a strong influence on demographic dynamics partly because marriage and reproduction are such an essential part of increasing membership of a group.

Ethnicity is also an important determinant of preferred economic activity. The former close correlation between ethnicity and actual economic activity has gradually been eroded over the last century with colonial interventions (such as abolition of slavery, forced labour), advent of schools and changing socio-economic and environmental conditions, but for many people their primary economic activity (and their attitudes to other ones) is still substantially determined by which group they adhere to. There may of course be an element of chicken and egg here; people who want to change their main economic activity may take up residence elsewhere, start to speak other languages and gradually change their ethnic identity.

In comparison with censuses and sample surveys what are the advantages and disadvantages of ethnic specific demography in the Northern Sahel, and what methodologies are most appropriate?

Language
Ethnicity and maternal language are fairly closely related at least in rural areas – which are the ones most concerned here. Thus if data are being collected in population x who speak xese, one can use enumerators who are also from x and xese speakers, households can be defined in xese using meaningful social and/or economic units rather than an arbitrary all-purpose definition of eating or cooking together. For other concepts which might change meaning in translation such as marriage there is less risk of ambiguity for the interviewers and a stronger probability that the subjects will be talking about similar procedures.

Social divisions
Conventional demographic measures used for distinguishing social class or socio-economic status are useless in the Northern Sahel. Few rural people are educated. Subsistence production along with much use of wild produce and irregular and erratic income means that it is impossible to get any estimates of household revenue. Declaration of ownership of animals is extremely unreliable. Few households have access to any public amenities such as water or electricity, and even ownership of particular material goods is unlikely to be a good guide to socio-economic status especially among the more nomadic pastoralist populations. This is not to say that people are socio-economically homogeneous, just that it is very difficult to classify them on the basis of a questionnaire-style survey. In many of the populations, however, there are named subgroups which, although far from indicating material wealth are often good indicators of social status and behavioural expectations – and may in the past have been indicators of economic status and activity. These indigenous classifications may in fact be demographically more homogeneous than any wealth defined groups in areas which have poor access to and utilization of health services, and where housing and water supply are determined more by expediency than resources. Such divisions may be the various social classes found within Tamasheq society (divisions which can be a major divide between free *illelan* and former slaves *iklan*, or more subtle divisions) or the *lenyol (pl lenyi)* clans in Fulani society. Demographic analysis along these divisions can only be done within an ethnic grouping.

Normative behaviour
Working within an ethnic group, it becomes possible to speculate about normative behaviour and social expectations. In some populations it is clear that there are types of behaviour which are expected of that social group. Although it is possible for people to behave differently – e.g. for someone to go on labour migration in a group that normally doesn't, or for someone from a group renowned for being herders to be a successful cultivator, in general,

within an ethnic subdivision the social expectations are similar – and devia-tions from these become factors or individuals who merit specific investiga-tion. In some cases, ethnic subgroup is still a fairly good guide to economic activity, partly because some activities are effectively excluded because they are seen as shameful. If people are found in those activities (e.g. a high status Tamasheq actually cultivating fields) then that is a good indication that the person/household has been through some very stressful period.

Endogamy
Because most marriages are ethnically endogamous, especially in the rural areas of the Northern Sahel, all members of a household are usually from the same ethnic group. Ethnicity (with the possible exceptions outlined above) is unchanging over life and thus a series of surveys over time which are ethnically based will tend to capture the same individuals or their descen-dents. It should, however, be noted that it is most likely that the poorest, the lowest social status and the disenfranchised will be the most likely to transform their ethnicity for the very reason that they are disenfranchised and only thus can they hope to change their lot. It is important to remember that reproduction is not only for the individual but the group. Fulbe Gaobe have Fulbe Gaobe children; a pastoralist does not necessarily have pastoralist children, or an educated woman, educated children.

Disadvantages of ethnicity-specific demography
A survey of one ethnic group only obtains the dynamics of a proportion of the population in an area. Most of the Northern Sahel is ethnically hetero-geneous. In one cercle there may be villages or camps of people from eight different ethnic groups all speaking different languages, each with a different dynamic. Thus ethnicity-specific demography only provides a very limited overall picture of a region.

It is harder to define ethnicity in urban areas, and the logistics of ethnic based data collection would be substantial. However, given that the issues we are attempting to address here are those of population growth in the rural zones, this should not be seen as a major obstacle. Obviously where there is substantial out-migration to local or distant urban areas this must be considered.

National sample surveys
It might seem that well-designed national sample surveys would be the solu-tion to demographic lacunae in the Northern Sahel. In fact this area is famed from its omission from studies which could serve this purpose; the 1962–3 Institut National de la Statistique et des Etudes Economiques (INSEE) sample survey in Mali omitted the then sixth Region which was the whole Northern Sahelian zone where most of the pastoralists live. The 1987 Mali DHS only

took urban samples from the two Northerly Regions (Gao and Tombouctou). The Mauritanian DHS only sampled the sedentary population (although there had been a supplement to the census for nomadic women). The recent series of migration studies in West Africa (Burkina Faso, Ivory Coast, Guinea, Mali, Mauritania, Niger, Nigeria and Senegal) explicitly excluded both refugee and nomadic populations both of which are important subgroups in the Northern Sahel.[3] Even in censuses, different methodologies are used for nomadic populations, which are likely to result in much poorer data: e.g. in Mali in 1976 nomads were told to gather at specific water points in order to be censused whereas villages were treated to enumerators arriving in their households.

Where sample surveys do include the Northern zones, the samples are usually too small for any meaningful analysis of population dynamics, and because of the ethnic heterogeneity, rarely include enough cases for any specific analysis of particular groups. Anyway, the more mobile populations are more likely to be excluded either deliberately or through the construction of the sampling frame.

Methodological issues in Northern Sahelian data collection
All the problems of demographic data collection outlined in *The Demography of Tropical Africa* (Brass *et al*, 1968) are still very much alive in the Northern Sahel: no vital registration, poor census data and real practical problems in collecting specific data. Literacy levels are very low, amongst men and women, and there is often total disinterest in the concept of age. Some groups are fairly remote from national events (especially women), event calendars are difficult to generate and use and age ranking is unreliable when the residential groups are fairly fluid. Many groups, especially the Fulani, have various interdictions on pronouncing names. A woman cannot say the name of her husband, and many couples will not mention the existence of their first child and are reluctant to name subsequent children.

The mobility discussed earlier has three main ramifications for demographic data collection. Firstly, if a relatively large number of individuals are to be enumerated, the only feasible methodology is a single round survey. Attempts at multi-round studies have either been abandoned because of logistic problems (e.g. Sodter, 1980, in Burkina) or have ended up with tiny samples (Loutan, 1985 and White, 1986, in Niger), or with large amounts of missing data for the more mobile sections of the population (K. Hampshire, personal communication).

Secondly, household membership may have to be defined rather more widely than is often the case in demographic studies. A six month cut-off for residents may omit people on seasonal labour migration to the coastal cities, who are definitely part of the household, and may also omit subsections of households who are on transhumance. This may engender a risk of double counting if the survey takes place over a large space and relatively long time period. Subsections of households may be enumerated as absent from their larger group at one place, but if they are camped with their own hut elsewhere they may be enumerated as a smaller, discrete household elsewhere. This problem is difficult to avoid, but probably not very serious. Such a wider-approach household definition also goes some way towards including the population who feel they have some right to live in the area

Sampling is a third problem. Although in some cases (Mali in the 1980s) it would theoretically be possible to draw up a sampling frame from tax registers, the practicalities of trying to locate selected mobile households in a huge, low population density area with no roads, and when they might be in one of many administrative districts, are enormous and the cost would be phenomenal. The INSEE 1966 nomad survey in Niger struggled with a variety of sampling methods but eventually abandoned them all. Given that most of the problems of demographic data collection in such environments consist of actually finding people to interview, and that the expense is mainly in terms of fuel and transport, and that there is no reason to assume that one geographical area of a population is demographically different from adjacent areas (with the same general ecology and climate), the most practical solution is usually total (or as close to total as can be obtained) coverage of particular water holes or a spatially defined area. Prior knowledge of people's location is not then essential because information can be obtained from each camp or village about the neighbouring ones, their ethnicity (and thus whether they are to be included) and their location. Clearly there is still potential for bias and omission, but this is probably unavoidable in nomadic demography, especially if a reasonable sample size is to be obtained.

Choice of season for study is of critical importance in these areas, and interpretation of results, and comparability between different surveys also depend on the season chosen. Seasonal issues differ according to whether the population is dominated by pastoralists or agriculturalists. Agriculturalists have a slack season from November through to June when nothing can be cultivated. Thus they are free to answer the demographer's questions – save that this slack season is the time of seasonal labour migration and thus much of the data on young adult men must be collected vicariously. Pastoralists do not have a slack season (White, 1986) but labouring is particularly intense towards the end of the hot season where watering and pasturing demands are heaviest. On the other hand, because of water shortage this is the season when they are most likely to be grouped together, which facilitates both locating them and interviewing large numbers. Thus again, probably much of the data on men will have to be gathered vicariously. Conditions mean that it is impossible to do any large-scale data collection in the wet season; anyway agriculturalists are busy and pastoralists very dispersed.

In most Sahelian countries (the exception being Mauritania) the populations who are found mainly in the Northern Sahel, in particular the more nomadic and mobile pastoral populations, are minority groups who are often underrepresented in the mainstream political system (whether from choice, circumstance or a combination of the two is debatable). A consequence of both their lifestyle and their marginal status is that usually educational levels are much lower than the national average (in many of these countries already very low in rural areas). This has practical consequences for undertaking demographic surveys – it is very hard to find suitable female interviewers. Educated women do exist, but they are usually members of families who for whatever reason have a long history of education and are usually urban dwellers, and are also usually from the elite social classes. Such women are reluctant or unable to cope with the unavoidable harsh conditions of a demographic survey in the rural pastoral areas, posing problems in collecting birth histories. If appropriate women are genuinely unavailable there are two solutions; use men to collect birth histories – with a concomitant diminution in the quality of the data, or abandon birth histories altogether and focus on using indirect Brass methods for estimations of fertility and mortality.

Population dynamics in the northern Sahel
Given all these constraints, what if anything is known about population dynamics in the Northern Sahel? Gross figures from censuses tell us that numbers of nomads are declining (see Pedersen, 1995; Randall 1995, 1998) and urban populations are increasing substantially, but this may well be a function of the fact that the last census round (1985 Burkina, 1987 Mali) was fairly soon after the 1984–5 drought which had a devastating effect on Sahelian livestock owners.

A picture of the population dynamics of different subgroups in the Northern Sahel is gradually being formed. Starting with a series of retrospective single round surveys in the early 1980s,[4] the two of these which probably contributed most to the lacunae of information about nomadic populations were those of Kel Tamasheq (Twareg) from two different zones in Mali; one group who spent the dry season in the inner delta (and thus included in the Tenenkou 1987, Table 9.3 above) and the other living mainly in the Gourma, some in Gourma Rharous (Table 9.4). These surveys, which faced many of the problems outlined above produced the first estimates of fertility and mortality for these nomadic populations (Table 9.6). Despite the fact that their fertility was lower than that of some sedentary populations elsewhere in Mali, it was possible to show that in terms of natural dynamic the Delta Tamasheq were a population growing at around 2.3 per cent per annum, the Gourma Tamasheq at 1.2 per cent per annum (figures suggesting that the census data either seriously under-enumerated these populations in 1987, or the out-migration provoked by the drought was extreme). It is unlikely that there was a significant amount of excess human mortality in the drought.

Table 9.6 *Estimates of fertility and mortality in Malian Tamasheq populations: 1981–2 by social class*

| | Delta Tamasheq | | Gourma Tamasheq | | |
	Nobles	Iklan	Nobles	Low status illelan	Iklan
TFR	6.7	6.4	4.5	5.2	5.6
TMFR	10.0	10.2	7.7	7.2	8.7
$_5q_0$	0.35	0.26	0.41	0.37	0.29
e_{15} female	41	44	< 30	32	39
e_{15} male	40	38	33	< 30	33

TMFR = Total marital fertility rate.

Several interesting features were identified in the 1981–2 Tamasheq demographic surveys. Firstly, in all the population subgroups the marriage pattern had a significant effect in reducing fertility – much more so than is normally observed in rural African populations. This is interesting in its own right, but also in the implications for future population growth and the potential for change to a rapidly growing population. The second unexpected finding was the substantial heterogeneity within the population between the social classes, particularly with respect to mortality. Despite irregularities in the data and problems with accurate ageing, it is clear that there are a variety of demographic regimes which cannot be determined by ecological factors given that these groups all live within the same areas (the exception being Delta versus Gourma), or by access to health care and good water (not applicable for any group). These results suggest that in Mali in the 1980s there was not 'a pastoralist/Tamasheq demographic regime', but several, and also that there were both high growth rate (Delta *iklan* with low mortality for adults and children) and low growth rate (Gourma Tamasheq nobles: low fertility, high child and adult mortality) regimes. But can one talk of a pastoralist demography?

In the light of the Tamasheq data one would tend towards a perception of heterogeneity, with population growth somewhat constrained by high mortality and the marriage pattern. Fulani data from Burkina Faso in the 1990s suggests that there are other pastoralist demographic regimes too. These data were also collected using single round retrospective surveys, focusing only on Fulfulde speaking groups in an ethnically heterogenous zone. Unlike the Tamasheq who, at the time of the 1981–2 surveys were all pastoral nomads, the Northern Sahelian Burkinabe Fulani stretch across a wider spectrum of pastoralism and cultivation, with most pure pastoralists being Djelgobe, most Gaobe and Fulbe Liptaako being agropastoralists with the Liptaako more sedentary and in larger more permanent villages than the

Table 9.7 *Estimates of fertility and mortality in Burkinabe Fulani populations 1995:*
by ethnic subgroup

	Fulbe Djelgobe	Fulbe Gaobe	Fulbe Liptaako	Rimaibe
Estimated TFR (1994–5)	9.2	6.3	6.4*	7.05
Reported parity for women aged 45–64	7.8	6.6	7.0	6.8
parity for women 45–64 after correction for under-enumeration of girls)	7.9	6.6	7.8	7.1
TMFR (1994–5)	10.1	7.3	6.8	7.6
$_5q_0$	.22	.24	.32	.32
e_{20} female	51	45	45	46
e_{15} male	n/a	n/a	n/a	n/a

* Corrected for under-enumeration of girls.

Gaobe, and the Rimaibe (former serfs and slaves of the Fulbe) being largely agriculturalists (Table 9.7).

Despite some reporting problems and inconsistencies[5] there is clearly a variety of demographic regimes here. Contrary to what was expected the most pastoral group, the Djelgobe, have the highest fertility (using either reported completed family size or age-specific fertility) and the lowest child mortality. Given the high reported fertility the low mortality (estimated from proportions dead of children ever borne) is unlikely to be a function of underreporting. The groups with lower reported parities actually report higher proportions of dead children.

CONCLUSIONS

Although such studies do not provide answers or solutions to the various baseline 'population problem' stories outlined earlier, they, and others like them can start to provide some real information on which to premiss any arguments. These studies demonstrate such a wide variety of demographic regimes that it is hard to envisage that a simplistic population-underdevelop-ment or population-environmental disaster scenario is ever going to be a realistic representation of the issues in the Northern Sahel. Certainly many of these groups clearly do have a substantial natural population dynamic, notwithstanding any evidence from censuses, which might ultimately cause problems but at present it is a rational response to the environment and production system in which they operate. The variability in fertility and mor-tality within a fairly homogeneous environment lacking health infrastructure or inputs also suggests an ability to manipulate population parameters to a certain degree, which must have proved evolutionarily advantageous in the recent past.

Thus far data are only available on a limited number of these Northern Sahelian pastoral and agropastoral populations. Yet if the development discourse is going to continue to hinge upon issues of population growth and transformation, it is essential that the data base be extended. Here the indirect methods pioneered by Brass are probably the only way forward. More recent sample survey methodologies, along DHS lines, with long questionnaires and detailed, demanding birth histories are just not practical in these environments. Old and tested indirect methods from rapid single-round surveys will have to continue to be used, because only thus can enough of the population be covered, and only thus will people be persuaded to participate. Ethnic homogeneity becomes part of the methodology for practical purposes – largely the mobility and marginalization of the populations concerned.

Even with more demographic data collection, some pastoralist population questions will remain enigmatic, because the determinants of growth of pastoralists are not the traditional demographic parameters of birth, death and migration, but economic transformation, life-cycle changes, seasonal fluctuations and responses to hardship which may be temporary or permanent.

REFERENCES

Blion, R. (1990) *Phénomènes Migratoires et Migration de Retour des Migrants Burkinabe de la Côte d'Ivoire*. Paris: Mémoire DEA, Panthéon Sorbonne.

Bonfiglioli, A.M. (1990) 'Pastoralisme, agro-pastoralisme et retour: itinéraires saheliens'. *Cahiers des Sciences Humaines*, 26 (1–2), pp. 255–66.

Brass, W., Coale, A.J., Demeny, P., Heisel, D.F., Lorimer, F., Romaniuk, A. and van de Walle, E. (1968) *The Demography of Tropical Africa*. Princeton, NJ: Princeton University Press.

Cisse, S. (1981) 'Sedentarisation of nomadic pastoralists and pastoralisation of cultivators in Mali', in J. Galaty, D. Aronson, P. Salzman and A. Chouinard (eds), *The Future of Pastoral Peoples*. Canada: IDRC.

Cordell, D., Gregory, J. and Piché, V. (1996) *Hoe and Wage*. Boulder, CO: Westview Press.

Gallais, J. (1967) *Le Delta Intérieur du Niger, et ses Bordures*. Paris: CNRS.

Gulliver, P. (1955) *The Family Herds: A Study of Two Pastoral Tribes in East Africa, the Jie and the Turkana*. London: Routledge and Kegan Paul.

Hampshire, K. and Randall, S. (1998) 'Pauvrêté et migration saisonnière au sahel', in *Crises, pauvrêté et changements démographiques dans les pays du sud* ed. Francis Gendreau. Aupelf-Uref, Editions Estem, Paris.

INSEE, SEDES Niger Mission Economique Pastorale (1966) Enquête Démographique et Nomades, vol 2: Démographie, budgets et consommation. Niger: Institut National de la Statistique et des Etudes Economique.

Lestaeghe, R. (ed) (1989) *Reproduction and Social Organization in sub Saharan Africa*. Berkeley, CA: University of California Press.

Loutan, L. (1985) 'Nutrition amongst a group of WoDaaBe (Fulani Bororo) pastoralists in Niger', in A.G. Hill (ed), *Population Health and Nutrition in the Sahel*. KPI.

Pedersen, J. (1995) 'Drought, migration and population growth in the Sahel: the case of the Malian Gourma: 1990–91'. *Population Studies*, 49 (1), pp. 111–26.

Randall, S. (1998) 'The consequences of drought for populations in the Malian Gourma', in J. Clarke and D. Noin (eds), *Population and Environment in Arid Regions*. (Man and Biosphere series 19). Paris: UNESCO, pp. 149–76.

Randall, S. (1995) 'Are pastoralists demographically different from sedentary agriculturalists?' in B. Zaba and J.Clarke (eds), *Environment and Population Change*. ORDINA.

République du Mali Recensement Général de la Population 1976, vol 1. Mali: Ministère du Plan.

République du Mali Recensement Général de la Population 1987, vols 5, 6, 7. Mali: Ministère du Plan.

Sodter, F. (1980) Enquête démographique sur la zone de la Mare d'Oursi (Haute Volta). ORSTOM Ouagadougou Mimeo.

Spencer, P. (1973) *Nomads in Alliance*. Oxford: Oxford University Press.

Thébaud, B. (1995) 'Pastoralisme et degradation du Milieu naturel au Sahel: mythe ou réalité, in A .Reenberg and S. Marcussen (eds), SEREIN Occasional Paper No 1.

Toulmin, C. (1992) *Cattle, Women and Wells*. Oxford: Oxford University Press.

UNDP (1996) *Human Development Report 1996*. New York: Oxford University Press.

White, C. (1986) 'Food shortages and seasonality in WoDaaBe communities in Niger'. *IDS Bulletin*, 17 (3), pp. 19–25.

Winter, M. (1984) Slavery and the pastoral Twareg of Mali'. *Cambridge Anthropology*, pp. 4–30.

Developed Country Demography

CHAPTER TEN

Accessions and abdications: men and women as family markers in linked data for England and Wales

Lynda Clarke

London School of Hygiene and Tropical Medicine

Heather Joshi

Institute of Education, London University

In 1983 the British Society for Population Studies held its Annual Conference on the theme of 'The Family'. Family demography had only recently emerged as an integrated topic of demographic study. Professor William Brass was one of the speakers invited to contribute. Characteristically, Brass gave a paper which investigated the mathematical relationships of determinants of family composition and size (Brass, 1983). He described the core of family demography as the investigation of the relationship between demographic factors and the numbers and composition of co-resident units in a population. Brass took the view that previous attempts at specifying the formal demography of the family (Ryder, 1977; Sweet, 1977; Burch, 1979; Bongaarts, 1983) to 'range widely and none attempts to constrain the scope tightly'. This he felt needed to be done.

Brass outlined a theory of the proximate determinants of the family. He developed a model for the impact of such demographic factors as fertility, mortality, divorce, ages at establishment and dissolution of families on mean size and family composition. He concluded that the age at which females set up separate establishments is critical and that divorce can be a significant influence. He assumed families could be identified across time by tracing one particular individual, or marker – a practice questioned by Murphy (1996).[1] His somewhat controversial recommendation was that this person should be female rather than male, as in the conventional concept of a family head.

Family demography has recently become an increasingly important area for demographic research on developed countries. The last two decades has witnessed much change in family dynamics. Increased childbearing outside marriage, the breakdown of marriages and cohabitations, as well as family reconstitution mean that the family is not the stable unit it was. Demographic research in the field of the family has grown but it has concentrated on analysing patterns of family formation and disruption (e.g. Kiernan and Eldridge, 1985; Ni Brolchain, 1993; Berrington and Diamond, 1997; Clarke *et al*, 1997) or quantifying household dynamics (Murphy, 1996). Brass contributed more broadly to an understanding of the processes of family formation and dissolution by establishing the quantitative importance of demographic determinants of the family. Whether his assumptions still hold and the models are enduring is a moot point. Brass himself concluded by saying:

> There is a need for further investigation of the validity of the models through comparisons with observations for appropriate populations with good data. Further refinement is possible, if justified, to achieve greater precision and extend the scope for application. Such extension might be to time paths of change in the numbers of families as well as the mean size. Since the models are developed with the age of marker as a key variable to which composition characteristics, such as numbers of children, could be attached the approach might lead to outputs more detailed than mean family size without destruction of its essential simplicity. (Brass, 1983)

In this paper we will test some of his assumptions, using empirical data from the Office of National Statistics (ONS) Longitudinal Study. We summarize the data on family continuity through three censuses using male and female family 'markers', to use Professor Brass's terminology, to test his assumption that females have greater stability as longest serving members of a co-resident group (core family heads), and are therefore preferable as markers. We also investigate how sensitive family continuity would appear to be in recent times in England and Wales using male as opposed to female family markers. The unit of interest is the group consisting of a couple, or a single adult with or without co-resident children of any age, as defined in the next section. We trace adults from leaving the parental home into and out of co-resident partnerships and examine how stable the family membership of adults is by age and between men and women.

DEFINITION OF THE FAMILY

For the purposes of this paper, the co-resident grouping is that of the family as defined in the Census of England and Wales, with other people outside families treated as separate units. Brass (1983) uses the terms household and family somewhat interchangeably, with households that consist only of one family very much at the core of his exposition. The particular definition of 'family' used here is a co-resident group of individuals related by 'marriage' or parenthood. 'Marriage' includes *de facto* conjugal partners, where identifiable. Parenthood includes all co-resident children of a couple or lone parent of whatever age provided the children have never married. Thus a family here consists of a couple with or without their 'children' or a lone parent with children. Rare cases of grandparents living with grandchildren are treated as a family by the census, but not here. We confine our definition of the family to two generations.

People who are not members of families are treated in these schemes as separate units whether they live alone, in households with other people or in institutions. These out-of-family states are treated as one-person 'families' when we come to report average 'family' size. This grouping of the population into 'families' resembles that of 'benefit units' used in the study of income distribution as well as the administration of benefits (Roll, 1991), except that children living at home do not have to be under any given age or be economically dependent. Provided they are not themselves married or lone parents they are counted as part of a second generation of the nuclear family.

The definition of a family also varies slightly from census to census, in respect of the treatment of cohabiting couples who were legally married. At the time of the 1971 Census, when the practice was at a low level (Brown and Kiernan, 1981), there is no information to identify unmarried couples. We can only count as couples, people who reported themselves as married. This probably includes some who were not actually legally married, but who preferred not to advertise the fact. If they did not claim to be married they would appear in the census as a lone adult or possibly a falsely lone parent. False lone fatherhood is the most likely outcome in the minority of cases with children present. By 1981 cohabitation had become more common and recognized, though not to the extent of being included as a possible condition of the census form. An indicator of '*de facto*' couples was generated after the census for cases writing in descriptions of their relationship which suggested non-marital conjugal unions. This procedure is not thought to give complete identification of cohabitees, so the problem of false lone fathers remains, possibly on a larger scale, given the rising prevalence of cohabitation and childbearing within such unions. In 1991 the census asked a direct question to identify cohabitation, so that, as the phenomenon grew in prevalence, so did its acceptability and its coverage in the census (Wright and Lynch, 1995). Hence couples as a whole are more extensively covered in 1991 than in earlier years.

MARKERSHIP

In Professor Brass's models one member of each family at any one time is uniquely specified as a 'marker'. He assumed that consistent rules for determining the marker could be framed. The concept of marker is similar to that of family head or 'head of household' as used in the classification of census or survey data, where the senior male is usually designated as the family or household head. Brass assumed, however, that

> it will normally be better to take the marker wherever possible as the senior female in the coresident family group where 'senior' relates to function in the household decisions and services rather than age.

Family markers come into being – Brass sometimes says they are 'born' or '*accede*' – and cease to be markers – 'die' or 'abdicate' – in the following exercise according to Brass's original specification.

> Markers are born at a rate b(x) (where x is age), defined in the conventional way; as the number of persons who become markers at age x divided by the number at risk, in this case taken as the total in the population of this age. Births will occur when a person leaves the parental home either to become a family of one or the marker in a group (primarily through marriage), through separation, divorce or widowhood of a non-marker and in a minority of other residence changes. There is no bar on a person being a marker more than once. Of course the implicit assumption that all persons aged x are at risk of becoming markers is a crude simplification but no different in kind from that made in the calculation of an age-specific fertility rate.
> Once 'born', markers disappear because they die or because they abdicate, the latter occurring mainly through marriage to another marker with priority for the title, or through joining an established household, for example old people moving to live with married children. Abdication will be measured by S(x) a function similar to the life table survivorship to age x, l(x). Thus the rates of abdication at each age are used to construct a decrement table with S(x)/S(a) giving the proportion who became markers at age a, still in that state at x conditional on their being alive. The major simplifications are that S(x) is only age dependent and does not vary with type of marker (for example male or female) or duration of time in that state (Brass, 1983).

Markership in the following exercise is assigned to men as a priority under the 'male scheme' and women as priority under the 'female scheme'. The extent of difference in family formation and dissolution experienced by men and women by age, and hence markership under each scheme, is, thus, critical to the comparison.

DATA

The assumptions made by Brass in his models will be tested using data from the ONS Longitudinal Study (LS). The LS is a 1 per cent sample of the population of England and Wales based on a sample of people born on four days selected from the calendar year. It links census records – beginning in 1971 – with vital registration data and is constantly updated with the addition of births and immigrations and records of deaths and emigrations via the National Health Service Central Register. Thus, in this LS, individuals' household and family position can be followed forward from the 1971 Census through two subsequent censuses. Full details of the history and structure of the LS are to be found in Hattersley and Creeser (1995). The sample size over three censuses was 594,036 LS members, born before 1976 and hence aged at least 15 in at least one of the three censuses covered, is shown in Table 10.1.

For every marker, the size of a unit group is:

One – if they live alone or with others not in a family.

Two – if they are one of a couple with no children, or a lone parent with one child.

Three or more – if a lone parent has more than one child or a couple has any children.

LINKAGE AND MISSING DATA

Table 10.1 shows attrition from the three censuses linkage and reasons for persons not having valid data. In total 294,732 males and 299,304 females were present in our linked sample in at least one census. Just under two-thirds were present at every census, or dead after having been present at least once: 64 per cent of males and 65 per cent of females. Reasons for not appearing at all censuses include being born between 1971 and 1976 and international migration. Apart from these valid and documented transitions, there are cases which are not found at the census. These arise from unrecorded emigration, census under-enumeration and failures to match an LS identifier with a census record. There are also cases present at a census but with missing information on co-residential status: for example those enumerated as a visitor in another household or where family relationships in the household are not clearly coded. Births since the 1971 Census account for a relatively small proportion (5 per cent) of the sample. Known cases of international migration (which includes Scotland as a source or destination of migration) account for a similar proportion.

The main reason for escaping complete coverage in the LS over this period is non-coverage in a census, in other words people not located at a

Table 10.1 Attrition. Who escapes complete coverage?

Age of cohort at 1981 (years)	Present at any census (N)	Valid at all three (incl. deaths)	Born in first decade	ratios to all present at any census Immigration	Emigration	Not found 1971 census (mutually exclusive)	Not found 1981 census	Not found 1991 census	Invalid at all three
Males									
5–9	18,482	0.000	0.893	0.054	0.000	0.053	0.000	0.000	0.000
10–14	24,531	0.560		0.048	0.016	0.118	0.083	0.111	0.064
15–19	25,955	0.584		0.053	0.011	0.121	0.080	0.112	0.040
20–24	24,147	0.567		0.071	0.011	0.122	0.104	0.077	0.047
25–29	22,013	0.563		0.074	0.019	0.124	0.113	0.058	0.049
30–34	23,162	0.586		0.058	0.023	0.126	0.107	0.048	0.051
35–39	19,765	0.646		0.041	0.024	0.115	0.098	0.046	0.030
40–49	34,835	0.693		0.030	0.018	0.103	0.091	0.041	0.024
50–59	34,291	0.762		0.015	0.011	0.082	0.073	0.031	0.026
60–69	31,005	0.781		0.009	0.010	0.074	0.074	0.024	0.028
70–79	23,716	0.855		0.004	0.007	0.038	0.051	0.013	0.032
80–89	10,079	0.897		0.002	0.005	0.017	0.045	0.004	0.030
90–99	2,563	0.924		0.000	0.002	0.008	0.025	0.000	0.041
100 plus	188	0.931		0.000	0.000	0.000	0.021	0.000	0.048
All ages	294,732	0.637	0.056	0.037	0.013	0.094	0.079	0.049	0.035

Table 10.1 (continued)

Age of cohort at 1981 (years)	Present at any census (N)	Valid at all three (incl. deaths)	Born in first decade	ratios to all present at any census					Invalid at all three
				Immigration	Emigration	Not found 1971 census (mutually exclusive)	Not found 1981 census	Not found 1991 census	
Females									
5–9	17,678	0.000	0.896	0.054	0.000	0.050	0.000	0.000	0.000
10–14	23,704	0.552		0.057	0.017	0.115	0.079	0.075	0.063
15–19	24,761	0.621		0.064	0.014	0.123	0.073	0.071	0.033
20–24	22,365	0.602		0.088	0.016	0.115	0.085	0.051	0.043
25–29	19,958	0.588		0.094	0.020	0.123	0.098	0.038	0.039
30–34	21,920	0.612		0.062	0.024	0.116	0.108	0.035	0.043
35–39	18,339	0.671		0.040	0.020	0.113	0.093	0.037	0.026
40–49	32,562	0.715		0.028	0.014	0.102	0.084	0.035	0.023
50–59	34,218	0.757		0.014	0.009	0.086	0.072	0.032	0.029
60–69	33,397	0.742		0.009	0.010	0.093	0.079	0.028	0.039
70–79	28,008	0.791		0.006	0.007	0.061	0.064	0.023	0.049
80–89	16,041	0.839		0.002	0.003	0.035	0.063	0.010	0.047
90–99	5,747	0.894			0.002	0.014	0.039	0.002	0.049
100 plus	606	0.899			0.002	0.008	0.045	0.000	0.046
All ages	299,304	0.654	0.053	0.039	0.012	0.094	0.075	0.036	0.037

particular census. The ages most likely to be missed for men and women in general are below 50. Men are less likely to be located at a census than women. However, the worst census coverage is for men aged 20–29 at the 1991 Census (shown aged 10–19 in 1981). Under-enumeration of young men of these ages in the 1991 Census has been established (Population Statistics Division, 1993). There was worse contact for those in non-family statuses in 1991, especially for males.

Non-coverage due to missing or bad data at any one census accounted for 3.5 per cent of the sample. This does not include the missing records on elderly people in 1971 and 1981 who subsequently died. Among the remaining cases with missing data, however, the likelihood of missing data at the 1971 Census is much higher for people in the oldest two age groups shown, men and women aged 80 and older in 1971, especially women. Nearly one-third (30.4 per cent) of women aged 80 and older and one-sixth (14.7 per cent) in 1971 had bad or missing data. This accords with the problems of dementia and fragility at these ages. Many of these elderly people had died by the time of subsequent censuses, in which case there is no uncertainty about how they should be classified. Note that missing data accentuates the underrepresentation of young adults.

FAMILY POSITION AND ITS STABILITY OVER THREE DECADES

The most common living arrangement was as a couple family with children, then as a couple without children, then as a child and then living alone, these latter two family positions obviously were related to age. Small proportions of people were living as lone parent families, as non-families or in institutions. Very few LS members were reported in what the census terms 'a lone parent family', which encompasses an elderly parent co-residing with adult progeny, as well as dependant children living with a sole parent. There were more lone mothers than fathers.

Of the various non-family forms of living arrangements, living alone was most common among older women. At younger ages very few LS members were found living alone, more being men than women. Institutions range over a variety of establishments, from nurses homes through barracks to residential homes for the elderly. The relative size of this group is tiny (1.2 per cent of the population).

Figures 10.1a and 10.1b summarize the experience of continuity in a given family position over three censuses by age in 1971. People for whom family status was not recorded at either of these censuses (not present at the census or enumerated as a visitor) do not enter these calculations, but those who are known to have died are not excluded, so that death during the 20-year period is one of the major ways of leaving a family position, particularly for cohorts who were over 50 in 1971 (see Figure 10.1).

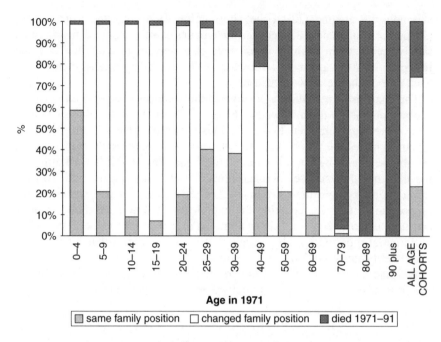

Figure 10.1a   Stability of family position, 1971, 1981, 1991: males

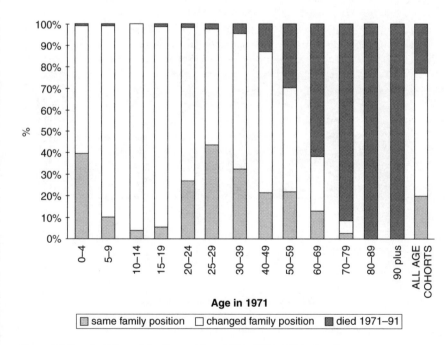

Figure 10.1b   Stability of family position, 1971, 1981, 1991: females

Among LS members of all ages (born before 1976) just under one quarter (23 per cent of males, 22 per cent of females) were reported in the same family membership position in all three censuses, another quarter died and just over half (53 per cent) were found in new living arrangements in at least one of the next two censuses.

The chances of repeating a position at three censuses depend on what the starting position was and gender. Figure 10.2 shows being one of couple with co-resident children to be the most retentive state. Taking all ages together, males are more likely to reappear in the same state than females, but this seems to be due to males' longer duration as child in a family. In most of the adult statuses, women outstay men. This is partly due to their lower mortality, and their lower rates of repartnering. This means that the proportion of women repeating the experience of lone parenthood at three censuses is more than three times higher than that of men (11 cf 3 per cent). Differential repartnering also means that men are more often found in the two-parent family position than women.

We also examined by the numbers in each family position initially and the proportion of them who remained in it for three censuses (data not

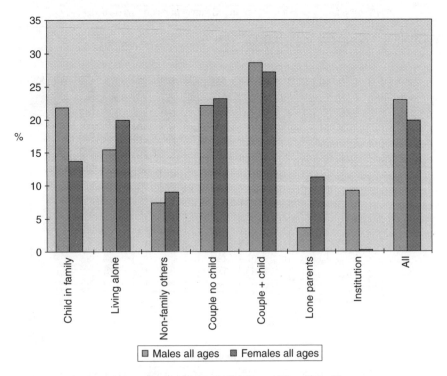

Figure 10.2   Percentage of cohort in same family position 1971–91

shown). Children living in a family at age 10–14 in 1971 would normally be expected to have left the parental home by the time they were aged 30–34 in 1991. This is reflected in a precipitous fall in the 1971 cross-sectional numbers (*ca* 14,000 each males and females at 10–14 to 1−2,000 at 25–29). It is also reflected in the very low 'staying-at-home' rates between ages 10–14 to 20–24. The greater propensity of males to stay at home, otherwise described as the earlier leaving home of females, is clear in the cross-section numbers and in the longitudinal summaries (Figure 10.2). The propensity to remain in the parental home rises at ages where most people have already left it, disability among either children or their parents may be implicated, the sex differences disappear, as does the category itself as the cohort members enter age groups where their parents are unlikely to survive 20 years.

Once a person has left the parental home, the most common destination is to form a new family. Living as one of a couple with no (co-resident) children is seldom a long-term situation for those observed in it under the age of 30, most of these couples proceeded to have children. It is at the age when children have left the home that the cross-sectional numbers peak (among couples aged 50–69) in 1971. The greatest chances of remaining for 20 years in this state were for those in couples aged 30–49 at the outset. Those whose children left home earliest had a good chance of repeating the 'childfree' state at two subsequent censuses. The sex differences in these rates reflect the age gaps between spouses. At ages under 40, female LS members are more likely than their male counterparts to be observed three times as part of a no-child couple. We attribute this to their younger average age than their male contemporaries. Beyond age 40–49, differential mortality and differential age of spouses mean that women's chances of repeat appearances in this category are lower than men's – they are more likely to have a spouse who dies.

The LS members who were in a couple with children were most numerous in ages 30–49. Those who had entered this state by the youngest ages (15–24 in 1971) were most likely to reappear in that state (*ca* two cases in three) at both subsequent censuses – their childrearing (or at least child-housing) careers lasting more than twenty years. At ages over 30, the children were increasingly less likely to stay at home for 20 years. A possible reason for fathers having higher repetition in this state than mothers could be their greater chance of repartnering and prolonging their family life with a second family.

Repetition of lone parenthood was mostly greater (up to 15 per cent) for lone mothers than lone fathers (whose age-specific rates did not exceed 5 per cent). At younger ages, spells were ended by the departure of children and the arrival of a partner, at ages 60 and over the dominant form of departure was death of the parent.

The chances of living alone (most prevalent form of non-family living) rise with age until mortality becomes important, and are greater for women than men because of men's greater chances of partnering in mid life. Living with others in a non-family or complex household is a smaller category than living alone, and more transient. It includes some young adults, and another cluster of older people. The greatest rates of repetition are among the small number of females aged 40–59 living with non-family in 1971. On the whole these arrangements are not a major way of life. Turnover of the institutional population is relatively high, especially through mortality at high ages, but is somewhat less at ages 25–59, particularly among women.

To summarize, greatest repetition of family position is found among young parents in two-parent families aged 35–50 in 1991 (under 30 in 1971), then amongst couples with no children aged 30–49 and among people (especially women) aged 30–59 and living alone. Otherwise living arrangement mobility is high at the young end of the life cycle, and at the upper end the longevity of a living arrangement is limited by the mortality of the persons living together. This underlying picture of mobility and stability of seven sorts of family position underlies the transitions people may make as adults between positions where they might be counted as the marker for their co-resident group.

MARKERSHIP

A person is treated as a marker for their co-resident unit if: (i) he or she is in a one adult unit, i.e. living alone, living with others apart from their two-generation family, if he or she is a lone parent, (ii) he or she is living in a couple and belong to the sex designated as a marker in the given scheme. Thus, in Brass's scheme females are markers even when they are living with a male partner. In a male markership scheme it is the man who is the marker for families headed by a couple.

The cross-sectional picture of allocation of family markership for men and women under the two schemes of markership priority are shown in Figures 10.3a to 10.3d. The figures show the proportions of men or women alive at each census in each age group who would be a marker given the scheme specified. The age group shown on the x axis is age in 1981 and, hence, the lines representing the 1971 and 1991 censuses need to be interpreted as 10 years younger and older respectively.[2]

The gender difference in the proportion of markers by age according to their respective priority schemes in each census reflects the differences in family position reported above. Higher proportions of women are markers under the female priority scheme than men are markers under the male priority scheme in the younger age groups, particularly below the age of 25. This is due to men's greater propensity to remain in the parental home.

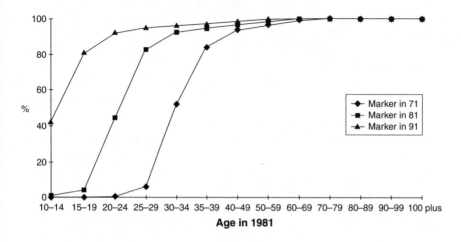

Figure 10.3a   Male markership under male scheme

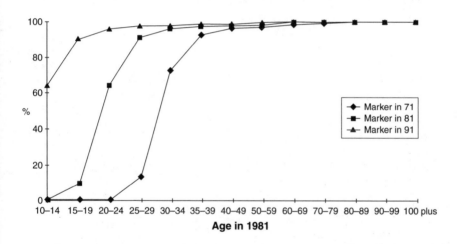

Figure 10.3b   Female markership under female scheme

In 1991, for example, 42.6 per cent of men aged 20–24 (shown as 10–14 in 1981 in Figure 10.3a) would have been markers under the male scheme compared with 64.8 per cent of women of the same age under the female priority scheme (Figure 10.3b). In 1971 the proportions of men and women who would have been markers under their 'own' scheme (50.9 per cent of men and 73.1 per cent of women) is larger at these younger ages than in the latter two census years.

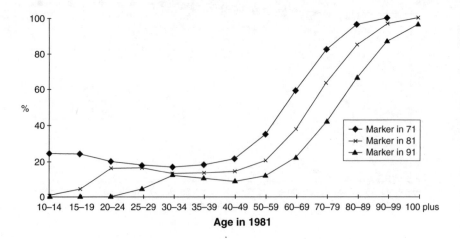

Figure 10.3c   Female markership under male scheme

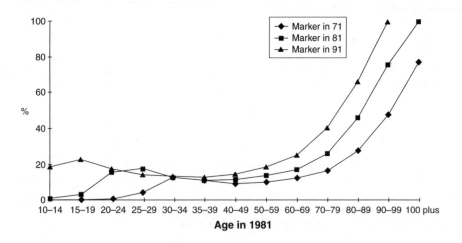

Figure 10.3d   Male markership under female scheme

Markership for the dominant or, to use Brass's term, 'star' marker becomes nearly universal (more than 9 out of 10) for men and women aged over 30. However, women show higher proportions of markers under the female scheme, generally in excess of 96 per cent, compared with 91 per cent of men under the male scheme. This means only 4 per cent of women are living with another adult woman who takes priority. This can only happen if she is living with a parent or in an institution.

The proportion of markers who are not of the priority gender, 'non-star' markers, are also higher for women than men (Figures 10.3c and 10.3d). Women are more likely to be markers under the male scheme than men are to be markers under the female scheme, particularly at ages over 50. This reflects the greater longevity of women, who become markers under the male priority scheme when their husband dies. For example, in 1981, 37.7 per cent of women aged between 60 and 69 would be markers under the male priority scheme, 63.3 per cent at ages 70–79, 84.9 per cent at ages 80–89 and 96.7 per cent at ages 90–99 years. This compares with only 26.1 per cent of men under the female priority scheme at ages 60–69 and 76.6 per cent at ages 90–99 years.

In the cross-sectional picture then, women appear to become 'star' or priority markers at an earlier age than men and to show a higher proportion of markership at all ages than men. Women also become 'non-star' markers under the opposing scheme more than men, particularly at older ages. How far this reflects longer duration in their markership or a greater rate of inflow is discovered by examining markership accession and abdication over the 10-year snapshots available to us.

FAMILY SIZE

The average family size of star and non-star marker families under the two schemes of markership allocation for the two decades are shown in Table 10.2. This covers all the co-residents of our markers, who are not necessarily LS members themselves. In using the LS to examine family size we are not using the total population. To take a sample of families from a sample of individuals we use the markers to ensure each family is represented only once.[3] The average size of families in a population should not change when different people are called markers as the number of families remains the same. The selection of men rather than women as marker will produce different average family size for star markers if men and women LS members have different numbers of coresidents. We would not expect any difference in principle so any differences in average family size between the two schemes shown in the LS result from sampling variation.

The trend over time shown by the LS calculations is for a fall in family size (including a possible bias against females in couples), shown for under both schemes when considering markership in total (Table 10.2). There is a clear downward trend for the star marker average family size under both schemes but not for the non-star marker family size. This is likely to result

Table 10.2   *Size of markers' co-resident group by markership scheme, sex of markers and year*

	Male scheme			Female scheme		
	Mean	*Standard deviation*	*N*	*Mean*	*Standard deviation*	*N*
1971						
Star markers	2.93	1.47	140,820	2.73	1.48	157,987
Non-star markers	1.36	0.82	42,084	1.17	0.60	21,798
All markers	2.57	1.35	182,904	2.54	1.40	179,785
1981						
Star markers	2.83	1.38	148,428	2.64	1.37	165,550
Non-star markers	1.39	0.85	48,002	2.64	1.37	26,649
All markers	2.48	1.27	196,430	2.44	1.29	192,199
1991						
Star markers	2.64	1.31	159,271	2.50	1.28	179,695
Non-star markers	1.43	0.83	57,648	1.11	0.43	32,471
All markers	2.32	1.20	216,919	2.29	1.19	212,166

from changes in family structure over the two decades, mainly in the prevalence and family size of lone parent families. Lone motherhood has become more prevalent, suggested by the number of non-star markers under the male markership scheme – i.e. females (Table 10.2).

If we look at the average family size of markers it can be seen that family size is about 0.03 larger under a male scheme of markership than a female scheme (for example, 2.57 compared with 2.54 in 1971). There are more markers identified under the male scheme than the female scheme of markership. There are fewer star markers but more non-star markers under the male scheme of markership. Star and non-star markers have a higher average family size under a male scheme than a female scheme. There is also greater variability for non-star markers under the male scheme (females) than under the female scheme (males). These all result from the fact that women are more likely to be lone parents and to live on their own at older ages. Thus, in the female scheme lone parents are included as star markers, so deflating the average family size of couple families. In the male scheme they increase the number of non-star markers, inflate the family size of non-star markers and increase the variability of family size.

ACCESSIONS AND ABDICATIONS

The 'birth' and 'death' of persons as markers, taking men and women together, in the two decades are shown in Figures 10.4 and 10.5. Accession rates are high below age 25. Under the male scheme accession rates peak

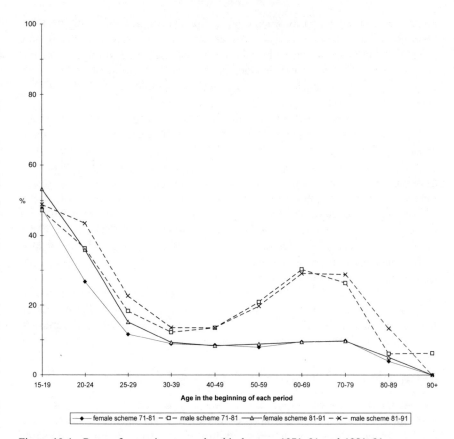

Figure 10.4   Rates of accession to markership by age, 1971–81 and 1981–91

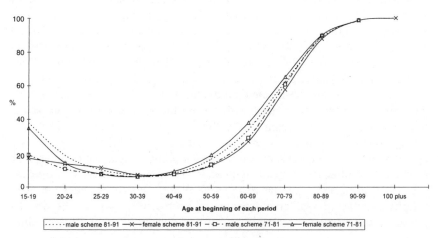

Figure 10.5   Rates of abdication (including deaths) from markership by age, 1971–81 and 1981–91

again between ages 50 and 79 due to the earlier age of death of men. Overall, there are more accessions under the male scheme than the female scheme. There are slightly higher rates of accession at younger ages for both schemes in the second decade. Women accede earlier than men and, overall, a higher proportion of women accede to markership than men (not shown).

Abdication rates, which include death, are low until age 50, after which age they rise steadily (Figure 10.5). There is little difference in the rates of abdication between the two schemes and the two decades. There is a rise in abdication rates for people under 25 in the second decade under both markership schemes. This could be due to higher rates of single living at younger ages before partnering. Abdication rates show only a minimal rise for the second decade for people aged over 50; however, the ordering of the two schemes in rates of abdication are reversed at these ages. There would be differences between the two schemes if abdication excluding deaths were considered, because these would then relate to differences in part-nering and repartnering between the sexes.

Overall, there are more transitions experienced with the male scheme of markership than the female scheme, mainly resulting from higher accession rates under the male scheme at older ages. How this relates to duration in markership is examined below.

STABILITY OF MARKERSHIP

Figures 10.6a to 10.6d summarize the stability or continuity of markership over three censuses for men and women in the LS according to the two priority schemes. We use the term stability to refer to repetition of the same state at successive censuses. We do not know of any changes which may have occurred between censuses, or indeed of any changes of identity of the people living with the LS member. The bars in Figures 10.6a to 10.6d represent the proportion of those recorded in a given position in 1971 and for whom subsequent information is complete, who were also observed in that state in 1981 and 1991. People for whom markership could not be allo-cated at either of these censuses (not present at the LS or enumerated as a visitor), do not enter these calculations, but those who are known to have died are not excluded, so that death during the twenty-year period is one of the major ways of leaving markership (see Figures 10.6a and 10.6c).

This longitudinal information shows that among all LS members, of any age, women are more consistent than men in family markership under their respective dominant schemes (Figures 10.6a and 10.6d). Over one third of men (38.9 per cent) were star markers at all three censuses under the male priority scheme of markership compared with nearly one-half of women (45.6 per cent) under the female priority scheme of allocating markership.

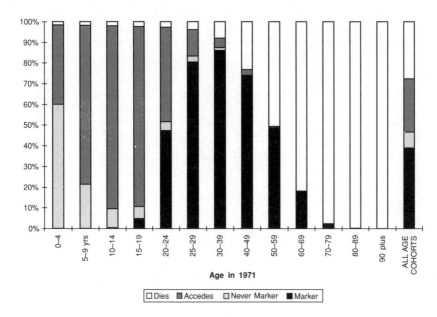

Figure 10.6a   Stability of markership for men under male scheme

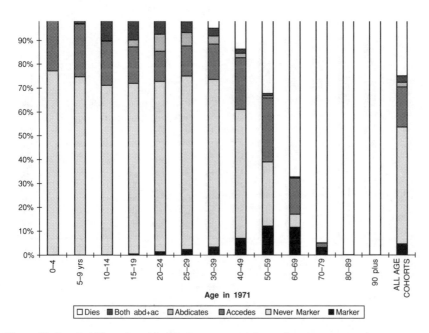

Figure 10.6b   Stability of markership for women under male scheme

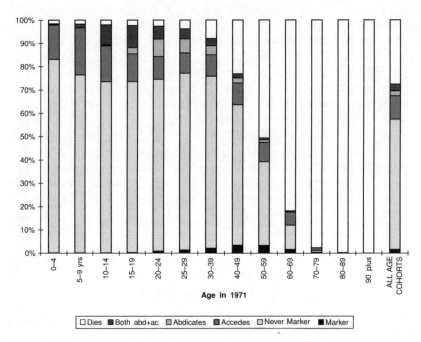

Figure 10.6c   Stability of markership for men under female scheme

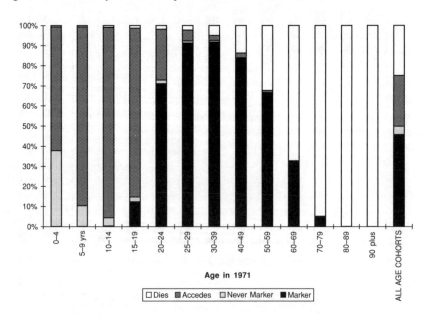

Figure 10.6d   Stability of markership for women under female scheme

Roughly one-quarter of men and women in their own priority schemes acceded to markership over the two decades and another quarter died (27.6 per cent of men and 24.9 per cent of women). Negligible proportions abdicated under their own priority scheme while still alive, and below 5 per cent abdicated under the opposing dominant scheme.

The ages of greatest stability for markership over the two decades for both men and women in the LS are their second quarter century, 25 to 50 years of age. This is related to the greatest repetition found for 'couples' and 'couples with children' in the family position linkage findings reported above (Figure 10.3a). Women have a larger age range of stability of markership under their own priority scheme than do men under their respective scheme – women from starting ages 20 to 69 years of age in 1981, compared with ages 20 to 59 for men.

The ages of making a single accession to markership over the two decades are similar to men, which relate to age at leaving the parental home and setting up an independent household. Men are more likely to remain as a 'child in a family' for longer durations than women. Men are most likely to make a single accession to markership over the twenty years under the male priority scheme below the age of 25 and women below the age of 20.

Women LS members also show a greater proclivity to be stable family heads – non-star markers – under the male scheme of markership priority than men under the female scheme. As many as 12 per cent of women LS members were allocated as consistent non-star markers at ages 50–69 in 1971, while a further quarter of 40–59 year old women experienced only accession over the two decades. The proportion of men experiencing non-star markership was minimal – below a maximum of 4 per cent – and accessions were only numerous in the young ages. This is partly due to men's higher mortality and their higher rates of repartnering after family breakup.

The stability of family markership for persons, taking men and women together, is greater under the female system of priority markership allocation as Brass conjectured, although the differences are not large (Figures 10.7a and 10.7b). Similar proportions of people remain as family markers (24 per cent under the female scheme and 21.5 per cent under the male scheme) and non-markers (29.5 per cent and 28.7 per cent respectively) under both schemes. However, there is more single accession to markership under the male scheme (21.2 per cent of people made a single accession to markership compared with 17.7 per cent under the female scheme), which means more transition. Under the female scheme there is more consistency of markership at young ages, in the early 20s, than under the male scheme. There is a greater likelihood for men to be missing at some point in the longitudinal study as previously shown (Table 10.1), especially men aged 20–29 at the 1991 Census and those in transitional, non-family states. However, the numbers involved would not render the findings invalid.

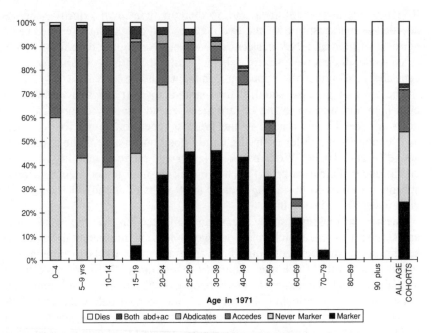

Figure 10.7a   Stability of markership for both sexes under female scheme

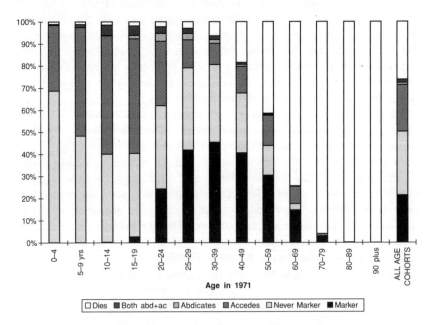

Figure 10.7b   Stability of markership for both sexes under male scheme

In summary, the general tendency for women to outstay men in most adult family statuses implies greater continuity as family markers. Men are less stable as both star and non-star family markers. This shorter duration as family markers for men results from remaining as a child in a family for longer, more repartnering and higher mortality than women. In other words, women make more accessions as non-star markers than men. Consequently, there are more transitions in markership under a male scheme than a female scheme.

CONCLUSIONS

Individuals' living arrangements normally change over the course of the life cycle. Therefore the group of people living together in a family or household has a changing membership over time. This poses a problem on how to define a household longitudinally. Brass's solution was to define the group by one individual, 'a member' whose co-residents, if any, formed part of the group whose existence continues until the marker dies or joins with someone who has a superior claim to markership (abdication). Brass suggested that for purposes of demographic projection it would be more convenient to follow females rather than males, despite the social and statistical practice of treating men as the representatives of their household.

The empirical test of the assumptions underlying Professor Brass's models of formal demography show that he was correct. Women have longer durations than men in most adult family statuses and, hence, are more consistent family markers. There is little difference in the results from the two decades, although some evidence of higher accession rates for both sexes at younger ages under both schemes of markership for the second decade. While overall men are more likely to remain in the same family status, this appears to be due to their tendency to remain as a child in a family for a longer time than women. Women accede to family markership at an earlier age, are more stable as star and non-star family markers and are more likely to accede as markers at older ages. This is because women leave the parental home earlier, are less likely to repartner and have lower mortality.

In cross-sections there are fewer markers and a smaller average family size under the female markership scheme than under a male priority scheme which are related to the differential stability of markership between the sexes. These findings are relevant for modelling the living arrangement of adults and their implications for housing demand and income over the life cycle.

ACKNOWLEDGEMENTS

This paper forms part of a programme of research on 'Livelihoods and Living Arrangements' funded by the Leverhulme Trust (Grant F353/G). We are grateful to the Office of National Statistics for permission to use the data from the Longitudinal Study. Judith Wright of the Longitudinal Study Support Programme then at City University, provided access to the data. Georgia Verropoulou helped with the manipulation of data. We would like to thank them for their assistance in the preparation of this paper. The views expressed are the authors', and not necessarily those of ONS or the LSSP.

REFERENCES

Burch, T.K. (1979) 'Household and family demography: a bibliographic essay'. *Population Index*, 43 (2).

Berrington, A. and Diamond, I. (1999) *Marital dissolution among the 1958 cohort: the role of cohabitation, Populatin Studies*,53, pp. 19–38.

Bongaarts, J. (1983) The formal demography of families and households: an Population. Liege.overview. *Newsletter*, 17. International Union for the Scientific Study of Population.

Brass, W. (1983) '*The formal demography of the family: an overview of the proximate determinants*' in *The Family*, British Society for Population Studies Conference Papers, University of Bath 1983. Occasional Paper 31. London: Office of Population, Censuses and Surveys.

Brown A. and Kiernan, K. (1981) 'Cohabitation in Great Britain: Evidence from the General Household Survey'. *Population Trends*, 35. London: HMSO.

Clarke, L., Joshi, H., Di Salvo, P. and Wright, J. (1997) *Stability and Instability in Children's Family Lives: Longitudinal Evidence From Two British Sources*. CPS Research Paper 97–1. London: Centre for Population Studies, London School of Hygiene and Tropical Medicine.

Hattersley, L. and Creeser, R. (1995) *The Longitudinal Study 1971–1991: History, Organization and Quality of Data*. London: HMSO.

Kiernan, K. and Eldridge, S. (1985) *Demographic Analysis of First Marriages in England and Wales: 1950–1980*. CPS Research Paper 85–1. London: Centre for Population Studies, London School of Hygiene and Tropical Medicine.

Murphy, M. (1996) 'The dynamic household as a logical concept and its use in demography'. *European Journal of Population*, 12, pp. 363–81.

Ni Bhrolchain, M. (ed) (1993) *Fertility Trends*. London: OPCS, HMSO.

Population Statistics Division, OPCS (1993) 'How complete was the 1991 Census?' *Population Trends*, 71, pp. 22–5.

Roll, J. (1991) *What is a Family? Benefit Models and Social Realities*, Occasional Paper No. 13. London: Family Policy Studies Centre.

Ryder, N.B. (1977) 'Models of family demography'. *Population Bulletin of the United Nations*, 9. New York: United Nations.

Sweet, J. (1977) 'Demography and the Family'. *Annual Reviews of Sociology*.

Willekens, F. (1988) 'A lifecourse perspective on household dynamics', in N. Keilman, A. Kuijsten and A. Vossen (eds), *Modelling Household Formation and Dissolution*. Oxford: Clarendon Press, pp. 87–107.

Wright, J. and Lynch, K. (1995) *Using the LS for Intra-household Analyses*, Update No. 12, November 1995. London: Social Statistics Research Unit, City University, pp. 12–16.

CHAPTER ELEVEN

A novel method of comparing regional trends in infant mortality applied to Italy 1950–89

John Osborn

Istituto di Igiene 'G Sanarelli', Università di Roma
'La Sapienza', Roma, Italy

Angela Spinelli

Istituto Superiore di Sanità, Roma , Italy

Maria Sofia Cattaruzza

Istituto di Igiene 'G Sanarelli', Università di Roma
'La Sapienza', Roma, Italy and Istitututo Dermopatico
dell'Immaculata, Roma, Italy

INTRODUCTION

The infant mortality rate is defined to be the proportion of live births that die before reaching their first birthday. This is usually estimated by calculating the ratio of the number of deaths at ages less than 1 year registered in one calendar year, to the number of live births in the same period.

Many biological, social and economic factors have been known to be associated with the risk of infant mortality for a long time. Biological factors believed to be of importance include maternal age, birth order, interval between successive births, multiplicity of births, the sex of the infant, maternal height, presentation of the fetus at delivery and mother's past obstetric history. Social and economic factors include legitimacy, housing and overcrowding, degree of urbanization, nutrition, maternal education, maternal smoking habits during pregnancy and father's occupation and income.

From an epidemiological point of view, it is interesting to study factors which may affect the risk of infant mortality and even try to separate their independent effects. From the point of view of public health, however, this is only interesting if it is possible to initiate an intervention in order to reduce the risk of infant death. For example, modern contraceptives enable couples to plan their families, delaying childbearing until the economic circumstances are right (but this involves increasing the mean age of the mothers at delivery and reducing the mean total family size) and to space their children to avoid having very many children together. Although there are many individual risk factors, those for which an intervention is possible are almost all associated with maternal education and standard of living. Indeed, these epidemiological findings are now used by sociologists and economists who use the infant mortality rate as an indirect indicator of the socio-economic–health status of a community.

In studying the medical, social and economic implications of the level of infant mortality, it is useful to divide the period of infancy into two parts: the neonatal period, which includes only the first 4 weeks of life, and the postneonatal period which includes ages from 4 weeks to 1 year. The reason for this is that the causes of death among neonates are generally 'biological' in the sense that they are related to the health of the mother during pregnancy, the process of delivery and the immediate health of the newborn. These causes of neonatal mortality tend to be related to the level of health care available from antenatal clinics, maternity hospitals, etc. In contrast, postneonatal mortality is usually caused by environmental conditions which affect the risk of infections of the respiratory system and the digestive system, but currently in developed countries accidents are increasingly important. These causes of postneonatal mortality are much more closely associated with the general standard of living than the specific provision of medical care. For example, infections of the respiratory system are more easily transmitted in overcrowded housing, when there are older brothers and sisters at school who become infected and bring the infection into the house of the infant. Infections of the digestive system will be more common in households with inadequate provision for hygienic food preparation and which lack satisfactory sanitary conditions and in which personal cleanliness is less common. Historically, postneonatal mortality was much more important than neonatal mortality, but with the massive reduction in mortality from infections, the postneonatal mortality rate is now a small component of the total infant mortality rate in developed countries.

The study of infant mortality has a long history, for example Holt (1913) gives a review covering the times from the Spartans, but the study of infant mortality nationally in Europe started during the last century as each country established national registers of births and deaths. For example, in England and Wales, the General Register Office was established in 1837 and the first national estimate of the level of infant mortality for the year 1838 was 180 per 1000 live births, (Farr, 1840). Crude infant mortality rates were published for 25 geographical regions of England and Wales and these gave an indication of the association between infant mortality and poverty. Farr (1885) gave the following as some of the principal causes of infant mortality: improper or insufficient food, bad management, use of opiates, neglect, early marriage, debility of the mother and bad sanitary arrangements. Brass and Laurie (1954), Laurie *et al* (1955a, 1955b, 1956) and Brass (1959) were among the first to try to separate the effects of associated factors which affect infant mortality or more generally, pregnancy wastage. Using data

from the East Africa Medical Survey they were able to estimate the independent effects of maternal age, parity and birth spacing on stillbirth and
infant mortality rates. This led Brass to develop multidimensional standardization which was the first methodological extension of indirect
standardization since the technique was introduced by Farr (1859) in the
20ᵗʰ Annual Report of the Registrar General for England and Wales for
1858! Osborn (1975) applied Brass's ideas to separate the confounding
effects of maternal age and parity on stillbirth rates in England and Wales.

An early review of the social implications of infant mortality in Italy was
described by Allaria (1950). For Italy, data on infant mortality are available from 1863, when the rate for the whole country (as then constituted)
was 231.6 per 1000 live births and varied from the regional minimum in
Liguria, 189.1 per 1000, to the maximum in Basilicata, 259.7 per 1000. An
important characteristic of infant mortality in Italy is the extent of the
regional variation in comparison with other European countries. For example,
in England in 1986 the infant mortality rate was 9.5 per 1000 live births
and the maximum regional rate was 10.7 per 1000 in the North Western
region and the minimum was 8.0 in East Anglia giving a ratio of 1.34. In
contrast, in Italy, in 1992, the national rate was 7.9 per 1000, with the
maximum regional rate being 10.2 in Sicilia and the minimum 5.3 in Friuli-
Venezia-Giulia (Figure 11.1), which gives a ratio of 1.92. A politician might
argue that regional differences in infant mortality (and thus inequalities in
health and welfare) have diminished in Italy during the last century because
the difference between the highest and lowest regional rates has reduced
from 70.6 per 1000 in 1863 to only 4.9 in 1991 (Figure 11.2), although
this reflects the fact that all the rates have diminished. Another politician,
with a different party allegiance, might argue that the relative risk of infant
death between the maximum and minimum regional levels has increased
from 1.37 in 1863 to 1.92 (Figure 11.3) implying that inequalities in health
have increased. In epidemiology, the difference between the risks is called
the attributable risk and is used when it is necessary to measure the impact
of regional differences on the the risk and number of infant deaths, whereas
the ratio, or relative risk is a better indicator for aetiological studies.

An alternative to these two measures would be to observe the time lag
between the maximum regional rate and the national rate and the lead time
between the minimum rate and the national rate. For example, in 1980, the
rate in Sicily was 18.45 per 1000, the same as the national rate midway
between 1976 and 1977, whereas in 1980 the rate was 9.16 in Friuli, a rate
not achieved nationally until 1988. Thus in 1980 Sicily lagged three and a
half years behind Italy in the war against infant mortality, while Friuli was
eight years ahead. An obvious disadvantage of the method is that for recent
years the lead time cannot be estimated because the lower regional rates
have not yet been achieved nationally.

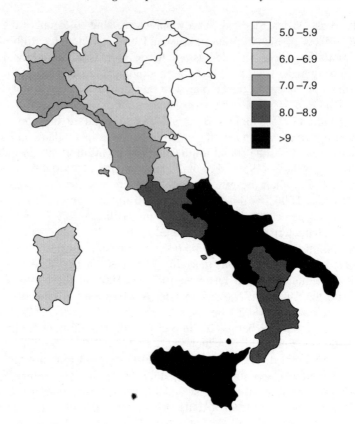

Figure 11.1   Regional infant mortality rate, 1992

METHODS

Regional data of infant mortality rates from 1950 to 1972 have been summarized in a volume published by the Italian Istituto Centrale di Statistica
(ISTAT, 1975) and data up to 1992 are available in 'Le Regioni in Cifre'
published annually by ISTAT. The time lags and lead times for each region
in each year can be estimated by measuring the horizontal distance between
the national and regional graphs of the infant mortality rate against calendar
year. A slight problem can occur because the national graph of infant
mortality from one year to the next does not always decrease. However,
where a rise was observed, this was relatively small and where necessary
the graph was smoothed by eye. Smoothing of the graph could easily be
achieved by using a 3- or 5-point moving average but this would have the
disadvantage of blurring the annual changes in the infant mortality rates.
The lag times and lead times for each region show considerable variability
from one year to the next and for this reason the times were averaged over

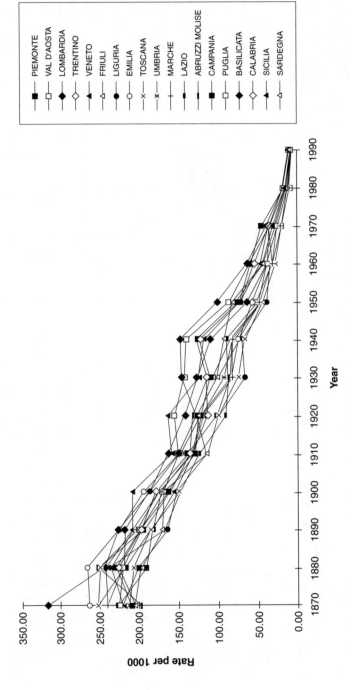

Figure 11.2 The absolute decline in infant mortality for the regions of Italy, 1870–1990

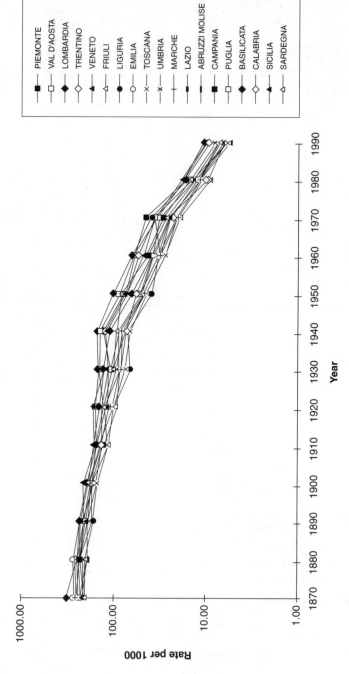

Figure 11.3   Relative declines in infant mortality rates for the regions of Italy, 1870–1990

five-year periods from 1950 to 1984. The lag times, and when possible, the lead times were also averaged for the five years 1985–9 and these five-year averages are shown in Table 11.1. The average annual change in the lag or lead times in each region during the period of observation can be estimated by calculating the simple linear regression of the lead/lag times on calendar year. The levels of statistical significance should be interpreted with caution because the changes in the times may not be linear, but they can be used to crudely discriminate between:

(a) the regions which had lower rates of infant mortality than the national figure and have maintained their advantage,
(b) the regions which had lower rates of infant mortality than the national figure but have tended to lose this advantage during the period of study; that is, the well-off regions which have moved towards the national average,
(c) the regions which had higher rates than the national average and managed to reduce their lag times during the period of study; that is, the disadvantaged regions which have moved towards the national average,
(d) the regions which had higher rates than the national average and have not managed to significantly reduce their disadvantage.

Regions which had lower rates early in the period of study which managed to significantly increase their lead times and similarly the regions which earlier had higher rates than the national average which increased their lag times would imply a widening of regional infant mortality differentials.

A national summary of the change in the variability of regional infant mortality rates can be achieved by tabulating the mean lead times and mean lag times in the calendar time intervals studied. If these means were to reduce with calendar time period, a reduction in infant mortality differentials would be implied; an increase would indicate a widening of the differentials.

RESULTS

Table 11.1 shows the estimated lead times and lag times for the 19 regions of Italy (in fact there are 20 regions in Italy, but historically Abruzzo and Molise were combined and they are combined in this analysis), in five-year intervals from 1950 to 1989. To maintain a sense of the implication of these lag times and lead times the infant mortality rates for Italy are also included together with the regional infant mortality rates in 1950 and 1992.

Applying the classification of the regions according to the values of the regression coefficients and the values of the lead times and lag times, it can be seen that:

Table 11.1 *Mean lead times (negative sign, infant mortality rate (IMR) lower than the national rate) and time lags (positive sign, IMR higher than the national rate) for the regions of Italy in five-year intervals between 1950 and 1989, the regional infant mortality rates in 1950 and 1992 and the slope, b, of the linear regression of the lag/lead times on calendar year intervals*

Region	1950–4	1955–9	1960–4	1965–9	1970–4	1975–9	1980–4	1985–9	IMR 1950	IMR 1992	b years/ calendar year
Piemonte	−5.3	−5.3	−2.2	−1.9	+0.5	+0.5	−0.4	nc	50.2	7.1	0.22**
Valle d'Aosta	+1.7	+0.0	−7.4	−0.3	+1.9	−1.4	−2.5	nc	52.7	6.9	−0.04
Lombardia	−1.3	−4.1	−3.8	−3.6	−2.1	−2.3	−2.9	nc§	63.3	6.2	0.00
Trentino AA	−3.2	−5.2	−4.2	−4.8	−3.2	−5.7	−4.4	nc§	57.0	5.5	−0.03
Veneto	−7.2	−9.1	−7.5	−6.9	−4.1	−3.2	−4.3	nc§	49.3	5.8	0.17*
Friuli VG	−8.5	−9.3	−8.8	−5.7	−3.6	−4.7	−8.4	nc§	45.3	5.3	0.10
Liguria	−10.2	−6.3	−7.9	−4.1	−2.3	−3.0	−3.5	nc§	38.7	7.0	0.23*
Emilia Romagna	−8.0	−9.6	−6.9	−4.7	−2.0	−3.2	−3.1	nc§	46.8	6.5	0.23**
Toscana	−10.0	−9.9	−10.2	−5.8	−3.0	−3.4	−3.7	nc§	43.7	7.0	0.28**
Umbria	−8.9	−6.2	−7.8	−4.0	−5.0	−5.7	−3.6	−1.2	46.6	6.4	0.17**
Marche	−8.0	−8.7	−8.2	−6.5	−5.2	−4.5	−4.1	−0.8	47.6	5.7	0.20**
Lazio	−5.6	−5.1	−4.4	−4.8	−1.8	−2.0	−2.3	nc§	49.2	8.2	0.13**
Abruzzo, Molise	+2.9	+1.7	−0.9	−4.4	−2.8	−0.7	−0.1	+1.9	77.2	10.1	−0.03
Campania	+2.9	+4.7	+8.1	+10.4	+8.9	+3.9	+3.0	+3.1	72.6	9.5	−0.05
Puglia	+5.4	+7.0	+8.2	+7.1	+2.1	+2.1	+3.1	+2.6	86.5	9.2	−0.15*
Basilicata	+9.6	+8.6	+8.9	+8.6	+4.1	+0.7	+3.8	+2.7	100.9	8.5	−0.24
Calabria	+3.0	+4.5	+6.2	+6.2	+3.0	+1.7	+2.1	+3.3	71.0	8.1	−0.06
Sicilia	+2.1	+3.1	+2.6	+3.8	+4.2	+2.1	+3.4	+3.6	71.2	10.2	0.03
Sardegna	+1.5	+2.5	+1.4	+2.1	+0.1	−0.1	−0.4	−0.7	81.1	6.8	−0.08*
IMR, Italy/1000	61.1	48.7	40.5	33.5	21.9	17.8	12.9	9.4	61.1	7.9	

§ nc indicates that the lead times were not calculable because low regional rates had not been achieved nationally by 1992.
* $P < 0.05$; **$P < 0.01$.

(a) the regions which had lower rates of infant mortality than the national figure and have maintained their lead times are: Valle d'Aosta, Lombardia, Trentino AA and Friuli VG,

(b) the regions which had lower rates of infant mortality than the national figure but which have tended to lose this lead time advantage significantly during the period of study are: Piemonte, Veneto, Liguria, Emilia Romagna, Toscana, Umbria, Marche and Lazio,

(c) the regions which had higher rates of infant mortality than the national figure and have managed to reduce their lag times significantly during the period of study were: Puglia, Basilicata and Sardegna,

(d) the regions which had higher rates of infant mortality than the national figure and have not managed to reduce their lag times significantly were: Abruzzo and Molise, Campania, Calabria and Sicilia.

There were no regions which have increased their lead times or lag times significantly between the five-year time intervals.

That this classification based on the statistical significance of the linear trend in the lead and lag times is crude can be seen by inspecting the trends in the individual regions. For example, Lazio seemingly lost a considerable part of its advantage between 1965–9 and 1970–4, with little change in the other periods; Abruzzo and Molise lost their lag time and gained lead time in 1965–9 but subsequently lost this advantage; Campania always had rates higher than the national average but its lag times increased exceptionally in the period 1960–1974. However, these regional changes in lead and lag times generally reflect the differing rates of economic development during the period 1950–89.

Sicilia is the region which usually shows the highest rate of infant mortality. The regression based on the five-year time intervals does not show a significant tendency for the lag times to increase, but the individual annual lag times for the 42 years, 1950–72 and 1974–92 (data for 1973 are unfortunately not available) seem to show two distinct trends. The lag times (in years) are shown in Figure 11.4. These tend to increase in the period 1950–72 (b = 0.127, SE(b) = 0.035, P = 0.003). Between 1972 and 1974 there was a great improvement when the lag times reduced from 5.5 to 1.5 but since then, the lag times have increased at an even greater rate (b = 0.241, SE(b) = 0.034, P < 0.0001). It would seem that if there is no intervention, there is no prospect for the Sicilian infant mortality rates to approach the national figure in the forseeable future; indeed, Sicilia seems doomed to lag ever further behind the rest of the country in terms of its infant mortality rate.

The results in Table 11.1 are summarized in table 11.2. The column of mean lead times implies that for the regions with levels of infant mortality lower than the national average, the mean lead times diminished between

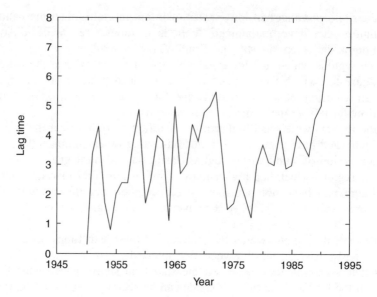

Figure 11.4   Lag times (years) for Sicilia 1950–92.

Table.11. 2   *The mean and standard deviation of the lead and lag times in Table 11.1*

Calendar years	Mean lead time (SD)	Mean lag time (SD)	Mean all regions (SD)
1950–4	−6.93 (2.81)	+3.64 (2.69)	−2.48 (5.99)
1955–9	−7.16 (2.16)	+4.11 (2.76)	−2.42 (6.19)
1960–4	−6.61 (2.39)	+5.19 (3.46)	−2.26 (6.45)
1965–9	−4.77 (1.36)	+5.50 (3.61)	−0.98 (5.59)
1970–4	−3.19 (1.18)	+3.10 (2.78)	−0.54 (3.74)
1975–9	−3.55 (1.44)	+1.48 (1.24)	−1.43 (2.87)
1980–4	−3.89 (1.65)	+2.04 (1.52)	−1.39 (3.38)
1985–9	nc	+2.87 (0.60)	nc*

* nc indicates that the lead times were not calculable because low regional rates had not been achieved nationally by 1992.

1950 and 1974 as their low rates tended to move towards the national figure, after which there has been an increase again. In contrast, the lag times (for the regions with higher infant mortality rates than the national figure) tended to increase in the two decades 1950–69, to reduce to a minimum in 1975–9 and to increase again by 1990. The standard deviation of the lead/lag times for all regions gives another indication of variability between the regions. The high values of the standard deviation in the periods 1950–64 imply much variability between the regions, but these tended to diminish between 1965 and 1979 to rise again slightly in 1980–4. Together these figures imply that the regional infant mortality differentials tended to reduce in the earlier part of the study period, 1950 to 1974 after which there seems to have been an increase in the difference between the advantaged and disadvantaged regions.

DISCUSSION

Time trends in rates can be compared absolutely or relatively, and when the values of the rate change, the two methods may give apparently conflicting impressions. If regional infant mortality rates are plotted on an arithmetic scale against calendar year, the only real conclusion that can be drawn is that in all regions infant mortality has been reduced dramatically, especially at the earlier dates when the rates were relatively high. Conversely, if the regional rates are plotted on a logarithmic scale one sees a band of approximately constant width which contains the graphs and one would conclude that there has been little relative change between the rates observed in the regions. One advantage of the lead time and lag time approach is that it is independent of the scale used for the graphs and produces an indicator which is readily understandable and interpretable; the Italian infant mortality rate is lagging about eight years behind that of Friuli. Sicily's rate is lagging about seven years behind that of the nation, and on average, since 1973 it has been getting an additional three months further behind every year.

There have always been regional differentials in infant mortality in Italy. Nowadays the regions in the North of the country have lower rates than in the South but it has not always been so easy to divide the country geographically. In 1863, when the earliest data were produced, Piemonte had the same infant mortality rate as Calabria. Lombardia, Umbria, Marche and Basilicata were all equal and Sicilia ranked fourth. The reasons for this homogeneity was that the economic advantages of the North were countered by its cold wet climate which predisposed its infants to postneonatal mortality from respiratory infections. The great reduction in infant mortality that has occurred in all regions, about 5 per cent per year since the Second World War, has been to a large extent due to the reduction in post-neonatal mortality and the South has been left to suffer the consequences of its relative poverty in comparison with the North.

In 1989, the infant mortality rate varied from 3.51 per 1000 in Valle d'Aosta (Valle d'Aosta is a small region with a low number of births and infant deaths but a generally low rate; the second lowest regional rate was 4.29 per 1000 in Friuli VG) to 11.62 per 1000 in Basilicata, while the PIL (*prodotto interno lordo*, the Italian equivalent of the GDP per capita) varied from 27.0 million lire in Lombardia to 12.0 million in Calabria (£ = 2,500 lire, $ = 1,500 lire). A scatter diagram (Figure 11.5) of the infant mortality rate against PIL is approximately linear with correlation coefficient 0.80

and linear regression equation IMR = 15.2 − 0.35PIL. To find a relationship between infant mortality and PIL is not a surprise. What is surprising is that in a country as rich as Italy one can find such extremes of levels of infant mortality and PIL. The infant mortality rates in the most favoured regions are about equal to the lowest national rates in the world (for example in Japan the rate is 4.4 per 1000) while in the poorer South of Italy the rates are more akin to those of poorer countries such as Greece. If wealth (and all the other associated technological, cultural and health-care advantages) were the only determinant of infant mortality, a simple calculation could estimate the number of infant deaths that could be avoided in Italy if all regions were as fortunate as Friuli VG. In 1989 there were 4822 infant deaths in Italy and the rate was 8.49 per 1000. If the rate observed in Friuli VG were experienced in all Italy, there would have been only 2437 infant deaths and 2385 would have been avoided. There are more than 6 infant deaths every day in Italy that are potentially preventable given the experience of Friuli VG and the other fortunate regions of the North of the country.

The death of an infant is a tragedy, not only for the parents but also for the extended family and the community at large. A baby dead because of parental neglect is regarded as justifiable headline news. In Italy, 6 avoidable infant deaths is an everyday event.

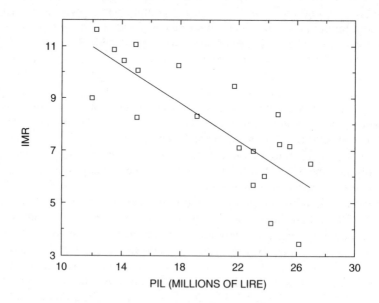

Figure 11.5   The association between infant mortality and *prodotto interno lordo* (PIL)

REFERENCES

Allaria, G. (1950) *Aspetti Medico-sociali della Mortalità Infantile*. Roma: Istituto di Medicina Sociale.
Brass, W. (1959) 'Differentials in child mortality by marriage experience of the mothers in six African communities'. *Proceedings of the IUSSP International Population Conference*. Vienna: IUSSP.
Brass, W. and Laurie, W. (1954) 'General introduction to the Monograph Series'. *East Africa Medical Survey Monograph No. 1*. Nairobi: East African High Commission.
Farr, W. (1840) *1st Annual Report of the Registrar General for England and Wales*. London: General Register Office.
Farr, W. (1859) *20th Annual Report of the Registrar General for England and Wales*. London: General Register Office.
Farr, W. (1885) *Vital Statistics*. N.A. Humphreys (ed), London: Offices of the Sanitary Institute.
Holt, L. (1913) 'Infant mortality, ancient and modern'. *Archives of Pediatrics*, 30, 885–915.
ISTAT (1975) Tendenze Evolutive della Mortalità Infantile in Italia. *Annali di Statistica, no. VIII*, 29. Roma: Istituto Centrale di Statistica.
Laurie, W., Brass, W. and Trant, H. (1955a) *A Health Survey of the Bukoba District. East Africa Medical Survey Monograph No. 2*, Nairobi: East African High Commission.
Laurie, W., Brass, W. and Trant, H. (1955b) *A Health Survey of the Kwimba District. East Africa Medical Survey, Monograph No. 3*, Nairobi: High Commission.
Laurie, W., Brass, W. and Trant, H. (1956) *A Health Survey of the Kisii Tribe, Kenya. East Africa Medical Survey, Monograph No. 4*, Nairobi: High Commission.
Osborn, J. (1975) 'A multiplicative model for the analysis of vital statistics rates'. *Applied Statistics*, 24, 75–84.

CHAPTER TWELVE

Demographic and socio-economic data in general practice in Britain; discussed using data from East London

Kath Moser* and Sandra Eldridge

St Bartholomew's and the Royal London School of Medicine and Dentistry at Queen Mary and Westfield College

INTRODUCTION

In recent years there has been an increased interest in the problems of the interactions of population and public health. It has come from a variety of origins, among which the following are important. The emphasis on the planning of health services has made it necessary for administrators to take a more precise account of demand and future demand, which depend heavily on population size, structure and distribution. With the reduction of mortality and morbidity from infections in the richer countries more attention has been paid to chronic diseases: the realisation of the powerful influence of social factors on these conditions has been accompanied by an acceptance that the factors operate in intimate conjunction with demographic features, such as family composition, dependency and so on (Brass, 1972).

As William Brass clearly states demographic and socio-economic information on the population provide baseline data essential for the purposes of health service planning and needs assessment, resource allocation and research. We need to know the population size and age–sex distribution, and, given the well-established relationships between social and material factors and health and mortality (Department of Health and Social Services, 1980; Marsh and Channing, 1986; Wilkinson, 1986; Whitehead, 1987; Goldblatt, 1990; Eachus et al, 1996; Drever and Whitehead, 1997), socio-economic characteristics too.

As a result of the current policy shift towards a primary care-led National Health Service (NHS) general practice and primary care are increasingly the focus for health care provision in Britain. There is a system of universal population registration with a general practitioner (GP), and 90 per cent of

---

* now, Office for National Statistics

illness presents through general practice. With the exception of accidents and emergencies, general practice is the link to the hospital system and secondary care, through referrals. All contacts with primary and secondary care are recorded in the patients' general practice record, with the consequence that the collation of information on health service use revolves around general practice. There is therefore a need to understand the relationship between demographic and socio-economic factors and morbidity and health service use at the general practice level.

The uses which can be made of the wealth of data on morbidity and health service use available from general practice are limited by the lack of population data. Practice list size and the age–sex distribution are available from practice registers but no socio-economic data are routinely collected. This is a major drawback given the richness of the data in so many other ways.

In this paper we outline the population data available from general practice. We examine the variation in the demographic characteristics of general practices in East London and discuss the implications of this variation for allocating resources and planning the provision of health care. We describe a method of creatively using census data and practice population registers to derive estimates of the socio-economic characteristics of practice populations, using a proportional allocation technique. We apply this method to East London data, and we discuss some methodological issues associated with its use.

Brass often spoke of serendipity, that is making the most of the data available. Although best known for his work on limited and defective data in developing countries the twin principles of serendipity and simplicity which he espoused in that work he also applied in less well known work on developed countries in relation to family and household demography (Brass, 1984). Our description of how these principles have been applied in estimating characteristics of general practice populations show how his ideas are pertinent to the field of public health data collection.

POPULATION DATA AVAILABLE FROM GENERAL PRACTICE

Data available from general practice registers
The age and sex of patients are routinely collected in general practice, but no socio-economic data are systematically recorded. All individuals registered with a GP are on the register of their local health authority, with information on their name, date of birth, sex, postcode of residence, NHS number and the GP with whom they are registered. These computerized registers, which cover almost all of the population throughout their lifespan, are continually updated as people are born, die, change GP or practice locally, or move to other health authorities. From this register the age–sex breakdown of

practice lists is available. The address postcodes enable individuals to be located in a ward and enumeration district, and hence linked with the census characteristics of their area of residence. Personal NHS numbers facilitate the linking of a range of health service data for any individual.

Survey data

The routine data described above are largely collected for administrative and financial purposes. However, there are surveys of general practice which have collected more detailed population information, in particular socio-economic information, and have demonstrated the potential for epidemiological work in general practice (Hart, 1992). Most of these studies focus on single or small groups of practices. The National Morbidity Surveys of general practice in England and Wales are an exception as they cover larger numbers of practices. To date there have been four such surveys at approximately ten year intervals, collecting a wide range of very detailed information on patients and their use of general practice. The latest, the Fourth National Morbidity Survey of 1991–92 (Royal College of General Practitioners, Office for Population Censuses and Surveys and Department of Health, 1995; Fleming *et al*, 1996) collected data from half a million patients registered at 60 volunteer practices. The objectives of the study included examining the pattern of general practice consultations by age, sex and socio-economic characteristics and to provide information designed to assist in allocating resources and planning health care services. Socio-economic information was successfully collected by interview from 83 per cent of patients registered at the survey practices. The practices which participated in the survey tended to be larger, employ more assistant and trainee doctors, and have younger partners, as compared to all practices in England and Wales. The patients from whom socio-economic data were collected were representative of the general population on most characteristics but ethnic minority groups, people living alone and metropolitan areas were underrepresented.

Local or small-scale studies have also used patient interviews to obtain socio-economic information. For example, a study of a group of practices in Tower Hamlets in East London (Atri *et al*, 1996) collected information on socio-economic status and ethnic group in an attempt to assess how equitable the provision of services was across such groups. Using a detailed questionnaire 500 sampled adults were interviewed at home. Other studies have used postal questionnaires to collect data on socio-economic status (Worrall *et al*, 1997). A study by Marsh and Channing (1986) examined the morbidity and use of preventive services of two neighbouring communities (a deprived council estate, and a more endowed private housing estate) both served by the same general practice. This approach assumes that individuals have the characteristics of their place of residence. Census data for the area where a practice is located has been used to describe the socio-economic characteristics of its population; this rests on the assumption that patients have the characteristics of the ward or enumeration district in which the practice is situated. A study of practices in the Glasgow area (Lynch, 1995) used 'neighbourhood types', determined from census data, for each practice location.

As described a variety of approaches have been adopted for acquiring socio-economic population data from general practice. These largely rely on local surveys, or studies of selective groups of practices. Although of great value in themselves the findings from such surveys cannot readily be extrapolated beyond the limits of the studies themselves. Time and money prevent similar labour-intensive studies being done more frequently or on a larger scale.

Use of census data – the proportional allocation method
An approach which has been gaining in popularity over recent years is that of using census data in conjunction with the postcode distribution of a practice's registered patients to estimate practice socio-economic characteristics. A proportional allocation technique is used whereby census data for electoral wards is weighted according to the proportion of a practice list resident in each ward. For example, if in a certain practice 20 per cent of patients live in Ward A, 30 per cent in Ward B and 50 per cent in Ward C, census data for Wards A, B and C are weighted in the ratio of 2:3:5 to estimate the practice value of the variable under consideration. The procedure can be applied to a range of census variables. However, in this paper we describe the estimation of two variables of particular relevance to East London; the percentage of households in rented housing, and the percentage of residents of Asian ethnicity.

To derive a practice estimate of the 'percentage of households in rented housing', we take the 'percentage of households in rented housing' for wards from 1991 Census data, and a breakdown of the practice population according to which ward people live in. Suppose h_i is the percentage of households in ward i that are in rented housing, and p_{ki} is the proportion of practice k living in ward i, then the estimated variable,

percentage of households in rented housing in practice k,
$$h(k) = (h_1 * p_{k1}) + (h_2 * p_{k2}) + (h_3 * p_{k3}) + \ldots$$

This procedure rests on the assumption that individuals have the average characteristics of the geographical area in which they live. The extent to which this assumption is valid will affect the accuracy of the resulting estimated practice variables. Methodological issues surrounding this approach are discussed later. The application of the method to data from East London, and the use of the estimated practice population characteristics in analyses of health service use are described below.

AN EAST LONDON EXAMPLE

East London is taken as the East London and City Health Authority (ELCHA) area, which is coterminous with the local authorities of Hackney, Newham and Tower Hamlets, plus the City of London. It is an inner city area characterized by high levels of poverty, population mobility and ethnic diversity. It is also an area which has historically had poor provision of primary care services (Widgery, 1991).

The population of East London in 1991 was slightly over half a million residents. Table 12.1 describes aspects of the age–sex structure and socio-economic characteristics of East London, compared with the population of Greater London, and that of Great Britain as a whole. East London has a relatively young age structure, and higher ratio of males to females. It is an area of high social deprivation in terms of unemployment, car availability, housing tenure and overcrowding, as well as being an area of great ethnic diversity.

Table 12.1 *Characteristics of the population of East London, Greater London and Great Britain (1991)*

	East London	Greater London	Great Britain
Age-sex structure			
% under age 5	9	7	7
% under age 16	24	20	20
% aged 16–44	46	46	42
% aged 75 and over	5	7	7
Sex ratio (100 males/females)	95.1	92.3	93.9
Socio-economic characteristics			
Male unemployment as % of all males 16–64	20	12	10
% households with no car	59	41	33
% households owner-occupied	34	57	66
% households overcrowded (> 1 person per room)	9	4	2
Ethnicity			
% Asian	20	10	3
% Black	15	8	2
% Other	3	3	1
% White	63	80	95

Sources: Office of Population Censuses and Surveys. 1991 Census: Great Britain. OPCS National Monitor CEN 91 CM 56.
1991 Census: Inner London. OPCS County Monitor CEN 91 CM 17/1. London: HMSO, 1992.

Demographic characteristics of practices and wards

Among general practices in East London in 1993 practice populations varied in size from 800 to over 13,500, with a positively skewed distribution (Figure 12.1); the median practice size was 3,562 and the mean 4,323. Of the 163 practices administratively accountable to ELCHA in 1993, 159 are included in the analysis; complete data sets were not available for the remaining four. Information on practice list sizes and age and sex distributions was obtained from the 1993 health authority registration data.

Figure 12.2 illustrates the heterogeneity of practice populations in terms of their age and sex distributions. It shows for all practices in East London the percentage of the practice population aged under 5 (Figure 12.2a), the percentage aged 75 and over (Figure 12.2b), female and aged 15–44 (Figure 12.2c), as well as practice sex ratios (Figure 12.2d). These age–sex groups were chosen as children, the elderly, women of reproductive ages and women in general have higher than average GP consulting rates (Royal College of General Practitioners, Office for Population Censuses and Surveys and Department of Health, 1995) and are therefore of great importance when considering GP workload and the provision of primary care. Table 12.2 summarizes the variation in practice demographic characteristics. For example, on average patients aged 75 and over constituted 4.7 per cent of the practice list but the inter-decile range (central 80 per cent of practices) was 1.5 to 8.0 per cent of the practice list, a fivefold difference. If the outer deciles are included the range was 0.5 to 11.8 per cent.

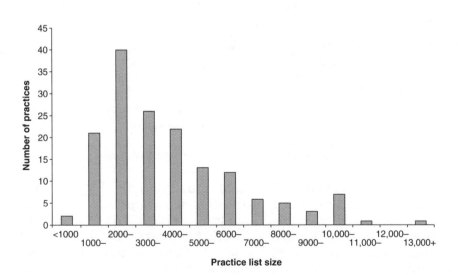

Figure 12.1   Distribution of practice list sizes: East London 1993

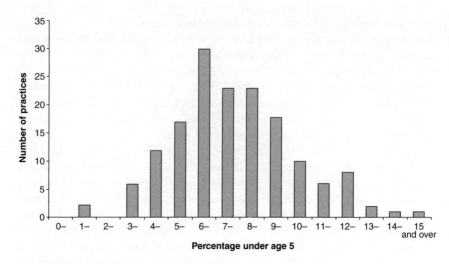

Figure 12.2a   Percentage of practice list under age 5: East London 1993

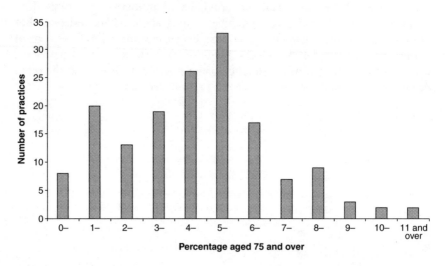

Figure 12.2b   Percentage of practice list aged 75 and over: East London 1993

The 67 wards in East London ranged in size from 4,000 to 16,000 people with a mean of 8,500, that is about twice the mean practice size (Figure 12.3). The data are taken from census-based estimates of the 1991 mid-year population (East London and the City Health Authority, 1993). Figure 12.4 illustrates the variability in the age–sex distribution of wards using the same groupings as used above for examining practice characteristics, i.e. percentages under age 5 (Figure 12.4a), aged 75 and over (Figure 12.4b), female

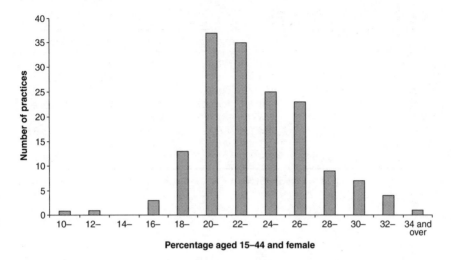

Figure 12.2c   Percentage of practice list aged 15–44 and female: East London 1993

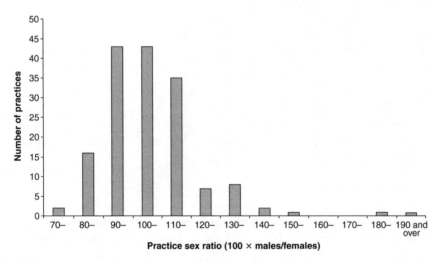

Figure 12.2d   Practice sex ratios: East London 1993

and aged 15–44 (Figure 12.4c), and the sex ratios (Figure 12.4d). These data are summarized in Table 12.3. Figure 12.5 summarizes the extent of the variability in components of the age distribution of practices and wards, and shows how much more variability there is in the former.

Practice populations have more extreme demographic characteristics than the (usually) larger geographical units of wards for reasons including the smaller size of many practices as compared to wards, and local variations

Table 12.2 *Variation in practice age and sex composition: East London 1993 (%)**

Age group	Mean	Median	Minimum	Maximum	Inter-decile range	
0–4	7.8	7.6	1.6	15.2	4.7	11.3
5–14	13.9	12.9	4.7	27.6	9.1	21.2
15–44	49.3	49.2	31.1	65.3	42.8	57.9
45–64	17.8	17.8	8.6	32.2	12.4	23.2
65–74	6.6	6.4	1.1	18.1	3.0	9.9
75+	4.7	4.8	0.5	11.8	1.5	8.0
Females 15–44	23.9	23.3	11.9	35.1	19.4	29.1
Sex ratio	106.1	104.8	72.2	196.0	88.8	124.0

* No. in age (sex) group as % of total practice list size, except for sex ratio = 100 * males/females.

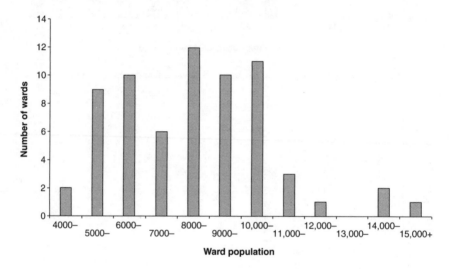

Figure 12.3   Distribution of ward populations: East London 1991

in population characteristics, childbearing and migration patterns. In addition variation arises because an individual can choose which practice to register at. In an inner-city area such as East London there are usually several nearby practices to choose between. There is likely to be some effect of, for example, women patients registering at practices with a female partner, and patients from particular ethnic groups at a practice with a GP from their culture and/or religion, and who speaks their language. All these factors contribute to variability in practice populations.

Health care implications of demographic variability between practices
Although it comes as no surprise that there is variability in practice age–sex distributions the resulting practical implications for health service

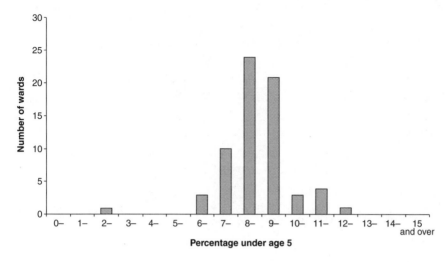

Figure 12.4a Percentage of ward population under age 5: East London 1991

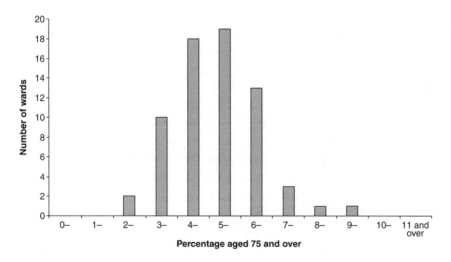

Figure 12.4b Percentage of ward population aged 75 and over: East London 1991

planning and use, workload, health promotion activities and finances are far reaching.

Children, women, especially those of reproductive ages, and the elderly are all groups with greater than average health needs, who consequently place more demands on the health service. Practices with a high proportion of patients in these groups will therefore have a greater workload, have higher prescription and referral rates, and have higher expenditure (Ben-Shlomo

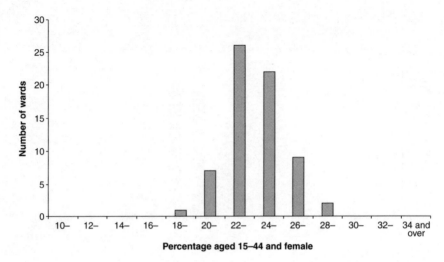

Figure 12.4c   Percentage of ward population aged 15–44 and female: East London 1991

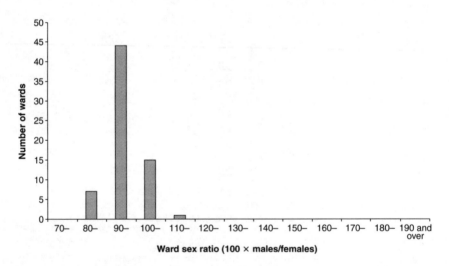

Figure 12.4d   Ward sex ratios: East London 1991

et al, 1992; Sleator, 1993; Royal College of General Practitioners, Office of Population Censuses and Surveys and Department of Health, 1995; Office for National Statistics, 1998). The adequate provision of health promotion services such as childhood immunization and cervical cytology screening will be affected by the age–sex distribution. A practice where women aged 15–44 comprise one-third of patients will have to work harder to screen for cervical cytology than one where women aged 15–44 comprise only 12 per cent

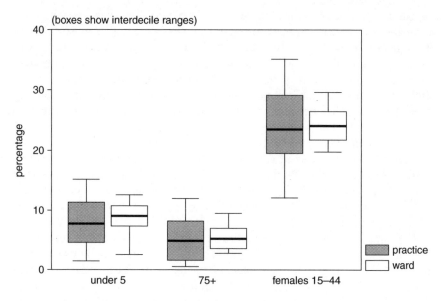

Figure 12.5   Variation in age composition of practices and wards: East London 1991

Table 12.3   *Variation in ward age and sex composition: East London 1991 (%)**

Age group	Mean	Median	Minimum	Maximum	Inter-decile range	
0–4	8.8	8.9	2.5	12.5	7.3	10.7
75+	5.3	5.2	2.7	9.3	3.5	6.9
Females 15–44	24.0	23.9	19.6	29.5	21.5	26.4
Sex ratio	96.5	95.5	86.1	113.4	89.7	105.1

* no. in age (sex) group as % of total practice list size, except for sex ratio = 100 * males/females

of the list. These variations will also affect the demand for contraceptive and maternity services, as well as baby clinics.

Some aspects of the age distribution are taken into consideration in the financial remuneration of general practice. GPs get paid a capitation payment for each patient on their list, and this payment varies with age with patients aged 65–74 attracting a fee about 30 per cent higher than those under 65, and those 75 and over 150 per cent higher. It has been suggested that GPs should also receive additional payments for children under 5 (Ben-Shlomo *et al*, 1992).

Some of the apparent demographic variability in practice populations may arise from inaccuracies in practice lists. Where local population mobility is high, as in East London, it is hard to maintain accurate age–sex patient registers and the resulting inflation of practice lists has repercussions throughout the organization of primary care (Bowling and Jacobson, 1989). This inflation may vary by age and socio-economic factors. In Tower Hamlets, one of the constituent boroughs of East London, an annual patient turnover of 30 per cent or more is not uncommon (Falshaw and Robson, 1992; Kalra, 1994); that is, almost one-third of a practice patient list changing over the year either because of patients joining or leaving the practice.

Socio-economic characteristics of practices and wards

As described under 'Use of census data' socio-economic data can be attributed to practices using routinely available data in the form of census data and practice registers. This section describes some socio-economic characteristics of wards in East London and then uses these data to derive estimates of practice characteristics.

The socio-economic characteristics of wards in East London are examined in relation to two census variables, the percentage of households in rented housing, and the percentage of residents of Asian ethnicity. Data come from the 1991 Census (East London and the City Health Authority, 1993). Figure 12.6 shows the distributions of these two variables among East London wards and illustrates the great variability of wards according to these characteristics. The percentage of households in rented accomodation varied between a quarter and over 85 per cent, with a mean value of 66 per cent. The percentage of residents of Asian ethnicity ranged from 1 to 67 per cent, with a mean value of 19 per cent.

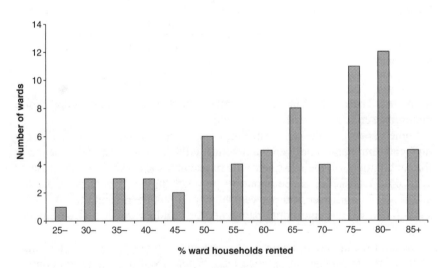

Figure 12.6a   Percentage of ward households rented: East London 1991

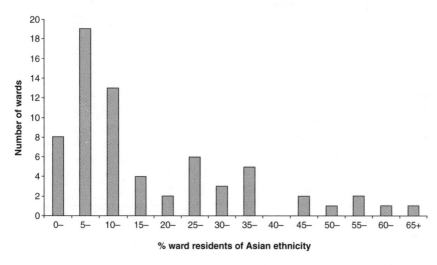

Figure 12.6b   Percentage of ward residents of Asian ethnicity: East London 1991

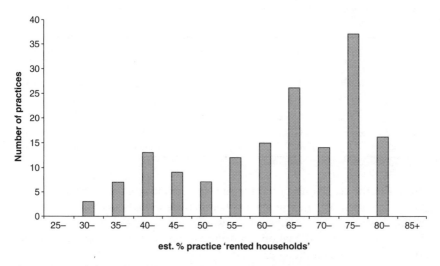

Figure 12.7a   Estimated practice 'rented households': East London

Figure 12.7 shows the estimated practice values for 'households in rented housing', and 'residents of Asian ethnicity' derived from 1991 ward census data and practice address lists in 1993. A comparison of these practice estimates and ward data is summarized in Table 12.4. For both variables the means of the distributions are very similar for wards and practices; however, there is greater variability among wards, and there is a smaller percentage of practices at the extremes of the distributions than wards. This is in direct

258   *Kath Moser and Sandra Eldridge*

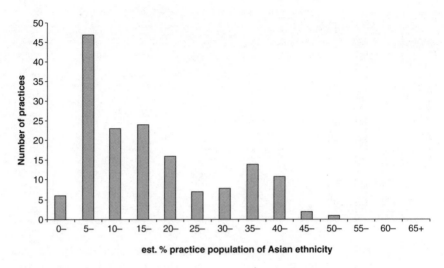

Figure 12.7b   Estimated practice population of Asian ethnicity: East London

Table 12.4   *Comparison of estimated practice socio-economic variables with ward data: East London*

	Mean	Median	Minimum	Maximum	Inter-decile range	
% of households in rented housing						
Practice estimate	64.5	66.9	31.5	84.4	41.4	80.0
Ward data	65.9	68.3	26.6	89.6	39.1	83.2
% of residents of Asian ethnicity						
Practice estimate	19.0	15.5	4.5	50.0	6.2	38.9
Ward data	18.8	12.0	1.1	66.8	4.6	46.1

contrast to the results observed for age–sex composition where greater variability was seen between practices than between wards. The attenuation of practice estimates as compared to ward values arises as a direct result of the proportional allocation procedure used in calculating the practice variables (see 'Methodological issues').

Studies linking practice population characteristics to measures of health service use
A number of studies have used estimates of practice socio-economic characteristics to examine relationships between practice populations, health needs and health service usage (Majeed *et al*, 1994, 1995a; Moser *et al*, 1994; Sturdy *et al*, 1995; Hull *et al*, 1996, 1997).

A practice-based study in East London examined variations in attendance rates at local accident and emergency departments (AEDs) in relation to features of practice organization, population characteristics and distance to hospital (Hull *et al*, 1997). The practice population characteristics were estimated using 1991 Census data. Both univariate and multivariate analyses indicated higher attendance rates in populations where owner-occupation of housing was low and where there were a high proportion of pensioners living alone; both variables are generally taken to be indicators of social deprivation. However, the relationship between some of the other population characteristics and attendance rates was not straightforward. No significant relationship was found between attendance rates and practice organization, and there was an expected negative association between distance to the nearest AED and attendance rates.

A study in south London (Majeed *et al*, 1994) found practice cervical cytology uptake rates to be negatively correlated with various measures of social deprivation including overcrowding, lack of car, unemployment and the percentage of 'non-White' ethnicity. Practice organization also played an important role; practices with a female GP had substantially higher uptake rates. A study in East London found similar results (Moser *et al*, 1994). There are other studies which have used census-derived estimates of practice population characteristics (Majeed *et al*, 1995a; Hull *et al*, 1996) including some which have found no association with the outcome variable of interest, for example a study of asthma prescribing in East London (Sturdy *et al*, 1995).

METHODOLOGICAL ISSUES

The proportional allocation technique for estimating practice population variables as described above has the great advantage of relying on routinely available data; hence it is cheap to use, can in theory be calculated for any practice or group of practices, and meaningful comparisons can be made between practices. However, there are several problems and limitations. These are described below alongside some discussion of how the technique may be improved. Since our unit of analysis is the practice some way of accounting for differences in general practice size (and demographic characteristics) may be required. There are the additional and perennial problems of data quality, and of highly correlated variables. These issues are discussed using data from East London.

Completeness of coverage and representation
The proportional allocation method combines census data with health authority registration data on the proportion of a practice list resident in each ward. Both data sources may contain inaccuracies and the socio-economic make-up of a ward may have changed since the last census. There may be issues concerning the completeness and accuracy of the census itself,

especially in an area such as East London where the average adjustment to 1991 Census data, to allow for under-enumeration, was +2 per cent ((East London and the City Health Authority, 1993). Poll tax evasion, as well as the considerable number of homeless people, recent immigrants and travellers, all contributed to this undercounting. High levels of population mobility can lead to inaccuracies in practice registers; people registered with a doctor may in reality have moved away or died, and others may have moved into the area but not yet registered.

The estimate of the mid-year population of East London in 1993 was 590,660; 708,900 patients were registered at practices in East London in 1993, 661,800 of whom were resident in East London. These figures suggest that practice list inflation was of the order of 12 per cent. If list inflation is concentrated in particular wards then these wards will be overrepresented in the derived socio-economic practice population characteristics.

The 'average inhabitant' assumption
Practice populations in East London are dispersed over a wide area with practice lists drawn from an average of 50 wards per practice. Only six practices have patients drawn from less than 20 wards, and seven practices have patients from over 100 wards. However, for each practice the bulk of patients are concentrated in a small number of wards. For example, one large group practice of about 10,000 patients has patients in 33 wards, but 80 per cent of their patients are drawn from just 5 wards. The weighting of ward census data to estimate practice population characteristics will obviously be dominated by the few wards where most of the practice population resides.

The main assumption underlying the proportional allocation method is that an individual has the average characteristics of the ward in which they live. The extent to which this is deviated from will obviously affect the accuracy of the estimates. Most wards in East London are far from homogeneous with people with very different characteristics (in terms of wealth and poverty, ethnic group, etc.) living side by side; for this reason individuals frequently do not have the average characteristics of the ward in which they live.

A direct result of the proportional allocation procedure is the attenuation of socio-economic differences between practices as compared to those between wards. This attenuation can be inferred from the equation in the section on 'Use of census data' since it is clear that the estimated practice variable, h(k), can never fall below the lowest, or rise above the highest ward value of the variable under consideration (h_i) (see Figures 12.6 and 12.7). If the *real* practice value is higher than the highest ward value then the *estimated* practice value will always underestimate the real value – and vice versa.

For example the elderly (aged 75 and over) as a percentage of the total practice population varies between 0.5 and 11.8 per cent (Table 12.2). A practice may have a particularly high percentage of elderly patients either because it serves wards which have an unusually high elderly population, or because it attracts elderly people out of wards which may not in themselves have a high proportion of elderly people. This latter situation may arise in the case of a doctor's list ageing with the doctor. Suppose, in addition, that the variable of interest varies with age as does, for example, the proportion of households in rented housing. In the case where a practice serves several relatively elderly wards the ward percentages of rented households, h_i, will reflect this, and hence the estimated practice variable, $h(k)$, will tend to reflect the real percentage. In the case where a practice particularly attracts elderly patients, the h_i from the wards in which these elderly live will not necessarily reflect the higher percentage in rented housing amongst the elderly, and consequently the estimated practice percentage rented will be too low.

This example highlights the fact that the attenuation effect of the proportional allocation procedure will be exacerbated when an estimated variable is related to a third variable (in this case age) and this third variable is 'clustered' in practices. Variables likely to be clustered in practices, are age, sex, ethnicity and socio-economic status. No account is taken of the age–sex distribution of the practice list in the proportional allocation procedure as applied here. If we can assume that a practice age–sex distribution is similar to that of the wards from which its patients are drawn then there is no problem. However, if this is not the case errors ensue. Theoretically, the proportional allocation procedure could be improved by taking account of age and sex in the calculations, in terms of both the practice registration data and the census data. Although this would increase the complexity of the calculations, it should remain well within the capabilities of modern-day computers. However, whether such refinements are warranted, given the crudity of the procedure in other ways, is an area for further study and investigation.

Validation of the estimates derived from the proportional allocation technique
There have been various attempts to validate census-derived estimates of practice characteristics. There are surveys which compare questionnaire data on social class with census-derived measures obtained using the proportional allocation method described here. A study in one Lincolnshire practice (Ward *et al*, 1994) compared data from a patient questionnaire on social class with census-derived measures obtained using the proportional allocation method.They found that the census-derived data (calculated as in this paper but using data for enumeration districts rather than wards) picked out

the same social class pattern as the patient questionnaire responses. They concluded that

> the use of small area statistics as a method of deriving local distributions of social class for health needs assessment is a useful asset in gaining the best (balancing cost, time and accuracy of results) insight into the socio-economic make-up of groups of patients in general practice (Ward *et al*, 1994).

The scale of the attenuation problem can only really be gauged by comparing actual and estimated practice characteristics in a validation exercise. This can most readily be done for practice age distributions obtained from patient registration data, and then compared with estimates derived using patient postcodes and ward census data. Work of this kind was carried out by Scrivener and Lloyd (1995) using data from Bradford. They used census data and proportional allocation techniques, similar to those described above, to estimate the proportion of patients aged 65 and over in each practice, and compared these estimates with the actual registration data. When census data at the ward level were used they found a correlation of 0.70 between the actual and estimated variables. The practice estimates of those aged 65 and over ranged from 10.5 to 18.8 per cent, while actual percentages ranged from 2.7 to 28.6 per cent, indicating a substantial attenuation in the estimates. They concluded

> Although predicted values correlated with actual values, the failure of the allocation procedures to correctly predict values, especially at the extremes, casts doubt on the validity of similar techniques for allocating census variables to general practice populations (Scrivener and Lloyd, 1995).

A comparison of the actual and estimated age distribution of patients in south London practices found the correlations ranging between 0.33 and 0.67 across the age range (Majeed *et al*, 1995b). The correlations for those aged 65–74, 75–84 and 85 and over were 0.58, 0.50 and 0.44 respectively. These correlations are weaker than those found by Scrivener and Lloyd and could indicate a higher degree of clustering within South London practices, or less homogeneous or larger wards.

An alternative way of validating the estimates is to see how well they support expected relationships within the data. General knowledge of the East London area suggests that those from certain ethnic backgrounds may be clustered in particular practices with ethnic minority GPs by choice. In addition, more affluent and mobile patients may be more likely to register with larger group practices often located within well-resourced health centres, and women may choose to be registered in practices where there is a woman GP. We were able to examine the second of these hypotheses using the proportionally allocated estimates. These estimates did not, however, support the hypothesis; estimated proportions of patients owning cars and living in non-rented housing tended to be higher in smaller practices. Either the estimates are severely in error, or our initial expectation of the relationship between affluence, mobility and practice size was incorrect. Without further evidence to support or reject the initial hypothesis our interpretation of this result is uncertain.

Regression analyses
Once socio-economic practice variables have been estimated, their relationship with measures of health service use can be investigated. The two major problems in carrying out practice-based regression analyses of this type are the inaccuracies in the values of the socio-economic variables as already described, and the variation in practice size. There is also the possibility of interaction between these two factors which may further complicate analyses.

Multiple regression analyses were carried out using the East London data. We looked at the relationships between the two estimated practice characteristics, living in rented housing and of Asian ethnicity, and the cervical smear uptake rate (percentage of women aged 25–64 having a cervical smear in the preceding 66 months). Two analyses were carried out, one in which each practice was given equal weight and a second in which the practices were weighted according to their list size. The association between the proportion of the practice population of Asian ethnicity and the cervical smear rate was not significant in either analysis. The association between the estimated proportion living in rented housing and the cervical smear rate was negative in both analyses. The unweighted analysis overestimated the importance of the proportion living in rented housing (-0.39: 95 per cent confidence interval -0.61 to -0.17) when compared with the weighted analysis (-0.30: 95 per cent confidence interval -0.49 to -0.11). Weighted analyses are generally to be preferred in situations like this, where the unit of analysis can vary considerably in size.

Taking account of the accuracy of the estimates is a more complicated issue. We hypothesized above that in East London certain types of patients would cluster in larger practices, in practices with ethnic minority GPs and in practices with women doctors. However, we have been unable to substantiate these hypotheses and even if we could the extent of the resulting inaccuracies in estimates would be difficult to gauge. It may be useful to have local or particular knowledge about population heterogeneity and patient clustering to try and assess any possible inaccuracies in the proportionally allocated estimates and thus any regression analyses. However, this is most likely to be a matter of discussing possible bias in results rather than any formal adaptation of the analysis procedure.

Correlations and their generalizability

Multivariate analyses of the relationship between socio-economic variables and health outcomes may be affected by strong correlations between some of the explanatory socio-economic variables (Table 12.5). These correlations are at a practice level, and cannot be assumed to apply at an individual or household level (English, 1992). The correlations are for East London and it may be inappropriate to generalize them to other areas or populations. For example, the strong positive correlation that exists in East London between households in rented housing and pensioners living alone (0.85) may not be found in a 'retirement town'. Thus while these two variables may be effectively measuring the same thing, and thus be almost inter-changeable, in an analysis pertaining to East London we cannot assume this will be true elsewhere. It is inadvisable to include too many highly related variables in a multivariate analysis. While the analyses may themselves indi-cate which variables should be included and which should not, to a large extent this decision is a matter of judgement and this may, at times, be difficult to make.

Improved spatial resolution

Improvements in the power of computers, leaps in the amount of data held on computer, facilities for linking datasets, and improvements in the link between postcodes and enumeration districts (EDs) have led to a great increase in analyses performed at the ED level (Carr-Hill and Rice, 1995). Consequently there has been considerable debate as to the relative advan-tages and disadvantages of using ED level data rather than ward level in the proportional allocation technique.

EDs are much smaller than wards and as a consequence tend to be more homogeneous. The 67 wards in East London are subdivided into about 1300 EDs, containing an average of 160 households each. The belief that aggre-gated ED data are more likely to reflect the circumstances of individual

Table 12.5 *Correlations between some estimates of practice socio-economic character-istics: East London*

	Male unemployment	Pensioners living alone	Households with no car
Male unemployment	1.00	*	*
Pensioners living alone	0.58	1.00	*
Households with no car	0.80	0.82	1.00
Households in rented housing	0.71	0.85	0.92

residents than are ward data is challenged by Carr-Hill who found no strong evidence for this (Carr-Hill and Rice, 1995). ED data are not always tabulated or available to the same degree of detail as ward data, and many Small Area Statistics tables are based on a 10 per cent coding of certain variables. Difficulties arise from postcodes which cross ED boundaries and so cannot readily be assigned an ED (Reading and Openshaw, 1993; Majeed *et al*, 1995b). One-sixth of postcodes in the Merton, Sutton and Wandsworth area of south London were found to lie in more than one ED (Majeed *et al*, 1995b) and consequently procedures have to be adopted for weighting ED data to derive postcode estimates. Population figures at ED level are not adjusted for under-enumeration (Scrivener and Lloyd, 1995) something of great importance in an area such as East London.

Because of their smaller size the characteristics of EDs are likely to be more variable than those of wards (and also practices). From this it directly follows that the estimates of practice characteristics derived using ED data will be more variable than those derived from ward data.

The validation exercises showed higher correlations between actual and estimated age distributions when ED data were used in the proportional allocation procedure rather than ward data. Scrivener and Lloyd (1995) found that when ED data were used to estimate the percentage of patients aged 65 and over the correlation with the actual data was 0.84 (as compared to 0.70 using ward data); the estimated range of practice values calculated with ED data (8.1 to 23.8 per cent) more accurately reflected the actual range (2.7 to 28.6 per cent) than did estimates using ward data (10.5 to 18.8 per cent). The authors concluded:

> Our results improved as the geographical areas used became smaller, with allocation for enumeration districts and postcodes producing the better results. It is not obvious, however, that the improved results were worth the extra work involved in achieving them.

Majeed *et al* (1995b) also found higher correlations between actual and predicted age variables when ED data were used rather than ward data.

SUMMARY

Information routinely available from health authority registers provides a rich source of demographic data. We have concentrated on describing its use at a general practice level, and have illustrated the large variability in the age and sex distributions of practice populations in East London. We have examined the practical effects and implications of this variability for health service planning and use, workload, health promotion activities and finances. Also important is the potential use of registration data at an individual level since this demographic data (originally collected for administrative and financial purposes) covers almost the whole population throughout their lifespan. Such data can be used to derive, or validate, estimates of the intercensal population, and to trace population movements and mobility (Haynes *et al*, 1995; Roberts *et al*, 1995).

Socio-economic data is another matter. There are no routinely available socio-economic data for general practice populations. Given the relationship between social factors and health this is a major problem when planning and implementing the provision of general practice and primary care.

We have described an increasingly widely used method for estimating general practice population characteristics using census data. Although this method has limitations, and there is limited direct evidence as to the accuracy of the estimates produced, it also has many advantages. It makes use of routinely available data, and hence is cheap to use; it can in theory be calculated for any practice or group of practices; and meaningful comparisons can then be made between practices. In the absence of better indicators of practice population characteristics it is sufficiently good to be used in practice (Aveyard, 1995; Lyons *et al*, 1995). The method follows well William Brass's principles of simplicity and serendipity, whereby creative use is made of the data available to obtain estimates of what we want and do not have – in this case socio-economic characteristics of practice populations.

An alternative is the collection of detailed survey data but this would be costly and necessarily restricted in time and space. Even if it were feasible on a large scale the results would still be subject to inaccuracies due to sampling variation and non-response. The ideal solution is the routine collection within general practice of patient socio-economic information. In the meantime more work is needed to assess the validity of the proportional allocation method of estimating practice population characteristics.

ACKNOWLEDGEMENTS

We would like to thank colleagues in the Department of General Practice, Royal London School of Medicine and Dentistry at Queen Mary and Westfield College for comments and advice; East London and the City Health Authority for data; Susan Dolan, formerly of the Department of General Practice, Imperial College School of Medicine at St. Mary's and Mike Chambers, formerly of the Department of Epidemiology and Medical Statistics, St. Bartholomews' and the Royal London School of Medicine and Dentistry, for providing the estimated socio-economic variables for practice populations. This work had close associations with the City and East London General Practice Database Project based at Queen Mary and Westfield College.

Funding: Work estimating the socio-economic practice variables was funded by the North East Thames Regional Health Authority locally organized research scheme.

REFERENCES

Atri, J., Falshaw, M., Livingstone, A., and Robson, J. for Healthy Eastenders Project (1996) 'Fair shares in health care? Ethnic and socioeconomic influences on recording of preventive care in selected inner London general practices'. *British Medical Journal*, 312, pp. 614–17.

Aveyard, P. (1995) 'Allocating census data to general practice populations: survey data have their problems too'. *British Medical Journal*, 311, p. 875 (letter).

Ben-Shlomo, Y., White, I. and McKeigue, P. (1992) 'Prediction of general practice workload from census based social deprivation scores'. *Journal of Epidemiology and Community Health*, 46, pp. 532–6.

Bowling, A. and Jacobson, B. (1989) 'Screening: the inadequacy of population registers'. *British Medical Journal*, 298, pp. 545–6.

Brass, W. (1972) 'The teaching of demography in relation to public health'. IUSSP Committee on Teaching of Demography and Training in Population.

Brass, W. (1984) 'A note on the estimation of family transition rates from census or survey data'. Seminar on The Demography of the Later Phases of the Family Life Cycle. Berlin: IUSSP Committee on Family Demography and Life Cycle.

Carr-Hill, R. and Rice, N. (1995) 'Is enumeration district level an improvement on ward level analysis in studies of deprivation and health?' *Journal of Epidemiology and Community Health*, 49(Suppl 2), S28–9.

Department of Health and Social Services (1980) *Inequalities in health*, report of a research working group chaired by Sir Douglas Black. London: DHSS.

Drever, F., and Whitehead, M. (eds) (1997) *Health Inequalities – Decennial Supplement*. Series DS No.15. London: The Stationery Office.

Eachus, J., Williams, M., Chan, P., Davey Smith, G., Grainge, M., Donovan, J., Frankel, S. (1996) 'Deprivation and cause specific morbidity: evidence from the Somerset and Avon survey of health'. *British Medical Journal*, 312, pp. 287–92.

East London and the City Health Authority (1993) *1991 Census Manuals*. London: ELCHA Information Unit.

English, D. (1992) 'Geographical epidemiology and ecological studies', in P. Elliott, J. Cuzick, D. English and R. Stern (eds), *Geographical and Environmental Epidemiology*. Oxford: Oxford University Press.

Falshaw, M. and Robson, J. (1992) *The Good Ghost Guide*. London: Healthy Eastenders Project.

Fleming, D.M., McCormick, A. and Charlton, J. (1996) 'The capture of socioeconomic data in general practice'. *British Journal of General Practice*, 46, pp. 217–20.

Goldblatt, P. (ed.) (1990) *Longitudinal Study; Mortality and Social Organisation 1971–81*, Office of Population Censuses and Surveys, Series LS no.6. London: HMSO.

Hart, J.T. (1992) 'Opportunities and risks of local population research in general practice', in D.P. Gray (ed.). *Forty Years On: The Story of the First Forty Years of The Royal College of General Practitioners*. London: RCGP.

Haynes, R.M., Lovett, A.A., Bentham, G., Brainard, J.S. and Gale, S.H. (1995) 'Population estimates from patient registers held by British family health services authorities'. *Journal of Epidemiology and Community Health*, 49, pp. 440–2.

Hull, S., Moser, K., Griffiths, C. and Jones, I. (1996) 'Night visiting rates'. *British Journal of General Practice*, 46, p. 375 (letter).

Hull, S.A., Jones, I.R. and Moser, K.A. (1997) 'Factors influencing the attendance rate at accident and emergency departments in East London: the contributions of practice organization, population characteristics and distance'. *Journal of Health Services Research and Policy*, 2 (1), pp. 6–13.

Kalra, D. (1994) *Patient List Turnover East London*. London: Medical Audit Advisory Group, City and East London.

Lynch, M. (1995) 'Effect of practice and patient population characteristics on the uptake of childhood immunizations'. *British Journal of General Practice*, 45, pp. 205–8.

Lyons, R.A., Monaghan, S., Heaven, M. and Willson, A. (1995) 'Allocating census data to general practice populations: reducing number of postcodes that cannot be ascribed would increase validity of method'. *British Medical Journal*, 311, p. 876 (letter).

Majeed, F.A., Cook, D.G., Anderson, H.R., Hilton, S., Bunn, S. and Stones, C. (1994) 'Using patient and general practice characteristics to explain variations in cervical smear uptake rates'. *British Medical Journal*, 308, pp. 1272–6.

Majeed, F.A., Cook, D.G., Hilton, S., Poloniecki, J. and Hagen, A. (1995a) 'Annual night visiting rates in 129 general practices in one family health services authority: association with patient and general practice characteristics'. *British Journal of General Practice*, 45, pp. 531–5.

Majeed, F.A., Cook, D.G., Poloniecki, J., Griffiths, J. and Stones, C. (1995b) 'Sociodemographic variables for general practices: use of census data'. *British Medical Journal*, 310, pp. 1373–4.

Marsh, G.N. and Channing, D.M. (1986) 'Deprivation and health in one general practice'. *British Medical Journal*, 292, pp. 1173–6.

Moser, K., Naish, J. and Chambers, M. (1994) Cervical smear uptake rates (letter). *British Medical Journal*, 309, pp. 476–7 and 674 (letter).

Office for National Statistics (1998) *Key Health Statistics from General Practice 1996*. Series MB6 No.1. London: ONS.

Reading, R. and Openshaw, S. (1993) 'Do inaccuracies in small area deprivation analysis matter?' *Journal of Epidemiology and Community Health*, 47, pp. 238–41.

Roberts, H.R., Rushton, L., Muir, K.R., Dengler, R., Coupland, C.A.C., Jenkinson, C.M., Ruffell, A. and Chilvers, C.E.D. (1995) 'The use of family health services authority registers as a sampling frame in the UK: a review of theory and practice'. *Journal of Epidemiology and Community Health*, 49, pp. 344–7.

Royal College of General Practitioners, Office for Population Censuses and Surveys and Department of Health (1995) *Morbidity Statistics from General Practice. Fourth National Study, 1991–92*, Series MB5 No 3. London: HMSO.

Scrivener, G. and Lloyd, D.C.E.F. (1995) 'Allocating census data to general practice populations: implications for study of prescribing variation at practice level'. *British Medical Journal*, 311, pp. 163–5.

Sleator, D.J.D. (1993) 'Towards accurate prescribing analysis in general practice: accounting for the effects of practice demography'. *British Journal of General Practice*, 43, pp. 102–6.

Sturdy, P., Naish, J., Pereira, F., Griffiths, C., Dolan, S., Toon, P. and Chambers, M. (1995) 'Characteristics of general practices that prescribe appropriately for asthma'. *British Medical Journal*, 311, pp. 1547–8.

Ward, P., Morton-Jones, A.J., Pringle, M.A.L. and Chilvers, C.E.D. (1994) 'Generating social class data in primary care'. *Public Health*, 108, pp. 279–87.

Whitehead, M. (1987) *The Health Divide: Inequalities in Health in the 1980s.* London: Health Education Council.

Widgery, D. (1991) *Some Lives! A GP's East End.* London: Simon and Schuster.

Wilkinson, R.G. (ed.) (1986) *Class and Health; Research and Longitudinal Data.* London: Tavistock Publications.

Worrall, A., Rea, J.N. and Ben-Shlomo, Y. (1997) 'Counting the cost of social disadvantage in primary care: retrospective analysis of patient data'. *British Medical Journal*, 314, pp. 38–42.

CHAPTER THIRTEEN

Health, health care and death among older adults in England and Wales: a hundred years' perspective

Emily Grundy

INTRODUCTION

In contemporary developed societies trends in the mortality, health and health care utilization patterns of older adults are now recognized as of major demographic and policy importance. In England and Wales, for example, 58 per cent of deaths occur among those aged 75 or over (OPCS, 1996) and those over 65 account for over half of all expenditure on hospital and community health services (Robins and Wittenberg, 1992). Mortality at young ages is in many populations now so low that the major scope for further gains in life expectancy at birth is through reductions in later life mortality. In Japan, for example, half of the increase of 1.4 years in female life expectancy at birth achieved between 1985 and 1990 was due to falls in death rates among those aged 75 and over (Kono, 1994). Moreover, as demonstrated by Preston *et al* (1989) and others, the further ageing of a number of already old populations with low fertility and mortality regimes is now largely mortality-, rather than fertility-driven. Professor Brass, as one of the foremost contributors to our understanding of population dynamics, of course foresaw the impact that changes in demographic parameters would have on the age structure on populations in both the developed, and eventually the less developed world. In his teaching in the late 1970s he was also among the first to emphasize that, although primary population ageing was the result of changes in fertility, declines in mortality at older ages also had a part to play, and that these would become more important. Before joining the Centre for Population Studies at the London School of Hygiene and Tropical Medicine his work in Aberdeen had included collaboration with geriatricians (Wilson and Brass, 1973) and his interests extended to studies of the health status of the older population, as well as on the processes of demographic change. Professor Brass was also very aware of insights that might be gained from the study of the demographic transition in the now developed world and, for example, made a major contribution to the question of the relationship between changes in infant mortality and fertility transition using historical data from England and Wales (Brass and Kabir, 1980). This chapter on the mortality and health of older adults in England and Wales from the mid-nineteenth to the mid-twentieth centuries thus reflects several of Professor Brass's many interests and owes much to the exposition of these in his teaching and research.

THE HEALTH OF OLDER ADULTS FROM THE MID-NINETEENTH TO THE MID-TWENTIETH CENTURY

As shown in Table 13.1, it was during the first decades of the twentieth century that the consequences of the fertility transition on the proportion of older people in the population became manifest. In the first forty years of the century, the proportion aged 65 and over doubled and England and Wales became one of the world's first populations in which one in ten people fell into this age band. Similar changes now occurring in a number of less developed countries have led to a growing interest in the mortality and health patterns of these countries' growing elderly populations (UNFPA, 1998). However, most studies of the mortality transition in the now developed world have focused, not surprisingly, on age groups experiencing the greatest change and less attention has been paid to patterns of mortality change at older ages. In the first section of this chapter we consider the course of mortality change in the older population between the mid-nineteenth and the mid-twentieth centuries. As noted by Schofield and Reher (1991, p. 7) 'little is understood of the relationship of morbidity to mortality during the [demographic] transition'. In the second part of the chapter we examine the rather limited evidence available on trends in morbidity at older ages during the same period. The chapter draws in parts on work undertaken as part of the Office of Population Censuses and Survey project *The Health of Adult Britain* which examined trends in health since 1841 (Grundy,

Table 13.1 *Percentage of the population aged 65–74 and 75+, England and Wales 1851–1951*

Year	65–74 (%)	75+ (%)	65+ (%)
1851	3.2	1.4	4.6
1871	3.4	1.4	4.6
1891	3.4	1.4	4.8
1901	3.3	1.4	4.7
1911	3.8	1.4	5.2
1921	4.3	1.7	6.0
1931	5.4	2.1	7.5
1941	7.1	2.9	10.0
1951	7.4	3.6	11.0
1991	8.9	7.1	16.0

1997a). Before considering the data available, a brief review of some of what is known and some of the main relevant theoretical debates is presented.

Mortality, morbidity and the health transition
As Preston (1976) and others have demonstrated, transitions from relatively high to relatively low mortality have in all populations which have experienced them been associated with transformations in the age, sex and cause structure of death. Substantial decreases in all cause mortality reflected major declines in death rates from infectious diseases (including respiratory tuberculosis, particularly important in England and Wales); bronchitis, pneumonia and influenza; diarrhoeal diseases; and maternal mortality (although in England and Wales declines in mortality from these latter causes occurred after the initial fall in infectious disease mortality). In England and Wales over half the gain in life expectancy at birth between 1871 and 1911 was due to reduced infectious disease mortality and over 20 per cent of the total gain was due to reduced mortality from respiratory tuberculosis (Casselli, 1991). These declines benefited the young more than the old and women more than men. The relatively slight improvement in death rates at older ages and the later stagnation of male mortality in some developed countries in the mid-twentieth century led to a predominant orthodoxy that death rates among elderly people were determined by largely immutable biological processes and that scope for improvement, once a certain level had been reached, was limited (Bourgeois-Pichat, 1952). However, recent marked declines in mortality at advanced ages in many developed countries (Manton and Vaupel, 1995), together with a better understanding of the biological processes underlying senescence, have led to a revision of this orthodoxy and its replacement with a new thesis. Recent analysts emphasize the plasticity of the ageing process – and so of mortality patterns at older ages – although a fierce debate about limits to this plasticity, and limits to the scope for further mortality reduction, persist (for a review of research on this topic see Grundy, 1997b).

Recent declines in mortality at older ages (and increased survival to later life) have also attracted particular attention because of uncertainties about relationships between mortality and morbidity in times of mortality change. While conventionally mortality has been used as an indicator of population health, it has been suggested that this is less appropriate in post health transition populations (Ruzicka and Kane, 1990). Although at the individual level health and risk of death are inversely associated, decreases in selective survival effects may, it has been suggested, result in a deterioration in the health of the older *population* as larger proportions with unfavourable health characteristics survive (Vaupel *et al*, 1979; Verbrugge, 1984). Populations which experience greater selective survival may thus have more favourable health characteristics in later life than ones subject to lower risks earlier in life. Related to this is the suggestion that declines in mortality at older ages in the 1970s may have been achieved through the prolongation of pre-death morbidity in those with health impairments rather than through the extension of 'healthy' life (Gruenberg, 1977; Kramer, 1980). Population surveys in a number of countries show recent increases in the reported prevalence of chronic conditions (Robine *et al*, 1992) which, if they reflect a change in health rather than in health expectations, would seem to support this argument.

More optimistically Fries (1980) has argued that the lifespan is biologically fixed and so future improvements in health will result in a 'compression of morbidity' as the onset of morbidity, but not death, is delayed. However, Fries's work has been challenged on methodological, theoretical and empirical grounds (Schneider and Brody, 1983). Even if there is a fixed biological limit to the life span, which many dispute (Gavrilov and Gavrilova, 1991) recent mortality data show a wider dispersion by age rather than signs of increasing concentration as hypothesised by Fries (Rothenberg *et al*, 1991). Moreover, a compression of mortality does not necessarily imply a compression of morbidity. There are, however, some recent studies from the United States which suggest an improvement in the ratio of active-to-total life expectancy in very old age groups, and a decline in serious, if not mild, disability (Manton and Stallard, 1994; Crimmins *et al*, 1997).

Most of these analysts have been concerned with recent trends. Riley (1990, 1997) and Alter and Riley (1989) have suggested a more general negative relationship between morbidity and mortality observable, they argue, in some historical as well as contemporary populations. Broadly speaking it is suggested that declines in mortality may lead to declines in the health status of populations through increased survival of frailer members and greater accumulation of health insults in longer surviving groups. Alter and Riley (1989), however, differ from some commentators in suggesting that future cohorts with a lower cumulative exposure to various insults may prove healthier.

Our aims in this chapter are to look further at both mortality and morbidity patterns in older age groups during the period under consideration and examine the thesis of a possibly changing relationship between the two.

MORTALITY TRENDS

Data

Civil registration of births, marriages and deaths was introduced in England and Wales in 1837; the General Registrar's Office had been established the previous year. Long series of vital statistics are therefore available and recently the Government Actuary's Department (GAD) has prepared life tables for cohorts and periods from 1841 onwards. These life tables have been based partly on the updating of the previous series prepared by the Chester Beatty Institute (Case *et al*, 1962). Needless to say, the source data for these series present some problems, in particular there is evidence of some age inflation among those over 75 in nineteenth and early twentieth century censuses (Lee and Lam, 1983). In the GAD life tables mortality data for those over 85 for the period 1841–1960 were estimated by fitting a model which ensured a smooth progression from this age onwards. For years before 1901, interpolation was used to derive values for single years of age and single calendar years between quinquennial points. The results presented here are drawn from the GAD data with no further adjustment.

Period trends in mortality at all ages
In most of this chapter we consider changes during the period from the mid-nineteenth to the mid-twentieth century and focus on those aged 65 and over. However these need to be seen in the context of longer-term trends in mortality in England and Wales in all age groups. These are shown for men and women respectively in Figures 13.1 and 13.2. The greater gains among the young in comparison with the old and among women in comparison with men are clearly evident. The figures also show that there have been changes in mortality at older ages as well, although these have been greatest in the more recent past. Period changes in life expectancy at birth, at age 30, and at age 65 1841–1951 (and, for comparison, 1991) are shown in Table 13.2.

Life expectancy at birth and at age 30 improved for both men and women between 1881 and 1901 and continued to improve in the first half of the twentieth century, apart from some stagnation in life expectancy at age 30

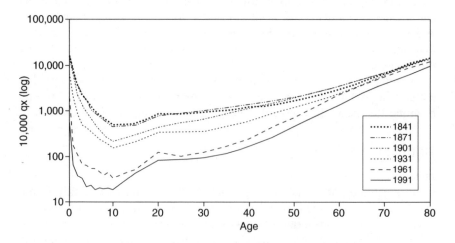

Figure 13.1   Period mortality rates (qx), males: selected years, 1841–1991

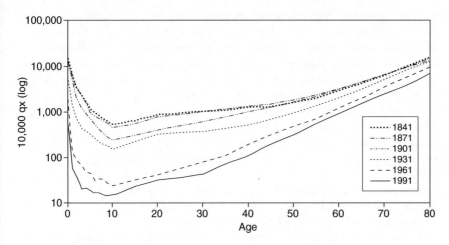

Figure 13.2   Period mortality rates (qx), females: selected years, 1841–1991

Table 13.2   *Life expectancy (period) at birth, at age 30 and at age 65, 1841–1951 and 1991*

Year	e_0		e_{30}		e_{65}	
	M	F	M	F	M	F
1841	41	43	33	34	10	11
1861	39	42	32	34	10	11
1881	42	45	32	34	10	11
1901	45	49	33	35	10	11
1911	50	54	35	38	11	12
1921	56	60	37	40	11	13
1931	58	62	37	40	11	12
1941	59	64	38	42	11	13
1951	65	70	39	43	11	13
1991	73	78	44	49	14	17

in the 1920s. Male life expectancy at age 65 showed no improvement in the nineteenth century, followed by an increase of a year early in the twentieth century. Gains for women were greater and continued into the mid-twentieth century. Certain episodic events, as well as underlying trends are relevant in interpreting these changes. These include the cholera epidemics of 1848–9, 1853–4 and 1866 and the influenza epidemics of 1847–8, 1889–92 and the pandemic of 1918–19. Gage (1993) has suggested the emergence of Asian influenza in the 1880s was associated with increased senescent mortality and exacerbated already high mortality from respiratory tuberculosis. This may account for the lack of improvement in life expectancy at older ages in the later nineteenth century. The 1918–19 influenza pandemic particularly affected young adults (see Figures 13.1 and 13.2). Young males were also obviously most directly affected by World War 1. Possibly the after effects of involvement in this war and exposure to the ensuing pandemic of influenza are a factor accounting for the lack of improvement in life expectancy at age 30 between 1921 and 1931.

An alternative way of conceptualizing the changes indicated in Figures 13.1 and 13.2 and Table 13.2 is to consider change in the age at which, on average, a specified period of life remains (Siegel, 1992). This has been done in Figure 13.3, which shows the age at which on average 15 years of life remained for the period under consideration and, for comparison, the recent past. Thus defined 'old age' for men in the mid-nineteenth century began at 55 or 56, compared with 58 for most of the first half of the twentieth century, 60 in 1971 and over 62 in 1991.

In the nineteenth century women attained this 'threshold' some two years later than men; by 1921 it had reached 61 for women (compared with 58 for men) and by 1971 there was a six year gap between the sexes.

Cohort perspectives

Table 13.3 shows survivorship to age 65 for cohorts born 1841–91, who reached the age of 65 between 1906 and 1956, together with cohort further expectation of life at age 65. Comparable data for those born in 1931, who reached the age of 65 in 1996, are also presented. Unfortunately, data for those born prior to 1841 are not available. The table shows marked increases among both men and women in survivorship to age 65 but no initial improvement in further life expectation from age 65 for those born 1841–61. Female cohorts

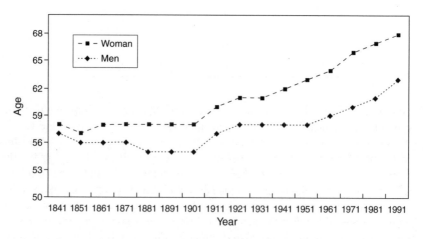

Figure 13.3   Age at which further expectation of life equals 15 years by period, 1841–199

Table 13.3   *Survivorship (% surviving) to age 65 and further expectation of life at age 65, by birth cohort*

Year of birth	% surviving to age 65		e_{65}	
	Men	Women	Men	Women
1841	28	34	11	12
1851	30	36	11	13
1861	34	41	11	13
1871	39	46	12	14
1881	42	51	12	15
1891	45	55	12	16
1931	68	78	16	19

born in 1871 and later did show continuing gains in further life expectancy. Male expectation of life at age 65 was one year higher for those born from 1871–81 than for those born 1841–61, but there was no improvement in this measure between cohorts born in the latter period. The table also shows clearly how slight these changes were in comparison to the improvements made between those born in the late nineteenth century and those born in 1931. Very much higher proportions of this later cohort reached the age of 65 and their subsequent life expectancy is projected (on the basis of recent trends in late life mortality) to be much higher, than in earlier cohorts, particularly for men.

These period and cohort mortality data suggest a slow but steady improvement in the chances of survival to later life for cohorts born in the nineteenth century (followed by more marked improvement in the twentieth century cohorts). Period data on mortality at older ages show no improvement until the end of the nineteenth century. Marked improvement followed, however, early in the twentieth century. Among women this was sustained while for men a period of relative stagnation followed.

If health status can be inferred from mortality data, it would seem that the older population, particularly the female older population, improved in health around the turn of the twentieth century. However, as noted earlier, alternative models of the relationship between mortality and health exist. Unfortunately, data on morbidity for this period are seriously deficient but in the following sections of this chapter we examine what data are available in order to see whether they can elucidate morbidity trends, and their association with mortality, during the period. The morbidity data considered are drawn from three sources: (1) census data on infirmities; (2) Friendly Society data on sickness spells from the mid-nineteenth to early twentieth centuries and (3) 1947–51 data from the national survey of sickness.

These data cannot be interpreted sensibly without some consideration of the major changes in social and health policy relating to the welfare and health care of older adults between the mid-nineteenth and mid-twentieth centuries. At the start of this period the predominant concern was with the deterrence of pauperism and the custodial care of the old and sick; by its end a National Health Service and all the other foundations of the modern welfare state had been established.

HEALTH AND SOCIAL POLICY

In the late nineteenth and early twentieth centuries the main 'services' with which elderly people had contact were those administered by Poor Law Boards of Guardians and the provision of care to elderly people with health problems was closely bound up with policy on pauperism.

The New Poor Law, introduced with the 1834 Poor Law Amendment Act, had as its guiding principle the deterrence of pauperism (reliance on payments from the poor rate) among the able-bodied. The destitute or near destitute were to be offered relief 'in the house' and out-relief payments were to be curtailed. Between 1852 and 1892 the numbers receiving outdoor relief (in all age groups) fell from 45 per 1,000 to 19 per 1,000 while the number of indoor paupers per 1,000 remained largely unchanged (fluctuating between 6 and 7 per 1,000). (RCADP, 1895, vol. 1, p. ix).

The Poor Law Guardians also had responsibility for the 'impotent' poor – those unable to support themselves as a result of age or infirmity. Many Poor Law Unions seem to have counted all paupers over 60 or 65 as 'not able-bodied', although practice varied and sometimes involved assessment by a medical officer (RCADP, 1895, vol. 1).

As the Poor Law Commissioners were at pains to point out in 1839 (cited in RCADP, 1895), out-relief payments to the aged and infirm were not forbidden by the 1834 Act and, they asserted, it had not been their intention to restrict support for these groups to in-relief. Although there was considerable local variation, widespread payment of out-relief to the aged seems to have continued after the 1834 Act, at least until the last decades of the century when there was a renewed campaign against out-relief (Quadagno, 1982; Thomson, 1984). Between 1872 and 1892 the number of 'not able-bodied' outdoor poor (in all age groups) fell from 16.2 to 8.8 per 1,000 population (RCADP, 1895, vol. 1, p. x). Census data show that the proportion of older people in workhouses (including sick beds) increased dramatically in the last decades of the nineteenth century. In the 1901 Census, for example, 9 per cent of men aged 75 and over were enumerated in workhouses, compared with fewer than 5 per cent in 1851.

The reliance of the elderly sick on the workhouse partly reflected the lack of provision elsewhere. The latter nineteenth century saw the rise of voluntary hospitals, which by 1921 accounted for a quarter of all beds in hospitals and related institutions for the physically sick (Pinker, 1966). These hospitals, however, to an increasing extent in the nineteenth century excluded both those with chronic illnesses and those with infectious diseases. Some provision for the latter group was made in specialist municipal hospitals.

In 1929 the Poor Law Unions were replaced by Public Assistance Committees and local authorities were empowered to take over poor law institutions. Many of those that did so converted the old workhouse into a hospital for the chronic sick, while the infirmary became the general hospital (Pinker, 1966). Even these general hospitals remained the poor relations of the voluntary hospitals.

Apart from inpatient care, which might be the result of poverty rather than poor health, other forms of health care in the nineteenth and early twentieth century were rudimentary. Voluntary hospitals provided outpatient clinics and in some areas Poor Law dispensaries existed. Members of Friendly Societies were entitled to medical consultations with 'club' doctors and membership grew rapidly at the end of the nineteenth century. From 1913, with the implementation of the 1911 National Insurance Act, insured workers were entitled to free consultations with 'panel' doctors and free drugs. This entitlement extended beyond the age of eligibility for a pension but applied only to insured workers and so largely excluded women. Prior to 1913, and for women and other uninsured elderly people thereafter as well, contact with Poor Law medical officers was probably more usual (Honigsbaum, 1979). These officers could prescribe 'medical out-relief', which might include food and drink, as well as medicine. The cost of medicines prescribed had to be paid for by the medical officers themselves, even so a return made in 1892 showed that some 15 per cent of the elderly population were in receipt of medical relief (RCADP, 1895, p. xii). Lack of access to doctors, apart from the overstretched Poor Law medical officers, may not have represented a particular disadvantage during this period, as arguably there was little of appreciable benefit that a personal physician could do for a patient until well into the twentieth century (Kunitz, 1991).

The early and mid-twentieth century saw several major milestones in the development of welfare and health provision for elderly people. Non-contributory means tested pensions payable at age 70 were introduced in 1908. Contributory pensions (from age 65) followed in 1925. Free health services for all were introduced in 1948 with the National Health Service Act under which ownership of all public and voluntary hospitals was transferred to the Ministry of Health. In the same year the National Assistance Act required, rather than empowered, local authorities to provide residential services to those in need, including disabled elderly people.

These changes in policy undoubtedly affected the health care available to elderly people, health related data and, particularly towards the end of the period considered here, health itself.

MORBIDITY

Evidence from Census data on impairments
From 1851 to 1911 the decennial censuses included questions on blind and
'deaf and dumb' people. From 1871 questions on 'idiots, imbeciles and
lunatics' in both private and non-private households were also asked. Table
13.4 shows the reported prevalence of these infirmities in the population
aged 65 and over. These, and more detailed data on age specific prevalence
rates of blindness published by Farr (Humphreys, 1885) for 1861, show a
strong relationship with age and overall high prevalence rate (comparable
with contemporary Mali).

The historical English data show a fall in the prevalence of blindness in
the later nineteenth century and a further drop between 1901 and 1911.
(This latter fall may partly reflect a change in the census question from
'blind' to 'totally blind'.) Improvements in hygiene and declines in infectious
diseases sometimes leading to blindness are likely to have been a factor
and possibly advances in treatment had some effect on prevalence rates.
Smith (1979) reports that successful cataract operations were carried out in
the 1840s and, although it is unclear how common they were, a number of
eye hospitals were opened in the mid-nineteenth century. By 1866 there
were six eye hospitals and seven ophthalmic clinics in London alone (Abel-
Smith, 1964).

The prevalence of deafness and muteness, by contrast, showed essentially
no variation by age in the nineteenth century and no changes in prevalence
in the age group considered here. However, the proportion of children
returned as 'deaf and dumb' or 'dumb' nearly halved between 1851 and
1911. This was attributed in the 1911 Census report to 'modern educative
methods' of helping deaf children to learn to speak and resulted in a marked
change in the age distribution of the 'deaf and dumb' population. For this
reason the prevalence of muteness would have been lower in cohorts reaching
older age groups in the twentieth century.

Table 13.4 *Prevalence (per 1,000 population 65+) of infirmities recorded in the
Census, 1851–1911*

		1851	1871	1891	1901	1911
Blind	M	8.9	7.2	6.0	5.6	5.1
	F	8.4	7.5	6.1	5.7	5.2
'Deaf and dumb'	M	0.5	0.5	0.5	0.5	0.5
	F	0.4	0.4	0.4	0.6	0.4
'Idiots, imbeciles	M		7.6	9.5	12.9	13.0
& lunatics'	F		4.9	5.5	6.4	6.7

Source: Census data.

Not surprisingly, underreporting of 'idiocy, imbecility and lunacy' was a problem in these censuses. Logan and Brooke (1957) noted that matching of mental hospital admissions records with census returns showed that many of those admitted had not been identified as 'defectives' in the census. The prevalence of mental health problems shown in Table 13.4 is broadly comparable with results from some of the early studies of mental health based on surveys of whole populations (Lin, 1953). However, it is clear that these surveys (and presumably the census) identified only the most serious cases. More detailed studies conducted in the mid-twentieth century in Britain estimated the prevalence of mental disorders amongst elderly people to be at least ten times higher (Kay *et al*, 1964). The data show an increase in reported prevalence between the late nineteenth and early twentieth centuries. However, this was due to the enormous increase in the proportions in lunatic asylums; the prevalence of identified mental health problems in the private household population remained unchanged. As a result, while in 1871 only just over half (53 per cent) of the male 'idiot, imbecile and lunatic' population was enumerated in asylums and other specialist institutions, by 1911 this proportion had increased to 73 per cent.

Overall these data suggest that blindness decreased in prevalence. In less developed countries blindness is a major cause of disability in elderly people so this change, although relatively modest, represents a clear health gain. The apparently alarming increase in mental illness almost certainly reflects changes in policy, resulting in greater institutionalization, and perhaps growing awareness of mental health problems, rather than a real deterioration in mental health.

Evidence from data on sickness spells
Of the limited morbidity data available for the later nineteenth and early twentieth centuries returns of sickness benefits paid by Friendly Societies constitute a major source. The potential value of these data were recognized by contemporaries and a number of investigations into the sickness and mortality rates of Friendly Society members were carried out (see, for example, Ratcliffe, 1850; Farr, in Humphreys, 1885). Information derived from returns from the largest society, the Manchester-based Independent Order of Odd Fellows (IOOF) were used to calculate contribution rates when the first compulsory national insurance scheme (for workers earning less than £160 per annum) was established in 1911. More recently, Alter and Riley (1989) have used IOOF data relating to periods between 1846–50 and 1893–7 to explicitly examine the relationship between male mortality and morbidity (in all adult age groups). They concluded that between the 1860s and 1890s morbidity rates in fact increased, while mortality fell, and used a model which incorporated both selective survival and insult accumulation effects to account for this.

As Alter and Riley (1989) point out, Friendly Society and other insurance-based, data have a number of strengths. As benefits are paid to those unable to work due to illness, the measure of morbidity is essentially a functional one. Both parties have incentives, on the one hand to claim benefits when incapac-itated and on the other to verify claims (often by a physician). However, against these strengths must be set a number of major weaknesses. Member-ship of Friendly Societies was (until 1911) voluntary and applicants consti-tuted a self-selected group. Members were predominantly better-off manual workers in their 20s and 30s (Smith, 1979). Farr (in Humphreys, 1885) noted that the average age of members in the 1836–40 returns was 32 and in 1846–8 those over 55 constituted only 1.5 per cent of insured lives (Ratcliffe, 1850). Further selection occurred at admission to a society, when the chronically ill were excluded; some societies also excluded those in hazardous occupations. Long-term members (likely, it seems safe to assume, to include many of the older members) represent an even more selected group as membership turnover was high (Farr, in Humphreys, 1885; Smith, 1979). The effects of these selective processes undoubtedly changed over time as membership grew. Ratcliffe's comparison of life expectancy of Friendly Society Members and population as a whole suggests that even between 1836–40 and 1846–8, the relative advantage of society members lessened (Table 13.5).

A further problem arises from possible age-related and other influences on actual claims by members. Some societies appear to have made payments to older members as a form of pension, rather than as sick pay (Helowicz 1987). Neison, who examined data from all English Friendly Societies for the period 1836–40 (results reported in Ratcliffe, 1850), noted that the ratio of sickness claims to deaths varied substantially by age group, being lowest among 30–40 year olds and highest for those in their 60s and 70s. Neison concluded that sickness and mortality were not connected as 'cause and effect'. Farr, however, disputed this and pointed out that for those in their 30s, both the gap between wages and sickness benefits and the likelihood

Table 13.5 *Expectation of life among men at ages 20–70; members of English Friendly Societies 1836–40, England and Wales 1841 and IOOF members 1846–8*

Age	English Friendly Societies 1836–40	England and Wales 1841	IOOF members 1846–8
20	44	40	41
30	37	33	34
40	29	27	26
50	22	20	19
60	16	14	13
70	10	9	9

Source: Ratcliffe (1850), p.29.
Note: These contemporary estimates overstate expectation of life at age 70.

of having dependants was much greater than for older workers. Farr's conclusion was that: 'there is no connection between the time men of different trades in friendly societies are in the receipt of sick-pay and the actual sickness which they experience' (Farr, in Humphreys, 1885, p. 505).

If this assessment is correct it clearly limits the usefulness of these data in elucidating health trends. These problems complicate the interpretation of differentials by age in sickness recorded by Friendly Societies and, to an even greater extent, the interpretation of trends over time.

Table 13.6 shows weeks of sickness per 1,000 by age for the periods 1834–40 to 1921–3. The data for 1846–8, 1866–70 and 1893–7 are drawn from Alter and Riley's (1989) presentation of IOOF data compiled by Watson in 1903; the 1834–40 data, included as an earlier benchmark, are derived from Neison's compilation of returns from all English Friendly Societies. The 1921–3 data also come from Friendly Societies, but relate to their administration of benefits payable under the compulsory national insurance scheme. Under this scheme (as amended by the introduction of disability benefit in 1914) those who had claimed sickness benefit for more than 26 (not necessarily consecutive) weeks in a year were moved on to disability benefits, paid at a lower rate, as were those who reclaimed within a year of coming off disability benefit. The data shown here include both sickness and disability benefit recipients. Those over 70 are not included in the 1921–3 returns as they were eligible for non-contributory pensions. It should be noted that the introduction of compulsory National Insurance did not compel the Friendly Societies to extend their membership to groups previously excluded. They continued to select members on health-related grounds while other schemes, run by trade unions and insurance companies, catered for other workers.

Table 13.6 *Weeks of sickness/incapacity per 1,000 weeks at risk, males 1836–40 to 1946–7*

Period	Age					
	55–9	60–4	65–9	70–4	75–9	80–4
1836–40[a]	63	107	206	341	478	542
1846–48[b]	62	97	125	233	322	374
1866–70[b]	59	91	139	232	325	396
1893–97[b]	77	121	204	335	484	621
1921–23[c]	53	84	146	–	–	–
1946–47[d]	46	48	49			

[a] Derived from Friendly Society data collected by Neison and reported in Ratcliffe (1850).
[b] Data from IOOF (Watson 1903) presented in Alter and Riley (1989).
[c] Derived from Appendix A of Royal Commission on National Health Insurance (1926).
[d] Derived from 'Survey of Sickness' (Stocks, 1949).

The returns for all the periods considered show strong relationships between age and weeks of sickness; at age 55–59 for example, sickness rates were generally over three, and in some periods nearly four, times higher than rates for 30–34 year olds. More caution should be applied to the rates for those over 75 as the numbers involved are small (the 1846–8 enquiry included only 105 'years at risk' for those aged 75 and over) and ages, particularly in the early period, are likely to have been overstated. However, weeks of sickness in these age groups were generally twenty or thirty times as great as those for 30–34 year olds. It should be noted that weeks of sickness per 1,000 as recorded in the IOOF data were massively greater at older ages than self-reported sickness recorded in 1946–7 (Stocks, 1949). This strongly suggests that the IOOF payments were being made as a form of pension.

In terms of changes over time, Alter and Riley have drawn attention to the increase in sickness rates between 1866–70 and 1893–7 and noted that this was particularly marked among those aged 70 and over. Sickness rates also seem to have been high in 1836–40 and, although high in 1893–7, declined between then and 1921–3. Alter and Riley suggest that the increase between the 1860s and the 1890s was due to the increased survival of the frail, together with a greater accumulation of insults resulting from previous illness among these survivors. Unfortunately, we know little about changes in the early survivorship of cohorts born between the end of the eighteenth and the mid-nineteenth centuries (although we do know that between the late 1860s and the mid 1890s rates of mortality among those aged 55 and over deteriorated slightly in the population as a whole and among IOOF members) (Alter and Riley, 1989, Table 2). It seems equally probable that either changes in the procedures of the IOOF over payments, or in the membership, account for the apparent rise in morbidity. Membership of Friendly Societies and other benefits societies grew very rapidly during the second half of the nineteenth century; the IOOF had some 60,000 members in 1836, nearly a quarter of a million in 1844 (Farr, in Humphreys, 1885) and in 1897 enrolled some 7 per cent of the adult male population (Alter and Riley, 1989). By the 1890s nearly a quarter of adult males were members of some society (Smith, 1979) and members thus represented a less strongly selected group than previously.

Changes between 1893–7 and 1921–3   The Royal Commission on National Health Insurance, which reported in 1926, undertook a comparison of claims for sickness benefit by IOOF members 1893–7, and claims under the national scheme 1921–3. This comparison (Table 13.7) showed a decrease in the proportions claiming sickness benefits (payable to those sick for less than half the year) but, particularly at younger ages, an increase in lengths of claims. It should also be noted that the short-term sickness rates reported for the 1921–3 period may be artificially low, because, as Watson *et al*

Table 13.7 *Sickness and disablement claims among men aged 45–64 1893–7 (IOOF) and 1921–3 (National Insurance)*

Benefit/usage	Period	Age			
		45–9	*50–4*	*55–9*	*60–4*
Sickness benefit					
Proportion claiming	1893–7	258	273	300	328
per 1,000 pa	1921–3	171	195	221	263
Average length of claim	1893–7	4.8	5.4	6.1	7.0
(weeks)					
	1921–3	5.3	5.7	6.3	7.1
Disablement benefit					
Proportion claiming	1893–7	27	42	69	119
per 1,000 pa	1921–3	23	29	47	81
Average length of claim	1893–7	67	81	91	110
(weeks)	1921–3	62	61	72	82

Source: Derived from Watson *et al* (1926). Appendix A of the Royal Commission Report, Tables 1, 2, 4 and I.

(RCNHI, 1926) noted, the insured population had an incentive to claim unemployment benefits (paid at a higher rate) rather than sickness benefits. Among those over 50 the proportion claiming disablement benefit and the length of disablement claims fell quite sharply, while the reverse was true in younger age groups. Watson *et al* (RCNHI, 1926) thought that the increase in length of claims and in the proportion reaching disablement benefit in younger age groups might be partly due to frequent claims from a small group with poor health at entry to the scheme; the size of this group would have been much smaller in the IOOF because of the need to satisfy a medical examination. However, it is unclear why the change in the older age group should have been in the opposite direction.

Evidence from the Survey of Sickness
The Second World War provided a stimulus both to enquiry and to policy change, in particular the first official survey of hospital beds undertaken in 1938 revealed the inadequacies of much hospital accommodation. The 'Survey of Sickness' was initiated in 1944 (although those over 65 were not at first included) and continued until 1951 (Stocks, 1949; Logan and Brooke, 1957). It thus straddles the immediate pre- and post-NHS period.

Respondents to the 'Survey of Sickness' were asked about periods of sickness (defined as a condition listed in the International Classification of Diseases and causing some disability); days of incapacity (defined as absence from work or confinement to the house due to illness) and medical consultations in the previous two (initially three) months. Table 13.8 shows

Table 13.8   *Reported monthly sickness (%reporting one or more episodes of sickness; days of incapacity per person per annum and monthly medical consultation rates per 100 registered patients 1947–51, males and females aged 65 and over*

Year	Reported monthly sickness		Days of incapacity (p.a.)		Medical consultations per 100 (monthly)	
	65–74	*75+*	*65–74*	*75+*	*65–74*	*75+*
Males						
1947	75	81	17.3	21.6	53	61
1948	74	82	16.3	24.0	58	71
1949	76	83	19.6	19.7	65	74
1950	76	85	18.8	19.0	73	81
1951	79	85	20.0	20.0	64	89
Females						
1947	84	89	19.7	24.4	56	76
1948	84	88	23.0	34.9	58	79
1949	86	89	20.2	28.6	62	72
1950	86	92	16.1	23.0	64	81
1951	86	91	18.2	19.8	64	84

Source: Survey of Sickness (Logan and Brooke, 1957).

the percentage of respondents reporting one or more episodes of sickness in a month, reported days of incapacity and reported medical consultation rates by sex and age group. Reported sickness was higher among women higher in the 75– age group than among 65–74 year olds. Although the rates of sickness reported appear very high, it is clear that respondents included very minor complaints. In 1946, 87 per cent of those over 65 who reported some sickness had not experienced any days of incapacity as a result and only 6 per cent had been incapacitated for longer than a week (Stocks, 1947). Women aged 75 and over generally also reported the greatest number of days of incapacity, although these fluctuated.

The proportion of older adults, including those aged 75 or more, reporting any illness, was generally higher in 1951 than in 1947, yet among women aged 75 or more the number of days of incapacity fell. This implies either a reduction in the incidence of incapacitating illness (or progression to incapacitating illness), or in the duration of incapacitating illness or both. The greater availability of penicillin after the war and changes in access to, and the practice of, general practitioners may have contributed to this.

The mean monthly medical consultation rates (consultations in a specified month per 100 surveyed) shown are *consultation-* rather than *patient-*based. As would be expected, the consultation rate was higher for those over 75 than for 65–74 year olds. Initially consultation rates were higher among women than among men, especially in the 75– age group. However, from 1949 this differential was either slight or reversed, reflecting the particularly large increase in consultation rates among men over 75. The overall increase in consultation rates may, to some extent, reflect increased access following the establishment of the NHS in 1948.

What is striking about these data is the very high rate of consultation – a rate which implies 10 doctor visits per year per person aged 75 or more. (Recent data from the General Household Survey implies only 6 consultations per year in this age group in the 1990s.) Given that local surveys show that some two-fifths of the elderly population did not consult at all in the course of a year (Sheldon, 1948), it is clear that others must have been frequent and regular surgery attendees. Subsequent national surveys of morbidity in general practice show marked falls in the consultation rates of elderly people between the mid-1950s and early 1970s due, not to any decrease in the proportion of people consulting at all, but to a halving in the number of consultations associated with each episode of illness (Logan and Cushion, 1958; BRU, 1976). Improvements in available therapies and in medical management probably explain this trend.

CONCLUSION AND IMPLICATIONS

What can be concluded from this review of mortality and morbidity data on older adults in England and Wales from the mid-nineteenth to the mid-twentieth centuries? During this period survival to and beyond the age of 65 increased, more so for women than men. In comparison with recent changes, the extent of improvement at older ages among men appears very modest and the restriction of change to the first two decades of the twentieth century is also puzzling. The lack of improvement in the nineteenth century may, as Gage (1993) suggests reflect the emergence of new viruses such as Asian flu. Possibly the harsher implementation of assistance schemes for the impoverished elderly population and other adverse economic factors may also have played a part. The early twentieth century saw several improvements in the status of elderly people, including the provision of pensions. Suicide rates at older ages declined substantially during this period (Murphy *et al*, 1986), which some have seen as a consequence of greater economic security. Later in the twentieth century economic slump, increased exposure to cigarette smoking, an increase in dietary fat intakes and unfavourable health legacies may have impeded further progress. All have been implicated in the rise in heart disease mortality which underlies the failure of all-cause mortality to improve (Charlton *et al*, 1997). Among older women the early twentieth century was also a period of particular improvement in survival but gains continued throughout the 1920s and 1930s. Women, in contrast to men, did not start smoking in great numbers until the 1920s. It has also been suggested that women's social ties afforded them

greater protection from the stresses resulting from continuing industrializa-
tion and urbanization (Waldron, 1986).

How were these changes related to changes in morbidity or in health?
Census data suggest a decline in the prevalence of blindness which, although
fairly small, represents a gain. (Possibly it may also indicate an improvement in the nutritional status of the population reaching old age, but this is
highly conjectural.) Mental illness appears to have increased, but undoubtedly the epidemic here was in institutionalization rather than madness.

Friendly Society data, I would suggest, are influenced by so many biases
that they form a shaky basis on which to build hypotheses about relationships between mortality and morbidity. There appears to have been an
increase in sickness between the 1860s and 1890s (when male mortality
was *also* increasing slightly). Sickness rates at old ages are so phenome-
nally high in these data – ten times as high as self reported in 1946–7 –
that it seems that sickness payments must have been made as a form of
pension. Possibly the harsher implementation of the Poor Law and reduced
availability of outdoor relief from the 1880s increased the pressure on
Friendly Societies to make such payments to their (relatively few) older
members. The evidence in support of increased morbidity would seem to
be very weak.

The data from the mid-twentieth century point to the high prevalence of
self reported illness (much of it minor) and high use of doctors by older
people. Since then rates of medical consultation have fallen substantially,
undoubtedly a reflection of improvements in available therapies and in
medical management.

Several questions remain unanswered, and perhaps unanswerable given
the paucity of data. Among these are the effect of lifetime experiences on
health and morbidity in later life. Barker's work (1992) suggests an important and continuing effect of early childhood factors on health throughout
life. However, some of these conclusions have been challenged (Elo and
Preston, 1992) and other analyses (for example Charlton *et al*, 1997) suggest
that period, rather than cohort factors, may have had a stronger effect on
trends in heart disease mortality. Possibly the answer may lie in some interaction of early life experiences and later exposures. Certainly the childhood
experiences of those born in the early twentieth century included high
exposures to poor nutrition and environmental hazards such as heavy air
pollution coupled in some cases with later occupational hazards and
'lifestyle' exposures such as fatty diets and smoking. The extent of 'plasticity' in the ageing processes that underlie both morbidity and mortality in
later life may now only just be becoming apparent as cohorts including
larger proportions with more favourable experiences at all stages of the life
course reach old age.

REFERENCES

Abel-Smith, B. (1964) *The Hospitals 1800–1948*. London: Heinemann.

Alter, G. and Riley, J.C. (1989) 'Frailty, sickness and death: models of morbidity and mortality in historical populations'. *Population Studies* 43, pp. 25–46.

Barker, D. (1992) *Fetal and Infant Origins of Adult Disease*. London: BMA Publications.

Bourgeois-Pichat, J. (1952) 'Essai sur la mortalité 'biologique' de l'homme'. *Population*, 3, pp. 381–94.

Brass, W. and Kabir, M. (1980) 'Regional variations in fertility and child mortality during the demographic transition in England and Wales', in J. Hobcraft and P. Rees (eds), *Regional Demographic Development*. London: Croom-Helm, pp. 71–88.

BRU (Birmingham Research Unit of the Royal College of General Practitioners) (1976) *Trends in National Morbidity*. London: Royal College of General Practitioners.

Case, R.A.M., Coghill, C., Harley, J.L. and Pearson, J.T. (1962) *The Chester Beatty Research Institute Serial Abridged Life Tables*. London: Chester Beatty Institute.

Casselli, G. (1991) 'Health transition and cause specific mortality', in R. Schofield, D. Reher and A. Bideau (eds), *The Decline of Mortality in Europe*. Oxford: Clarendon Press, pp. 68–96.

Charlton, J., Murphy, M., Khaw, K.T., Ebrahim, S. and Davey Smith, G. (1997) 'Cardiovascular diseases', in J. Charlton and M. Murphy (eds), *The Health of Adult Britain 1941–1994*, vol II. London: The Stationery Office.

Crimmins, E., Saito, Y. and Reynolds, S. (1997) 'Further evidence on recent trends in the prevalence and incidence of disability among older Americans from two sources: the LSOA and the NHIS'. *Journal of Gerontology: Social Sciences*, 52B, S59–71.

Elo, I.T. and Preston, S.H. (1992) 'Effects of early life conditions on adult mortality: a review'. *Population Index*, 58, pp. 186–212.

Fries, J. (1980) 'Aging, natural death and the compression of morbidity'. *New England Journal of Medicine*, 303, pp. 130–5.

Gage, T.B. (1993) 'The decline in mortality in England and Wales 1861–1964'. *Population Studies*, 47, pp. 47–66.

Gavrilov, L.A. and Gavrilova, N.S. (1991) *The Biology of Life Span: A Quantitative Approach*. London: Harwood Academic.

Gruenberg, E.M. (1977) 'The failures of success'. *Millbank Memorial Fund Quarterly*, 55, pp. 3–24.

Grundy, E. (1997a) 'The health of older adults 1841–1994', in J. Charlton, M. Murphy (eds), *The Health of Adult Britain 1841–1994*, vol II. London: The Stationery Office, pp. 183–204.

Grundy, E. (1997b) 'Demography and gerontology: mortality trends among the oldest old'. *Ageing and Society*, 17, pp. 713–25.

Helowicz, G. (1987) 'A look at the past', in B. Benjamin, S. Haberman, G. Helowicz, G. Kaye and D. Wilkie (eds), *Pensions: the Problems of Today and Tomorrow*. London: Allen & Unwin.

Honigsbaum, F. (1979) *The Division in British Medicine*. London: Kogan Page.

Humphreys, N.A. (ed.) (1885) *William Farr. Vital Statistics. A Memorial Volume of Selections from the Reports and Writings of William Farr*. London: Edward Stanford.

Kay, D.W.K., Beamish, P. and Roth, M. (1964) 'Old age mental disorders in Newcastle-upon-Tyne. I: a study of prevalence'. *British Journal of Psychiatry*, 110, pp. 146–58.

Kono, S. (1994) 'Demography and population ageing in Japan', in *Ageing in Japan*. Tokyo: JARC.

Kramer, M. (1980) 'The rising pandemic of mental disorders and associated chronic diseases and disabilities'. *Acta Psychiatrica Scandinavica*, 62, Suppl 285.

Kunitz, S.J. (1991) 'The personal physician and the decline of mortality', in R. Schofield, D. Reher and A. Bideau (eds), *The Decline of Mortality in Europe*. Oxford: Clarendon Press, pp. 248–62.

Lee, R. and Lam, D. (1983) 'Age distribution adjustments for English censuses 1821 to 1931'. *Population Studies*, 37, pp. 455–64.

Lin, T. (1953) 'A study of the incidence of mental disorder in Chinese and other cultures'. *Psychiatry*, 16, pp. 313–36.

Logan, W.P.D. and Brooke, E.M. (1957) *The Survey of Sickness 1943–1952*. London: HMSO.

Logan, W.P.D. and Cushion, A.A. (1958) *Morbidity Statistics from General Practice*. London: HMSO.

Manton, K. and Stallard, E. (1994) 'Medical demography: interaction of disability dynamics and mortality', in L.G. Martin and S.H. Preston (eds), *Demography of Aging*, Washington, DC: National Academy Press.

Manton, K.G. and Vaupel, J.W. (1995) 'Survival after the age of 80 in the United States, Sweden, France, Japan and England'. *New England Journal of Medicine*, 333, pp. 1232–5.

Murphy, E., Lindsay, J. and Grundy, E. (1986) '60 years of suicide in England and Wales'. *Archives of General Psychiatry*, 43, pp. 969–76.

OPCS (Office of Population Censuses and Surveys) (1996) *Population Trends No 83*. London: HMSO.

Pinker, R. (1966) *English Hospital Statistics 1861–1938*. London: Heinemann.

Preston, S.H. (1976) *Mortality Patterns in National Populations*. New York: Academic Press.

Preston, S.H., Himes, C. and Eggers, M. (1989) 'Demographic conditions responsible for population aging'. *Demography* 26, pp. 691–704.

Quadagno, J. (1982) *Aging in Early Industrial Society: Work, Family and Social Policy in Nineteenth Century England*. London: Academic Press.

Ratcliffe, H. (1850) *Observations on the Rate of Mortality and Sickness Existing Among Friendly Societies, Particularized for Various Trades, Occupations and Localities*. Manchester: Manchester Unity of the Independent Order of Odd Fellows.

RCADP (Royal Commission on the Aged Deserving Poor) (1895) *Report, vol 1*. London: HMSO.

RCNHI (Royal Commission on National Health Insurance) (1926) *Appendix A: Reports of the Departmental Actuarial Committee*. London: HMSO.

Riley, J. (1990) 'The risk of being sick: morbidity trends in four countries'. *Population and Development Review*, 16, pp. 403–32.

Riley, J.C. (1997) *Sick, Not Dead: The Health of British Workingmen During the Mortality Decline*. Baltimore, MD: Johns Hopkins University Press.

Robine, J.M., Blanchet, M. and Dowd, J.E. (eds) (1992) *Health Expectancy. 1st Workshop of the International Healthy Life Expectancy Network (Reves)*. Studies on Medical and Population Subjects No. 54. London: HMSO.

Robins, A. and Wittenberg, R. (1992) 'The health of elderly people: economic aspects', in Central Health Monitoring Unit, *The Health of Elderly People, An Epidemiological Overview: Companion papers*. London: HMSO.

Rothenberg, R., Lentzner, H. and Parker, R. (1991) 'Population aging patterns: the expansion of mortality'. *Journal of Gerontology*, 46, pp. S66–70.

Ruzicka, L. and Kane, P. (1990) 'Health transition: the course of morbidity and mortality', in J. Caldwell, S. Findley, P. Caldwell, *et al* (eds), *What We Know About Health Transition: The Cultural, Social and Behavioural Determinants of Health*, Vol. 1. Canberra: Health Transition Centre, Australian National University.

Schneider, E. and Brody, J. (1983) 'Aging, natural death and the compression of morbidity: another view'. *New England Journal of Medicine*, 309, pp. 854–6.

Schofield, R. and Reher, D. (1991) 'The decline of mortality in Europe', in R. Schofield, D. Reher and A. Bideau (eds), *The Decline of Mortality in Europe*. Oxford: Clarendon Press, pp. 1–17.

Sheldon, J.H. (1948) *The Social Medicine of Old Age*. Oxford: Oxford University Press.

Siegel, J.S. (1992) *A Generation of Change: A Profile of America's Older Population*. New York: Russell Sage Foundation.

Smith, F.B. (1979) *The People's Health*. London: Croom Helm.

Stocks, P. (1949) *Sickness in the Population of England and Wales 1944–1947*. Studies on Medical and Population Subjects no. 2. London: HMSO.

Thomson, D. (1984) 'The decline of social welfare: falling state support for the elderly since early Victorian times'. *Ageing and Society*, 4, pp. 451–82.

UNFPA (United Nations Fund for Population) (1998) *The State of World Population 1998*. New York, UNFPA.

Vaupel, J.W., Manton, K.L. and Stallard, E. (1979) 'The impact of heterogeneity in individual frailty on the dynamics of mortality'. *Demography*, 16, pp. 439–54.

Verbrugge, L. (1984) 'Longer life but worsening health? Trends in health and mortality in middle-aged and older persons'. *Millbank Memorial Fund Quarterly*, 62, pp. 475–519.

Waldron, I. (1986) 'What do we know about causes of sex differences in mortality? A review of the literature'. New York, *Population Bulletin of the United Nations*.

Wilson, L.A. and Brass, W. (1973) 'Brief assessment of the mental state in geriatric domiciliary practice. The usefulness of the mental status questionnaire'. *Age and Ageing*, 2, pp. 92–101.

Notes

CHAPTER 2. ADJUSTMENT METHODS FOR BIAS IN THE INDIRECT CHILDHOOD MORTALITY ESTIMATES

1. Strictly speaking this is an approximation since the cumulated children born by age 20, $F(1)$ would be more correct (with $F(i)$ denoting cumulated fertility to the upper limit of the age group i); however, average parities are more convenient and simpler to use as this is how data are presented in surveys and censuses. They performed better in regressions of simulation results, as the proportions dead similarly refer to averages for age groups.

CHAPTER 3. ESTIMATION OF ADULT MORTALITY FROM DATA ON ADULT SIBLINGS

1. This range is chosen because there are few birth intervals of less than two years – this cannot be represented by a normal curve. Equally, closed birth intervals of more than 22 years can only be experienced by women aged more than 35 years. There are relatively few such women and the dates of their very early births may be more subject to reporting errors than those of more recent births.

CHAPTER 6. EVIDENCE OF CHANGES IN FAMILY FORMATION PATTERNS IN PAKISTAN?

1. A sample of the complete set of respondents of the PDHS 1990–1 was re-interviewed and their responses were used for verification of the fertility and contraceptive use status level (Curtis and Arnold, 1994). The findings of the re-interview survey confirm a serious deficit in the number of births reported for the last five years but a much better compatibility in the contraceptive use levels for the survey. This re-interview survey supports the claim that the PDHS showed a much higher than actual fertility decline for the five years preceding the survey.
2. As Brass readily acknowledged, there are virtually no objective criteria for determining which models constitute the 'best' fit to the data, particularly when the latter are as distorted as are those from the PDHS. The trends in period rates obtained from the model fitting are in fact quite sensitive to the choice of models. Thus by manipulating the parameters it is possible to obtain almost any desired trend in fertility, and the analyst must resist the temptation of choosing those which will fit his or her preconceived ideas. Nevertheless, the procedure still constitutes the most effective method of correcting for dating errors in birth histories currently available to demographers.
3. Blacker and Hakim (forthcoming) have in fact applied the method to the PFFPS.

CHAPTER 7. A COMPARATIVE ANALYSIS OF FERTILITY IN ARAB COUNTRIES: EXPLAINING THE ANOMALIES

1. As part of the Demographic and Health Survey (DHS) or Pan Arab Project for Child Development (PAPCHILD) programmes. Indeed a country like Egypt has had as much as four major national surveys in a span of seven years (DHS (88), MCHS (91), DHS (92), DHS (95)).
2. This is either because no birth history was collected in their recent survey or only the preliminary brief report has been published or is accessible.
3. PAPCHILD refers to the Pan Arab Project for Child Development that included the collection of the Maternal and Child Health Surveys (MCHS) in nine Arab countries. The Gulf Health Surveys programme has undertaken both the Gulf Child Health Surveys (GCHS) in the Gulf countries and Iraq and the Gulf Family Health Surveys (GFHS).
4. In particular, the UN revised edition did not include: Egypt DHS (95), Libya MCHS (95), Sudan MCHS (92–3), Tunisia MCHS (94–5), Syria MCHS (93). It also appears that GHS findings for Bahrain (89), Iraq (89), Oman (88),Qatar (87) and Emirates (87) were not considered.
5. Using Table (A.2) and the extrapolated rates for 1990–4.
6. It is noted that the level of TFR of 6.2 for Sudan is much lower than what one would expect at pretransitional levels. Also, the WFS estimate is much lower than those derived from the birth history of the surveys conducted by PAPCHILD and DHS and of those presented in the UN report. The current level of analysis cannot disentangle the reason for discrepancies between the different sources. Nevertheless, even if WFS TFR is an underestimate, this would tend to be associated with overestimate of SMAM, contraceptive prevalence rate and breastfeeding prevalence but is less likely to affect the distribution of factors responsible for the change across time. This is particularly true given the remaining 1990's low levels of contraceptive prevalence and universal and quite long durations of breast-feeding.
7. It is important to note that the difference in Cm across countries is not enough to imply that the proportions married in different age groups are the source of variations in TFR. For this to be true, marital fertility rates by age need to be similar. Such an observation does not hold for the other indices (Ci and Cc) as they have direct links with duration of breast-feeding and contraceptive prevalence and mix.
8. It should be remembered that this factor is not fully accounted for in the calculation of age specific marital fertility rates as no nuptiality history is collected in either the DHS or PAPCHILD surveys. Also, the statistics in Table 7.10 are a proxy indicator of dissolution since they are also affected by remarriage.
9. A movement that encourages specification of a targeted number of children and allows the exercise of planning and aspirations, which in turn argue for and prompt a reduction in the number of children.

CHAPTER 8. FERTILITY TRENDS AND POPULATION POLICY IN KENYA

1. The original procedure consisted in subtracting the births which had occurred in the five years before the survey, and thus reconstructing the parity distributions of the women five years before, when they were five years younger. The changes which had occurred in the five years for each cohort are then chained

together to project the parity distributions of younger women up to the end of childbearing. In the present case the parity distributions from the 1993 DHS were used in lieu of the back-dated 1998 data.

2. The calculations could not be made for the 1962 census on account of the high level of non-response to the question on children ever borne.

3. There is an unexplained discrepancy between the mean lengths of breast-feeding, amenorrhoea, abstention and insusceptibility given in Brass and Jolly (Table 5–5, p. 100) and those in the report on the 1989 KDHS (Table 2.7, p. 15), despite the fact that they were apparently calculated in the same way.

4. Brass and Jolly (1993, pp. 102–3, 108) adopted an Ip value of 1.01 for 1989, since the proportion of childless women shown by the DHS was less than Bongaarts's 'natural' level of 3 per cent. However, we believe the DHS data to be somewhat suspect. The census data on childlessness are also unreliable on account of the large numbers of women who were 'not stated' as to children ever borne, but after the application of the El Badry correction figures in the region of 5 per cent were obtained from the 1969, 1979 and 1989 censuses.

CHAPTER 9. POPULATIONS OF THE NORTHERN SAHEL: DEMOGRAPHIC PROBLEMS AND SOLUTIONS

Acknowledgements
Demographic studies in Mali 1981 and 1982 were funded by ILCA (International Livestock Centre for Africa) and the Population Council under the Determinants of Fertility Programme. The data for N. Burkina Faso were collected by Kate Hampshire as part of an EEC funded research programme on 'Household viability and migration in the Sahel' EU DG XII Programme STD3, reference 921028.

1. In the Human Development Report (UNDP, 1996), Mali, Burkina Faso and Niger figured in the bottom five countries world wide, and all were in the bottom 15 per cent countries for human development.

2. Administratively Mali in 1987 was divided into seven Regions. Each Region has between 5 and 8 cercles which are divided into arrondissements (the lowest level of administration). A town is defined as 'urban' once it has a population of over 5,000. The administrative centres of the cercle (usually with the same name) are also 'urban' whatever their size. Thus Kidal, with a population of 2,230 in 1976 was urban.

3. 'Il faut souligner que les populations réfugiées et les nomades ne figurent pas dans les échantillons', p. 7. Resultats preliminaires: Migrations et urbanisation en Afrique de l'ouest (MUAO) July 1995.

4. These surveys were commissioned by the International Livestock Centre for Africa under their socio-economic research programmes, and supplementary research was financed by the Population Council under the Determinants of Fertility programme.

5. Particular reporting problems in these surveys were: Fulbe Liptaako underreported females both in terms of actual residents and in children ever borne. The sex ratios of Fulbe Liptaako residents was about 1.23 for under-15s, adults 15–59 and over 60. The sex ratio of children ever borne to women was 1.25 and to men was 1.20. Estimates of adult male mortality from orphanhood data were not possible. For all groups the reported fathers surviving was implausibly high. Adult female mortality estimates seem very low, especially in comparison to child mortality levels, but many West African populations do have very high

child mortality. The extremely high age-specific fertility for the Djelgobe is probably a function of small sample size and random annual fluctuation. Reported parities do, however, suggest that this group does have higher fertility than the others.

CHAPTER 10. ACCESSION AND ABDICATIONS: MEN AND WOMEN AS FAMILY MARKERS IN LINKED DATA FOR ENGLAND AND WALES

1. This poses a problem as to how to define a household longitudinally. Willekens (1988) proposes 'an orthodox approach ... based on individual as a unit of analysis and in which changes in the household position and status of these individuals are analysed using mainstream demographic and statistical approaches such as lifetable and hazards models' (Murphy, 1996).
2. In the allocation of markershhip people who were a child in the family or in an institution were excluded. In the allocation of family unit we grouped co-resident family units according to our definition. The fact that non-family units are treated atomistically is because they fall outside our main focus. Hence, lodgers or one person units are treated as separate even though they may be co-resident with other family units. We have not estimated yet how many multi-unit households there were as this is complicated by the fact that the 'head of household' was self-defined in the census.
3. Sampling bias results from the fact that LS members are more likely to be selected from large families.

Index